C0-AMV-445

Women and National Development

Women and National Development: The Complexities of Change

Wellesley Editorial Committee
Ximena Bunster B.
Carolyn M. Elliott
Michelle McAlpin (chair)
Achola O. Pala
Hanna Papanek
Helen I. Safa
Catharine R. Stimpson
Niara Sudarkasa
Roxane Witke

The University of Chicago Press
Chicago and London

Based on a conference on women and development held June 2—6, 1976. Sponsored by the Center for Research on Women in Higher Education and the Professions, Wellesley College; the African Studies Association; the Association for Asian Studies; and the Latin American Studies Association. This volume originally appeared as the Autumn 1977 issue of *Signs: Journal of Women in Culture and Society* (Volume 3, Number 1).

The University of Chicago Press, Chicago 60637
The University of Chicago Press, Ltd., London

Printed in the United States of America

Library of Congress Cataloging in Publication Data
Main entry under title:

Women and national development.

"Based on a conference on women and development held June 2-6, 1976, sponsored by the Center for Research on Women in Higher Education and the Professions, Wellesley College; the African Studies Association; the Association for Asian Studies; and the Latin American Studies Association."

"Originally appeared as the Autumn 1977 issue of Signs, journal of women in culture and society (volume 3, number 1)."

Includes bibliographical references and index.

1. Underdeveloped areas—Women's employment—Congresses. 2. Underdeveloped areas—Economic policy—Congresses. 3. Women in community development—Congresses. 4. Women's rights—Congresses. I. Wellesley College. Center for Research on Women in Higher Education and the Professions.

HD6223.W65 331.4'09172'4 77-15038
ISBN 0-226-89314-6
ISBN 0-226-89315-4 pbk.

Contents

Foreword

On June 2–6, 1976, a conference on women and development was held at Wellesley College, coordinated by the Wellesley Center for Research on Women. Its purpose was to bring together people interested in the issues that women must confront in Latin America, Africa, Asia, and the Middle East as their countries undergo profound social, economic, and cultural changes. Over 500 people attended. Eighty papers, organized into twenty panels, were given, and films were shown. In addition, several plenary sessions were held.

The sponsors of the conference, in addition to the Center, were the African Studies Association, the Association for Asian Studies, the Latin American Studies Association, and Wellesley College. Designing the conference was a program committee, its members drawn largely from the Committees on the Status of Women of the various area studies associations. They included Carolyn M. Elliott (convenor), Margaret Crahan, Nancy Hafkin, Margaret Jean Hay, Michelle McAlpin, Marysa Navarro, Hanna Papanek, Helen I. Safa, Ann Seidman, Annemarie Shimony, Roxane Witke, and Catherine Muther (conference coordinator).

Helping to underwrite the conference were a number of institutions: the conference sponsors themselves, the Agricultural Development Council, the Ford Foundation, the Johnson Foundation, the Lilly Endowment, the Pathfinder Fund, the Rockefeller Foundation, the Tinker Foundation, and the United States Agency for International Development. In addition, the Ford Foundation contributed to the cost of publication of the *Signs* issue.

Some months before the conference, the program committee arranged with *Signs* to publish selected papers, which were to be revised for a book edition. At the June meeting, an editorial committee was chosen, consisting of representatives from *Signs,* from the program committee, and from the regions represented at the conference. Its members were Ximena Bunster B., Carolyn M. Elliott, Michelle McAlpin (chair), Achola O. Pala, Hanna Papanek, Helen I. Safa, Catharine R. Stimpson, Niara Sudarkasa, and Roxane Witke. Mely Tan was also elected to the Editorial Committee but was unable to participate because of distance. This committee both finally conceptualized the volume and chose the papers. It regretted that limitations of space and the demands of the volume as a whole kept it from publishing full proceedings.

The editors believe that the question of development, whether or not that term is entirely appropriate, is of extraordinary importance, concerning, as it does, the structure and substance of life of much of the world's population. Moreover, the changes that development demands are complex, subject neither to easy analysis nor to quick judgment. For these reasons, this volume is dedicated wholly to material that the Wellesley conference both presented and provoked.

MICHELLE MCALPIN, *Chair, Wellesley Editorial Committee*

CATHARINE R. STIMPSON, *Editor, Signs*

DOMNA C. STANTON, *Associate Editor, Signs (International Contributions)*

Preface

Ester Boserup

In recent years numerous research projects, conferences, and seminars have been devoted to the theme "Women and Development." This is no wonder, for the theme lies at the juncture of two major streams of present-day social research: women's condition and economic development. Moreover, the increasing number of local studies on women in Third World countries has revealed their lot in the labor market, especially in rural areas, to be peculiar; on one hand, women are overburdened with work, and on the other, their efforts partly go to waste, because they have even less training and use even more primitive equipment than the male labor force in their communities. Hence, there is need for additional research that aims to improve the working conditions of Third World women, including domestic work, and to provide them with better access to the labor market.

A frequent objection to studies of "Women and Development" is that their emphasis on labor market problems and labor productivity is unwarranted. Many studies of women in Third World countries show their social status to be low where they are actively engaged in agriculture, crafts, trade, or construction, and where they support themselves and their children by such work. Therefore, or so the argument continues, the study of women's status, especially their status in relation to male family members, should have priority over labor market studies. However, in these Third World communities female subservience to male relatives derives from legal or customary rules which women are unable or disinclined to change. Thus, economic self-support coexists with low family status. But in societies of another type, where women are legally independent, opportunities for economic self-support are of crucial importance to actual female status in relation to male relatives. In recent decades, many Third World countries have made important changes in women's legal status. For example, women have obtained the right to divorce and to guardianship of themselves and their children in case of divorce and widowhood. But, apparently, these achievements in the legal sphere have made little change in the real family status of women, unless opportunities for economic self-support in case of divorce or widowhood also existed.

Economic change is also occurring in most Third World countries. This change, however, is making it less and less feasible for women, even for those who live in rural areas, to support themselves and their children by means of subsistence activities. If women have no opportunity to earn money incomes, their dependence upon male relatives will increase with divorce and widowhood and their family status may deteriorate in spite of legal independence. By contrast, where legal independence and opportunities for earning money incomes go hand in hand, the family status of women who do not divorce or leave the family in case of widowhood is also likely to improve because male relatives will treat them better knowing that they have an alternative to staying with them. Therefore, it is pointless to argue whether priority in research concerning Third World women should be given to studies of family status or to studies of labor market conditions. Both are indispensable.

Research on women and development must be integrated with studies of the development process itself. Studies of this process undertaken in various parts of the world have shown that certain groups may reap a disproportionate share of the benefits of development, while other groups may become victims of development, because the products they were selling or the services they were performing are replaced by new and more productive activities. Although both men and women may become victims of development, it is more difficult for women to adapt to new conditions, because (1) family obligations make them less mobile than men, (2) their occupational choice is more narrowly limited by custom, (3) they usually have less education and training, and (4) even without these handicaps they often face sex discrimination in recruitment. Moreover, in Third World countries, a much larger percentage of the female than of the male labor force is engaged in traditional occupations, which are precisely those gradually replaced by modern enterprises in economic development.

It is likely, then, that large numbers of women in developing countries will be victims of development. Some research projects on women and development have already revealed unexpected side effects of technological change for rural women and their local income opportunities. Research must be undertaken to foresee such cases and explore possibilities of creating alternative income opportunities. Because of the speed of technological change in many developing countries, we must train both women and men, not for the labor market structure of today, but of tomorrow.

There are striking contrasts between the speed of economic growth and modernization in different developing countries, and most generalizations about the current process of change are misleading. In any given country or region, the possibilities for improving women's income-earning opportunities are of course related to differences in natural resources, the stock of human and physical capital, foreign relations, and government policies. In countries where economic growth is swift and labor shortages appear, attitudes toward women's work outside the home are also swiftly changing, and part of the female labor reserve is pulled into the labor market. By contrast, in countries where population growth is rapid and growth of the economy is slow, women from poor families are pushed into already crowded occupations, such as market trade and domestic service, to help to support their large families. In both cases, research aimed at helping women adapt to and improve their status must be based on solid investigation of economic conditions and other factors in the countries in which those women are living. Application of overall "development models," either "western" or "alternative," makes little sense when economic conditions, institutional patterns, and attitudes to women's work vary so widely.

Many of the features which accompany the development process, especially rural modernization and rural-urban migration, are likely to result in the modification of cultural attitudes and the abandonment of traditional marriage systems and other customs. However, with the notable exception of fertility and attitudes to birth control, few systematic studies have been undertaken of the interrelationship between technological, demographic, and cultural changes affecting women. Studies of the effects of development on aspects of women's lives and status other than childbirth are needed. Indeed, a broader attitude to research in this field is required.

Many look to development as a means of undermining customs and of changing cultural attitudes which they consider unfavorable to women. Others, women as well as men, fear the possible effects of development in the cultural field. Factual research which aims to sort out the various effects on women of traditional culture and customs may help throw more light on these controversial and highly emotional problems and may be a useful supplement to the studies of the effects of development on such institutions.

Solid national and local studies are indispensable, because economic conditions and cultural attitudes vary so widely among countries and even among local communities within the same country. At the same time, knowledge that is useful to women in other countries—and to development policies in other countries—risks getting lost unless national and local studies are made available internationally. Likewise, there is a very real need for coordination in planning and carrying out research. International conferences and seminars on the theme of women and development, like the ones in Wellesley and Wingspread,[1] have a crucial role to play, not only as inspiration for individual scholars, but also as a stimulus for international exchange and coordination of research.

Charlottenlund, Denmark

1. This was a follow-up conference held at Wingspread Conference Center, Racine, Wisconsin, U.S.A. Sixty-three participants, the majority from overseas, discussed research needs in their countries and the possibility of cooperation among them. *Women and Development,* a report of the conference, may be obtained from the Johnson Foundation, Racine, Wisconsin 53401, U.S.A.

Toward Models of Development

Theories of Development: An Assessment

Carolyn M. Elliott

Critics of women's secondary status in modern society have traced the subordination of women to the beginning of history and culture. Now students of development are demonstrating that the position of women has not significantly improved as their societies have incorporated modern technology and organization. Indeed, women may be worse off in important ways because the benefits of modernization have accrued mainly to the male half of society. The papers in this volume seek to document and explain women's position in national development by close examination of evidence from one or more cases. They raise questions that show the need for new theories, methodologies, and research. However, they also draw from several intellectual traditions, and in order to assess them it is useful to point out their informing perspectives. They are: (1) cultural dualism, which Simone deBeauvoir utilized to examine the position of women; (2) social evolutionary thought, which generated both modernization theory and the Marxist analysis of stages in the development of capitalism; (3) developmentalism, which identified obstacles to women's participation in national development; and (4) dependency theory, which also analyzed the logic of capitalist growth.

Cultural Dualism

A perception of the universality of woman's secondary status has propelled many students of culture to look for explanations in pancultural facts of human existence. One such student is Simone de

Beauvoir.[1] She locates the origins of woman's subordination, in part, in her relationship to nature and nature's relationship to culture. She finds in the concept of humanity a universal opposition between nature and culture. Human beings are distinguished from animals by their efforts to transcend the limitations of perishable nature through culture. Man is freer than woman to pursue transcendence because he is not constrained by the tasks of reproducing and sustaining life. Yet man cannot live without woman, just as he cannot abolish nature, which includes and contains sexuality. Knowing this, man's attitude toward woman is deeply ambivalent. He at once celebrates her and denigrates her. He does not dare to bind her to the extent of endangering her creativity, but he wishes to control her. Susan Wadley's paper argues that this ambivalence permeates Hindu culture.

There are, however, cultures where women play the dominant role in regulating nature and sexual behavior. Among the Sande of Sierra Leone, according to Carol MacCormack's essay, women bear the major responsibility for restricting sexual intercourse to sanctioned places, times, and partners. MacCormack's analysis utilizes Lévi-Strauss's notion of the opposition between nature and culture but argues against the necessary identification of women with the sphere of nature.

In assessing dualistic theories, it must be acknowledged that there do appear to be certain commonalities in the social and cultural position of women across virtually all known societies, based primarily on the continuing sexual division of labor. Anthropologists have found no society, of foragers or of industrial giants, in which women play a major role in warfare or formal religion. Students of development can find little guidance from dualistic theories, however, because they give no attention to variations in these purportedly fundamental patterns of human existence, nor are they concerned with change.

Social Evolutionary Theory

The question—is women's position becoming better or worse as societies change—animates those who draw from social evolutionary theory to study women's roles. It provides them with an explanation of the dynamic producing social change and an evaluation of its direction. The notion of social evolution perceives societies as propelled by changes in the population/resource balance and competition with neighbors to move along a scale of increasing division of labor and differentiation.[2] Those in which the same persons or institutions do a

1. Simone de Beauvoir, *The Second Sex* (New York: Alfred A. Knopf, Inc., 1952).

2. For an example of this perspective, see Talcott Parsons, *Societies: Evolutionary and Comparative Perspectives* (Englewood Cliffs, N.J.: Prentice-Hall, Inc., 1966); see also Gerhard Lenski, *Human Societies: A Macro-Level Introduction to Sociology* (New York: McGraw-Hill Book Co., 1970).

multitude of tasks are at one end of a continuum, in the category of simple societies; those in which social units specialize in only a few tasks are at the other, in the category of complex societies. Higher levels of technology and more formal institutions, as well as greater occupational specialization, characterize complex societies. That this best describes Western society is no accident, for social evolutionists took the West as their measure of progress.

By drawing on the notion of division of labor, social evolutionary theory provides an explanation for inequality, both among and within societies. With specialization, each laboring group becomes more efficient, and overall productivity increases. Generally, societies seeking a higher level of productivity move toward greater specialization. Therefore, simple societies, with less differentiation among social units, are less productive and poorer. Within complex societies, those groups who perform less specialized roles are less productive. This explanation of inequality has been the premise for much stimulating work on sexual inequality, particularly among economists. Accepting the linkage between specialization, technology, and rewards, Ester Boserup demonstrates that women have been relegated to jobs in the backward sectors of the economy. Because they fall on the lower side of the "productivity gap" they suffer inequality.[3] The same analysis has been made about the effect of social differentiation on political participation. As differentiation increased the distance between domestic and public arenas, women were relegated to the more particularistic concerns of domestic life and lost the opportunity to participate in community-wide decisions. The growth of the specialized state, with its professional armies and bureaucracies, enhanced their subordination.

Providing empirical documentation for the long-range societal change contemplated in evolutionary theory is exceedingly difficult. Most studies drawing on an evolutionary model array a number of disparate contemporaneous societies along a scale of complexity and infer a process of movement along the scale. Utilizing the wide range of communities in Turkey, however, Deniz Kandiyoti has been able to trace the dynamic impact of increasing social complexity on women's roles. Remi Clignet shows how colonialism in West Africa created a more complex society with greater sex-role segregation.

Historically, social evolutionary theory has generated several variants which have significantly informed studies of women and development. Both modernization theory and Marxism draw from the pool of evolutionary notions, though in quite different ways.[4] Criticisms of these

3. Ester Boserup, *Woman's Role in Economic Development* (London: Allen & Unwin, 1970).

4. For a statement of how modernization will break down all ascriptive criteria, including the assignment of roles by sex, see S. N. Eisenstadt, "Modernization: Growth and Diversity," in *Tradition, Change and Modernity* (New York: John Wiley & Sons, 1973), pp. 22–46.

schools, which are widespread, have in turn yielded revisions which now stand at the forefront of theory on women and development.[5] I will turn first to the work of developmentalists and then to the dependency theorists, both of whom are represented in this volume.

Developmentalism

Perception that modernization has had differential effects on men and women has led planners to seek to describe the obstacles preventing women from participating in development. The 1975 United Nations conference in Mexico City focused worldwide attention on the need for "intensified action to ensure the full integration of women in the development process."[6] Implicit in the UN call and the developmentalist perspective are three notions about social change that differ from the assumptions of modernization theory. (1) Society is not seen as a single organic unit such that changes in one sector will generate compatible changes throughout. New technologies introduced to raise productivity may remain encapsulated, just as development programs addressed to men often fail to spin off benefits for women. (2) There are contradictions in the process of social change. Policies to increase women's employment may only increase exploitation if wages and working conditions are not improved at the same time. (3) External forces and national leaders play a key role in producing social change. Because developmentalists do not see a pervasive internal dynamic carrying societies toward modernization, they look for conscious policies to move them in desirable directions. Pnina Lahav considers the effectiveness of law as an instrument of change in family relations. Her paper is a model for analyzing how existing institutions (e.g., religious courts) modify policy initiatives and constrain the implementation of a law.

Failure of implementation has led revisionist developmentalists to consider decision making by individuals as well as governments. They point out that few development decisions are implemented by direct intervention. Most are enacted by altering the structure of situations in which individuals make decisions. Therefore, they examine how price supports affect farmers' decisions to invest in new technology, for example, or how work opportunities affect women's decisions to have children. Mary Chamie extends the analyses of the context of decision making on fertility into a new arena. She examines how patterns of com-

5. June Nash's essay discussing the political implications of modernization theory shows why Third World women are so hostile to it (see "A Critique of Social Science Roles in Latin America," in *Sex and Class in Latin America,* ed. June Nash and Helen Safa [New York: Praeger Publishers, 1976], pp. 1–2).

6. Point 14 of the introduction to the "Report of the World Conference of the International Women's Year" (Mexico City, June 19–July 2, 1975), UN Publication Sales no. E. 76. IV. 1 (New York: United Nations, 1976), pp. 9–43.

munication between sexual partners about coitus affect women's decisions on contraception.

By looking at women as rational decision makers, and not simply conservative holdouts from change, developmentalist studies of women have identified many previously ignored reasons for development failures. They have also generated a critique of the entire conception of development in the 1950s and 1960s. They argue that concentration on increasing the value of the GNP, an aggregate measure of marketable goods and services, undervalues the full production of a society and ignores the question of distribution. Neglect of nonmarket work done in households, subsistence agriculture, and the informal labor market, all done by women more often than men, has led to policies which impede its productivity. Little is invested in upgrading nonmarket work, and the costs of the incursions of the market are ignored. Women suffer an increasing narrowing of social roles and capacity to generate income. Society also suffers by losing the household as an adaptive low-cost productive center which can shield its members from the vicissitudes of the market economy.[7] Expanding the definition of the GNP to include women's work is a strategy proposed by Ester Boserup and others to include assessment of their costs in the formation of development goals.

Unfortunately, much of the developmentalist literature disembodies information and attitudes from economic structure and power relationships. It rests on the assumption that more enlightened planning will remove the obstacles to women's participation. If false views are exposed, new statistics gathered, and better arguments devised, development can benefit women. One must question, however, whether the obstacles to "including women in development" are not greater than these planners recognize. Furthermore, the survey of women's attitudes which provides the basis for many social education and training programs must be questioned. Too many studies have located women's perceived passivity and resistance to change in female nature instead of examining how their life experience in positions of powerlessness may have made them distrust new initiatives.[8]

Dependency Theory

Dissatisfaction with the capacity of modernization theory to explain continued poverty and backwardness in Third World countries led some observers to look for systemic connections among the contradictions

7. Nash.

8. Many studies of modernization are constructed on the assumption that women are resistant to change and take men's attitudes as the measure of social change. Alex Inkeles surveyed male factory workers in six nations to study modernization but did not consider women (Alex Inkeles and David H. Smith, *Becoming Modern: Individual Change in Six Developing Countries* [Cambridge, Mass.: Harvard University Press, 1974]).

noted by developmentalists. As they pursued these linkages through the societal infrastructure of the countries in question, they became increasingly impressed with the constraints placed on development by international forces. Even though formal control over governments had been abandoned by colonial powers, industrialized nations still held economic hegemony through control of markets and technology. Colonialism was largely over, but neocolonialism persisted. In the same manner, urban and landed elites within nations created the backwardness of the rural sector by skewing national plans toward investment in export-crop agriculture, heavy industry, and urban growth.

Another source of dependency theory as it relates to women is the dissatisfaction of internationally minded Marxist feminists with the model of patriarchy which has dominated feminist thinking. Following standard Marxist theory, Norma Chinchilla argues that one cannot understand power relations between men and women without seeing them in the context of the mode of production. But, as several papers in this volume point out, how the mode of production affects Third World women is part of an international system based on dependency. This factor alters the classic Marxist explanation of women's subordination, that is, that women are relegated to the domestic economy and denied the opportunity to participate in production of goods for exchange in the larger society. Thus, Ann Stoler argues that the labor-intensive sugar plantation economy of colonial Indonesia drew both men and women into the colonial labor force. Similarly, Martha Mueller finds in African Lesotho that export mining drew men from the villages, leaving women more opportunity for participation in community life. Both caution, however, that the options of these women remained severely restricted by the economic position of the whole community, which was ultimately determined by the international system.

A new theory of women's subordination in development has been constructed out of these critiques. Paralleling the analysis of the systematic linkage between advanced and backward nations, it posits that capitalism depends on the backwardness of the household. According to Brazilian sociologist Heleieth Saffioti, for example, the household maintains women as a reserve labor force available to join capitalist production when required, as in wartime.[9] Furthermore, it eases the social tensions when unemployment rises, enabling capitalism to survive its chronic cycles of inflation and depression.

If industrial capitalism places women on the periphery of the economy, the capitalism of the dependent nations makes their position even more difficult. Contrary to the experience of core capitalist economies, capitalism in dependent countries is dislodging workers

9. Heleieth B. Saffioti, "Female Labor and Capitalism in the United States and Brazil," in *Women Cross-culturally: Change and Challenge*, ed. Ruby Rohrlich-Leavitt (The Hague: Mouton & Co., 1975), pp. 59–94.

from agriculture faster than they are being absorbed into industry. Therefore, female labor force participation in countries like Brazil has declined with development, as Glaura Miranda demonstrates. Characteristic of these dependent economies is the growth of a large service sector. Women hold a disproportionate number of jobs in this sector, particularly the low-status ones not usually counted in the GNP. Dependency theorists have called these jobs—domestic servants, street vendors, prostitutes, etc.—the informal labor market. Documenting and assessing the consequences for women of this informal labor market is the subject of several papers in this volume. Lourdes Arizpe, for example, draws on informal labor market theory to argue that the large number of domestic servants (40 percent of all nonrural female workers) and other marginal workers in Latin America reflects the structure of opportunities open to women, not their choice or the constraints of family obligations.

Dependency theory is intellectually compelling. It is coherent, and it eliminates the invidious distinction between "socially productive" and domestic work. There is a wide range of questions, however, that it has yet to address. It has not reexamined the relationship between income and power within and outside the home, a question of great importance to advocates of women's participation in the labor force. Yolanda Moses finds that, contrary to a common assumption, providing family monetary income does not give women power within West Indian families. Nor can dependency theory offer much insight into why particular ideological notions about women, such as pollution, seem especially gripping. Like its Marxist forebears, it has little interest in and few tools for examining the content of cultural statements. For a more sophisticated view of the internal dynamic of culture, cultural dualist theory may still provide the most useful analysis.

* * *

These critiques, both empirical and theoretical, are the material for theory building. While it is difficult to perceive what a new theory of women and development might look like, it is possible to state some factors it should incorporate. It must evaluate women's work by its production, not by the presence of technology or monetary rewards. Such an evaluation will show women contributing to family survival and social production in cooperation with men. Second, it must examine the political role of women with an expanded notion of politics. Just because women are infrequently found in formal political organizations, their role in constructing linkages among families to integrate the community must not be neglected. The notion of family must also be expanded to include female-headed families with their many adult male participants and their extensions into other households. One would further like such a notion of family to include consideration of sexuality, intimacy, and affection.

A theory of women and development must perceive many different kinds of linkages among various parts of the world system. One current hypothesis requiring systematic examination is that world markets so constrain the internal economies of participating countries that each lower level of the system has less and less autonomy for decision making. Because women participate at the lowest levels, in subsistence agriculture and the informal labor market, they have the least autonomy.[10] Yet others have surmised that women have more freedom from centrally sanctioned norms by their not participating in paid work and other public institutions of modern life.[11] Just how and where societies allow for deviance and flexibility is a question that proponents of systemic theories must confront.

Finally, a theory of women and development must explain change, or lack of change, in women's roles. If social change has not largely benefited women is this a failure of development or an indication of a need for a deeper reformulation of social goals to meet human needs? The double burden of combining housework with wage labor which is carried by women in the labor force of most advanced industrialized societies does not seem like a desirable goal for development. In other societies the liberation of upper-class women appears to depend on the subordination of lower-class women as domestic servants. The relation between sex and class as modes of allocating social rewards remains a problem for theories of women and development.

Center for Research on Women in Higher Education and the Professions
Wellesley College
Wellesley, Massachusetts, U.S.A.

10. "Report on Women and Development: Workshop Convened by the Center for Research on Women, Wellesley College, in Co-operation with the Johnson Foundation," June 8–10, 1976. Available from the Wellesley Center for Research on Women, Wellesley, Massachusetts 02181.

11. Hanna Papanek, "Comment on Joseph R. Gusfield, Review Essay on Inkeles and Smith, *Becoming Modern*," *American Journal of Sociology*, in press.

TOWARD MODELS OF DEVELOPMENT

Definitions of Women and Development: An African Perspective

Achola O. Pala

In this brief paper, I do not propose to engage in a discussion of what development is or what an African perspective means. Rather, I wish to draw attention to points which I consider to be central to an understanding of the contemporary position of African women. It is reasonable to say that in Africa today the position of both women and men can be largely described as an interplay between two parameters. The first, which we may call dependency, comprises economic and political relationships through which our peoples have found themselves increasingly involved with metropolitan Europe (e.g., England, France, Germany, Belgium, Spain, and Portugal) and the United States of America, especially since the sixteenth and seventeenth centuries, starting with the slave trade and colonialism and continuing up to contemporary neocolonial links. The second embraces indigenous African socioeconomic norms (e.g., in food production, family ideology, property rights, and perceptions of respect and human dignity), insofar as these continue to regulate social behavior.

In other words, the position of women in contemporary Africa is to be considered at every level of analysis as an outcome of structural and conceptual mechanisms by which African societies have continued to respond to and resist the global processes of economic exploitation and cultural domination. I am suggesting that the problems facing African women today, irrespective of their national and social class affiliations, are inextricably bound up in the wider struggle by African people to free themselves from poverty and ideological domination in both intra- and international spheres.

Neither research on African development potential and problems nor specific emphasis on issues relating to the participation of African women in local economies is new. The British colonial government, for instance, commissioned and/or supported a number of studies specifically to investigate the role of women in African societies, in order to formulate policies which would "integrate" women more effectively into the colonial development. Even a quick perusal of local newspapers in a given colonial period will reveal a "concern" by the colonial government, backed by women's associations (usually made up of wives and sisters of colonial administrators and missionaries), for the education and training of African women. More recently, in the last two decades, African women's national organizations have taken up the cry for equal opportunities for women in such matters as employment and training. In every instance, it will be found that research or social protest launched on behalf of or by women themselves is invariably motivated by economic and political considerations rather than feminism per se. In some instances, the issue of women's rights is used as a means of social control; in others, it serves to consolidate the political position of individual men and women. In all cases, it is a reliable indicator of ideological alignments within a particular national or international situation.

It cannot be stated too often that up to this time research on African problems has been greatly influenced by intellectual trends from outside the continent. Like the educational systems inherited from the colonial days, the research industry has continued to use the African environment as a testing ground for ideas and hypotheses the locus of which is to be found in Paris, London, New York, or Amsterdam. For this reason, the primary orientation to development problems tends to be created on the basis of what happens to be politically and/or intellectually significant in the metropoles. At one time, it may be family planning; at another, environment; at yet another, human rights and women's social conditions. At one time, there is funding for a particular type of study; at another time, money for yet another research topic. Such continual redefinition of research priorities means that African scholars are forced into certain forms of intellectual endeavors that are peripheral to the development of their societies. Such a redefinition of research problems and programs concerning Africa sometimes manifests itself in the emphasis of research orientations which have little to offer African women. I have visited villages where, at a time when the village women are asking for better health facilities and lower infant-mortality rates, they are presented with questionnaires on family planning. In some instances, when women would like to have piped water in the village, they may be at the same time faced with a researcher interested in investigating power and powerlessness in the household. In yet another situation, when women are asking for access to agricultural credit, a researcher on the scene may be conducting a study on female circumcision.

There is no denying that certain statistical relationships can be established between such variables as fertility, power, initiation rites, and women's overall standing in the household/community. What I am trying to emphasize, however, is that a statistical relationship per se, which can be established as an academic exercise, does not necessarily constitute relevant information or a priority from the point of view of those who are made the research subjects. In essence, research efforts which seek to enhance the participation of women in contemporary Africa, whether or not they emanate from the continent, should be formulated in relation to the socioeconomic realities which African women confront today. Furthermore, as we stand between the corridors of international intellectual corporations and national ethnic class divisions, the struggle which is being waged by women at various levels for equity in access to land or educational opportunities, better nutritional standards, or lowered infant-mortality rates is by no means separate or different from efforts made at the level of analysis to understand the nature of real or putative problems facing African women today.

Two further points may illustrate some of the analytical mileage to be gained when the two basic parameters outlined above are brought to bear on understanding African women. First, in considering the issue of the impact on women of colonial and/or neocolonial socioeconomic processes, it is well to bear in mind that, although such processes have enclaved women in the reserves and exploited their labor while withdrawing men to work in wage-earning jobs, in reality wages alone cannot constitute an argument that men have benefited from those systems of oppression. In fact peoples who are dominated by a repressive regime, whether they are men or women, share a similar subordinate structural position vis-à-vis the dominant culture. What we must look for, then, is not how African women lost their development opportunity during colonial or contemporary neocolonial periods (since our men have also suffered the same loss) but, rather, the differential impact of such socioeconomic conditions on men and women.

In this respect, I am reminded of men in our villages who were once recruited as plantation workers or infantry soldiers to fight in colonial wars. They left their villages thinking that they would earn money or make some other fortune from earning wages in work or benefits from the army. Meanwhile, their wives worked on the land to keep the family on its feet at home. Now these men (some of them at least) are retired at home with no benefits, having spent their youth feeding the industrial and military machines of their days. In actuality they are no better off than their wives, who had to till the land to feed their children.

The alienation experienced by low-paid African (Senegalese) dockworkers and their womenfolk at the hands of French colonials is also well documented by Sembene Ousmane in his novel *God's Bits of Wood.* In another novel, *Mine Boy,* Peter Abrams vividly depicts the situation of

Ma Leah, a strong African woman in the slums of Johannesburg who earns a living by brewing and selling illicit liquor. She tries to evade the police but is finally arrested and jailed. In the same story her "daughter" Eliza, who is well educated, is estranged from the slum community in which she grew up. Yet she is excluded from the community of others (white people) who have comparable educational experience. Meanwhile Xuma, a man from the rural hinterland, arrives in Johannesburg to look for work. He gets a job and even becomes a leader of his co-workers in the mines. However, he is haunted by the idea of his friend who is dying of tuberculosis, having spent all his youth in the service of the mining industry. The three—Ma Leah, Eliza, Xuma—are all earning wages, but their position as Africans in a discriminatory job market remains in reality the same.

The second point I want to consider here is a problem with the notion of "integration of women in development," an expression developed by the United Nations and largely adopted by international aid agencies. One may well ask, "Integrating women into what development?" Historically, African women have been active in the provisioning of their families. This is a role which they play today, although they are being constricted in their efforts to feed their families by multinational corporations in food processing and agribusiness as well as by national land reform and crop programs. These women are well "integrated" into the dependent national economies. While it is possible to anticipate some structural changes through the implementation of some of the UN recommendations for special women's programs and women's bureaus or commissions, it is also likely that such institutional arrangements may serve in some instances to restrict rather than enhance the participation of women in their societies. Member states that pursue a program of development that negates equity can only be paying lip service to the issue when they agree to establish a women's bureau or commission. Such concepts as "integration of women in development" therefore require close scrutiny, in view of the fact that the majority of African peoples still operate within dependent economies. In such circumstances local participation tends to be characterized by what is sometimes referred to as "resistance to change," "apathy," or "indifference." Whenever a people have to use much of their creative energy for resistance, it means they are set back one step each time they approach a problem. The majority of Africans (men and women) find themselves in this situation. Thus questions of autonomy and self-determination still remain critical to an understanding of the problems surrounding female participation in contemporary Africa.

In ending this brief statement, I wish to reiterate what I consider to be central in understanding the position of African women today.

a) Any analysis must embrace the relationship between the international and national economic systems and women's position, including expectations of women in society and the contradictions associated with and arising from these expectations at the international, national, and domestic level.

b) African scholars, and especially women, must bring their knowledge to bear on presenting an African perspective on prospects and problems for women in local societies.

c) Scholars and persons engaged in development-research planning and implementation should pay attention to development priorities as local communities see them. This means an effort to bring these priorities to the attention of national governments and research groups and to encourage participation by local communities in identifying issues which they consider primary in their daily lives. In this way, there need not be an artificial boundary between practical and academic research, or between policy and theoretical research, on the role of women in development.

I would close by recalling a peasant woman in rural Kenya, who said the following when I asked her what development means to her: "During the anticolonial campaigns we were told that development would mean better living conditions. Several years have gone by, and all we see are people coming from the capital to write about us. For me the hoe and the water pot which served my grandmother still remain my source of livelihood. When I work on the land and fetch water from the river, I know I can eat. But this development which you talk about has yet to be seen in this village."

Institute for Development Studies
University of Nairobi
Nairobi, Kenya

Toward Models of Development

Development Planning for Women

Hanna Papanek

In 1975, delegates from United Nations member nations met in Mexico City. They considered "the integration of women in the development process as equal partners with men," defining development in terms of its broadest objectives: "to bring about sustained improvement in the well-being of the individual and of society and to bestow benefits on all."[1] If such goals could even be partly met, women and men throughout the world would benefit greatly.[2] Yet there are immediate obstacles in the way. In this brief essay, I discuss some of them and offer some remedies.

Some of the obstacles are political. Although some governments recognize the importance of women in a superficial sense, no government now in power stands or falls on its policies toward women. They do not constitute a single political constituency on issues of social and economic development, though other causes, such as reform of mar-

Discussions with fellow participants at the Wellesley Conference and with colleagues and friends in Asia and the United States helped to develop the ideas presented here. With respect to specific issues, I found recent conversations with Elinor Barber, Warren Ilchman, Rounaq Jahan, Gustav Papanek, Soedjatmoko and Catharine Stimpson particularly stimulating. I thank them all.

1. United Nations, World Conference of the International Women's Year, Mexico City, June 19–July 2, 1975, E/CONF.66/5, Provisional Agenda, item 11, paragraph 13.

2. Background papers and reports of discussions at an international seminar on women and development held in conjunction with the UN meetings in 1975 appear in Irene Tinker and Michele Bo Bramsen, eds., *Women and World Development* (Washington, D.C.: Overseas Development Council, 1976). See also Ester Boserup and Christina Liljencrantz, *Integration of Women in Development: Why, When, How* (New York: United Nations Development Programme, 1975).

riage laws, often unite them. Women's interests are usually overshadowed by broader allegiances to class or political movements. In the process of bargaining that is involved in development planning, or any other kind of social or economic policymaking, women's interests are therefore rarely considered. Indeed, they are generally thought to be subsumed by others, or to run counter to those of men.

Other obstacles are attitudinal. In societies that are changing very rapidly, ambiguous signals are presented to women. Fears are often translated into attempts to prevent changes in their roles. They become the repositories of "traditional" values imputed to them by men in order to reduce the stresses men face. Resistance to women's greater participation in economic and political life may be felt especially strongly among groups most exposed to rapid social change and most ambivalent about it. Politicians, intellectuals, and development planners are usually drawn from these groups. Women may also share these feelings and express them in their own conflicts about modern life. At the same time, women may feel economic and other pressures which lead them to nontraditional actions.

Still other obstacles are conceptual. First, a curious ambiguity in the concept of *integrating* women in the development process hampers the achievement of this goal from the start. For women *are* full participants in all processes of social change, in spite of the fact that they may be affected differently than men. However, these differences often seem to confirm the false notion that women are less central to major social processes than men. In turn, this misperception leads many to assume that women are a backward sector of society that needs to be "integrated" in order to be "modernized." This false and patronizing view is not a good basis for development policies. At the same time, women have, of course, been excluded from the development process in a political and technical sense. They have not participated in the decisions that affect both sexes. Where women must be integrated in development is development planning—the process by which many governments seek to advance the growth and distribution of available resources.

Second, governments may make wrong assumptions about the social responsibilities of men and women. They may act as if men supported families, rather than as if men and women *together* do so, or women do so *alone.* This affects employment practices in many nations, in both the public and private sectors, and plays a crucial role in development policies. For example, the employment of women is widely considered "supplemental" to that of men.[3] As a result, wages for women are generally much lower than those for men. Although many governments recognize the need to plan for male employment, few rec-

3. Nadia Haggag Youssef, *Women and Work in Developing Societies,* Population Monograph Series, no. 15 (Berkeley: Institute of International Studies, University of California, 1974).

ognize similar obligations toward women who support families.[4] Arguments about the need to provide earning opportunities for women are often brushed aside by planners concerned exclusively with male employment and unemployment.

A third conceptual obstacle is directly related to the second. In most societies the family with a male head is considered the primary institution where women and children are concerned. This implies a fundamental difference in the assumption of social responsibility by governments concerning the needs of men as compared with those of women and children. As long as women are considered the dependents of men, in the economic and legal sense, it will be difficult to consider women's needs *directly* in development planning. An important structural consequence of seeing women as dependents of men is the location of women's programs in the administrative structures of many governments. They are usually located in social welfare ministries or other bodies dealing with remedial action, on the assumption that governments can only intervene when families have failed. Development planning for women cannot be based on a social welfare approach, however, nor should it be located primarily in a social welfare ministry.

Underlying these conceptual problems is a misperception of the relations between men's and women's work, particularly the changes that occur in these relations in the process of social change. In many instances women's work is expected to substitute for that of men, and direct monetary rewards go to men. One example of this substitution effect as an institutionalized pattern, rather than a matter of individual choice, is the concept of the "unpaid family worker." The statistical offices of many nations use the category to describe those who work for another family member without pay to produce items that are ultimately sold. These terms usually refer to women, such as the carpet weavers of the Middle East, who receive subsistence but no wages from male family members who market the product.

By its very nature, the substitution of women's work for men's cannot be explained or measured in purely economic terms because it is dependent on the existence of noneconomic bonds between women and men. Both the demands for the work and the rewards for its performance are channeled through these noneconomic links, serving to enhance or diminish them. The expectations which govern these relationships between men's and women's work are clearly expressed in the paradoxical situation that while there are no ready measures to analyze women's contributions through their "nonproductive" labor to a family's or nation's ability to produce no one expects to get along without these unmeasurable contributions.

In addition, both domestic and nondomestic arenas of work are not

4. Tinker and Bramsen, pp. 158–59.

seen as part of a single system but are usually sharply distinguished in the analysis of work and its rewards. Yet the enormous variation in the respective limits of the two arenas in different classes, societies, and time periods suggests that a single system would be more useful for analysis than a dualistic approach. Existing concepts give insufficient permeability to the boundaries between the family and the rest of society; movements between the family and the rest of society are granted insufficient frequency. Available methods of analysis make it difficult to understand such interactions, in part because they draw a sharp distinction between work that results in a product that can be sold and work that does not. This entails a parallel distinction in terms of reward systems. "Market" activities receive wages; "nonmarket" activities do not. This has also led to economic analyses that differentiate between the "modern" sector, entirely market oriented, and the "traditional" sector, partly involved in subsistence. The preoccupation with wage labor in economic analysis and development planning, while relevant to industrial societies, may be much less so for largely agricultural nations. New analyses which meet their needs are particularly relevant for women.

In general, for studying women's work it is more realistic to develop systems of analysis that accommodate the interplay between types of work which occur in different arenas and are differently rewarded. An interactionist approach would also, by definition, stress the reciprocal relationships between the work of women and men, usually within the context of household or family. Such an approach would be particularly useful for studies of informal labor markets, barter exchanges, do-it-yourself work, work in child care and socialization, and so on. It also directly challenges two common assumptions: (1) much of women's work, particularly housework, is a nonoccupation in many societies, since "with the separation of the workplace from the home, housework [has] lost its economic value,"[5] and (2) women's social marginality is based on the marginality of women's work in the home.[6] On the contrary, an interactionist approach fosters the idea that women and their work are central to social and economic events.

An interactionist approach to women's and men's work is particularly important for development planning because the social transformations aimed for almost always involve shifts in the reciprocal relationships between men and women with respect to work and its rewards. Changes in the resources available to members of a particular class and shifts in class membership of individuals are implicit goals of much development planning. But the preconditions and effects of such shifts

5. Tamara K. Hareven, "Modernization and Family History: Perspectives on Social Change," *Signs: Journal of Women in Culture and Society* 2 (Autumn 1976): 190–206; quotation is from p. 201.

6. For an extensive discussion of these issues, see Eli Zaretsky, *Capitalism, the Family and Personal Life* (New York: Harper & Row, 1976).

on women are usually not well understood. As a result, development programs for women may be designed from the middle-class perspective of planners who assume that poor women "do nothing" and need government assistance "to give them something to do and earn a little money." When programs like this fail it is considered evidence that women's development programs are a mistake, rather than showing a lack of political will or understanding of conditions on the part of planners.

Planners need to understand the extent to which important changes in women's work occur in connection with broad shifts in the economy and society or when an individual or family moves into another class. This would make it possible to specify the conditions under which women enter or leave the paid labor force and the broader economic significance of women's paid and unpaid work in both the domestic and nondomestic arenas. As is beginning to be recognized, much of the economic activity of poor women in both rural and urban areas is not adequately understood by planners. Because upward social mobility into the middle class is accompanied by a withdrawal of women from the paid labor force in many societies, this pattern is often considered the norm for all classes. In these countries, the economic activities of middle-class women take another form. Instead of bringing outside resources into the family, they concentrate their work on managing the more complex consumption needs of the family and on maintaining the family's status through attention to children's schooling. Many middle-class women also create earning opportunities for themselves from a domestic base in response to rising aspirations or declining income from other sources without being classified as "economically active." In short, a clearer recognition of the class differences in women's work and its rewards must underlie development planning in order to generate policies relevant to the interests of people at all class levels.

A final obstacle to the integration of women in development is the argument that knowledge about women is so scarce that analyses and policies cannot be formulated. Yet development planners in many nations work, as a matter of course, in situations of very imperfect knowledge about many aspects of economy and society. While data on women are often insufficient, or buried in the wrong classifications in available reports, it would be a mistake to assume that development planners have no factual materials from which to work, so that all new programs must be based on completely new studies. Some conceptual frameworks can and must be transferred from existing models in the social sciences to originate a rigorous approach to the study of women along with the creation of innovative systems of analysis. New methods of data collection and classification can certainly be developed as well. Much of the research on women in affluent industrial countries can be useful in these efforts, particularly on topics like occupational segregation,[7] legal reform, health care, child care, single-parent families, female supported households, and the exclusion of women from decision-making positions.

If governments are to be genuinely concerned with women in development planning they must respond to certain arguments in which questions of their political survival and self-interest are addressed. One such line of argument is that a nation as a whole incurs certain losses when women are poorly educated, in bad health, or barred from many activities. These losses may be related to more general problems of economic growth, either as cause or as effect. As a result, including women intelligently in development planning might increase not only their individual well-being but the total of national resources. It is now clear, of course, that not including women in development planning so far has hurt women. As Ester Boserup[8] and others have pointed out, as a consequence of economic development many women have had to bear increased work loads, the loss of existing employment, or changes in the social and economic rewards associated with women's work, the value of which is almost always underrated.[9]

Development planning for women is congruent with other broad changes in the thinking of development planners in many nations. Past failures of development in many countries have combined with political pressures to reinforce the demands of social critics that development must mean more than greater productivity or more industrialization.[10] Such critics have urged wider distribution of the benefits of economic growth through more investment in education, provision of health and social services, and the development of "human resources," of which women are a particularly important aspect. In some of the poorest countries a lack of natural resources means that economic improvement must be based on labor-intensive activities that require the development of all human resources. Even in countries which are somewhat better off a strategy linking human resource development with planning for women has several advantages. First, it provides a context of support for

7. Martha Blaxall and Barbara Reagan, eds., *Women and the Workplace: The Implications of Occupational Segregation* (Chicago: University of Chicago Press, 1976).

8. Ester Boserup, *Woman's Role in Economic Development* (London: George Allen & Unwin, 1970; reprint ed., New York: St. Martin's Press, 1975).

9. The costs of public programs designed to substitute for the work of women in families may give a more accurate idea of the extent to which women's work is undervalued than the more usual practice of "pricing" housework in terms of wages earned by domestic servants. Class biases are likely to affect the costs of such programs, as those substituting for the work of middle-class women are usually more expensive. Inferences about the work of women from public costs, therefore, reflect class distinctions as well as broader social and political considerations.

10. A broad selection of recent papers in this area appears in Manning Nash, ed., *Essays on Economic Development and Cultural Change* (Chicago: University of Chicago Press, 1977). See also Mahbub ul Haq, *The Third World and the International Economic Order* (Washington, D.C.: Overseas Development Council, 1976).

women's programs. This is politically useful in overcoming some kinds of opposition to women's participation. Next, women's work is important in human resource development because of its relation to the service sector in many countries. Paid or unpaid, it is concentrated in services rather than production. Expansion of the service sector, however, will not automatically provide greater opportunities for women. There are many historical examples of men replacing women in "traditional" women's occupations, especially in the service sector. Women's opportunities will have to be carefully planned for to prevent such losses. Finally, linking women to human resource development would move development planning for women out of a segregated position to a central unit in the government. In general, *all* development programs should be examined for their impact on women, not just those thought to have a "women's angle." For instance, the introduction of new harvesting technology may result in unexpectedly widespread displacement of women whose work in this activity has been overlooked.

In some countries family planning programs may provide another important starting point for development planning for women. Many of the nations concerned about high rates of population growth and scarce resources have already recognized the importance of better knowledge about women to family-planning programs. Indeed, research projects established in this context have provided much information with important implications for women.[11] However, since women are generally not included among those who design and implement family-planning policies, the interests of the women who are the "targets" of these programs are often neglected or even harmed.

International agencies may be useful in the process of integrating women in development planning. For example, efforts of the United Nations, both during International Women's Year and in follow-up efforts, have already provided an important stimulus which must continue. International agencies could also arouse national planning boards by requiring accurate data and analyses of women's condition as a prerequisite to obtaining financial assistance for programs. Voluntary agencies can play important roles as well. In general, more money is now available to charitable organizations in affluent countries than can be absorbed by existing community self-help programs in poor countries. Although this situation may be temporary, these organizations can be very useful to the needs of women's programs. They may be more responsive to innovative ideas than large government agencies. In affluent

11. William P. McGreevey, Nancy Birdsall, James M. Creager, Anne S. McCook, and Bernice Slutsky, *The Policy Relevance of Recent Social Research on Fertility,* Occasional Monograph no. 2 (Washington, D.C.: Interdisciplinary Communications Programs, Smithsonian Institution, 1974); and Ronald Ridker, ed., *Population and Development: The Search for Selective Interventions* (Baltimore: Johns Hopkins Press, 1976).

countries special efforts should be made to influence these organizations to pay attention to women's needs in development projects.[12]

Of course, in any government or agency training will also be needed for people working on development planning for women, particularly if their prior advancement in professional work has been slowed down by prejudice against women. Positions generally should be filled by women, not only because they are most likely to feel a deep concern for women's problems but also because more representation of women in government is an important goal in itself. Very few women are now in the top levels of development planning staffs in most countries. This is partly due to the fact that they are staffed mainly by economists, a profession which on the whole contains very few women. To equip interested people with the necessary skills training programs should be worked out with international agencies, voluntary organizations, and universities in both the agricultural and the industrial nations.

In short, the integration of women in development should follow the same principles voiced by many critics of development planning: those whose lives are to be affected by social and economic policies must have a say in these decisions. Many of the political and structural obstacles in the way of integrating women in development can only be solved within each nation. But solutions to the conceptual, attitudinal, and methodological problems can be drawn from a much broader international context of research and experience. Women's work, in effect, is vital to the survival of families as well as to the implementation of status aspirations. It is crucial to the process of development itself and must be seen to be indispensable to it.

Department of Sociology
Boston University
Boston, Massachusetts, U.S.A.

12. Boserup and Liljencrantz, pp. 40–41; and Subcommittee on Women in Development of the Committee on Development Assistance, ACVAFS, *Criteria for Evaluation of Development Projects Involving Women* (New York: American Council of Voluntary Agencies for Foreign Service, 1975).

Changing Modes of Production

Introduction

Helen I. Safa

Although studies of Third World countries have increasingly questioned the benefits of development, the implications for the division of labor by sex have only begun to be explored. The essays in this section make an important contribution to this task. The pioneering work by Boserup,[1] to which several of these essays refer, concludes that women are often victims of development, that their status declines with their diminished productive role in the transition to an urban industrial economy based on wage labor. While generally confirming this hypothesis, these essays also show the process of development to be far more complex and suggest that each case be examined in its own particular cultural and historical context.

In Java, for example, Dutch colonialism did not push women out of rice production or lead to sharpened sexual dichotomies in the division of labor. However, according to Stoler demographic pressures and technological changes have increasingly stratified the village economy, with different effects for women in landless or small subsistence peasant families than for those in large landowning ones. Thus mechanization has eliminated many of the supplementary sources of employment on which poor women depended. In Stoler's view, "female autonomy and social power are a function of access to strategic resources within the domestic and social sphere" which are defined differently for each class within peasant society. Stoler refutes those who view peasant women as a

1. Ester Boserup, *Women's Role in Economic Development* (reprint ed.; New York: St. Martin's Press, 1975).

homogeneous social group. Sexual inequality, she argues, must be examined within the context of class inequality, for in a stratified society, both gender and class determine access to strategic resources.

Like Stoler, Chinchilla and Arizpe insist that it is impossible to analyze fully the impact of changing modes of production on women's status outside of a class context. Chinchilla documents the changes in female occupational patterns in Guatemala with the advent of monopoly capitalism based on foreign investment, particularly from the United States. She shows that poor, uneducated Guatemalan women, particularly in cities, are increasingly confined to the tertiary sector, largely as domestic servants. Women from middle and upper classes, on the other hand, are entering the same occupations which have generated expanding female employment in the United States, namely, white-collar jobs as clerks, office workers, and professionals. The percentage of women in white-collar jobs is still much smaller in Third World countries than in the United States and, as Arizpe observes, consists largely of young and unmarried women with at least a high school education; in Latin America, then, this would appear to be the only group of working women who have clearly benefited from the development process.

In Mexico, according to Arizpe, most women remain locked in the informal sector, in menial and poorly paid jobs as petty vendors and domestic servants. Domestic service provides the government with an excuse for not adopting a policy to increase and improve female employment. Education is clearly no panacea, for, as Arizpe demonstrates, women with the same schooling as men still experience higher unemployment rates. However, whereas middle- or upper-class women can choose not to work if they do not find suitable employment, poor women in the informal labor market are forced to work as a matter of survival, while their job options are severely reduced. Women's job options, Arizpe insists, must be examined within a class context.

Over and above structural impediments to sexual equality, such as education, class structure, and occupational segregation, we must also examine the cultural and ideological factors which keep women subordinate. Cultural factors are particularly emphasized by Kandiyoti, who compares the status of Turkish women in nomadic tribes, peasant villages, rural towns, and cities. The influence of the patrilineal extended household is pervasive in all sectors, but less so in towns and cities because of neolocal residence and the diminished importance of elders. Though urban women are more likely to head their own households, they play a sharply reduced role in the productive process when compared to peasant and nomadic women. The latter, however, do not receive any recognition for their own labor, not even their offspring, which belongs to the patrilineal extended family. Thus, we cannot speak of a simple decline in women's status with the transition to an urban wage labor economy. Their diminished role in production may be offset by other factors, which are, however, increasingly specific to certain class sectors.[2]

As these papers demonstrate, the growth of wage labor under capitalism not only widens the sexual division of labor but also increases class inequalities, placing the primary burden on proletarian women, who are doubly exploited as members of a subordinate class and sex. For most Third World women, class barriers are equally if not more important obstacles to genuine equality than sexual oppression. This is not to deny the importance of occupational segregation by sex but to argue that it must be examined in a class context, in the United States and other advanced capitalist societies as well as the developing countries. A closer examination of the class differences in sexual inequality in our society should dissuade us from assuming, as Arizpe points out, that the present occupational structure for women in advanced capitalist societies is an ideal toward which Third World countries should strive.

Department of Anthropology
Livingston College, Rutgers University
New Brunswick, New Jersey, U.S.A.

2. See June Nash and Helen Safa, *Sex and Class in Latin America* (New York: Praeger Publishers, 1976).

Changing Modes of Production

Women in the Informal Labor Sector: The Case of Mexico City

Lourdes Arizpe

In recent years, the informal labor sector has increasingly represented a testing point for theories of development. The proliferation of informal jobs in developing countries has been considered alternately a stage in the process of development and a blind alley leading a country back into underdevelopment. But social scientists and policymakers have rarely recognized that the majority of those left out of the formal occupational structure are women. It is, however, very difficult to establish the heuristic boundaries of the informal labor sector, particularly with respect to women. Are we referring to the intermittent part-time activities of women outside the household both in cities and in rural areas? But men also engage in such activities, for example, as street peddlers. Is the unpaid work of the wife and young unmarried daughters in a family enterprise such as a store an informal job? If unpaid labor is to be included in the informal labor sector, then women's voluntary community service and their unpaid domestic labor must also be taken into account. Moreover, since informal labor also comprises work not regulated through a contract, all low income, noncontractual jobs registered as formal occupations, such as paid domestic service, belong to this classification. Many low income and low productivity jobs included in the formal occupational structure and registered in national censuses, even when such a contract does exist, can be considered as a continuation of informal jobs as well and thus must be analyzed within the informal labor sector.

This paper assumes that the nature of the informal labor sector in a developing economy is a direct outgrowth of the type of industrialization a country is undergoing. Within this framework, this paper explores the degree of occupational choice that women have within the structural margins of employment. In recent years, the question of choice has become central to an analysis of women's participation in economic and political activities. Noting a decline in women's economic participation as development proceeds in certain underdeveloped countries, Ester Boserup asks whether this is due to difficulties in finding jobs or to voluntary withdrawal because of family obligations.[1] A definite answer is perhaps empirically unverifiable, because of the ideological nature of assumptions on which decisions are made. However, understanding the nature of the occupational options open to women will clarify the issues.

The Nature of the Informal Labor Sector

An individualistic theoretical viewpoint would assume that the types of jobs taken, the sex distribution, and the size of the informal labor sector are a result of random individual decisions. Research based on such a viewpoint would center on the way in which women weigh their options and decide on a course of action, but could not explain why those options alone were available. The usefulness of this individualistic approach in studying the informal labor sector is therefore quite limited. It can help show why certain women choose particular kinds of jobs at certain times, but not why women as a group tend to enter the informal labor sector rather than formal employment. The answer can only be found in understanding how capitalistic development affects women's economic roles.

According to developmental theory, labor shifts from agriculture to the modern sector and is absorbed by manufacturing industries, following the pattern of industrial growth in developed countries.[2] Although the informal labor sector is not explicitly referred to, we must infer that it is regarded only as a bridge over which workers pass in shifting from one sector to another. In most Latin American countries, as well as those in Africa and Asia, however, data show that the displaced labor from agriculture enters the informal labor sector, most often in the cities which provide a large market for such jobs, and remains there.[3] "The excess population (which in a system operated by peasants lives on the family farm) shows itself . . . mainly in domestic service, trading, and

1. Ester Boserup, "Employment of Women in Developing Countries" (paper presented at the International Population Conference, Liège, 1973), p. 387.

2. The main exponent for this theory is W. W. Rostow (*The Stages of Economic Growth: A Non-Communist Manifesto* [Cambridge: Cambridge University Press, 1960]).

3. Rodolfo Stavenhagen, *Sociologia y subdesarrollo* (México City: Nuestro Tiempo, 1972); F. H. Cardoso y Enzo Faletto, *Dependencia y desarrollo en America Latina* (México City: Siglo XXI, 1973); André Gunder Frank, *El Desarrollo del subdesarrollo* (México City: Escuela Nacional de Antropologia e Historia, 1972).

casual jobs."[4] Whereas these informal activities constituted a secondary source of income for the peasant household, they become a primary source of income as agriculture is increasingly dominated by wage labor, and people become wholly dependent upon them economically. At best, workers go into the service sector rather than manufacturing. Even in countries with moderate industrial growth, such as Brazil and Mexico, the jobs created by industrialization have been unable to compensate for the loss of employment in agriculture.[5] Rapid demographic growth has made this situation even more acute.

An alternative theoretical explanation to the expansion of the informal labor market in Latin America is provided by the concept of marginality. According to Quijano and Nun, the population displaced from agriculture has been unable to find a place in the modern sectors of developing economies because of the nature of their industrial growth.[6] Whereas the industrial reserve army in central capitalist economies provides an accommodating supply of labor, in underdeveloped countries labor absorption in industrial employment has not expanded at an adequate rate in proportion to the increase of available labor, so that large numbers of workers have no possibility of finding formal employment. This marginal population, waiting to enter the formal occupational sector, survives by low income, intermittent wage or self-employment. In other words, workers are pushed into the informal labor sector and into the services as a result of insufficient demand in the manufacturing sector, and they are destined never to leave them.

Recent studies, however, tend to cast doubts on some aspects of this theory. There has been a slow but steady absorption of workers, even unskilled ones such as rural migrants, into the formal sector in Brazil, Argentina, and Mexico, which have a moderate industrial growth rate.[7] Moreover, it has been argued by E. Hobsbawm that marginality has always existed in capitalist economies and that the difference between the industrial reserve army and the marginal population is not qualitative but quantitative. It has been suggested that "marginals" do fulfill specific functions within the economy. In Brazil, for example, full-employment policies have not prevented street vendors from pursuing their activities.[8] In Mexico City, certain manufacturers, who could not

4. Gunnar Myrdal, *Asian Drama* (New York: Twentieth Century Fund, 1968), p. 2042.

5. Paul Singer, *Economía política de la urbanización* (México City: Siglo XXI, 1975); E. Suarez Contreras, "Migración interna y oportunidades de empleo en la Cd. de Mexico," in *El perfil de México en 1980,* ed. J. Martínez Ríos, vol. 3 (México City: Siglo XXI, 1973).

6. Anibal Quijano, "Redefinición de la Dependencia y Proceso de Marginalización en América Latina," mimeographed (Comision Economica para America Latina, 1970); and José Nun, "Sobrepoblación relativa, ejército industrial de reserva y masa marginal," *Revista Latinoamericana de Sociologia,* vol. 69, no. 2 (1969).

7. Orlandina de Oliveira, *Absorción de mano de obra a la estructura ocupacional de la Ciudad de México* (México City: El Colegio de México, 1976).

8. Faria Vilmar, personal communication, February 1976.

place their products in supermarkets because of monopolistic trade practices, used street vendors successfully to increase sales. Finally, participation in the informal labor sector does not automatically result from lack of jobs in the other sectors. Some informal activities are traditional in an urban society and usually fulfill specific functions. Indeed, participation in some traditional urban informal jobs seems to be unaffected by fluctuations in labor demand. For although increase in surplus labor adds a greater number of workers to those traditional informal activities, it also creates new ones.

Women in Development: Their Participation in the Informal Labor Market

Statistically, the distribution of women in the labor force does tend to reflect the level of development of a country.[9] A detailed analysis of female labor participation according to the level of development of the Mexican states showed that "for every unit increase in the index of economic development, there is a corresponding increase of about three percentage points in the aggregate level of women's labor force activity."[10] However, the overall rate of participation can vary simply because of differences in statistical definitions. As Boserup has observed, "Official statistics in a developing country may show female activity rates increasing or decreasing over time without any real difference in the work performed by women being involved."[11] Some countries take women's labor in agriculture into account, while others do not. Usually neither part-time work outside the home nor work for a family enterprise is included in national censuses. The Mexican census, for example, only records women's primary activity, and since this is assumed to be domestic work, the frequent, and in many cases constant, involvement of women in the informal labor section does not appear in official statistics. Since women's domestic work is not classified as an economic activity, 79.9 percent of women in Mexico thus appear to be "economically inactive."

By and large, women's productive activities decline when they are no longer involved in the agricultural tasks and the cottage industries of a peasant economy. This is particularly evident where rural-urban migration is involved.[12] By the same token, the introduction of new technology, both in the agricultural sector and in industries, displaces women

9. Marta Tienda, "Regional Differentiation and the Sector Transformation of the Female Labor Force: Mexico, 1970" (Ph.D. diss., University of Texas, 1974); Boserup.

10. Tienda, p. 15.

11. Boserup, p. 388.

12. Ibid.

and restricts their access to new jobs.[13] During the first stage of industrialization, the types of industries that are established, mainly textiles and leather, are labor intensive and provide additional employment for women. But when mechanization advances, employment goes predominantly to men. For example, whereas women in 1900 comprised 45.3 percent of the Brazilian labor force, by 1970, notwithstanding industrial expansion, women represented 21 percent of the labor force.[14] Industrial growth, in fact, intensifies sectorial sex inequality in both developed and developing economies. As Schmink has remarked, "occupational segregation has, if anything, shown a tendency to increase in Venezuela."[15] Cultural factors must then be taken into account to explain differential sex distribution in the economy, especially the sex labeling of jobs and women's attitudes toward work.[16] More specifically, age and marital status influence the possibility of formal or informal employment for women. In Mexico, for example, "the level of participation of single females does seem to vary systematically with development levels, while the rates for ever-married females remains relatively unaltered by degree of development."[17] This may mean that divorced, widowed, or separated women work whether employment is expanding or not, while single women stay at home until industry offers them adequate jobs. Thus the increase in jobs does not benefit the most needy women who support their children, but the young women who will normally leave the labor force when they get married. In Latin America women's involvement in the labor force declines steadily after the age of twenty-five. Is this due to voluntary withdrawal, or to the unavailability of jobs for older women? I suggest that in Latin America, and perhaps in other developing regions, women's participation in formal employment declines with age while it increases in informal activities.

Women in the Mexican Labor Force

Women represent 20.6 percent of the Mexican labor force.[18] This is

13. Elsa Chaney and Marianne Schmink, "Las mujeres y la modernización: Acceso a la technología," *La Mujer en América Latina,* vol. 1 (México City: Sepsetentas, 1975).

14. Heleith Saffioti, "Relaciones de Sexo y Clases Sociales," *La Mujer en América Latina,* vol. 1. (México City: Sepsetentas, 1975).

15. Marianne Schmink, "Dependent Development and the Division of Labor by Sex" (paper presented at the Fifth National Meeting of the Latin American Studies Association, San Francisco, 1974), p. 15.

16. Ibid., p. 18; Nadia Youssef, "Social Structure and the Female Labor Force: The Case of Women Workers in Muslim Middle Eastern Countries," *Demography* 8, no. 4 (November 1971): 427–39; and Boserup, p. 387.

17. Tienda, p. 16.

18. R. Ruiz Harrell, "Aspectos demográficos, educativos y laborales de la mujer en México, 1960–1970" (paper presented at International Women's Year Conference, México City, 1975), p. 76.

a low percentage compared to that for other developing nations, which averages 26 percent.[19] This low figure stems partly from the inadequate registration of women's labor in rural areas. Because most of the women are engaged in agricultural tasks intermittently, particularly during seeding, weeding, and harvest time, they are classed only as housewives and are considered "economically inactive." However, if we add the "economically active" women to the "economically inactive" housewives, 94.7 percent of the female population over the age of twelve is involved in work, as compared to 89.7 percent of the male population. Significantly, only 17.5 percent of the women receive a wage for their labor, as compared to 90.3 percent of the men.[20] Keeping in mind the inaccuracy of figures for agriculture, the sectorial sex distribution in the Mexican economy is shown in table 1. Women are overwhelmingly employed in the tertiary sector of the Mexican economy, and about 40 percent are engaged in jobs of extremely low productivity and income.[21] In the manufacturing sector, they are concentrated in dress manufacturing, food, electrical equipment, and textile industries, primarily as administrative personnel.[22] Women rarely hold high administrative or professional posts; 60 percent are workers and employees, as compared to 37.1 percent of the men. Status differences between men and women are even more conspicuous in the modern sector of the economy; in Mexico City 25.1 percent of male office workers are classified as professional or technical in comparison to 14.6 percent of female office workers.

Sharp differences exist between the male and female unemploy-

Table 1

Sexual Distribution in Mexican Economy

Sector	Women (%)	Men (%)
Agriculture	10.0	47.2
Manufacturing	16.9	16.8
Services	64.5	26.8
Sector not specified	2.5	9.5
Insufficiently specified	6.1	2.7
Total	100	100

SOURCE.—R. Ruiz Harrell, "Aspectos demográficos, educativos y laborales de la mujer en México, 1960–1970" (paper presented at International Women's Year Conference, México City, 1975), p. 134.

19. International Labor Organization, *Womanpower* (Geneva: International Labor Organization, 1975).

20. Ruiz Harrell, p. 134.

21. Gloria Gonzalez Salazar, "La participación de la mujer en la actividad laboral en México," *La Mujer en América Latina,* vol. 1 (México City: Sepsetentas, 1975), p. 120.

22. Ruiz Harrell, p. 130. I am indebted to Ruiz Harrell for the remaining statistics in this section.

ment rates in Mexico. In recent decades, women's unemployment has risen at a faster rate (14 percent) than that of men (5.7 percent). By 1980, in Ruiz Harrel's estimation, female unemployment will overtake male unemployment, and 60 percent of all unemployed will be women.[23] Women have greater difficulties than men in finding a job for the first time, particularly in the thirty to thirty-nine age group, and according to the national census women take a longer time to find a job at all ages. As table 2 suggests, this situation persists even though women seeking employment have more years of education. Although educational background does generally correlate with unemployment, women with the same level of schooling as men have higher unemployment rates.

Women in the Labor Force in Mexico City

More women work in Mexico City (29.7 percent) than in the rest of the country (17.8 percent).[24] Women's participation in manufacturing has increased since the 1940s with the expansion of industries. In fact, they have been employed at a faster rate than men, who nonetheless hold double the number of middle-professional and technical jobs. In the 1960s, however, the rate of labor absorption in manufacturing decreased in Mexico City, while the service sector expanded, particularly in self-employment for craft production. As a result, unemployment increased in Mexico City during the sixties, particularly for women; female unemployment is twice as large in Mexico City as in the rest of

Table 2

Education and Unemployment

Educational Level	Unemployed Women (%)	Unemployed Men (%)
No schooling	11.0	24.2
Primary school:		
Grades 1–3	31.4	36.3
Grades 4–6	33.5	26.8
Grade 6	12.1	6.4
Secondary school	5.5	4.2
Middle education	4.8	1.2
Professional	1.7	0.9

SOURCE.—R. Ruiz Harrell, "Aspectos demográficos, educativos y laborales de la mujer en México, 1960–1970" (paper presented at International Women's Year Conference, México City, 1975), p. 134.

23. Ibid.
24. Suarez Contreras, p. 406 (see n. 5 above).

the country (46 percent vs. 20 percent).[25] Suarez Contreras has concluded that urban women, who have educational levels that are 20 percent higher than in the rest of the country, refuse to accept jobs of inferior status. On the other hand, in Mexico City, while the rate of female unemployment has increased, the rate of female participation in domestic labor has decreased between 1950 and 1970. In the rest of the country, significantly more women are now in domestic work per family than in 1950. This may be due to the fact that rural women who can find no work stay in the house to help with domestic tasks, whereas Mexico City women in the same situation consider themselves unemployed.

In Mexico City, 72.2 percent of working women as compared to 53.9 percent of men received less than the official minimum salary in 1970.[26] In the services, which employ 42.9 percent of the total female labor force, the figure is 72.9 percent. Of the total salaried labor force between twenty-one and sixty years of age in Mexico City, 18.1 percent of the men are in these low-income jobs, as compared to 35.6 percent of the women.[27] Table 3 shows the sex composition by occupation. It is these jobs, especially those of street peddler and unskilled worker in the services, that must be closely examined in relation to the informal employment of women.

The Strategies of Women in the Informal Labor Sector of Mexico City

The informal activities of women in Mexico City cover a broad range from private tutoring in foreign languages to dishwashing. However, a definite stratification of such tasks exists, related to at least two

Table 3

Composition of Marginal Labor Force by Sex

Occupation	Women (%)	Men (%)
Street peddlers	40.2	59.8
Unskilled workers in services (mainly salaried domestics)	71.8	28.2
Unskilled production workers	21.7	78.3
Unskilled construction workers	...	100.0
Peasants and agricultural peons	5.8	94.2

Source.—H. Muñoz, Orlandina de Oliveira, and Claudio Stern, "Migración y marginalidad occupacional en la Ciudad de México," in *El perfil de México en 1980,* ed. J. Martinez Rios (México City: Siglo XXI, 1973), 3:325–58.

25. Ibid., p. 387.
26. Gonzalez Salazar, p. 120.
27. H. Muñoz, Orlandina de Oliveira, and Claudio Stern, "Migración y marginalidad ocupacional en la Ciudad de México," in Rios, ed. (see n. 5 above).

clearly defined social groups: middle-class women with certain educational and social advantages, and working-class and "marginal" women with no schooling.

Mexican middle-class women generally consider work outside the home undesirable. According to social norms, their fulfillment, dignity, and respectability lie in home and children. Only a minority, usually university graduates, accept salaried work, notably of a professional kind, as a part of a woman's life. Thus it is only women whose husbands do not earn enough who generally engage in part-time activities to earn money. Most can be done at home, or in other women's homes, such as baking, embroidery, sewing or knitting, private tutoring in languages or school subjects, and craftsmanship, such as dolls, boxes, paintings, or leather work. Interestingly, all of these activities are normally done freely for friends and relatives; the only difference between such informal jobs and domestic or family tasks is wages.

Self-employment by middle-class women outside the home usually involves having a small restaurant, or a small shop that sells cakes, china, flowers, knitting, children's clothes, books, and records. A more traditional business is the neighborhood shop that sells everything from charcoal and candles to flour and sweets. The old shopkeeper who knows all the local gossip is still an institutional figure in some neighborhoods today. The women who can afford it might establish small song, dance, gymnastics, yoga, or "personality" academies—a full-time activity for the owner, a part-time activity for women teachers. Significantly, the clientele and the workers in these establishments are almost exclusively women; they constitute an all-female supply and demand labor market.

Lower-class women, in contrast, carry out their activities primarily in the streets or in other women's homes. These activities involve personal services and trade, but most especially domestic service. Domestic service functions as an economic safeguard for migrant and poor urban women because it is always available. However, because it partakes of the traditional female preoccupations with house, children, and kitchen, domestic work is not conceptualized as "a job." Since there is no contract, women can be fired with ease and can enter or leave domestic service at various times during their lives. Young women become chambermaids or nannies while they wait to marry; unmarried or separated mothers become domestics in order to support their children. Women between the ages of thirty-five and fifty can still get work as servants, provided they have no more than one child and no man; only rarely is the husband employed in the same house as gardener, chauffeur, or handyman. It is extremely rare for old women to enter domestic service; the possibility of inefficient work and illness makes employees reluctant to hire them.

Would domestic workers accept an eight-hour work schedule with higher wages if they were offered alternative employment? Given the fact that a female servant's wages are far below the official minimum salary, that she must be available for work day and night with only Sundays off, and that she is often mistreated, one could reasonably assume that she would be eager for another type of job. Indeed, most young women in domestic service today say that they would like to find other types of jobs. However, free room and board for herself and sometimes for her small child often makes domestic work a woman's best option.

Some women live with their husband or children and provide part-time household services, such as washing clothes, windows, and floors, mending clothes, looking after children or the house, and helping out at parties and celebrations. They go to the employer's house, sometimes to seven different houses a week, and return at night to their own homes. Such jobs are sought after and found through friends and relatives. Young lower-class girls can sometimes get a job in a factory or a shop, especially if they have "good appearance" (*buena presentación*). Or they help in the family enterprise—a restaurant, market stall, or shop.

Middle-aged and elderly women tend to go into petty trade or the sale of food in the streets. Whereas female petty trade usually involves edibles, such as sweets, chewing gum, fruit, and chocolates, in keeping with the traditional image of women as providers of food, men vendors sell clothes, belts, jewelry, and toys. Some women are provided with small carts by the city government; unauthorized street sellers, who move fast to avoid the police, are predominantly rural migrants, many of them Indians. Still other women sell food that they cook in charcoal burners outside their homes, near bus stations, sports grounds, university campuses, or factories. These two types of street vending have proliferated in Mexico City in recent years. However, they tend to offer an unnecessary service and to create their own demand, since a street vendor who sells what she just bought in the market two blocks away is not fulfilling a real demand. It is reasonable to suppose that if they had other alternatives, these women would not engage in such activities.

Data from my own research on a group of underprivileged migrant Indian women in Mexico City suggest that they have few choices open to them. These Mazahua peasants, who started migrating from their villages some 300 kilometers outside of Mexico City in the 1960s, cannot find alternative work. Because most of the men work only intermittently as construction peons, market porters, and in similar low-paid, informal positions, women are obliged to earn additional income through street selling. Widows and divorced or abandoned women who have migrated to the city with their children are also street vendors. Their blatant poverty has aroused public attention and led to a repression of their activities by city police. City officials have wondered why these women have not conveniently disappeared into domestic service. Indeed, domestic service is used as a shield against protest over women's high unemployment rate and over the government's unwillingness to do anything about it. A simple analysis shows the limited range of occupational choices open to lower-class women in Mexico City. Most of these migrant women have children and/or husbands and are thus disqualified from residential domestic service. Even if they were willing to be separated from their families, their wages would be lower than those paid to urban women, and they would probably be ill-treated by their employers. Irregular domestic service is also unavailable to them because they lack the necessary skills and the social contacts to find such jobs. As dishwashers and kitchen help in restaurants, they know that they would be exploited, sometimes working up to fifteen hours a day for extremely low pay. Young urban girls are usually preferred as waitresses. Finally, these migrant women lack the knowledge to sell in established markets; this requires an appropriate license for a stall, an ability to cope with market administrators and inspectors, and established business contracts to obtain their merchandise at wholesale prices. Outright begging is subject to police harassment, and Mazahua women consider it degrading. Thus, they prefer to sell fruit or sweets in the streets, an activity which they already know from their peasant villages. The network of former Mazahua migrants in the wholesale fruit and vegetable section of the Merced, the main city market, gives Mazahua women access to wholesale prices. In addition, street selling can be taken up and left at any time, either in order to return to the village or to stay at home when a child or husband is ill. Another advantage is that small children remain with their mother while she sells, at times that are convenient to her and in places where she can talk and joke with her friends and relatives. Even more important, income from sales in "good spots" is higher than her husband's unstable earnings as a construction worker or porter. Thus some husbands have stopped working altogether and only help their wives out by carrying the crates of fruit to the house, or by hiding the bulk of it in case the police arrest their wives. Others simply wait for their wives to bring home some money with which to get drunk. As this brief description suggests, given their occupational options, street selling provides the greatest advantages to these migrant women. Guided by decisions that are very rational, they make the most out of their hopeless, underprivileged situation.

Finally, another informal occupation open to women of all classes is prostitution. Data on prostitution are virtually nonexistent. According to one unpublished psychiatric study conducted in Mexico City, prostitutes are either extremely neurotic or mentally retarded, an explanation given in medical circles throughout the world. Although a serious attempt at a sociological survey was stopped by gangsterial opposition, bits of information suggest that young girls from middle-class families occasionally go into prostitution before marrying because they can make more money in one evening than in two weeks of secretarial work. For some, prostitution is a reaction against the tediousness and repression of their family life. The lack of reliable studies means that we can only speculate about the reasons why lower-class women become prostitutes. Judging from occasional data, it would seem that prostitution is a major informal source of income for women, but it is never taken into account in discussions of female economic participation or survival.

Conclusions

Informal activities in developing capitalist economies must be understood within the total pattern of employment in a given country. Whether temporarily or permanently, informal activities are usually taken up when formal jobs are unavailable. For women especially, the dividing line between formal and informal jobs is, as we have seen, very tenuous. On the one hand, formal employment implies a long-term, full-time contractual job, but this does not apply to paid domestic work, petty trade, and small craft production, all of which have large numbers of female workers. These jobs are considered informal if they are carried out intermittently on an irregular basis. On the other hand, the boundary between women's wage labor in the informal sector and unpaid household and community tasks is even more tenuous. A woman not needing an income will do exactly the same tasks—baking, sewing, embroidery, crafts, and tutoring—without pay that other women who need an income do for a wage. Indeed, at the formal end of the spectrum, women servants who earn a salary are considered economically active and are included in the GNP; midway, women do the same tasks on an informal basis—part time and intermittently—and yet are paid for them without being considered economically active and without being included in the GNP; at the other end of the spectrum, housewives do full-time domestic work with no payment and are considered outside the economic system. All of these women obviously are doing exactly the same type of work. Thus there is a very real need to reconceptualize women's work.

The analysis of female work in Mexico City has suggested that when women are in economic need, they press the system for payment of their domestic services—but not those done for their own families. Instead, women turn domestic duties into economic activities by offering such services to other women. This represents an all-female supply and demand market. At the same time, our analysis indicates that as long as women can enter paid domestic service, female unemployment will not be officially or publicly acknowledged. Government officials can claim that there is no female unemployment problem since lower-class women can always become servants.

As the data on Mexico City suggest, women withdraw from the

labor force by the age of thirty to raise a family, but later on are unable to reenter the labor force, primarily because of the unavailability of jobs. Since women with schooling have higher unemployment figures than their male counterparts, education, contrary to what is frequently argued, does not represent the determining factor in women's unemployment. Age is an important factor; expanded job opportunities in Mexico have gone to young women between the ages of fifteen and thirty. After thirty, the census indicates, women have more difficulty finding jobs than men. In such a situation, the notion that women should remain at home will tend to be reinforced, even by women themselves. Data showed an inverse correlation between women's unemployment and their participation in domestic tasks. Importantly, this means that female unemployment figures are far from accurate, since many women stay on sharing household duties rather than consider themselves unemployed when they are unable to find work.

When women who need to work cannot find jobs, they compensate for their unemployment by taking up informal activities. Middle-class women take up jobs they can carry out in their own homes or in those of other women. The largest number of women in Mexico City, though, the lower-class women, usually have to engage in informal activities even if their husband has a steady income. And of course, elderly, divorced, widowed, or single women depend entirely on informal activities. The ever-increasing number of women who sell fruits and sweets or snacks in the streets do not fill a demand within the urban economy, but create their own demand out of desperation, since they have no other economic alternative. Immigrant women in Mexico City have the most restricted range of options. The Mazahua women street sellers merely choose the activity that gives them the most advantages within their set of options. Indeed, if we were to ask them why they chose to work at such a low-income, harassed activity, most probably they would answer, "Well, one must carry on one's little fight, mustn't one?" [Pues tiene uno que hacer su luchita, ¿no?].

Center for Sociological Studies
El Colegio de México
México City, México

Industrialization, Monopoly Capitalism, and Women's Work in Guatemala

Norma S. Chinchilla

For different reasons, Marxists, feminists, and developmentalists have called attention to the alarming numbers of women in Third World countries who can neither depend on a "family wage" nor find employment in economies in which cash income is becoming increasingly necessary.[1] Surprisingly, very little is really understood about the political economy of women's work, the factors which determine when and where women are employed, and the social and political consequences of particular configurations of "women's work." Sex segregation in the labor force or exclusion from employment altogether is most often attributed to "tradition" or "male chauvinist attitudes" with little con-

I want to thank Susanne Jonas, David Tobis, Eric Wright, Pete Clecak, Raul Fernandez, Domna Stanton, and the Wellesley Conference Editorial Committee for their valuable comments on an earlier draft of this paper. I also want to thank the personnel at the Instituto de Investigaciones Económicas y Sociales (Universidad de San Carlos), Dirección General de Estadística, Sección Industrial de Censo, and Departmento de Estudios Economicos del Banco de Guatemala for helping me gain access to Guatemalan data, although they are not responsible for my calculations or the interpretation I give them. My research for this paper was supported by a grant from the Social Science Research Council.

1. See, e.g., Frederick Engels, *Origin of the Family, State, and Private Property* (New York: International Publishers, 1972); and Charlotte Perkins Gilman, *The Home: Its Work and Influence* (New York: Maclure, Phillips & Co., 1903). Two authors who make reference to the connection between decreased fertility and women working outside the home are Nadia Haggag Youssef, *Women and Work in Developing Societies,* Population Monograph Series, no. 15 (Berkeley: University of California, 1974), p. 2; and Nora Scott Kinzer, "Priests, Machos, and Babies: Or Latin American Women and the Manichaean Heresy," *Journal of Marriage and the Family* 35, no. 2 (1973): 300–312.

sideration of historical changes in the occupational structure and changes in the allocation of work by sex. All too often it is assumed, although with less frequency now than a few years ago, that women in "traditional" societies are always confined to "traditional" roles, that is, restricted to domestic production in the home. The possibility that industrial growth and "modernization" might actually bring about greater restrictions on the ability of females to contribute directly to family economics and create the need for ideologies that justify the continued work of the majority of women in the home is one that has been discussed only recently.

It makes little sense to study changes in women's work independently from that of men, just as it gives an incomplete understanding to study occupational structures or industrial growth independently of an international context of investment, production, and control.[2] Industrialization almost universally destroys or weakens artisan industries, which are usually in the hands of women. But whether industrialization then absorbs the women displaced from productive roles in the home or traditional precapitalist economy into manufacturing depends on the total political-economic context in which it occurs and the extent to which it breaks down feudal or precapitalist relations, creates a demand for labor in the dynamic sectors of the economy, and redistributes wealth internally. The fate of women, the way they carry out their daily tasks, and the view of the world they derive from these experiences depends, in the final analysis, not so much on the policies of their governments or the "enlightenment" of the men around them as on the function that the economy of which they are a part serves in the world system.

Guatemala is a case of rapid recent industrial growth in which, unlike industrialization in late nineteenth century Mexico and early twentieth century Argentina, women have not been pushed into manufacturing industries in large numbers and have even declined proportionally in industries considered "female."[3] Although more women are working than ever before, the proportion of women officially classified as working has changed very little. Those who work remain largely in the most backward sectors of the economy, except for the rapidly expanding clerical, sales, and professional strata. Industrial growth is mostly capital intensive, based on foreign monopoly capital, and exploitative of a cheap labor force. This industrialization, rather than de-

2. Much work, including the present research, has been stimulated by Harry Braverman's provocative study, *Labor and Monopoly Capital: The Degradation of Work in the Twentieth Century* (New York: Monthly Review Press, 1974).

3. See Margaret Towner, "Monopoly Capitalism and Women's Work during the Porfiriato," and Nancy Caro Hollander, "Women Workers and the Class Struggle: The Case of Argentina," both in *Latin American Perspectives* 4 (Winter 1977): 90–105 and 180–93, respectively.

stroying the large agricultural sector, has held intact a sector which produces cash crops for export but which relies on traditional, labor-intensive methods of production, including a large seasonally employed work force. This study is designed to explore, within this particular historical context, the changes in occupational structure, demand for labor, division of labor by sex, and inequality of employment by sex during industrial expansion.

Foreign Capital, Industry, and Women's Work in Guatemala before 1944

Capitalist relations of production came late to Guatemala. Before World War II the proportion of the population that was working for wages was very small. The coffee boom of the 1880s relied on forced labor of the indigenous population. This revival of feudal institutions from the Spanish colonial period insured cheap and "willing" workers to harvest coffee. The Liberal state not only supported the claims of the coffee growers that it would be impossible for them to pay wages, but itself took advantage of the Indian labor to build the infrastructure of a modern economy and to maintain the army.[4] When not "serving time," the indigenous agricultural population was engaged in small cultivation for consumption or limited trading on a local market. Commerce as well as artisan crafts were largely in the hands of non-Indians (*ladinos*) and some foreigners.

Foreign control of the Guatemalan economy was established very early and was not successfully challenged, and even then in a limited way, until the revolution of 1944. Manufacturing and modern forms of industrial organization began after the liberal reforms of the 1880s and were made possible by the establishment of public education, communications, a banking system, and new roads and ports.[5] These advances, together with a centralized government administration (most often presided over by a dictator) and a large reserve of labor, made Guatemala an attractive site for foreign investment—first German coffee and banking interests, then large banana, electric, and railroad monopolies from the United States. Although the first manufacturing establishments, founded with the profits of the coffee boom and encouraged by the government's vigorous diversification policy, were in native hands, the

4. Susanne Jonas, "Guatemala, Land of Eternal Struggle," in *Latin America: The Struggle with Dependency and Beyond,* ed. Ronald Chilcote and Joel Edelstein (Cambridge, Mass.: Schenkman, 1974), pp. 103–93; Chester Lloyd Jones, *Guatemala: Past and Present* (Minneapolis: University of Minnesota Press, 1940); and Jaime Diaz Rozzotto, *El Caracter de la Revolución Democratico Burgesa Corriente* (Mexico: Ediciones Revista "Hoirizonte" Costa Amic, 1958).

5. Jones.

native bourgeoisie remained weak due to its dependence on the boom-bust market of exports like coffee. The state also depended on unstable exports for its income, and when the coffee fortunes declined around the turn of the century, its treasuries were depleted. Even during the coffee boom, German creditors, with their access to European banks, were able not only to appropriate many coffee farms but to monopolize grain export to the extent of fixing its price on the internal market.[6]

Lured by concessions offered by the dictator Cabrera, three large U.S. companies—the United Fruit Company, Electric Bond and Share, and International Railways of Central America—entered Guatemala and were able to dominate its economy and politics until 1944. Among them, they had the power to enthrone and dethrone presidents and to exploit local labor.[7] They brought modern forms of industrial organization and a modern occupational structure and recruited the first politically important class of wage laborers. Their workers formed the workers' organizations which were the forerunners of modern unions. Conflicts between the workers and the companies and between the rest of society and the companies finally resulted in the ouster of dictator Ubico in the revolution of 1944 and the demand that the remaining barriers to full industrialization be removed.

In the context of a largely agricultural economy in which most of the population worked under precapitalist relations of production, it is not surprising that female suffrage was never seriously considered in the package of reforms that characterize the Liberal period. One of the leading intellectuals opined that there was no point in introducing political equality for women in Guatemala since it clearly had "not worked" in the countries where it had been tried: "The right of suffrage ought not to be granted to the woman for nature created her for the home and she is only fitted to be occupied with the multitudinous and difficult family cares, in feeding and educating the children, in teaching them morals and to know the rights and duties which they will later have as citizens. The destiny of the mother does not permit her to busy herself with politics."[8]

Yet contrary to this idealized image, the contribution of women to social production in an economy in which the boundaries between home and work were still unclear must have been great. Women undoubtedly raised food for family consumption or exchange and made clothing, pottery, candles, and cooking utensils. When forced labor was reinstituted in the last quarter of the nineteenth century, rural women must have shared if not assumed completely the responsibility for cultivation while the men were away. The 1921 census records that women made up more than half (58 percent) of the nonagricultural labor force and 18

6. Diaz Rozzotto, p. 27.

7. Ibid.

8. Rafael Montufar, cited by Jones, p. 105.

percent of the total number of workers.[9] Furthermore, women were employed in the sectors of the economy with the largest numbers of workers: 45 percent of those in food; 20 percent of the public employees (including teachers, nurses, and nuns); 10 percent of those in "electricity"; 9 percent of those in "specialized arts and industries" (musicians, office workers, typesetters, fireworks makers); and 0.8 percent of those in "furs and skins" (see table 1). The largest number of female employees, then as now, were domestic workers—63 percent. Even when this figure is removed from the statistics, women still made up 26 percent of all nonagricultural, nondomestic workers, a proportion which has declined with industrialization.

While the census data are of unknown reliability, it would appear

Table 1

Female Occupations in Guatemala, 1920

Occupation	% Female	Total (Male and Female)
Pottery making	85.9	2,287
Specialized arts and industries (artists, acrobats, mattress makers, collectors, midwives, impresarios, book binders, musicians, florists, innkeepers, typists, evangelical missionaries, masseuses, office workers, hair stylists, fireworks makers, typographers, secretaries)	9.0	4,865
Alcoholic and fermented beverages	52.0	295
Food and rations (caterers, atole makers, charcoal suppliers, juice makers, soap makers, bakers, tortilla makers, tamale makers, provisions [e.g., mess halls, etc.])	45.0	7,519
Commerce (peddlers, merchants, candle sellers)	19.0	17,147
Electricity (telephone operators)	10.0	156
Clothing (embroiderers, dressmakers, designers, tailors, hat makers)	72.0	13,618
Miscellaneous manufacturing (basket makers, torch makers, fence makers [*enrejadoras*], industrialists, gourd makers [*jicareros*], mat makers [*petateros*], rope makers)	87.0	2,180
Cakes, pastry, and candy (barquilleras, candy makers)	88.0	509
Furs and leather (shoemakers)	1.0	
Professionals (pharmacists, librarians, translators)	0.8	1,380
Domestic services (ironers, housekeepers, cooks, chambermaids, governesses, domestics, wet nurses, baby-sitters, servants)	97.0	63,998
Government services (public employees, nurses, Sisters of Charity)	32.0	4,435
Tobacco (cigarette and cigar makers)	100.0	2,628
Weavers in silk, wool, and cotton (combers, weavers, knitters, dyers)	88.0	7,766
Total (19% of total work force)	...	519,183

SOURCE.—Calculated from *Censo de la población de la Repúbliva* (Guatemala: Tipografiá Nacional, 1921).

9. Dirección General de Estadística, *Censo de población* (Guatemala: Tipografiá Nacional, 1921).

that the contribution of women to nondomestic production prior to industrialization was great. Accurate representation of rural as well as urban occupations would only increase evidence of that contribution. While it would be important to substantiate such a conclusion with further historical research, the evidence raised here suggests that Guatemalan women had an economic role not unlike that of women in preindustrial, precapitalist Mexico, Argentina, and the United States —an important and varied one.

Nationalist Capitalist Industrialization, 1944–54

By 1944 the repressed demands for industrial expansion and agrarian reform had exploded into the "revolution of 1944," based on a multiclass movement in which urban women, especially teachers, played an important role.[10] The early reforms extended bourgeois democracy and legal protections for workers. Programs included expansion of education, establishment of rural schools, creation of social security for workers, encouragement of unions, indemnification for dismissed workers, regulation of exploitative working conditions (especially for women), guaranteed maternity leave, recognition of "illegitimate" children, and political equality.[11] The government strategy for industrial growth reflected the dual goals of the multiclass movement: "social justice" for workers and peasants and competitive opportunities for national "progressive" capitalists interested in producing for the expanding internal market. Foreign investors were to be welcomed as long as they obeyed indigenous labor laws. The Guatemalan state was to assume a larger role in planning, directing, and regulating investment.

Although landlord and foreign capitalist opposition to agrarian reform and regulation of foreign investment created uncertainty and hindered industrial expansion, the index of manufacturing increased a healthy 13.1 percent in four years (1946–50), due to growth in the tobacco, chemical, nonmetallic mineral, and food industries. Output declined slightly in textiles, clothing, and wood. Industries appeared in new areas of production, including cement, food processing, clothing, and transformation of raw materials.[12] At the beginning of the period, the largest concentrations of workers were still in traditional industries:

10. The teachers founded a permanent national association, the STEG, on January 15, 1945, which became second only to the railway workers' union in political importance; see Diaz Rozzotto; and Edwin Bishop, "The Guatemalan Labor Movement, 1944–1959" (Ph.D. diss., University of Wisconsin, 1959).

11. Diaz Rozzotto; and Susanne Jonas, " 'The Democracy That Gave Way': The Guatemalan Revolution of 1944–54," in *Guatemala,* ed. Susanne Jonas and David Tobis (Berkeley, Calif.: North American Congress on Latin America, 1974), pp. 44–56.

12. Mario Monteforte Toledo, *Centro America: Subdesarrollo y Dependencia,* (Mexico: Universidad Nacional Autónoma de Mexico, 1972), 1:274.

food, clothing, footwear, and textiles. These, in addition to chemicals (especially fireworks and match-making), were also the highest categories of female employment (see table 2). Although we lack reliable data on the number of new workers who entered the work force during this period, it seems likely that more women were drawn into industrial employment at the same time that women's wages in manufacturing increased (see table 3).

Industrialization with Redistribution, 1954 to Present

The revolution of 1944 was overturned ten years later and with it the "soft line" on industrialization. Faced with increasingly militant workers and peasants on the one hand and the active opposition of landowners and U.S. investors (most notoriously United Fruit) on the other, the multiclass alliance crumbled. Counterrevolution and the "hard line" on industrialization took its place. The "soft line" policy had been characterized by agrarian reform, increased consumption, improvement of the standard of living, alleviation of gross inequities, regulation of foreign investment, and policies favoring public investment and the middle class. To return to this policy after the Arbenz government was overthrown in 1954 would have meant a return to working-class militancy. "Hard line" industrial strategy seemed the only means to contain class struggle (in the short run) and leave existing dominant groups intact. The strategy of no confrontation and minimum state interference depended on the establishment of the Central American Common Market in order to expand demand without internal redistribution.[13] Generous incentives were given through it to industries which developed new exports (cattle, flowers, seeds, and nonessential oils) and those which assembled products previously imported (drugs, cosmetics, etc.). National investors were guaranteed no tax reforms and minimal state interferences, while foreign investors were promised free repatriation of profits.[14]

The hard line industrial strategy has yielded increased output, but the benefits of increased production have accrued to a very few. The market remains very small, and the jobs created few. As a result, the number of people working in agriculture and the service sector remain high, and both foreign investors and large landowners have a vested

13. Susanne Jonas, "Master-minding the Mini-Market: U.S. Aid to the Central American Common Market," in Jonas and Tobis, pp. 86–103.

14. As much as 66 percent of all direct investments came from the United States in 1969, an increase of 128.8 percent over 1950, as compared to an increase of 37 percent during the 1950s (see Gert Rosenthal, "The Development of the Central American Common Market [Ph.D. thesis, Gúatémála, 1971], chap. 3, pp. 4, 5, 10, cited by David Tobis, "The U.S. Investment Bubble in Guatemala," in Jonas and Tobis, p. 132, n. 3).

Table 2

Indices of Manufacturing Production, Total Employment, and Female Employment, 1965 (1946 = 100)

Industry	Production		Employment (1965)			% Female (1965)	
	1965	1973	Overall	Male	Female	1946	1965
Foods	204.3	242.5	445	510	263	26	16
Beverages	140.6	201.8	82	81	92	5	6
Tobacco	203.5	266.5	76	202	35	75	53
Chemicals	610.8	728.2	338	300	227	36	24
Furs and leather	121.1	64.9	102	97	262	3	7
Textiles	182.0	253.3	138	151	115	35	30
Clothing and shoes	279.8	524.4	89	123	144	28	45
Electricity	736.2	1,583.5	...	...	...	...	...
Wood and cork	135.6	255.2	106	104	319	1	3
Nonmetallic minerals	666.0	914.0	148	146	310	1	3
Paper	...	...	174	433	250	63	9
Printing	...	...	233	242	166	11	8
Rubber	...	...	556	684	297	33	18
Metal products	...	...	204	296	518	...	...
Machinery	...	...	74	73	180	2	6
Electrical appliances	...	...	(528)*	(397)*	(231)*	...	31
Transportation	...	...	(976)*	(944)*	(132)*	...	4
Furniture	...	...	(913)*	(860)*	(153)*	...	...
Misc. manufacture	...	...	178	150	351	14	3
Total	247.7	380.3	187	298	150	22	18
Durable Goods Index	...	568.1	...	...	...	...	...

SOURCE.—Calculated from data in First and Fourth Industrial Census, as reported in letter from Banco de Guatemala, November 15, 1976.
*These categories reported no workers in 1946.

Table 3

Index of Wage Inequality by Sex in Selected Industries, Guatemala, 1946, 1965, and 1973

	1946				1965				1973			
	Wages of Skilled Female as % of Male & Q/mo.		Wages of Unskilled Female as % of Male & Q/mo.		Wages of Skilled Female as % of Male & Q/hr.		Wages of Unskilled Female as % of Male & Q/hr.		Wages of Skilled Female as % of Male & Q/hr.		Wages of Unskilled Female as % of Male & Q/hr.	
Foods	32.0	(88.92)	36.5	(51.85)	79.6	(0.49)	70.4	(0.27)	55.6	(0.54)	77.4	(0.31)
Beverages	...	...	...	...	74.5	(0.55)	100.0	(0.32)	40.6	(0.64)	...	...
Tobacco	60.2	(106.03)	45.2	(80.79)	114.4	(0.79)	64.0	(0.50)	25.2	(1.15)	145.6	(0.99)
Textiles	24.5	(135.05)	43.9	(77.68)	72.1	(0.43)	128.0	(0.25)	71.7	(0.46)	87.1	(0.27)
Clothing and shoes	49.1	(67.30)	54.3	(61.02)	95.0	(0.40)	88.9	(0.27)	86.8	(0.38)	87.1	(0.27)
Printing	19.2	(192.82)	79.7	(69.00)	31.3	(0.67)	77.8	(0.27)	54.4	(0.63)	86.1	(0.31)
Rubber	...	...	...	...	57.4	(0.47)	59.5	(0.37)	74.6	(0.59)	117.6	(0.40)
Total (all industries surveyed)	35.4	(106.66)	41.8	(72.30)	54.5	(0.55)	89.7	(0.29)	57.0	(0.63)	86.8	(0.33)

SOURCE.—These figures are calculated from data presented in the First Industrial Census of Guatemala, December, 1946, and Reports to Dirección de Estadística, Sección Industrial.
NOTE.—Quetzal (Q) = 1 U.S. Dollar ($).

interest in keeping it that way. Most industries lured by such a scheme are capital-intensive, multinational giants which consolidate or eliminate existing industries, replace old job categories with some new ones, and create little overall employment. A few industries, particularly those in clothing and textiles, are labor-intensive "run-away shops" that take advantage of the large labor pool. While there are no available statistics on the capital-labor ratio for industry alone, a United States AID study reported that U.S. investment in Guatemala accounts for 11 percent of the total direct investment, but only 1 percent of the labor force; the national average of people employed per $100,000 of total assets is 658, as compared to fifty-eight for U.S. capital.[15]

Land and Rural Labor

In the two decades since agrarian reforms were abolished, agricultural land ownership has reconcentrated. By 1964, 62.6 percent of the arable land was held by 2.1 percent of the farms, while almost 98 percent of the units represented only 37 percent of the arable land.[16] Furthermore, while concentration of ownership is high, proportional use is low; multifamily large farms utilize only 5 percent and multifamily medium farms only 9 percent of the area they control. Farming continues to be extensive, labor intensive, and oriented toward unstable international markets. Severe repression of union activities and the few alternatives for employment assure low wages, which is clearly beneficial to landlords and foreign investors.

Although agricultural production has become large and modern, working conditions are almost as harsh as they were under forced labor. Seasonal workers, recruited on large *fincas,* often work as a family unit to pay off loans incurred earlier in the year. Their hours are long, their rations meager, their housing sparse. Women and children risk transportation in open trucks and often die in accidents or of carbon monoxide fumes. They live primitively, with as many as 500 workers in large open-air dormitories that have dirt floors and laminated roofs, no sanitary facilities, electricity, or portable water. They sleep on the ground, in hammocks, or on straw mats. They are given about twelve to fourteen pounds of corn per week, one to two pounds of beans, and occasionally some sugar and rice. Children receive half rations and women none if they do not work because of their young children. Sickness among workers who migrate from the highlands to the coastal lowlands is com-

15. Phil Church, "Foreign Investment: The Operation of U.S. Direct Investment in Guatemala" (unclassified U.S. AID document, CERP D, Guatemala, A-107, June 16, 1972, pp. 4–5), cited by Tobis, "U.S. Investment Bubble," in Jonas and Tobis, p. 133, n. 11.

16. The data are from the *1964 Censo Agropequário,* cited by Carlos Figueroa Ibarra, *El Proletariado Rural en el Agro Guatemalteco* (San Carlos, Guatemala: Instituto de Investigaciones Económicas y Sociales, University of San Carlos, 1976), p. 76.

mon. Insecticide poisoning is frequent, and the amount of DDT in mothers' milk has been found to be dangerously high. Women earn the same wages as men and are an important part of the rural labor force, although only 7 percent are officially registered as agricultural workers (see table 4). Even with all of its members working, however, an entire family earned an average of $1.00 a day in 1966, and about half of that was actually taken back after the migration.[17] Only food from the subfamily plot and occasional cash income from the sales of handicrafts and wood can help rural families survive on the low wages of seasonal labor.

Employment and Industrialization

Agriculture remains the most important sector of the economy in terms of foreign exchange and employment; in 1973 it employed 65.5 percent of all male workers. Nevertheless, because the absolute increase in male workers is very small, it is clear that for the growing rural population, agriculture as a source of *new* employment has fallen behind. The index of manufacturing, on the other hand, has climbed steadily since 1960, and the index of durable goods has climbed even faster (see table 2). Manufacturing and construction have attracted large amounts of new investment and have increased the absolute number of jobs. In 1973 there were 279,639 workers in this sector of the economy, or 18.1 percent of the labor force (see table 4). The number of new occupational specialties has created a demand for new labor which men have filled in much greater proportion than women, even in industries, such as textiles and tobacco, that have traditionally hired women.

The reasons for this decline of female workers in the productive sectors of the economy become clearer when the statistics on wage labor are examined. In the 1973 census 48 percent of the employed were said to be working for wages or salaries (the rest were either self-employed, unremunerated family laborers, or owners [1.2 percent]). Among these workers, the rate of wage labor was much higher for women than for men (66 percent as compared to 45 percent) because of the large proportion of men who work in agriculture and the probable underreporting of women who do not work for wages or salaries. In the manufacturing sector, however, the proportions are reversed: 32.4 percent of the women and 57.6 percent of the men work for wages (57 percent and 34.7 percent, respectively, are "self-employed"). It would appear to be the destruction of independent artisan industries, without an increased demand for factory labor, that has seriously affected the employment of

17. Lester J. Schmid, "El Papel de la mano de obra migratoria en el desarrollo económico de Guatemala," *Economia* 15 (1968): 68–70; and Escuela Facultativa de C.C. Económicas de Occidente y Comité Interamericano de Desarrollo Agrícola, *Tenéncia de la Tierra y Desarrollo Socio-Económico del Sector Agrícola en Guatemala* (Guatemala: Editorial Universitária, 1971).

Table 4

Labor Force by Sex and Basic Sector, 1950, 1964, and 1973 Index (1950 = 100)

	1950			1964			1973		
	Male (%)	Female (%)	Total (%)	Male (%)	Female (%)	Total (%)	Male (%)	Female (%)	Total (%)
Primary (agriculture, silviculture, hunting, fishing, and mining)	76.2	14.6	68.3 (660,991)	73.3	12.1	65.8 (895,119)	65.5	7.0	57.3 (885,989)
Secondary (manufacture, construction, electricity, gas, water, sanitary services)	12.4	28.1	14.4 (139,209)	12.5	21.4	13.6 (187,074)	17.5	21.7	18.1 (279,639)
Tertiary (commerce, transportation, communication, services)	11.0	57.0	16.9 (163,618)	14.2	66.5	19.9 (270,757)	15.0	67.9	22.4 (347,273)
Undetermined	0.4	0.3	0.4 (3,996)	...	...	0.8 (10,719)	1.9	3.4	2.1 (32,757)

SOURCE.—Calculated from 1950, 1964, and 1973 *Censo de población de la República.*
NOTE.—Total of workers in each category is in parentheses.

women in the manufacturing sector. Moreover, the industrial censuses of 1946 and 1965 report a decline in female workers from 22 to 18 percent (see table 2). The largest declines are in tobacco, textiles, chemicals, rubber, foods, and paper. For male workers, on the other hand, employment is rapidly increasing in the areas of chemicals, paper, rubber, and metal products, as well as electrical appliances, transportation, and furniture, which first appear in the 1965 census. Thus, not only have new industries created a disproportionate demand for male labor, but men are replacing women in some industries. In absolute terms, overall male employment climbed much higher than overall female employment in this period—an index of 298 compared to 150 in the industrial census (see table 2) and 215 to 134 in the population census (see table 5).

Since many workers classified under manufacturing are not engaged directly in production, the statistics on skilled and unskilled labor by sex are perhaps a better indicator of actual changes in those occupations. We might expect occupations in manufacturing to expand considerably with industrialization. It is true that in absolute terms the operative and unskilled categories increased for women (27 and 7 percent, respectively) as well as for men (37 and 11 percent) between 1946 and 1973 (see table 6). But the increase in operative jobs for women is lower than the overall 30 percent increase of females in the work force, although it is still much higher than the increase of males (11 percent in the twenty-seven-year period). The proportion of nonagricultural male and female workers in skilled labor, on the other hand, declined between 1950 and 1973, from 32.5 percent to 20.9 percent for women and from 48.8 percent to 43.2 percent for men. The proportion of unskilled or manual laborers for both sexes has remained the same (see table 6). Thus, while significantly changing the distribution of investment, the expansion of industries in manufacturing and construction has clearly done little to change the overall distribution of employment. There has been only a slight overall increase in the proportion of workers in this sector in twenty-three years, from 14.4 percent in 1950 to 18.1 percent in 1973 (see table 4).

Since the population continues to increase, and agriculture and manufacturing absorb relatively little labor, the residual category, that is, the tertiary sector, composed of commerce, transportation, communication, and services, must act as the "sponge" for the remaining labor. This sector now employs 22.4 percent of all workers, as compared to 16.9 percent in 1950 and 19.9 percent in 1964 (see table 4). The increases are not as dramatic for women, who have been concentrated in this sector since the 1921 census as domestic servants or teachers. While two out of three women worked in the tertiary sector in 1973, the majority were not employed in commerce, transportation, or communications (as were 44 percent of male workers), but in domestic service; 64 percent of all

Table 5

Index of Employment by Sex and Sector, 1964 and 1973 (1950 = 100)

Sector	Females		Males	
	1964	1973	1964	1973
Agriculture	...	...	136	135
Mining	...	...	140	132
Manufacturing	103	134	145	215
Construction	...	...	138	242
Electricity	...	...	126	330
Commerce	142	216	169	219
Transportation	158	277	192	256
Services	157	205	173	198
Unspecified	520	172	238	712
Total	134 (166,924)*	175 (216,928)	142 (1,196,745)	158 (1,328,730)

SOURCE.—Calculated from 1950, 1964, and 1973 *Censo de la población de la República.*
*Total number of persons in each sector.

Table 6

Labor Force Participation by Occupational Group and Sex, 1964 and 1973 (1950 = 100)

Occupational Group	Females				Males			
	1964	Non-ag (%)	1973	Non-ag (%)	1964	Non-ag (%)	1973	Non-ag (%)
Professionals	186	8.3	343	9.4	216	5.8	376	7.2
Managers	130	4.5	60	1.5	194	5.1	152	2.9
Clerical workers	236	5.5	408	6.9	589	6.1	791	5.9
Sales	167	11.0	344	16.5	179	12.2	278	13.4
Agriculture	112	...	82	...	136	...	136	...
Miners	...	...	...	...	108	...	114	...
Transportation workers	97	0.1	166	...	207	7.5	309	7.9
Operatives	95	22.4	121	20.9	145	44.3	199	43.2
Unskilled	121	1.7	130	1.3	209	9.1	233	7.3
Service	152	46.5	186	43.4	131	9.9	225	12.1
Total	134	100	175	100	142	100	158	100
	(167,024)		(216,928)		(1,196,745)		(1,328,730)	

Source.—Calculated from 1950, 1964, and 1973 *Censo de la población de la República.*

female tertiary sector workers are classified as maids. Thus, while industrial growth has created new employment areas for men and women —clerical, sales, and professional—the proportion of all women who are domestics has not dropped below 40 percent, and the absolute number of women in this category has actually increased by 28.9 percent since 1964.

Industrialization and Occupational Structure

The continuing concentrations of workers in domestic service and agriculture conceal some important transformations in the occupational structure which have resulted from the type of industrial growth Guatemala has experienced in recent years. Large corporations with world-wide markets, banks involved in world-wide transactions, and even landowners who read daily computer printouts require a corps of technical experts and office workers. Moreover, expanded commercial activity requires clerks and salespeople.

Women are in fact desirable as "white collar" workers in Guatemala, as in the United States, because they can dress to "sell" the product or service, they have education and skill (facility in several languages, for example), and will accept low pay with little possibility of advancement when there is a large reserve of women who can replace them. The proportion of women in clerical work rose to 34 percent in Guatemala in 1973 (see table 7), although they were concentrated in secretarial rather than in skilled or unskilled office work categories. It is unlikely, however, that women will dominate this category of employment in Guatemala, as they do elsewhere, since it is one of the few expanding sources of employment for male high school graduates who are expected to support their families.

While the administrative, owner, manager category of employment has declined sharply for both men and women in the recent period of foreign penetration—by 77 percent for males and 99 percent for women

Table 7

Nonagricultural Occupations by Percentage Female, Guatemala

Category	1950	1964	1973
Professionals	42.8	39.2	32.6
Managers	36.2	28.0	18.8
Clerical workers	20.4	28.7	34.1
Sales	30.2	28.9	35.1
Craftspersons, operatives	25.9	18.7	18.8
Manual laborers	12.3	7.8	7.2
Service	66.8	72.4	67.6

SOURCE.—Calculated from 1950, 1964, and 1973 *Censo de la población de la República.*

since 1964 (see table 6)—the demand for professionals and technicians has risen dramatically and created a new stratum of employment for those few women with technical and professional training, which is reflected in census statistics (see table 7). To what extent this trend will continue is difficult to predict, since the fiscal crisis of the Guatemalan state makes expansion of services virtually impossible without major reforms, and professional and technical employment depends on state employment, especially for women. Moreover, although one of every three "technical or professional" workers is a female, and the percentage of all women workers in this area rose to 11 percent in 1973 (see table 6), the proportion of women to men is declining as the category expands, and the degree of sex segregation within the category may be increasing overall. Indeed, the large proportion of "professional" women obscures their concentration in three sectors of employment—teaching, nursing, and social work—which require no university degrees and are poorly paid. Three out of every four professional women are actually teachers, the majority in public schools. If nonuniversity teaching were treated separately, professional work would clearly constitute a male sector of employment.

Inequality by Sex

While it is true that women have entered the labor force at a faster *rate* than men since 1950, because of lower base (see table 7) it is also true that the occupational structure has become increasingly segregated by sex, except for the expanding areas of sales and commerce. The ratio of male to female workers has actually increased from 1.93 to 2.29 (see table 8). The increased segregation by sex has been high among artisans and operatives, unskilled laborers, and transportation workers—those categories most directly affected by expanded industrial output. Only in services do women outnumber men, by a slightly declining margin (0.66 men to one woman, compared to 0.55 to one in 1950; see table 8). Although the wages of women relative to men in manufacturing are slightly more equal in the skilled category and considerably more equal in the unskilled category, the wages of everyone are depressed to such an extent that it makes little difference. (Note, for example, the very small increase in overall wages of men and women in manufacturing between 1965 and 1976 in table 3.) Industrial growth has meant increasing inequality of wealth and opportunity overall and greater inequality of employment by sex.

* * *

Having examined in detail one case of industrial growth and its effects on employment, the occupational structure, and the division of labor by sex, what can we conclude about the effect of industrialization

Table 8

Occupational Segregation by Sex (Ratio of Male to Female Workers)

Category	1950	1964	1973
Professionals	1.34	1.55	1.47
Managers	1.76	2.56	4.32
Office workers	3.96	2.49	1.94
Sales	2.30	2.46	1.86
Agriculture	38.50	46.90	66.00*
Mines	89.50	...	160.00
Transportation	109.50	255.10	221.90
Artisans, operatives	2.87	4.36	4.70
Unskilled	7.14	12.30	12.90
Service	.55	.47	.66
Total	6.79	7.16	6.13
Total nonagricultural	1.93	2.24	2.29

SOURCE.—Calculated from 1950, 1964, and 1973 *Censo de la población de la República.*

*Changes in rural female employment are often the result of different census recording practices and are thus unreliable indicators.

on women's lives in underdeveloped countries? The first and most important conclusion is that there is no *universal* homogeneous consequence of industrialization, but that there is a cluster of consequences that are conditioned by the mode of production and by the function of the economy in an international economic system. Under conditions of competitive capitalism (in the developed countries) and early national (dependent) capitalist development (in Latin America), the demand for labor in a previously agricultural economy was great. In the United States, Argentina, Mexico, and perhaps elsewhere, large numbers of women workers were drawn into the first factories, where they were at the center of the most militant political and economic struggles of their day. To a smaller extent this was also true of that nationalist phase of industrial growth in Guatemala, where the expansion of the market and the promise of agrarian reform put a premium on the labor of women willing to work for wages.

Yet under industrial growth conditioned by the needs of monopoly capitalism, the period of a large industrial work force composed in large part of women is skipped. Thus in Guatemala the dramatic increases in industrial production are accompanied by only modest increases in employment, hardly sufficient to cover the number of traditional jobs eliminated or the increase in population. The level of unemployment is high; to advocate, as a matter of government policy, incentives for employing females would only extend their superexploitation. Most workers, male and female—but especially female—remain locked into the most traditional and backward sectors of the economy (subsistence agriculture and domestic service). Lacking adequate employment outside the home and lacking sufficient income coming into the home, the role of women in the daily reproduction of labor power becomes more important than ever for survival.

Industrial growth, once the liberal panacea to poverty and backward ideas about "women's place," becomes linked to increased poverty and feudal patriarchy. Modernity and backwardness in employment and in the status of women arrive in the same package. The solution is not more of the same, that is, more industrialization, more modernity within the same framework, but the necessity for a new framework in which industrialization has the truly liberating effect on backbreaking labor and the control of women as property that it was meant to have.

Industrial growth under imperialism thus generates and accentuates many of the contradictions it was supposed to solve and in so doing creates its own opposition. Women as consumers, direct producers in the countryside, and urban workers increasingly become part of this opposition to unemployment, rising food prices, and increased repression. It is not surprising that in Guatemala, in the absence of a large female industrial work force, the mobilizations of professional and semiprofessional women (such as teachers, nurses, and social workers) in alliance with other social groups have had strategic importance. While their participation so far has been directed toward political and economic demands on behalf of classes, rather than social and cultural demands that speak to the special oppression of women, it is not inconceivable that at some point in the struggle "women's consciousness" and "class consciousness" might intersect. In the meantime, however, the struggle of women is inseparable from the struggle of the majority of the population for survival.

Program in Comparative Culture
University of California at Irvine
Irvine, California, U.S.A.

Changing Modes of Production

Sex Roles and Social Change: A Comparative Appraisal of Turkey's Women

Deniz Kandiyoti

An analysis of the impact of development on women implies an understanding both of the concrete contexts within which sex roles are enacted and of the processes of transformation which affect them. Turkey offers a variety of such contexts differing widely in complexity, from the nomadic tribe to the large metropolitan center. The purpose of this paper is to adopt a comparative perspective on women in order to conceptualize different components of sex-role behavior and to analyze their manifestations within each of the social settings to be considered —the nomadic tribe, the traditional peasant village, the changing rural environment, the small town, and the large urban center. It must be emphasized that this approach is used primarily as a heuristic and analytical device rather than an attempt to achieve representativeness. Currently, the few nomadic tribes that exist are under strong pressure to sedentarize. The subsistence village is also a thing of the past and is increasingly drawn into a market economy. On the whole, these simpler forms of community have come under greater scrutiny than small towns or larger urban centers which require both different approaches and greater methodological resources. Despite some imbalances in the distribution of available data, the attempt to put sex roles into comparative perspective should prove one of the best ways to understand contemporary change.

Women in the Nomadic Tribe

The nomadic tribe represents a nonstratified society, even though households differ with respect to the number and quality of household implements and the number of animals. The essential form of wealth and property is sheep, and livelihood depends on herding. Kinship ties and the division of labor among the sexes are the key to social and economic functioning in the tribe. Kinship is patrilineal, and tribal life is based on belief in descent from a common male ancestor. This ancient form of tribal existence is under extreme pressure since sedentary life has spread. Adjustments to this pressure range from changes in the size and composition of camp units to partial and complete sedentarization. Increasingly mechanized agriculture has led to an ever-narrowing supply of pastureland rented at high prices from local authorities and villages. Bates, studying the Yörük of Southeastern Turkey, has convincingly argued that the present tribal structure is as much an adjustment to cash economy as to the material prerequisities of herding.[1] However, the striking uniformities in women's roles produced by this herding economy suggest that sex roles may be the least affected and the slowest to react to change.

In the nomadic tribe, marriage always involves the payment of the brideprice (*başlik*) by the groom's father to the bride's father. This sum, which was estimated at approximately $650 in 1967 for the Alikan tribe,[2] but which can sometimes be as high as $1,450 among the Yörük, constitutes a great financial burden on the groom's family (the average Turkish annual per capita income is $400 according to 1970 figures). Even elopement or kidnapping, which are mechanisms for bypassing the accepted procedures of parental matchmaking, do not result in the waiving of the brideprice.

It is generally agreed that the brideprice prevails when the woman's contribution to production is very high and her control over the marriage situation she is entering is very limited. Conversely, it has also been argued that the dowry could be used as a means of female control.[3] In the Middle East, however, the brideprice is used as a security fund in case of divorce, when the bride returns to the family of origin. But as Stirling points out, those funds are effectively restituted to the bride in the form of an elaborate trousseau in villages; therefore, this practice increasingly takes the form of conspicuous consumption.[4] According to Bates, the trousseau has started among sedentarized Yörüks, but it does not equal the *başlik* as it is generally practiced in the villages. Despite the varying applications, a nationwide survey carried out in 1968 by Timur

1. D. Bates, "Nomads and Farmers: A Study of the Yörük of Southeastern Turkey," Anthropological Papers, no. 52 (Ann Arbor: University of Michigan, Museum of Anthropology, 1973).
2. I. Beşikçi, *Doğuda Değişim ve Yapisal Sorunlar* (Ankara: Sevinç Matbaasi, 1969).
3. E. Friedl, "The Position of Women: Appearance and Reality," *Anthropological Quarterly* 40 (1967): 97–108.
4. P. Stirling, *Turkish Village* (New York: John Wiley & Sons, 1965).

confirms the overall association of the brideprice to regions such as Eastern Turkey, the Black Sea Coast, and Central Anatolia, where women's economic contribution to production is high and where the patriarchal extended family is most prevalent.[5] In the nomadic tribe where the number of laborers in the household is a crucial variable, Beşikçi, who has provided a cogent and detailed analysis of women's roles in the Alitan tribe of Eastern Anatolia, sees this payment as a direct compensation to the girl's household for the loss of her labor.[6] Woman's contribution to production is very high. She has to bear a number of children because of their economic value in a herding economy. She also prepares the food, carries the water and firewood to the tent, which may involve miles of walking, feeds the animals, keeps their quarters clean, and weaves both all the family's clothing and the tent itself, which needs renewal and upkeep. Among the Yörük the wool tent has been replaced by one made of store-bought cloth, but all the other duties of women are essentially the same. It is she who sets up and takes down the tent, packs up for seasonal migration, and does the bartering.

The men of the Alikan tribe believe that a woman is tougher than a man and can withstand the hardships of nature better. Paradoxically, this is the very claim upon which many societies justify male superiority. The women perform tasks that are considered shameful by men. In comparison to women's industrious lives, men's work load is light. They have to shepherd the flocks, milk the animals, shear the sheep, look after sick animals, and make contact with merchants concerning the sale of their produce. Nonetheless, shepherding is a valued and specialized skill—in fact, the only sphere of specialization in an otherwise simple economy. Aside from negotiations with local authorities to rent pastures, contacts with merchants are the only significant public dealings of a rather isolated community. As Rosaldo has suggested, whatever the actual distribution of the workload in quantitative terms among the sexes, it is the males who control both the public sphere and the specialized activities considered socially significant.[7] Here, the asymmetry is further bolstered by a visibly patriarchal setting. In the ideal household of this extended patrilocal type, a woman has control neither over the produce of her own labor, nor over her offspring, who in principle belong to the patrilineage. Despite her apparent "beast of burden" role, a woman enjoys high status, according to Beşikçi, and is an outspoken participant in family affairs. He attributes this respect and status to her hard work and her contributions to production. This interpretation may well be challenged, however, by his own admission that a woman is valued principally in terms of her procreative capacity. If a woman is unable to

5. S. Timur, *Türkiyede Aile Yapisi* (Ankara: Sevinç Matbaasi, 1972).

6. See n. 2 above.

7. M. Z. Rosaldo and L. Lamphere, *Women, Culture and Society* (Stanford, Calif.: Stanford University Press, 1974).

provide an offspring, the fault is believed to be hers. The value of giving birth to a child, preferably a male, is so high that only as a mother can a woman cover her head with the white headscarf called *kofi,* the ultimate sign of status. Whatever their other domestic achievements may be, women who have not borne children feel clearly inferior.

Male authority is evident in all walks of life. Within the tent, children and women sit farthest away from the heart (*ocak*) where the head of household sits. They also take their meals separately and eat whatever is left over. Girls have no inheritance rights, in contradiction to both the Islamic and Republican Civic Code, and they address their male siblings as "older brother" (*abi*) regardless of real age ranking. Although clear male-female heirarchies exist, nomadic life does not seem to enhance the much-publicized Islamic physical segregation of the sexes into different quarters. If anything, tent life fosters extensive visibility, which Beşikçi mentions as a problem. Female seclusion clearly has no place in this life style.

In conditions of social change, the fortunes of tribal women are closely linked to those of the tribe itself. Where there is group sedentarization, the women of land-owning rich lineages may lead secluded lives and devote themselves to domestic tasks exclusively. Poorer tribeswomen may have to join the ranks of rural wageworkers or eventually of the urban poor. From then on, their lives are directly affected by their position in the larger society.

In a sedentarized, land-owning lineage community located on the Turkish-Syrian border, Aswad reports that noble women of the same patrilineage as their husband may control a significant amount of land and enjoy the political status that goes with this control under certain conditions.[8] This role shift occurs when a man dies leaving small children and more than one wife, and when one of the widows is his patrilineal relative. The husband's share of land is managed by his brothers until one of his sons becomes eleven years old. Then the widow heads the patrilineal segment previously headed by her husband, assumes control of the property, and retains it until one or all sons are married. Occasionally, she may continue to retain economic and political control for a whole extended family of grown sons and their families. In four and a half generations, seventeen out of sixty-eight men in the community have had their property managed nineteen times by women. The preconditions for this authority by default are very constraining, however. Aside from the fact that the widow must be of the same patrilineal group as her husband and have under-age children at his death, she must remain a widow and relinquish all further sexual function. She must also function within her husband's network of interest, even though she may be indebted to her own family, who helped raise her

8. B. Aswad, "Key and Peripheral Role of Noble Women in a Middle Eastern Plains Village," *Anthropological Quarterly* 40 (July 1967): 139–52.

children in the years of her widowhood before one of her sons became eleven years old. Despite her control and authority, she is still barred from public functions and cannot form major patron-client alliances in situations external to the village—for example, with landlords and merchants of the towns. Effectively, then, her power is restricted to negotiations of marriage unions and alliances within the village. This confers considerable authority as long as the community remains a self-contained unit. However, integration into a market economy erodes these women's status.[9] New power is conferred on young males who are better equipped to mediate between the community and the outside world.

Women in the Village

The peasant village that depends on the cultivation of a subsistence crop and the raising of livestock, with an ox-and-plough technology, is a very old form of sedentary existence in Anatolia according to all archaeological and historical accounts. Despite regional and climatic variations, the ecological, technological, and demographic constraints under which the peasant village functioned gave it great resilience and made it capable of perpetuating itself without any internal impetus to change, until it came into contact with market-oriented production. Stirling's study, conducted in two central Anatolian plateau villages in 1949–50, conveys a vivid account of rural conditions, as well as a detailed consideration of sex roles.[10] Once again, in a setting that gives no evidence of clear-cut social stratification—although there is ranking according to age, kinship, and wealth—segregation among the sexes is strongly emphasized. As compared to the nomadic life, the life of the sedentary peasant has more props to bolster this segregation. Some of these are physical, such as the walls which surround every household, preventing unrelated men from entering. A man spends as much time as possible away from his house, either working in the fields, or leisurely talking in groups out of doors or gathering in guest rooms (*oda*) patronized by wealthier households. The *oda* are barred to women, with the possible exception of postmenopausal women, whose presence is sometimes tolerated. The patrilocally extended household, which is based on land

9. In a different but possibly directly related context, Abadan states that women's political participation in terms of female representation in parliament has steadily declined since the foundation of the republic, especially after the transition to a multiparty system (N. Abadan, "Turkey," in *Women in the Modern World,* ed. R. Patai [New York: Free Press, 1967]). This is readily understandable if we think of it as a shift from a single-party system where the appointment of women by an "enlightened" vanguard, in line with party ideology, is possible to a situation of multiparty democracy where patron-client relationships in the male world play a key role in political competition.

10. See n. 4 above.

wealth transmitted through males only and in which patrilineal descent predominates, leaves women a very restricted role. This pattern generates and is further reinforced by an ideology that cuts across the boundaries of Islam and other religions and can be found in other types of peasant society.[11]

In the female nexus of the traditional household, the most critical relationships are between in-marrying strangers and the male-headed household. A girl comes to her husband's household, as her title *gelin* (the one who comes) indicates; she has learned from childhood that she will have to leave her house of origin and go to *el* (strangers). In the case of village endogamy, isolation from her kin may not be as extreme as the word *el* suggests, but when she marries into another village her contacts with her own family may be very restricted. Within the household there is a clear hierarchy—the newest bride is subordinate to her mother-in-law, and to all her sisters-in-law with more seniority. Childbearing, especially of a male child, will give her fuller acceptance in her husband's family. Only when her father-in-law dies will she establish her separate nuclear household. However, the apex of her influence and power comes when she, in turn, has grown sons who bring her brides. A woman's relationship with her son is therefore absolutely crucial. Not only is husband-wife interaction quite limited; there are also severe restrictions placed on any display of affection or even of mild interest in one's spouse in front of others. There is even a taboo against direct references to one's wife. A man's relationship with his mother is generally stronger than that with his wife, and in cases of conflict, his allegiance may easily be with the former. The mother-son relationship is intimate and affectionate; the woman indulges her son, sometimes protects him against a punitive father, and looks to him for future security and protection. This mode of socialization may carry an implicit investment toward future security in widowhood and old age; it also helps to perpetuate a system which results in women's submission. The traditional promise of security through sons' loyalty may break down under conditions of social change and create serious role strain.

Against this background, specific forms of the division of labor among the sexes do not particularly enhance our understanding of female submission. Depending on economic and geographical conditions, some women are totally involved in household duties and home production, which in a premarket economy constitutes a considerable burden. At the other end of the spectrum, some women are involved in traditional crafts, such as carpet weaving; others work full-time in the fields with the men during the production season; and still others, in regions of traditional male out-migration such as the Black Sea, may be in total charge of agriculture, especially harvesting. However, female

11. E. Wolf, *Peasants* (Englewood Cliffs, N.J.: Prentice-Hall, Inc., 1969).

labor does not receive social recognition, regardless of the extent of economic contribution. In fact, since the seclusion of women and the restriction of their activities to daily household duties is considered prestigious and more "urban," it is not unusual to hear village males state that "their women do not work." A closer look at the actual situation, however, reveals a pattern of heavy, unrecognized labor.

Women and Rural Change

The absorption of villages into the national market economy has occurred with increasing speed since the 1950s and has undermined the functioning of traditional household economy. Whether there was farm mechanization, change to cash crops, or both, small peasant enterprise has become untenable. Marginality or submarginality on land has meant that household members cannot subsist from their land and have increasingly had to turn to other sources of income, generally wage work. One of the most well-known outcomes has been massive migration to town centers. However, within the village itself, these changes have had direct implications for household formation and functioning, among them the undermining of the role of the father as the sole holder of economic resources, that is, land. This has created friction and, as numerous studies reveal, has resulted in the son's decision to separate from the father's household early and to set up a separate nuclear family after he has contributed the cost of his wedding to the paternal household. In fact, Kiray regards the household as a very flexible institution, since in an instance of severe economic pressure after agroeconomic change, she found households harboring matrilineal kin and cases of in-marrying men (*iç güveysi*)—a major deviation from the culturally expected pattern.[12] By modifying the economic base of traditional existence, rural change has greatly modified authority relations *within the male domain,* as the decline of respect to elders and the assumption of leadership roles by younger married males suggests.

The effects of this process of social change on women have rarely been directly analyzed. According to Boserup, change in rural areas widens the productivity gap because men monopolize the new equipment and agricultural methods and leave women to perform simple manual tasks.[13] In Turkey, however, the monopolization of specialized tasks by males and the underrating of female labor exist even in the simplest type of community, such as the nomadic tribe, where the woman is valued for her allegedly superior muscular power. Further-

12. M. Kiray and J. Hinderink, *Social Stratification as an Obstacle to Development* (New York: Praeger Publishers, 1970).

13. E. Boserup, *Women's Role in Economic Development* (New York: St. Martin's Press, 1975).

more, the connection between female productivity and relative status does not apply to women who never controlled the products of their own labor. Indeed, where women did enjoy free laborer status, as in Africa, or where the shift to cash economy occurred through colonial enterprise of the plantation type, as in Latin America, female status suffered greater erosion and stress than in many parts of the Middle East and Asia. In Turkey, rural change intensified not the already existing asymmetry between the sexes but the social stratification among males. Those who controlled the new agricultural technology and land resources consolidated their economic position; the rest were pushed into a marginal category. The changes for women merely complemented the changing relations in the male world. A study of Sakarya, a mechanized Anatolian plateau village, showed that bachelors became freer of parental control in choosing a marriage partner, for example, and that this prerogative led to maidens being consulted more on their preferences.[14] Thus there has been an increase in marriages by mutual consent. Moreover, a young couple looks forward to a certain amount of independence from their elders. Nonetheless, the changes in the status of women are minimal when contrasted to the rapidly changing authority relations in the male world. Village brides still take a place subordinate to all the males and older females in their new households. Female status is still defined according to the traditional criteria of age and childbearing. The one significant and common change is the early separation from the paternal household, which puts women at the head of their own households at a younger age.

Another significant side effect of mechanization in Sakarya for women is the emergence of leisure. Traditionally, although both men and women worked fully during the production season, men had considerable leisure in the winter, while women carried on their time-consuming household activities. Female leisure was an unknown phenomenon. Mechanization has greatly reduced the need for labor in general and has pushed women out of agricultural production except for such activities as feeding chickens and milking cows. More important, however, there has been a rapid decrease of home production in favor of store-bought goods. Clothes previously made by women are now store-bought; even ready-made bread, canned food, and household detergents have made their appearance in the village. The accessiblity of the town center and the presence of cash have made these purchases possible. Of course, no such evidence of leisure would be found in the destitute wage-working families of the southern plains where women

14. D. Kandiyoti, "Social Change and Social Stratification in a Turkish Village," *Journal of Peasant Studies* 2 (January 1974): 206–20; "Social Change and Family Structure in a Turkish Village," in *Kinship and Modernization,* ed. J. Peristiany (Rome: American Universities Field Staff Press, 1975).

pick cotton, one of the few manual jobs in a highly mechanized area; nor would it be evident in the case of labor-intensive crops such as hazelnuts, tobacco, or strawberries, where women are very much part of the work force. However, leisure does exist in Sakarya and is employed mainly for afternoon visits among neighbors, where tea is served and embroidery practiced. In the lives of these women we see an emulation of small-town life.

Women in the Small Town

Although sex roles and household formation have been closely studied in rural communities, both nomadic and sedentary, there is a considerable gap in our knowledge of the small, nonrural settlement, the *kasaba.* And yet, as Benedict suggests, small towns have played a crucial role in Turkey, historically and socially.[15] Many have served as mediating points between the rural hinterland and the large Ottoman towns, flourishing market towns, or specialized centers for traditional crafts, such as silk, carpet weaving, and copperware. Now in modernizing society these towns are often reduced to administrative units which function as restricted service and market centers. The local notables (*esraf*), who dominate and regulate the economic and business life of small provincial towns mainly as traders and artisans, perpetuate traditionalism in all walks of life—religious, political, and familial. The greater functional complexity of the small town, however, provides a much wider network within which to locate households and sex roles.

Kiray's analysis of Ereğli on the Black Sea coast is perhaps the first notable study of a small town.[16] Prior to the installation of heavy industry in the area, Ereğli displayed some variety in the distribution of occupations. Most household heads were traders, small manufacturers, or artisans, less often civil servants (both civilian and military), skilled workers, and professionals. Unlike the rural settings, female labor in Ereğli was not organized in any particular way. In lower socioeconomic groups, women did some gardening or often worked as domestics, doing housecleaning and laundering jobs, but this was not considered "work" by men, despite the cash income they received. Dressmaking, seamstressing, and embroidery for money were also habitual female occupations. Some women worked in the two food preserve industries. Others worked as janitors in the local schools. The most prestigious occupations for women were teaching, civil service, or secretarial work. Most of the

15. P. Benedict, "The Changing Role of Provincial Towns: A Case Study for Southwestern Turkey," in *Turkey: Geographic and Social Perspectives,* ed. P. Benedict, F. Mansur, and E. Tumertekin (Leiden: E. J. Brill, 1974).

16. M. Kiray, *Ereğli: Ağir Sanayiden Evvel Bir Sahil Kasabasi* (Ankara: State Planning Organization, 1964).

working women were single; only 17 percent of the married women were employed. The men studied regarded the work of single girls with more tolerance: 42.1 percent did not object as compared to 40.9 percent who did. However, 68.8 percent were opposed to any employment outside the home for married women. Despite this resistance, a surprising number of Ereğli dwellers conceded that women could be doctors, lawyers, engineers, or judges—in fact, that they could enter any profession. Thus, reluctance to let women work was not coupled with a belief that women cannot have a successful professional life. In his study of Susurluk, a town in the northwestern region of Anatolia, Magnarella reports similar perceptions of female occupations and similar degrees of resistance to employment of married women.[17] The reasons for this resistance tend to be uniform as well. Outside employment may mean neglect of home and family, enhances the dangers of promiscuity through contact with unrelated males, and may involve increased economic power that challenges male authority. As long as a female contributes to family production and does not receive payment in cash such a threat is not perceived. When cash payments are forthcoming, due both to economic necessity and the increasing availability of job opportunities, their importance to household economy is downgraded, while at the same time men keep careful watch that wages are properly "turned in" and spent according to their wishes. Unavoidably, however, women gain increasing budget control. In Susurluk, this tendency was enhanced when women began doing the shopping, traditionally a man's activity which gave him access to the market and discretion over the disposal of funds. Under the impact of a sugar refinery, men were prevented from shopping because of the refinery working hours and imitated the professional, nonlocal cadres who allowed their wives greater freedom in such respects.

One of the most striking findings of the Ereğli study is a change in attitudes toward female children. Whereas the male child has traditionally been regarded as a security for old age and an inheritor of property, in Ereğli the "greater loyalty of the daughter" was stressed, and more parents than in the past thought they might spend their remaining days with their daughter and son-in-law. The actual evidence of family extension around a married daughter was 7.8 percent of households, a significant shift from the traditional pattern. Nonetheless, the mother-son relationship continues to be crucial; the same pattern of privileged status and overindulgence in the socialization of sons prevailed.[18]

Although husband-wife relationships showed considerable variabil-

17. P. Magnarella, *Tradition and Change in a Turkish Town* (New York: John Wiley & Sons, 1974).

18. M. Kiray, "Changing Roles of Mothers: Changing Intra-Family Relations in a Turkish Town," in *Mediterranean Family Structure,* ed. J. Peristiany (Cambridge: Cambridge University Press, 1976).

ity, men and women live in two separate worlds, the latter in a female network of relatives and neighbors, segregated from male networks.[19] In a provocative paper on sex roles in Edremit, a small coastal town of Western Anatolia, Lloyd and Margaret Fallers in fact suggested that Turkish women are in many ways psychologically more independent of men than are Western women who have not experienced segregation.[20] It is when such women step into public roles that their different orientation becomes most evident. "These Turkish women in the public sphere bring with them from the traditional separated world of women a sense of independence from men which makes them more able to concentrate on the tasks at hand in the public world," Margaret Fallers writes.[21] They do not act as "females" but as professionals whose habits of behavior do not require orientation to men as males. However, those who emerge from the private to the public world are few in number. On the whole, women in the small town lead more secluded lives than do rural women, but behind this seclusion they apparently lead rich social lives.

The special visiting patterns instituted in the small town as a by-product of female leisure create female networks that are different both in function and composition from the rural domestic and neighborly networks. Studies of the reception day (*kabul günü*, also referred to as *istiqbal* in other parts of the Middle East), a specific day when women receive guests on a regular, almost rotational, basis, suggest that structured visiting among women serves important extradomestic, social functions. In Tütüneli, a small town which gained a cadre of nonlocal professional civil servants in 1954 when it acquired central government administrative status, the *kabul günü* was initiated by the nonlocal women, wives of the nonlocal civil servants who felt alienated in their new social surroundings. However, within the first couple of years, Benedict's study shows, the circle was widened to include the wives of local landowners (*agas*) and those of wealthy merchants who were influential at the level of town and provincial politics.[22] The nonlocal

19. The Western middle-class ideal of conjugal union based on companionship, mutual interest, and shared activities may have been greatly overrated. Among the working class, there is evidence that the husbands still go out with the "boys," and women confide in and feel closer to their mothers, sisters, or female neighbors (M. Komarovsky, *Blue Collar Marriage* [New York: Vintage Books, 1967]; L. Rainwater, R. P. Coleman, and G. Handel, *Workingman's Wife* [New York: Mc. Fadden-Bartell, 1962]). Bott further suggests that segregation of conjugal roles may be indirectly related to social class, depending on the connectedness of the family's network of social relations. A highly connected network, which is often seen in established working-class communities, seems to lead to greater segregation (E. Bott, "Urban Families, Conjugal Roles and Social Networks," *Human Relations* 8 [November 1955]: 345–84).

20. L. Fallers and M. Fallers, "Sex Roles in Edremit," in *Mediterranean Family Structure,* ed. J. Peristiany (Cambridge: Cambridge University Press, 1976).

21. Ibid., p. 255.

22. P. Benedict, "The Kabul Gunu: Structured Visiting in an Anatolian Provincial Town," *Anthropological Quarterly* 47 (January 1974): 28–47.

civil servant wives, who were more cosmopolitan, transmitted their cultural tastes to the local women. Not only was the social gap between the town notables and nonlocals bridged, but a considerable amount of male influence on the kinds of information transmitted at these gatherings was apparent. Men can use their wives to transmit knowledge about local events to other men when it would be improper for them to communicate such information face-to-face. Moreover, since the wife's position in the *kabul* is determined by her husband's standing in the community, female hierarchy mirrors exactly the ranking in the male world.

The visiting patterns among the traditional elite families in Antakya (the wives of local notables or *ashraf*), which Aswad has studied, serve to retain the cohesion of this group.[23] Visiting takes place mainly among persons who are considered kin, and new women enter this network through marriage ties. Nonetheless, the *kabul* also serves to extend the power of the elite, since women from a lower socioeconomic background may be invited and patronized by wealthier female relatives; men, however, do not like obtaining favors and establishing patronage through their wives.

No less significant within the Antakya elite which dominated both of the leading national political parties at the time, half of the marriages had been *across* party lines. Thus the party alignments which divide the male members of the elite were crossed by marriage and subsequently by the *kabul,* which established important cohesive lines within the elite, as well as vertical ties of a patron-client type. In contrast, the middle-class *kabul* patterns were confined to people of the same political party.

A simple comparison of Benedict's and Aswad's findings shows that the *kabul,* over and beyond its structural similarities, can be used to perform specific functions suited to a specific social context. The asymmetry and social distance that exist between the sexes in simpler, nonstratified communities can be accompanied by complementarity not only of conjugal roles, but of function in the social and political spheres. The informality and the entertainment value of women's associations often mask these latent functions, which are given uneasy recognition by males. In comparison, female economic contribution in the rural setting may go completely unrecognized.

Although village women of the area perceive their counterparts in small towns as leading imprisoned lives, and indeed they do seem to lack all contact with the nonresidential, public parts of town, the fact remains that there are considerable regional variations regarding physical segregation. This is suggested in Mansur's study of Bodrum, a small town on the Aegean coast that contains two culturally distinct communities —the "locals" who have traditionally lived off the land and the Cretans, Turks who fled the Cretan massacres of 1897 and who came after

23. B. Aswad, "Visiting Patterns among Women of the Elite in a Small Turkish City," *Anthropological Quarterly* 47 (January 1974): 9–27.

1923.[24] Analyzing recognized differences between these two communities, which have a very low rate of intermarriage, Mansur speaks of the contrasting economic bases of "local" and Cretan livelihood. The "locals" who make a living from the land and get lump sum incomes at harvest time need the labor of women. The Cretans, a seafaring people, have more unstable incomes which are in no way based on the labor of women. Even tasks such as mending nets and trimming sponges are easily done at home in odd moments. In addition, Cretan women, who may be left alone for weeks or even months while the men are at sea, have to make decisions in emergencies, arrange the budget as they see fit, and do their own shopping. This gives them considerable independence in their daily life, as well as greater exposure and mobility. Interestingly, the work of local women in the fields seems extremely hard to the Cretan women, and the local women find the insecurities of Cretan life unbearable. Thus, even within the bounds of the same small town, cultural differences influence different sex role patterns.

Mansur reports the same rigidly defined *kabul* structuring the leisure of the town's elite women, mainly the wives of civil servants and some of the locals, but female leisure is much more unstructured in lower socioeconomic groups. Whereas the Cretan women sit by the seashore watching passersby, no women are visible in the local quarters. Ceremonial occasions, especially religious feasts, seem to offer another focus for female gatherings, in comparison to rural areas, where formal religion and ceremonial participation is clearly in the male domain, while women are more involved with superstitious practices. In the small town, the women's involvement in formal religions not only invests them with knowledge and learning, but provides them with legitimate grounds for social gatherings. Another example of such gatherings is the *mevlut* prayer (recitation of the life story of the Prophet), a tradition which seems prevalent throughout the Middle East. Indeed, one could easily hypothesize that the *mevlut* is most prevalent in social classes where female activity outside the household must be seen as serious to gain legitimacy. Although it is also practiced in large urban centers, the *mevlut* may well provide legitimacy to the women of small towns, who are more visible and who spend more time establishing their reputations. However, it may be argued that, considered at the neighborhood level, larger urban centers do not provide the alleged anonymity and lower visibility attributed to city life. This may be especially true of nonindustrial countries where a sense of small, face-to-face community may be retained in the squatter districts, among the new immigrants to the city, very much as it evidently was in working-class or ethnic neighborhoods in industrialized countries.[25] This makes a discussion of sex roles within the

24. F. Mansur, *Bodrum: A Town in the Aegean* (Leiden: E. J. Brill, 1972).

25. H. Gans, *Urban Villagers* (New York: Free Press, 1962); M. Fried, *The World of the Urban Working Class* (Cambridge, Mass.: Harvard University Press, 1973).

larger metropolitan centers a very difficult proposition indeed: it is crucial to establish exactly which social class and which level of urban integration one is discussing. Since there are no adequate data at present, a more global approach to women in the urban context must be adopted.

Women and Urbanization

It is now widely assumed that urbanization, whether or not it is accompanied by the material culture of industrialization, promotes the "ideology" of the conjugal family, a system which allegedly favors women.[26] In the case of a traditional patriarchal society like Turkey, theory has focused on changing authority relations within the male world, largely under the rubric of "modernization," which leads to a conceptual underdevelopment in the area of women's roles. Because scholars have set themselves rather modest standards, anything resembling the Western model of conjugal union by mutual consent was labeled "egalitarian," "emancipated," or "modern." Schnaiberg, for example, exploring modernity on a sample of Ankara women, isolated a so-called emancipation factor consisting of participation in mass media and egalitarian family structure that allows women greater freedom of movement and a greater role in decision making.[27] The problem with this and similar approaches, however, is that it gives little insight into the actual concrete dynamics of the situation. The same intricate mechanisms which link livelihood to family structure and attitudes continue to operate, even though the framework is more heterogeneous and complex. Comparing different types of households in the urban setting, for example, Timur emphasizes that, whereas neolocality is encouraged for the professional in the highest income brackets, poorer families must pool their resources in extended families to mitigate the high costs of urban living.[28] This may represent a reversal of the rural pattern, where the extended family was associated with more landed wealth and patriarchal attitudes. Thus, superficially similar residential patterns may perform different functions in different settings; hence the difficulties of attitudinal inference.

The diverse life opportunities to which women are exposed when they immigrate from rural areas to large urban centers have by no means been satisfactorily explored. In her study of migrants to Cairo, Abu-Lughod points out that, while informal associations for male migrants, such as the coffee shop, are available in the city, no such associa-

26. W. Goode, "World Revolution and Family Patterns," in *Urbanism in World Perspective,* ed. S. Fava (New York: Thomas Y. Crowell Co., 1968).

27. A. Schnaiberg, "Measuring Modernism: Theoretical and Empirical Explorations," *American Journal of Sociology* 76 (November 1970): 399–425.

28. Timur (n. 5 above).

tions exist for women.[29] In addition, whereas in the village, and possibly the small town, religious festivals, births, deaths, and the like are important occasions on which women have major roles to play, within the city these events become more private, with the result that women's life is confined more and more to the immediate neighborhood. This may be equally true of Turkey, and yet large urban centers do offer more diverse job opportunities and greater access to education, which may eventually affect the mobility of women. Unfortunately, female employment in industry and the urban informal labor market have not as yet been studied. However, observation suggests that women employed in industry are primarily single and engaged in the lowest-paid, unskilled jobs, which are mostly available in the textile and food-processing industries. There is also a market for women in domestic and office-cleaning jobs. Unlike the rural environment, where women's contribution to production can be more easily observed, it is difficult to assess the stability and extent of the urban female labor force, with the possible exception of civil service jobs. A survey carried out among male industrial workers in the towns of Istanbul and Izmit showed that only 2 percent of their wives were engaged in any form of employment; the relatively stable income of industrial workers meant that they could keep their wives at home.[30] Even when there was more than one breadwinner in the household, that person tended to be either a grown child of either sex, or an in-living male relative. In addition, the young age of industrial workers' wives meant a high proportion of preschool children in their care, in the absence of child-care facilities and less support from female kin. Nonetheless, there are female networks of mutual support and help at the neighborhood level, most clearly in cases of emergency such as sickness, death, or childbirth. An intriguing but so far untested hypothesis in Turkey suggests that urbanization may bring about a shift toward greater solidarity with women relatives as opposed to patrilineal kin. If such findings which have been reported in other studies[31] were to be replicated in the Turkish context, they would have far-reaching implications.

There is at least one case study[32] that analyzes the conditions under which a shift to a more matrilocal definition of the household occurs. This condition, one of the most noticeable outcomes of social change in

29. J. Abu-Lughod, "Migrant Adjustment to City Life: The Egyptian Case," *American Journal of Sociology* 67 (July 1961): 22–23.

30. D. Kandiyoti, "Characteristics of Turkey's Industrial Workers in the Istanbul-Izmit complex" (paper presented at the OPSSME Workshop on Problems of Development, Khartoum, February 1976).

31. D. Sweetser, "The Effect of Industrialization on Inter-generational Solidarity," *Rural Sociology* 31 (December 1966): 156–70; S. Vatuk, *Kinship and Urbanization* (Berkeley: University of California Press, 1972).

32. M. Kiray, "The Family of the Immigrant Worker," in *Turkish Workers in Europe, 1960–1975,* ed. N. Abadan-Unat (Leiden: E. J. Brill, 1976).

Turkey, is the migration of "guest workers" to Western Europe, especially Germany. More than the temporary or seasonal migration of men to urban centers, this type of migration disperses the family unit for considerable periods of time and reunites them in a cyclical pattern. The onus to hold the family together as a unit falls on the women; unlike the patrilocal definition of the household, "home" is where the woman is. Even if she remains in the village of origin, she will set up a separate household with her own children. From a dependent, subservient role in her husband's extended kin, she becomes coordinator and decision maker on all matters concerning her children. Socialization by these mothers-in-command may actually influence male personality, although it is too early to speculate about such outcomes. The mother alone manages the cash income she receives from abroad and she has to enter into contact with impersonal, secondary institutions such as banks, post offices, and government agencies. These public dealings, both new and unforeseen, bring her greater sophistication. The women who migrate to Germany seem to adjust better to the new situation than the men; it may be that their socialization as in-marrying brides trained them for entering a potentially hostile environment. This situation demonstrates women's potential for flexibility and rapid adaptation to change.

In comparative perspective, components of sex-role behavior and the different patterns they produce seem clearer, and possibly freer of the subjective interpretations of "betterment" or "worsening" of status. As my review of different case studies has shown, the components of women's roles form different configurations in each setting. The nomadic tribe is highly patriarchal, high on female participation in production, and low on actual physical segregation. The traditional village is also patriarchal, varies regionally in terms of types of female participation in production, is higher on physical segregation than the nomadic tribe, but apparently less so than the small town. In all of the cases, however, the determinants of female status are invariant, namely, childbearing and advancing age. Whatever women's place in production may be, their labor goes largely unrecognized and the specialized areas and public dealing remain in the male sphere. This clearly indicates that the labor productivity of women has no direct impact on their status, unless they have control over the marketing of their own labor. In the above mentioned cases, women have no control over production or reproduction; the products of both belong directly to the patrilineage. In that sense, the breakdown of the traditional, land-based, patriarchal system has a potentially liberating effect on women. However, this effect has remained largely potential, since there has been no shift from an unrecognized, underprivileged laborer status to that of a free and emancipated one. Rather, as the female has become freed from her traditional toil and begun to enjoy leisure, she has increasingly turned into a conspicuous consumption item for males and not into a productive member of the community. Rural change led to a redefinition of male authority relations and has affected women through complementarity by putting them at the head of nuclear households at a younger age. It has also meant a decrease of participation in production where labor-saving techniques are available, and important decreases in home production due to increased contact with markets. In small towns, which show more structural heterogeneity than the rural areas, female labor can be more varied despite greater resistence to the work of married women. Cash earnings, over which women could have potential control, must have created an unprecedented threat to male authority which did not exist in the rural areas. In small towns, women also created more formal networks. Segregation from public places seems higher, but here again, variations exist and can be traced to the circumstances of livelihood as in the case of the Cretan women of Bodrum. The determinants of status among women in the small town are more directly related to their husbands' position, and are evident in the hierarchic nature of the *kabul.* In the larger urban centers, there is a whole range of very different life contexts for women—from the shanty-town at one end to the upper-middle class on the other, whose orientations in terms of education, work aspirations, marriage patterns, and leisure have a distinctly "Western" cultural backdrop. The chances of having access to education and of entering a wider variety of gainful occupations are obviously enhanced in large urban centers. As can be expected, role conflict and strain are maximized under those conditions. The social and psychological implications of urban patterns have been least explored, and constitute the area where most remains to be done.

Social Sciences Department
Boğaziçi University
Istanbul, Turkey

CHANGING MODES OF PRODUCTION

Class Structure and Female Autonomy in Rural Java

Ann Stoler

Ethnographic studies have emphasized the unusually high "status" of women in Southeast Asia.[1] Although the various definitions of status frequently confuse norms, jural rights, and actual behavior, the favorable position of Southeast Asian women has generally been interpreted as a function of their contribution to the household and rural economy. Indeed, in the case of Java, neither the colonial period nor the postcolonial developments appear to have lessened the relative economic and social independence of rural women. This paper, which is based on fieldwork in a Javanese village, considers two questions: (1) by what means and to what extent have women gained and maintained access to economic independence and social power[2] in Javanese rural society, and

This paper is based on fifteen months of field research carried out by myself and Benjamin White in a south central Javanese Village from August 1972 to December 1973. I am grateful for the detailed, extensive, and helpful criticisms of Lina Brock, Bette Denich, Lawrence Hirschfeld, Nancy Lutkehaus, and Benjamin White. A shorter version of this paper was delivered at the Seventy-fourth Annual Meeting of the American Anthropological Association, San Francisco, December 1975.

1. See, e.g., Robbins Burling, *Hill Farms and Padi Fields: Life in Mainland Southeast Asia* (Englewood Cliffs, N.J.: Prentice-Hall, Inc., 1965); Hildred Geertz, *The Javanese Family* (New York: Free Press, 1961); E. J. Michaelson and Walter Goldschmidt, "Female Roles and Male Dominance among Peasants," *Southwestern Journal of Anthropology* 27 (1971): 330–52; James Peacock, *Indonesia: An Anthropological Perspective* (Pacific Palisades, Calif.: Goodyear Publishing Co., 1973); Cora Vreede-de-Stuers, *The Indonesian Woman: Struggles and Achievements* (The Hague: Mouton, 1960).

2. To avoid the ambiguities inherent in definitions of "status," I shall use the concepts (1) "female autonomy," the extent to which women exercise economic control over their

(2) what are the effects of increasing demographic pressure and economic stratification on production relations and the role of women within them?

The question of class relations is, in my view, analytically prior to an investigation of male-female relationships within classes. And yet, studies of the economic determinants of female autonomy in both nonclass and class societies have focused on the intra- and intersexual organization of labor. According to one theory, female cooperative work patterns are an essential means by which women isolate themselves from male supervision and control.[3] This "strength in unity" argument (also advanced by Brown, Johnson and Johnson, Sacks, and others),[4] however, assumes that the organization of labor accurately indicates which members of society control the production process. Whether this assumption holds in nonclass societies is debatable;[5] it certainly does not apply to a stratified society such as Java. Although the division of labor in Javanese rural society is fairly well defined along sexual lines, the relationship of both men and women to the production process is not indicated by gender alone but, more important, by access to strategic resources which crosscut sexual distinctions. The following analysis shows that women gain autonomy and economic independence through the nature and flexibility of the sources of income available to them.

In examining female autonomy within class societies, a number of authors have maintained that transformations in traditional economic organization cause an increased dichotomization of sex roles and concomitant sexual inequalities. Engels, for example, insisted that the development of private property created a division of labor which diminished the value of female production from social use to private use

---

own lives vis-à-vis men (e.g., in disposing of the fruits of their labor), and (2) "social power," the extent to which women exercise control over the lives of others outside the domestic sphere (e.g., in appropriating the product of another person's labor). Although these are more limited categories than that of "status," they allow us to distinguish two dimensions of the economic role of women which are often confused.

3. Yolanda Murphy and Robert Murphy, *Women of the Forest* (New York: Columbia University Press, 1974), p. 211.

4. Judith Brown, "Economic Organization and the Position of Women among the Iroquois," *Ethnohistory* 17, nos. 3–4 (1970): 151–67; Allen Johnson and Orna Johnson, "Sex Roles and the Organization of Work in a Machiguenga Community" (unpublished manuscript, Columbia University, 1974); Karen Sacks, "Engels Revisited: Women, the Organization of Production, and Private Property," in *Women, Culture and Society,* ed. M. Rosaldo and L. Lamphere (Stanford, Calif.: Stanford University Press, 1974).

5. Emmanuel Terray, *Marxism and "Primitive" Societies* (New York: Monthly Review Press, 1972); but compare Scott Cook, "Production, Ecology and Economic Anthropology," *Social Science Information* 12, no. 1 (1973): 25–52; Jonathan Friedman, "Tribes, States, and Transformations," and Maurice Godelier, "Modes of Production, Kinships, and Demographic Structures," both in *Marxist Analyses and Social Anthropology,* ed. M. Bloch (New York: Halsted Press, 1975).

of the household unit.[6] A derivative theory suggests that capitalism augments the exploitation of women by excluding female domestic labor (which remains unpaid but "socially necessary") from social production.[7] More specifically, Boserup and others have argued that increased production of cash/export crops demanded by the colonial powers from an indigenous economy progressively excluded women from export production and confined them to the subsistence sector.[8] This suggests that whatever the particular nature of colonial exploitation, the most severely affected members of peasant society are women.

Despite their different terms, each of these theories assumes that domestic production and subsistence production involved limited social relations and networks, as compared to those resulting from social production. The introduction of private property, the emergence of class stratification, and the imposition of colonial rule have frequently produced sexual dichotomization, but they do not *necessarily* do so. Javanese society is a case in point which does not disprove the general validity of these distinctions, but questions the universality of their application.

Historical Perspective on the Sexual Division of Labor in Java

The historical conditions of Javanese precolonial and colonial periods can shed an essential light on the determinants of female autonomy and, more specifically, on the reasons why agroeconomic change has not been accompanied by increased sexual inequalities. As Boserup points out, we must consider the traditional sexual division of labor in order to understand the response of men and women to these changes. Prior to the colonial period, Javanese peasant households were primarily engaged in production for use. Both men and women participated in agriculture as well as numerous handicraft industries, and even indigenous forms of exploitation extracted both male and female labor.[9] Although many different kinds of crops were grown under colonial rule, and through many different systems of extraction of land, labor, and/or

6. Friedrich Engels, *The Origin of the Family, Private Property and the State* (1884; reprint ed., New York: International Publishers, 1972).

7. Margaret Benston, "The Political Economy of Women's Liberation," *Monthly Review* 21 (1969): 13–27; Wally Secombe, "Housework under Capitalism," *New Left Review* 83 (1973): 3–24.

8. Ester Boserup, *Women's Role in Economic Development* (London: George Allen & Unwin, 1970); Dorothy Remy, "Underdevelopment and the Experience of Women: A Nigerian Case Study," in *Towards an Anthropology of Women,* ed. R. Reiter (New York: Monthly Review Press, 1975).

9. Sir Thomas Raffles, *The History of Java* (London: John Murray, Publishers, 1817), 1: 163; J. van Gelderen, "Economics of the Tropical Colony," in *Indonesian Economics: The Concept of Dualism in Theory and Policy,* ed. W. F. Wertheim (The Hague: W. van Houve Uitgeverij, 1961); W. F. Wertheim, *Indonesian Society in Transition: A Study of Social Change* (The Hague: W. van Hoeve Uitgeverij, 1956), p. 237.

produce, none of them confined female labor to the subsistence sector alone. The structure of the indigenous economy in Java was kept basically intact, and commercial crops such as sugar were ecologically and economically superimposed upon it.[10] The fact that colonial extraction worked *within* the framework of Javanese household economy had profound implications for the sexual allocation of labor. Through village leases with the plantation estates, a household was allocated a certain amount of land to grow wet rice and sugar. The ecological compatibility of sugar cultivation and wet rice cultivation made it possible "to conscript maximum amounts of land and labor into the commercial sector on a temporary basis while leaving that sector 'morally' free to contract whenever market conditions so indicate."[11] While cheap Javanese labor enriched the colonial economy, the maintenance and reproduction of labor power remained the responsibility of the indigenous economy.[12]

Both the African and Asian patterns of labor extraction under colonialism, Boserup points out, depended on reducing labor costs in the export sector to an absolute minimum. In Africa it was possible to extract solely male labor as women basically could and did carry out the main subsistence activities themselves.[13] In Asia, on the other hand, both male and female labor were required for wet rice cultivation; therefore, the patterns of labor recruitment in Asia utilized the entire family labor force, rather than fragmenting the household production unit. Dutch recruitment of labor strictly adhered to this principle by localizing export production and by integrating it ecologically into the peasant farm system.[14] Under the period following the Cultivation System (1830–70), when larger tracts of land were put over to sugar and greater amounts of labor were demanded for cultivation and processing, both male and female Javanese labor contributed directly to export production. Female labor accounted for "a great deal of the seasonal work including the

10. Clifford Geertz, *Agricultural Involution* (Berkeley: University of California Press, 1968), p. 47.

11. Ibid., p. 57.

12. Keith Buchanan, *The Southeast Asian World* (Garden City, N.Y.: Anchor Books, 1968); J. Khan, "Imperialism and the Reproduction of Capitalism: Towards a Definition of the Indonesian Social Formation," *Critique of Anthropology,* vol. 2 (1974); W. Roseberry, "Rent, Differentiation and the Development of Capitalism among Peasants," *American Anthropologist* 78, no. 1 (1976): 45–58; Benjamin White, "Demand for Labor and Population Growth in Colonial Java," *Human Ecology* 1, no. 3 (1973): 217–36.

13. Boserup, p. 77.

14. Clifford Geertz, *Peddlers and Princes: Social Development and Economic Change in Two Indonesian Towns* (Chicago: University of Chicago Press, 1963), p. 87. Other plantation export crops grown in large quantities in irrigated and nonirrigated areas (tea, coffee, rubber, tobacco, and sugar) also used large quantities of female labor; see, e.g., tables on average daily earnings in field and factory tasks for men and women in the Coolie Budget Commission, *Final Report: Living Conditions of Plantation Workers and Peasants on Java in 1939–1940* (Ithaca, N.Y.: Cornell University Modern Indonesia Project Translation Series, 1956).

strenuous work at the centrifuges in the sugar factories."[15] Moreover, decreasing access to arable land for subsistence production caused increased labor intensification in wet rice production. In proportion to the amount of male labor extracted from the subsistence economy, there was not only an increased demand for female labor in agriculture, but an increased demand for child labor as well.[16] The entire household labor force was mobilized to intensify subsistence production. Thus increased sexual inequalities which emerged as a result of a dichotomization of sex roles in other colonial situations did not occur in Java.

An analysis of the relationship between the peasant class and its colonial exploiters must not ignore the socioeconomic distinctions *within* the peasantry, sharpened by the colonial experience. For if precolonial Java displayed a relative homogeneity in landholdings, as population grew and land became increasingly scarce, variations in amounts of land held were transformed into critical advantages.[17] As the primary means of production, land, became less available, slight differences in land wealth became translated into differential access to all strategic resources and thus represented the genesis of intrapeasant class distinctions. These distinctions, over and beyond the historical conditions we have described, have determined the range of opportunities available to women and the role of women within the organization of household economy.

Peasant Class Structure and the Economic Role of Women

Although the anthropology of women has addressed cross-class differences, it has tended to view peasant women as a homogenous social group[18] and has dealt inadequately with the differences between women at different socioeconomic levels in peasant economy. Assuming that female autonomy and social power are a function of access to strategic resources within the domestic and social sphere, the primary strategic resources of land and capital reveal significant differences for each class[19] within peasant society—for both men and women. And yet the concept of "shared poverty," the "division of the economic pie in smaller and smaller pieces"[20] through land, labor, and food sharing, which

15. Wertheim, p. 249.

16. C. L. van Doorn, cited by Alice Dewey, *Peasant Marketing in Java* (New York: Free Press, 1962), p. 198; White.

17. G. H. van der Kolff, *The Historical Development of the Labour Relationships in a Remote Corner of Java as They Apply to the Cultivation of Rice* (Report C. in the International Research Series of the Institute of Pacific Relations, 1937), p. 1.

18. Remy, in Reiter, ed.

19. "Class" here is defined as a group who share the same relationship to the means of production.

20. Clifford Geertz, "Religious Belief and Economic Behavior in a Central Javanese

has been used by Geertz and subsequent authors, obscures the fact that Javanese society has always been stratified (and has always stratified itself) through differential access to strategic resources. It is surprising, then, that the "shared poverty" concept remains the most popularly held characterization of Javanese rural society, despite the existence of many studies which document the more relevant theme of class stratification based on differential access to land.[21]

In the central Javanese village of Kali Loro,[22] in which my own research was conducted, *sawah* (irrigated rice land) provides a major subsistence resource and work related to rice agriculture is an important, though secondary, source of employment. However, the distribution of landholdings indicates great variation in levels of participation in rice production and a correspondingly wide range of income differences. Of 478 households surveyed, 6 percent own more than half of all the *sawah,* 37 percent are landless, and another 40 percent work farms too small to produce their basic rice requirements.[23] In other words, at least 75 percent of the households have to meet their subsistence needs either primarily or completely through sources other than ownership and cultivation of rice land. Among these alternate income-producing activities are agricultural wage labor, various forms of market trade, handicraft production, and mixed garden cultivation for sale and consumption. While some of these activities are in part gender specific, the

---

Town: Some Preliminary Considerations," *Economic Development and Cultural Change* 4 (1956): 141.

21. The following is an incomplete selection of such studies: Svein Aass, "Chayanov and Java—a Discussion on Chayanov's Micro and Macro Theory of Peasant Economy" (unpublished manuscript, Storhove, 1975), Adiwilaga, *Land Tenure in the Village of Tjipagalo* (Bandung: Kantor Perantjang Tata Bumi, Djawa Barat, 1954); G. H. van der Kolff; J. M. van der Kroef, "Land Tenure and Social Structure in Rural Java," *Rural Sociology* 25 (1960): 414–30; Ina Slamet, *Pokok 2 Pembangunan Masyarakat Desa* (Jakarta: Bhratara, 1965); Ann Stoler, "Some Socio-Economic Aspects of Rice Harvesting in a Javanese Village," *Masyarakat Indonesia* 2, no. 1 (1975): 51–87; Ernst Utrecht, *De Onderbroken Revolutie in Het Indonesische Dorp* (Amsterdam: University of Amsterdam, 1974); Benjamin White, "Population, Employment, and Involution in Rural Java," *Development and Change* 7 (1976): 267–90; Margo Lyon, *Bases of Conflict in Rural Java* (Berkeley: Center for South and Southeast Asia Studies, Research Monograph no. 3, 1970).

22. Various aspects of the economy of Kali Loro have been reported in A. Stoler, "Rice Harvesting in Kali Loro: A Study of Class and Labor Relations in Rural Java," *American Ethnologist* (August 1977), in press, and "Garden Use and Household Consumption Patterns in a Javanese Village," *Agricultural Development in Indonesia,* ed. G. Hansen (Ithaca, N.Y.: Cornell University Press, in press); Benjamin White, "The Economic Importance of Children in a Javanese Village," in *Population and Social Organization,* ed. M. Nag (The Hague: Mouton, 1975), "Production and Reproduction in a Javanese Village" (Ph.D. diss., Columbia University, 1977).

23. Under present conditions of cultivation in Kali Loro, one-fifth of a hectare of double-cropped *sawah* is the minimum to produce enough rice to feed a household of average size throughout the year.

amount of time men and women spend in each, the scale of their activities, and the combination of activities they engage in reflect the demands of each particular household economy.

Neglect of the consequences of such socioeconomic inequalities within village society would result in two biases against women. First, an emphasis on *sawah* farmers could obscure the fact that female employment provides crucial income sources for a majority of the households in Kali Loro. Second, we would have to assume that all women are subject to the same social and economic constraints on their activities and thus theoretically should have equal access to social power within village society. An examination of several activities in which women are involved (rice harvesting, trade, and ceremonial exchange)[24] will illustrate that, although village women as a whole perform similar activities, not all women participate equally or with the same degree of control in the production process.

Rice Harvesting

The traditional rice-harvesting system in Kali Loro involves a labor-intensive technology and large numbers of women, who are paid in kind with a share (*bawon*) of the harvest.[25] It is cited by Javanese as the stronghold of mutual cooperation (*gotong-royong*) and by students of Javanese society as the prime example of "shared poverty." However, closer examination reveals a delicately balanced set of exchange relationships which determines both differential access and returns to harvesting opportunities.

Women harvest rice with a small single-bladed implement (the *ani-ani*) which cuts each panicle individually. Whereas ploughing, hoeing, and harrowing (all male tasks) require only a limited number of man-days and can be spread over a relatively long period of time, harvesting is the most labor intensive of all agricultural activities, demanding large supplies of labor at concentrated periods. However, the large

24. These activities by no means exhaust female resources. Although Islamic and Javanese customary (*adat*) law both prescribe that on the death of a parent a son will inherit twice as much as a daughter, in fact neither law is strictly adhered to. In Kali Loro sons and daughters alike inherit rice land; however, no hard and fast rules determine who will receive how much, although generally women do not inherit house-garden land. Women retain rights to land in marriage and in the event of divorce take the property they have brought with them to the marriage. Whereas *adat* also prescribes that men should retain twice as much as women of the communal property, in fact the division is usually more equal. Thus women have full rights and access to the strategic resources upon which social power is based.

25. Although studies have noted the contribution of female labor in rice production, they have not recognized the importance of harvest wages as a source of income for Javanese women and their households.

number of women mobilized for harvesting, even on relatively small farms, is not simply a function of the requirements of wet rice production. By paying members of a neighboring household in kind with a relatively large share, a farmer spreads the risks of cultivation and is assured of reciprocal employment opportunities for the female members of his or her household. Two factors directly determine the size of the harvest share: the amount of land the harvester herself controls, and her social proximity to the host household. Three degrees of social proximity can be distinguished. Close relatives receive anywhere from one-fourth to one-half of what they harvest, although a poor relation may be given the entire amount. Shares of one-sixth to one-eighth are given to women from neighboring households who fall within the social network of reciprocal labor exchange. The final group includes anyone outside the first two categories, that is, distant villagers and nonvillagers, who generally receive shares from one-tenth to one-twelfth.

The small landowner (who meets labor demands principally by recruiting kin and close neighbors) is forced to give higher shares than the large landowner (whose labor demands are greater and who thus can employ a greater proportion of women outside the first two categories). Whereas a small landowner and harvester exchange labor with one another, larger landowners, who are independent of these reciprocal relationships, have a stronger bargaining position vis-à-vis the harvesters. Thus the *average* share paid by a large landowner is lower than that paid by a smaller one.

Quantitative data on harvesting activities and incomes were gathered from a sample of seventy-five households which approximately reflects the distribution of landholdings in the village as a whole. The distribution of harvesting work and wages in table 1 shows that landless families harvest for the greatest number of woman-days (i.e., the total number of days all the women harvested in a given household) and bring in the largest total income in harvest wages, but receive the least amount of rice for each time they harvest, that is, the lowest returns to labor. Women from larger landholding households, on the other hand, receive the highest average returns to labor and harvest the fewest number of woman-days. Why are women in poor households forced to accept lower wages for the same work?

The varied types of income-producing activities available to women in each of these groups provide an explanation. For women in poor households rice harvesting is by far the most productive source of income. Mat weaving and some small-scale trading, for example, have much lower returns to labor and do not compete with time allotted to harvesting. During the harvest season, many women stop trading temporarily, but more often they combine each of these activities to maximize the opportunities available. Women from larger landholding households, on the other hand, have a different set of options. Basic rice

Table 1

Number of Woman-Days of Paid Harvesting per Household and Total Income from Harvesting according to Landholdings in Rainy Season Harvest, April 1973 (N = 75 Households)

Harvested Area of Hh's own Rice Farm (in Hectares) (1)	N Hh Who Did Not Harvest (2)	Average N Days Harvesting per Hh (3)	Average N Times Harvesting per Hh (4)	Average Total Harvesting Income per Hh (5)	Average Income per Woman Day of Harvesting (6)	Average N Harvesters per Hh (7)
None (i.e., landless) (N = 16 hh)	1	43.8 (N=15 hh)	53.1	111.1 kg	2.5 kg	2.5
≤0.2 hectares (N=40 hh)	1	25.3 (N=39 hh)	32.8	77.8 kg	3.1 kg	2.0
>0.2 hectares (N=19 hh)	5	14.8 (N=14 hh)	22.9	59.6 kg	4.0 kg	1.8

NOTE.—Hh = household; harvesting incomes in cols. 5 and 6 are given in kg of threshed but undried and unhulled paddy (*gabah teles*), the most common form in which paddy is measured directly after the harvest; 1 kg of *gabah teles* yields about 0.56 kg of hulled rice.

requirements can be met within the household, and as traders with much larger capital investments, they can ensure profits far beyond what they could earn from harvesting. Furthermore, they oversee the harvest operation, control the number of harvesters invited or admitted, decide on the share each harvester receives, and preside over the threshing, bundling, and distribution of shares which takes place at the home of the landholder. Indeed these women do not harvest unless invited and thus receive much higher shares. Landless women, on the other hand, lack the economic flexibility to choose when and where they harvest. If they do not harvest for close neighbors, where they are assured a larger share, they are forced to seek harvest opportunities further afield in order to meet consumption needs. They receive less rice per harvesting time, simply because they have to harvest more often. And because they have nothing to exchange but their labor, they can earn the right to harvest only by obligating themselves to a patron household.

Harvesting opportunities are a vital resource for poor households, and control over harvesting opportunities reflects a direct control over the labor and lives of others. Insofar as owning or farming rice land gives a household control of a much demanded "good" (wage labor opportunities), it is (1) women in the farming households who control the distribution of this "good," and it is (2) women harvesters who obtain this "good" for their households. Vertical dyadic relationships thus cross-cut the possible strength women might gain by exerting collective pressure on a wealthy landowner.[26] The Javanese harvesting system illustrates that it is not *participation* in collective social labor which gives women economic power[27] but rather a woman's ability to mobilize the social labor of others.

Trade and Markets

The Javanese market system provides another important source of female employment. In Kali Loro almost 40 percent of the adult women were engaged in some form of trade and probably another 30 percent had traded at some point in their lives; only 8 percent of the men were traders. Because of an abundant labor supply and a scarcity of capital there is a highly specialized division of labor:[28] the majority of traders (*bakul*) deal in a limited number of goods, take small risks, and obtain small profits. For small-scale traders (*bakul eyek*) who deal in small quantities of locally grown produce for local consumption, capital investments range from Rp 500 to Rp 700, and average daily profits are as little as Rp 50 and frequently less.[29] Because they are usually women

26. See Stoler, "Rice Harvesting in Kali Loro."
27. Compare Sacks, in Rosaldo and Lamphere (see n. 4 above).
28. Dewey (see n. 16 above).
29. Rp 415 = U.S.$1.00.

from landless and small landholding households, they can neither withhold their earnings from the household economy nor accumulate enough capital to increase their trading activities.

Kali Loro does not have a conveniently located intermediary market town to which small traders and producers can bring their goods. The result is a prevalence of village-based, medium-scale traders who act as middlewomen between the village and the city of Jogjakarta some thirty kilometers away. These traders, with capital of about Rp 2,000–5,000, buy up local produce (mats, eggs, chickens, and coconuts) directly from producers or small traders and sell them to larger wholesalers in the city; or they may buy dry goods (tea, tobacco, soybeans, etc.) in the city for sale in the village. Because of the costs of transport, such traders are limited to women whose capital allows them to deal in quite quite large volumes of these relatively high priced, compact goods. Even though these women acquire a strong degree of independence and their profits are important supplements to the household economy, their activities give them neither power over other traders nor enough wealth to buy land. Thus these activities are a source of economic independence but not necessarily of economic power.

Significantly, the small majority of large-scale traders (both men and women) are also among the largest landowners in Kali Loro. Their capital investments range from Rp 20,000 to Rp 200,000 ($50–$500), and their debts to city-based wholesalers are often large.[30] While some travel long distances to buy and sell, others are strictly "armchair entrepreneurs"; their profits simply reflect their control over cash resources. Several of these market entrepreneurs actively buy up rice land, or rent land for fixed periods of time, then sharecrop it out; three of these wealthy traders are also moneylenders who appropriate the debtors' land or services upon default. Thus these armchair entrepreneurs not only command the most strategic resource in the market (cash) but invariably use their profits to buy land and control labor.

Trade at the village level then (unlike the town marketing system described by Dewey) is intricately affected by socioeconomic relationships in the village economy (and vice versa). A woman's economic independence is not simply a function of the fact that she trades, but that she earns a regular and reliable income from her activities. Among poor households, the woman's earnings provide her with an important position *within* the household economy; among wealthier households, such earnings provide her with the material basis for social power.

Domestic Production and Interhousehold Exchange

Although certain types of female labor are "productive" in the tradi-

30. C. Geertz, *Peddlers and Princes,* p. 37.

tional sense, household labor which does not *directly* produce wages or items of measurable value has been systematically underestimated in peasant economic literature. However, Marx[31] has argued that we must consider both the day-to-day maintenance of laborers and the transgenerational maintenance of labor (reproduction). By excluding women's household work from our measurements, we exclude an essential input in the production process.[32] The fact that women often have "nothing to show" for their efforts does not render their labor less important.[33]

Javanese *adat* (customary law) recognizes the female contribution to household economy. As Geertz writes, "Since husband and wife are an economic unity, even though the wife may not participate directly in the acquisition of income, her performance of household tasks is considered part of the productive economic enterprise. . . . For this reason all goods acquired during the marriage, other than by inheritance, are thought to be community property."[34] The household, as the basic unit of production and consumption, is in practice under the unequivocal authority of women. Women and young girls usually cook; child care is shared by women, older siblings, and less frequently men; household marketing is done by women and children; water is fetched by young girls and women. Men and young children usually collect firewood (which is often scarce and thus a time-consuming task) and care for animals. Tasks are allotted among all the household members, but authority is not. According to Jay, Geertz, and Koentjaraningrat,[35] women clearly control family finances and dominate the decision-making process. Although an emphasis on female control in the domestic domain often implies male control in the public/social domain, Javanese rural society, based on extensive symmetrical and asymmetrical socioeconomic ties, shows "domestic" activities to encompass the "social" sphere. Daily "domestic" decisions concerning cash expenditures for wages and labor exchange clearly belong to the social domain as well.[36]

Foreigners often have the erroneous impression "that the Javanese wife holds an inferior status in the household" because she "retires" to the rear of the house when formal guests arrive.[37] The husband is in fact the household head and mediates between the family and the outside world. However, the discrepancies between appearance and reality are

31. K. Marx, *Capital* (New York: International Publishers, 1967), passim.

32. Secombe (see n. 7 above).

33. See White, "Production and Reproduction," for a discussion of this problem, specifically the problem of assigning.

34. H. Geertz, p. 49 (see n. 1 above).

35. Ibid., p. 11. Compare Robert Jay, *Javanese Villagers: Social Relations in Rural Madjokuto* (Cambridge, Mass.: M.I.T. Press, 1969); R. M. Koentjaraningrat, "The Javanese of South Central Java," in *Social Structure in Southeast Asia,* ed. G. P. Murdock, Viking Fund Publications in Anthropology no. 29 (Chicago: Quadrangle, 1960).

36. Jay, p. 92, my emphasis.

37. Koentjaraningrat, p. 104.

exemplified in the core ritual of Javanese rural society, the *slametan* or ceremonial feast, which is given for births, weddings, deaths, harvests, and in "response to almost any occurrence one wishes to celebrate, ameliorate, or sanctify": "The ceremony itself is all male. The women remain *mburi* (behind—i.e., in the kitchen), but they inevitably peek through the bamboo walls at the men, who squatted on floor mats (in front—i.e., in the main living room) perform the actual ritual, eating the food the women prepared. . . . [M]ost of the food remains uneaten. It is taken home, wrapped in the banana leaf dishes, to be eaten in the privacy of their houses in company with their wives and children. With their (the men's) departure the *slametan* ends."[38] However, in Kali Loro, the ceremony itself was often perfunctory and the distribution of food the centerpoint of activity. Focusing our attention on the distribution of food, rather than the symbolic aspects of ritual, it becomes clear that the real mediators of interhousehold relationships in the *slametan* are the women and not the men. The women buy, cook, and make the decisions as to how the food will be distributed, the latter a task often more complex than Geertz's description might imply. Men who appear for the ceremony at the host's house are given a rice package along with various small quantities of vegetables and condiments (the size of the package varies but is usually enough to feed two adults and several children).

Households who have not sent a representative in some cases have food sent to them. If food is left over, the women who participate in the cooking and who are fed once or twice (depending on how long the cooking takes) decide to whom it should be sent. If the amount of food has been underestimated, again the women decide which households can most inconspicuously be excluded. The distribution of food is an affirmation of symmetrical and asymmetrical socioeconomic ties: the invited guests belong to households with which the host household exchanges labor for harvesting, for housebuilding, and for other productive activities. We might, then, view this aspect of the *slametan* complex as one in which men, rather than women, "retire" to their "rigmarole" and in which women assume the center as mediators. Of course this is not true of all *slametan;* in house-building parties or at funerals both sexes often represent the household in their own domains. But the essential role of women within the *slametan* complex, their participation in "collective social labor," must not be ignored. At the same time, we must not forget that collectivity consists of people in subordinate, equal, and powerful positions vis-à-vis other members of the group. In Kali Loro, wealth differences crosscut alliances based on sex. Thus, although poor women from landless and small landholding households have the right to represent their household, it is important to remember (because it has been largely neglected) that what they represent is the subordinate position of their households in social production.

38. C. Geertz, *The Religion of Java* (New York: Free Press, 1960), pp. 11–14.

Agricultural Change and Its Impact on the Female Labor Force

Despite the obvious need for detailed studies concerning the effect of technological change on the economic role of women,[39] interest in this field has come only recently with the elimination of certain female employment opportunities that accompanied the "Green Revolution." In Indonesia as in other countries, the introduction of new high-yielding rice varieties, hulling machines, expensive pesticides, and fertilizers to increase agricultural production has primarily benefited the already secure members of rural society and has increased rural income inequalities.[40] Poorer village households have become more impoverished, not simply by their exclusion from the benefits, but directly by having their employment opportunities further limited. Thus, poor women have not been "released" from agriculture, as Boserup suggests for wealthier village women,[41] but rather forced out of agriculture and obliged to seek nonagricultural employment. Two principal changes have affected female economic activities in the poorest segment of village society—women have not been affected equally, nor have they responded by sharing the limited opportunities available equally among them.

One of the most rapid and widespread changes in Indonesia in recent years has been the replacement of traditional home pounding by rice hullers. While the earliest analyses of the effects of this change indicated a benefit to village society in general,[42] subsequent studies have shown a marked difference in the advantages of rice hullers to the richer and poorer members of village society.[43] For large landowners the hullers save costs, and more important, preserve rice better than pounded rice and facilitate sale. Thus, although a few large landowners still hire client women for daily pounding, hulling machines have almost completely replaced this labor. Rice pounding for a wage was formerly a major and regular source of income for women in poor households, with returns per hour comparable to those from harvesting. For 75 percent of the households in Kali Loro who do not cultivate enough rice even for subsistence, let alone enough to sell, the rice hullers, then, severely limited employment opportunities. In recent years the necessity of seeking alternate sources of income has, on one hand, set off an influx of these

39. Hanna Papanek, "Women in South and Southeast Asia: Issues and Research," *Signs: Journal of Women in Culture and Society* 1, no. 1 (1975): 193–214.

40. Dwight Y. King and Peter D. Weldon, "Pembagian Pendapatan dan Tingkat Hidup di Jawa 1963–1970," *Ekonomi dan Keuangan Indonesia,* vol. 23, no. 4 (1975).

41. Boserup (n. 8 above).

42. Peter Timmer, "Choice of Technique in Rice Milling in Java," *Bulletin of Indonesian Economic Studies* 9, no. 2 (1973): 57–76.

43. William L. Collier, "Choice of Technique in Rice Milling on Java: A Comment," *Bulletin of Indonesian Economic Studies,* vol. 10, no. 2 (1974).

women into local small-scale trade, and on the other, has increased the importance of their harvesting incomes.

Recent changes in more densely populated areas of Java also indicate that harvesting wages may not remain a secure income source. In order to cut harvesting costs and escape the "traditional obligations" of higher shares, large farmers are selling their rice before the harvest to middlemen from outside the village who assume the responsibility of harvest management, bring in outside harvesters, or drastically reduce the number of local harvesters. While harvesting costs have been cut by as much as 42 percent, this process has caused the loss of jobs on a huge scale. Even more drastic reductions in harvesting opportunities have occured where middlemen employ a small group of male harvesters using sickles rather than the traditional tool (the *ani-ani*) which cuts stalks individually. Under such a system, which reduces the number of harvesters by as much as 60 percent, women from large landholding households benefit in that they are freed from the job of harvest management and in fact are "released" (as Boserup suggests) to invest their time and capital in lucrative trading enterprises. For the poorer majority of village society, both men and women suffer as more and more land is concentrated in the hands of the wealthier households. However, the decline in female employment opportunities is more easily observable.

With all of these limitations on female employment, we would expect, as Boserup and others suggest, that the position of women would be inversely correlated to changes in economic development. And yet Java rural women from small landholding and landless households have been traditionally involved in alternate income-producing activities outside of rice cultivation. It is men, in fact, who have a smaller set of viable alternatives to agricultural labor. Women are, in a sense, better equipped to deal with the situation of increasing landlessness[44] and can manipulate a more familiar set of limited options. Figure 1 indicates that within two groups of households below the 0.2-hectare threshold, the purely female income sources (female trade, handicrafts, and agricultural wage labor) contribute one-third of the household's total income. For households above that threshold, however, female income sources comprise less than 15 percent of total income. This does not mean that women in the latter group necessarily make a smaller contribution to household income.[45] Their earning power is a function of their control over land and capital and not of their participation in the labor-intensive employment activities of poorer women.

We cannot, then, view women as a homogenous group in village

44. William L. Collier, Gunawan Wiradi, and Soentoro, "Recent Changes in Rice-Harvesting Methods," *Bulletin of Indonesian Economic Studies* 9, no. 2 (1973): 36–45.

45. Budhisantose, "Beberapa tjatatan mengenai keluarga matrifokal di desa Tjibuaja Djawa Barat" [Notes on the matrifocal family in the village of Tjibuaja, West Java], *Berita Antropologi* 2 no. 4 (1971): 70–80.

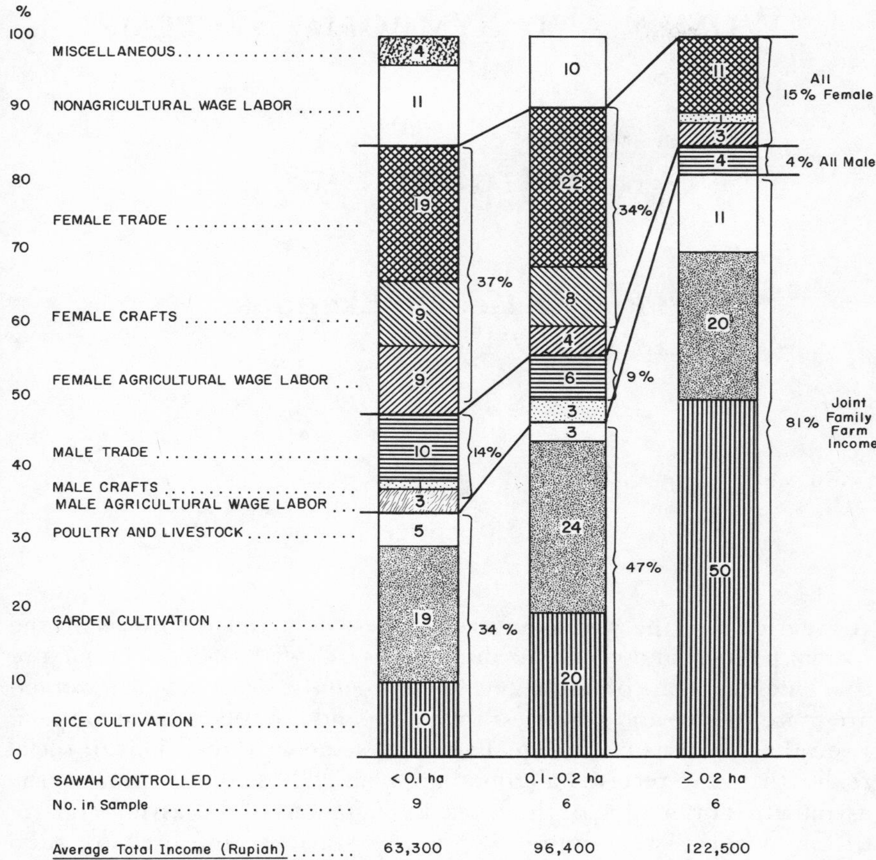

FIG. 1.—Sources of income as a percentage of total annual income for households grouped according to area of Sawah controlled.

society, nor can we assume that exploitation will occur primarily along sexual lines. Changes in the structure of precolonial, colonial, and present Javanese rural economy did not catalyze an increased dichotomy of sexual roles, but rather an increased scarcity and concentration of strategic resources. These changes adversely affected both men and women in the lower strata of village society. Thus the simple generalization that women in Java have a relatively high position obscures fundamental differences in their access to and control over productive resources. Poverty is indeed shared, but only among the already impoverished men and women of rural Java.

Department of Anthropology
Columbia University
New York City, U.S.A.

Women and Symbolic Systems

Introduction

Felicia Ifeoma Ekejiuba

A great deal of the vast literature on sex-role patterns focuses on the formal political and economic dimensions of social reality. The picture that emerges is one of a relationship between the sexes in which women are more passive and powerless than men and are subordinate to them. Even those aspects of the equally crucial symbolic dimensions of social reality that have received attention are mainly those that rationalize the asymmetrical valuation of the sexes. Explanations of this asymmetry are often materialistic, made within the static framework of such dichotomies as private/public, nature/culture, domestic/social. Men's activities are portrayed as more highly valued because they are cultural and public, while women's activities are seen as domestic, nearer to nature than to culture. The implication for social change and development is that "men should be integrated into the domestic sphere, giving them an opportunity to share in the socialization of children as well as in the more mundane domestic tasks . . . women's esteem will be elevated only when they participate equally in the public world of work."[1]

The three papers in this collection by Carol MacCormack, Fatima Mernissi, and Susan Wadley examine aspects of the symbolic and ideological dimensions of social reality. They also provide various indexes of the power and values that are traditionally associated with women among the Sande of Sierra Leone, Muslim Maghreb of North Africa, and Hindus in India. The papers go on to depict male attitudes toward

1. Michelle Rosaldo and Louise Lamphere, *Women, Culture and Society* (Stanford, Calif.: Stanford University Press, 1974), p. 41.

the paradox posed by the power of women. In recognition of the paradoxical nature of women's power, many societies seem more concerned with the separation of the sexes than with the domination of one by the other. Hindu and Islamic ideologies fear the mystical power of women, which may make men impotent. They thus harness, restrict, and confine it, prescribing its control by men but using it when needed, especially in revolts and rebellions against foreign domination and exploitation. Others, such as the Sande, recognize women's power as complementary to men's power. Consequently, they set up parallel institutions and avenues for the separate development of the sexes.

The three papers, in addition, explore structural and historical processes that erode the power of women and shift the balance of power in men's favor: the territorial displacement of women through marriage from one group to another, orthodox religions, colonization, capitalism with its competition for scarce resources, migration, industrialization, modernization, and development. These processes transform male superiority and power from the symbolic and fragile to real domination by integrating the formerly separate world of the sexes and making the knowledge, skills, professions, and products of these processes first available to men. In consequence, men are placed in a position where they define these as scarce and prestigious commodities and discriminate legally and informally, through male-created myths of female inferiority, against women's participation in these processes. Indeed, the lag in the differential exposure of the sexes to these scarce commodities widens the cultural and technological gap between the sexes, which then concretizes the differences between them.[2]

Finally, the papers demonstrate the strategies through which women as active participants in social processes exploit the power attributed to them, through which they perceive and close the gap which historical change tends to widen, and through which they acquire the knowledge and skills that give them increased access to the products and professions associated with change. Manipulation of female power leverage counteracts the advantages concomitant with male control of formal economic and political institutions.

Collectively, the three papers underscore the need to rethink the relationship between the sexes and to create a diachronic analytic framework that will integrate data from the materialistic and formal aspects of social reality with data from the symbolic and ideological domains. The latter give women a positive image, one that makes them equal to or more powerful than men. Such a framework will see society at any point in time, not as functionally integrated, but in Weberian

2. Evelyn Sullerot, *Woman, Society and Change* (London: World University Library, 1971); Ester Boserup, *Women's Role in Economic Development* (New York: St. Martin's Press, 1970), pp. 55–57.

terms, as composite of social groups, each with its own interest and each differentially exposed to historical processes of change.

It is true that social science has better-developed theories and tools for the analysis of formal economic and political institutions than it has for the symbolic aspects of social reality. But the seminal work on symbolic analysis by Victor Turner, Mary Douglas, Edmund Leach, and others provides valuable insights that should be incorporated into an analytical framework for a more balanced view of cross-cultural sexual differences and sex-role patterns.

Department of Sociology
Simmons College
Boston, Massachusetts, U.S.A.

Women and Symbolic Systems

Biological Events and Cultural Control

Carol P. MacCormack

The women come in from the fields and forest, laden with cocoyams and firewood, streaming with rain, screaming with fatigue at their husbands. They come from the wild, entering inside the village fence, inside house walls, within the boundaries that mark the domain of domesticated animals and the society of men. They come from nature to culture. In thus describing Bakweri women of Cameroon, Ardener continues with an analysis of their puberty rites, and concludes that these women have a model of the world which conceptually includes themselves with nature, while men bound mankind off from nature. Women's reproductive powers are their essence, and human reproduction is a thing of nature.[1]

Ardener's structural analysis rests upon Lévi-Strauss's hypothesis that it is the bounding off of culture from nature that accounts for our very humanity. Rather than mating within the consanguineal family as animals do, men at some point in evolutionary history renounced their sisters in the great gamble that some other men would also do the unnatural. By exchanging women, separate consanguineal groups became interwebbed with ties of affinity, and human society was born. Quite explicit in his structural analysis of society is the active role in exchange attributed to men and a passive role for women.[2]

Bakweri women's puberty rites symbolically confirm for Ardener

1. E. Ardener, "Belief and the Problem of Women," in *The Interpretation of Ritual,* ed. J. S. LaFontaine (London: Tavistock Publications, 1972), pp. 135–58.

2. C. Lévi-Strauss, *The Elementary Structure of Kinship* (1949; reprint ed., Boston: Beacon Press, 1969). U. Junus ("Some Remarks on Minangkabau Social Structure," *Bijdragen tot de Taal-, Land- en Volkenkunde* 120 [1964]: 293–326) questions the universality of Lévi-Strauss's assumptions, especially in matrilineal-matrilocal societies where men pass in

the concept that Bakweri women see themselves within the domain of nature. While he mentions that each initiate has a sponsor to teach her women's "mysteries," he does not elaborate upon the social context of the teaching or the content of the lessons.[3] Yet in other women's initiation rites the very point of the rite of passage is to teach girls to bring the biological events of their lives under careful cultural control.[4]

For example, officials of the Sande society, a women's religious society in Sierra Leone, instruct their pubescent initiates during weeks or months of seclusion.[5] Following that period of liminality the newly knowledgeable women are reincorporated into society with the status of adults. Henceforth they do not have sexual intercourse in any place, at any time, with any person they wish, as animals do. Such "natural" behavior would be a grievous offense to ancestral spirits, whose wrath might rain disease and infertility on the people and the land. Successful bearing and rearing of children is informed by Sande knowledge about hygiene, nutrition, medicine, and myriad other practical techniques rather than being a careless matter of doing what comes naturally. Should a man look on voyeuristically at women while they bathe, as people look at animals, ancestral wrath might strike him down. His only salvation would be to go to the officials of the Sande society, publicly confess, and submit to a ritual cleansing. Not only men, but women who trespass against Sande laws are sanctioned by ancestors or Sande officials.

Rather than being uncontrolled reproduction machines, Sande women, with their secret knowledge, public laws, legitimate sanctions, and hierarchical organization, bring women's biology under the most careful cultural control. Those very laws, sanctions, and organizations give Sherbro and Mende women in Sierra Leone a solid base of conceptual thought, practical experience, and social cohesion from which to launch out still farther into the cultural domain of thought and technology, the stuff of national development.

Sande Organization

Sande is an acephalous system of corporate groups organized on the

marriage between descent groups. S. de Beauvoir (*The Second Sex* [New York: Alfred A. Knopf, 1953], p. 239) and S. B. Ortner ("Is Female to Male as Nature Is to Culture?" in *Woman, Culture and Society,* ed. M. Z. Rosaldo and L. Lamphere [Stanford, Calif.: Stanford University Press, 1974], pp. 67–88) also speculate on the equation of women with nature and men with culture and on its consequences.

3. Ardener, pp. 149–50.

4. A. Richards, *Chisungu: A Girl's Initiation Ceremony among the Bemba of Northern Rhodesia* (London: Faber & Faber, 1956).

5. Information, unless otherwise specified, pertains to the Moyamba District of Sierra Leone. Sande occurs throughout Sierra Leone and in parts of neighboring Guinea and Liberia.

residence rather than the descent principle. Local chapters are not unified into an overarching hierarchy of officials. It derives its authority from the power and ongoing concern of founding ancestresses, made manifest on ritual occasions as masked figures.[6] In each local chapter, senior adult members, in a hierarchy of offices, provide leadership, and the sodality renews itself when a class of initiates is ritually "born" into the corporation which exists in perpetuity.[7] The most important corporate property which Sande owns is the secret knowledge transmitted to women at the time they are initiated. It also owns ritual objects and "medicine." Conceptually, "medicine" includes physical substances with effective pharmacological properties and physical substances which link persons with sources of power in the universe. If an initiated woman uses Sande knowledge and Sande medicine to treat an ill person, the fee she receives is not her own but is given to the officials of her local chapter. She has used corporate "capital," and the "profit" returns to the group, in the care of its officials.

Although a woman will most likely be initiated into her mother's Sande chapter, giving a matrilineal character to Sande organization, marriage usually follows quickly after initiation, and the woman will most likely go away to reside virilocally in her husband's town, transferring her active allegiance to the chapter where she lives. Initiation into Sande is just the beginning of a woman's lifelong active participation in her local chapter, where women gather for weeks or months during the initiation season. Initiations are held yearly in some towns and less frequently in sparsely populated areas. Officials of the chapter will spend a great deal of time in the initiation grove, while younger women, unless they are sponsoring a daughter's initiation, will spend less time in such activities. Aside from the initiation season, Sande women do not constitute a formal congregation, although they do interact informally and may dance together on public holidays.

A woman will, if possible, return to her natal village to give birth, maintaining a vital link with her mother's Sande chapter. Before hospitals provided an alternative, all Sande women gave birth in the Sande "bush," a cleared place in the forest, or in a house which only Sande women may enter. The woman in labor is given social support by her mother and other Sande women. She is given ritual protection by Sande "medicine," and the chapter headwoman attends her as midwife. The midwife, as headwoman, may be the very woman who supervised her transformation into responsible womanhood at initiation.

6. W. L. d'Azevedo ("Mask-Makers and Myth in Western Liberia," in *Primitive Art and Society,* ed. A. Forge [London: Oxford University Press, 1973], pp. 126 ff.) briefly describes a male principle, manifest as the black masked figure in Liberian Sande. In the Sherbro and Mende areas of Sierra Leone that mask represents the spiritual power and serene beauty of womanhood.

7. In Lungi, Moyamba District, Sande women are buried in a great mound in the village. The mound reminds inhabitants of the power of women to bless and succor, their power existing in unbroken continuity from the living to the ancestors.

By residing with their husband's people following marriage, these women are "in between" their natal descent group in which they do not renounce membership and their husband's group into which they are not completely absorbed.[8] They also link their mother's Sande chapter with that of their mother-in-law. Contrary to the Lévi-Straussian model of women as passive objects transferred between groups of men, in Sande, women link corporate groups composed exclusively of women. Marriages are arranged with the consent of the bride and in consultation with male and female kin of both the bride's and groom's group. In the Sherbro ceremony of requesting a bride, the groom's group specifically consults the bride's mother, giving a gift "for the sake of the lappa," the garment in which a mother carries an infant on her back. "Carrying" is shorthand for nurturing the fetus through pregnancy and the child into maturity. Not only the mother but other ranking female kin of the bride are consulted and their approval sought before the marriage is finally contracted. In Sande, and in marriage, women physically move back and forth between groups, interpreting events, often in their own self-interest, to the other camp, generating information which ties corporate groups together in a bond of common interest.

The headwoman of a local Sande chapter is referred to in Mende by the title *majo*. She is ultimately responsible for the quality of each initiate's training in the skills of womanhood. As midwife and adviser on gynecological problems, she is instrumental in assisting women to fulfill their culturally defined adult role through childbearing. Headwomen link the separate chapters together in an informal fashion by moving about the country to assist in each other's initiation ceremonies. Some women, because of their demonstrated adeptness in guiding other women to sound physiological and psychological health, are known over a wide area. They may travel across linguistic and ethnic boundaries, making their rank known through personal testimonials and manipulation of the symbols of their office.

A woman destined for a commanding role in Sande will acquire more knowledge and demonstrate her growing adeptness in womanly skills. This is learned behavior, socially transmitted, and therefore by definition cultural, not natural. Increased knowledge and adeptness is acknowledged by rites which elevate some women to higher grades within Sande. A woman who dies before the rank has been ritually conferred will have it conferred posthumously as the first stage of the funeral ceremonies which Sande chapters conduct for their members. Although some women rise to higher grades within Sande, there is no automatic promotion based upon age alone, nor the kind of age grading

8. M. Strathern (*Women in Between* [London: Seminar Press, 1972]) gives a case study of women actively linking corporate descent groups.

of women in society at large, as there is among Nyakyusa men, for example.[9]

Poro is the male equivalent of Sande, concerned with religious belief, socialization of adolescent males, and adeptness in manly skills. It is more overtly political than Sande, functioning at the local level to counterbalance the largely secular power of chiefs, who may be men or women.[10] Sande women, as individuals or as officials of their sodality, also enter the political arena, exerting significant direct political force upon the larger society.[11]

It is important to stress that Sande is not a "counterinstitution" to men's authority. Poro and Sande complement rather than oppose each other. Poro officials perform such duties as seeing that wells are kept clean or that disputes do not escalate into fights. Sande officials perform other duties, for example, treating certain illnesses or enforcing a prohibition against sexual intercourse with lactating women, assuring some spacing of children. Each sodality has its own domain of social control, laying down explicit laws of behavior known to the entire community. If a law is breached, all parties in the crime are at fault. Sande and Poro provide their laws for the health and well-being of the entire community, not for their own group alone. When Sande begins an initiation season, Poro, out of respect, remains quietly in the background. When Poro is initiating, Sande women show their respect by remaining ritually quiescent.

Initiation: A Rite of Passage

For analytical purposes, the female life cycle might be divided into four stages. The first is girlhood, from birth until the onset of menstruation. The second stage is that brief liminal period between the onset of menstruation and marriage when a female is no longer a girl but not yet by cultural definition a woman who might procreate. The third stage is adulthood, following Sande initiation and marriage or cohabitation with a man. The final stage is ancestorhood, following physical death.

The second stage is publicly marked when a group of girls, who have reached menarche, are ritually separated from the larger society

9. M. Wilson, *Good Company* (London: Oxford University Press, 1951).

10. K. Little, "The Political Function of the Poro," pts. 1 and 2, *Africa* 35 (1965): 349–65, and 36 (1966): 62–71.

11. For political structures and strategies used by Mende and Sherbro women, see C. P. Hoffer (MacCormack), "Mende and Sherbro Women in High Office," *Canadian Journal of African Studies* 6 (1972): 151–64, and "Madam Yoko: Ruler of the Kpa Mende Confederacy," in Rosaldo and Lamphere (n. 2 above), pp. 173–87; and C. P. MacCormack, "Sande Women and Politics in Sierra Leone," *West African Journal of Sociology and Political Science* 1 (1975): 42–50.

for weeks or months. Under the sponsorship of their mother or other kinswoman, they enter through a portal into the Sande "bush," a cleared place in the forest or a secluded part of the town.[12] There the group of girls, in a classical liminal state, discard the clothing of childhood, smear their bodies with white clay, and dress alike in brief skirts and many strands of small beads.[13] Mature Sande women intensively train them to womanly responsibility, making them vividly aware of their incipient womanhood and their value to the larger society, especially as farmers and bearers of children. In this institutional setting women dramatically pass on a strong, positive self-image to other women.

Shortly after entering the Sande bush, girls undergo the distinctive surgery of a Sande woman, in which the clitoris and part of the labia minora are excised. Sande women explain that excism helps women to become prolific bearers of children. Conceptually, it is the *majo* with "a good hand" who brings forth the procreative potential in a woman. Neither conception, childbirth, nor other biological matters such as hygiene are left to natural process.

Informants also said that the initial surgery made women clean. One might speculate along the lines Douglas has developed that by excising the clitoris, a rudiment of maleness, all sexual ambiguity is removed from the incipient woman. She then fits purely and "safely" into the social structure, free from the impurity and "danger" of categorical ambiguity.[14]

In most societies with initiation surgery, the resultant visible scar or body modification is a sign that the initiated adult has been brought within a moral sphere. For a member of Poro, the pattern of scars on a man's back signify that he is one of "those who may procreate." In the Poro bush he was instructed in the social responsibilities that go with sexual intercourse and has sworn an oath to behave responsibly or suffer the consequences that an affront to the living and the ancestors would engender.

For a Sande woman, her scars and body modifications can only be known through intimate contact, by the partner with whom she is sharing a sexual relationship. He, upon knowing she is a Sande woman, can be confident that she is also trained in the moral and practical responsibilities of a potential procreator.

Initiation begins with a painful and dangerous ordeal, endured in a context of intense social support, a metaphor for childbirth which may

12. Lest entry into the "bush" be interpreted as women's particular propensity to revert to nature, Poro men also enter a different clearing in the forest when they conduct initiations.

13. See A. Van Gennep (*The Rites of Passage* [1909; reprint ed., Chicago: University of Chicago Press, 1969]) and V. Turner (*The Ritual Process* [Chicago: Aldine Publishing Co., 1969]) for discussion of passage and liminality.

14. M. Douglas, *Purity and Danger* (London: Routledge & Kegan Paul, 1966).

occur in the same place among supportive Sande women. During the initiation period girls also experience intense positive gratification with abundant food, Sande songs, dancing, and storytelling, the stories often ending with an instructive moral linked to Sande laws. Those shared risks and pleasures help to bond the initiates into a cohesive social group. They swear an oath on Sande "medicine" before they leave the initiation grove, vowing never to reveal any fault in another Sande woman.[15] This solidarity training helps to mitigate co-wife rivalry and the potential divide-and-rule powers of polygynous husbands.

Most of the farming and household work girls do during initiation is not new to them. Since they have assisted their mothers from an early age, it is not new skills, but new attitudes toward work, that they learn. In childhood they worked in the role of daughter, but in Sande they begin to anticipate the role of wife in which they will have to work cooperatively with their co-wives and husband's kin. During the initiation period they work on the *majo*'s farm, the *majo* being a nonconsanguine, just as their husband's kin who control farm land in their marital residence will be nonconsanguine authority figures. They also cook, wash clothes, and daub mud houses in the manner of a married woman working cooperatively with her co-wives. Although attitudes toward work change, the nature of work in girlhood and womanhood remains largely the same. The image of death and rebirth is not as prominent in Sande initiation ceremonies as it is in Poro, where boys give up a more carefree childhood in taking on adult tasks.

The initiation period concludes when a "medicine," made by brewing leaves in water, is used to wash the initiates ritually, removing the magical protection they enjoyed since entering the initiation grove. In their liminal state, under magical protection, they were dangerous to any man who approached them sexually. Following the washing and final rituals of status transformation, all ambiguity about their womanhood is removed. They have become mature women in knowledgeable control of their own sexuality, eligible for marriage and childbearing.

The time of initiation for most women is determined biologically by puberty. However, an older woman, perhaps an in-marrying stranger or trader who takes up residence within the geographical sphere of Sande influence, may be initiated at any time.

Analytically, the belief system which underlies the Sande society might be explained with methods used by Lévi-Strauss in *Mythologiques* rather than those of more "humdrum ethnographic aim."[16] We might

15. This is the ideal. An occasional dispute between Sande women may go outside their moral community into the Native Administration court. In such cases, Sande "medicine" may be used for swearing an oath to tell the truth in court.

16. C. Lévi-Strauss, *The Raw and the Cooked* (Boston: Beacon Press, 1969; originally published in 1964 as *Le Cru et le cuit*). The quote is from Ardener (n. 1 above), p. 145.

choose to see all human society structured in contrastive categories of female-male, nature-culture, passive-active, uncontrolled-controlled, and copier-creator. If we do, however, then there logically can be no place for women, except at the most menial levels of production and reproduction, in the development plans of nations.

Department of Social Anthropology
University of Cambridge
Cambridge, England

Women and Symbolic Systems

Women, Saints, and Sanctuaries

Fatima Mernissi

. . . The next morning I went to see my mother. I had a snack with her and the children and then I went to spend the day at the Marabout [a sanctuary]. I lay down there and slept for a very long time.

Q: Do you go to the Marabout often?
A: Yes, quite often. For example I prefer to go there on the days of *Aïd* [religious festivals]. When one has a family as desperate as mine, the shrine is a haven of peace and quiet. I like to go there.
Q: What do you like about the shrine? Can you be more precise?
A: Yes. The silence, the rugs, and the clean mats which are nicely arranged . . . the sound of the fountain in the silence. An enormous silence where the sound of water is as fragile as thread. I stay there hours, sometimes whole days.
Q: The day of *Aïd* it must be full of people.
A: Yes, there are people, but they are lost in their own problems. So they leave you alone. Mostly it's women who cry without speaking, each in her own world.
Q: Aren't there any men at the shrine?
A: Yes, but men have their side, women theirs. Men come to visit the shrine and leave very quickly; the women, especially those with problems, stay much longer.
Q: What do they do and what do they say?
A: That depends. Some are happy just to cry. Others take hold of the saint's garments and say, "Give me this, oh saint, give me that.

Gathering of historical data on saints, mainly female saints, was done with the collaboration and critical supervision of the Moroccan historian, Halima Ferhat, a Maître de Conférence at the University Mohammed V.

. . ." "I want my daughter to pass her exam . . ." [she laughs]. You know the saints are men, human beings. But sometimes, imagine, the woman gets what she asks for! Then she brings a sacrifice . . . she kills an animal and prepares a meal of the meat and then offers it to the visitors. Do you know Sid El Gomri?
Q: No.
A: [laughs] Salé is full of shrines . . . full, full. You know, there is a proverb, "If you want to make a pilgrimage, just go around Salé barefooted . . ." [laughs]. They do say that. . . . All of Salé is a shrine. There are so many that some don't have names [laughs]. My father is a native of Salé. He knows the shrines and talks a lot about them. When you are separated from someone or when you have a very bad fight, the saint helps you overcome your problem. When I go I listen to the women. You see them tell everything to the tomb and mimicking all that took place. Then they ask Sid El Gomri to help them get out of the mess. They cry, they scream. Then they get hold of themselves and come back, join us, and sit in silence. I like the shrine.
Q: Are you ever afraid?
A: Afraid of what? In a shrine, what a question? I love shrines.
Q: And when do you go?
A: They are shut in the evenings except for those that have rooms, like Sidi Ben Achir, for example. You can rent a room there and you can stay a long time.
Q: Rent a room for how much?
A: Oh, fifteen dirhams.[1]
Q: Fifteen dirhams a night?!
A: No, for ten dirhams you can stay as long as you like, even a month. You know, they call Sidi Ben Achir a doctor. Sick people come with their family; they rent a room and stay until they are well. You know, it's not Sidi Ben Achir that cures them, it's God, but they think it's Sidi Ben Achir.
Q: Can anybody rent a room?
A: Not any more. Now you have to have the authorization of the *Mokkadem* [local officials]. They want to know where you live and be sure that you are really sick. Once a woman rented a room and told them she had a sick person, but it was her lover. Since then they've made renting rooms more difficult.
Q: Are there young people your own age at the shrine?
A: Yes, but they don't come for the shrine, only for the view. A lot of young men from the neighborhood come to the shrine for picnics during the spring and summer. You should see the shrine then: the Hondas, the motors roaring, the boys all dressed up, the girls with short skirts, all made up and suntanned. It's beautiful. It's relaxing . . . the silence inside of the shrine, and life outside . . . it's crawling with young people. You know they have even made a slide in the wall that goes down to the beach. I will show it to you when

1. A dirham is roughly equivalent to $0.20 (U.S. dollars).

> we go. It's faster. You jump off the rampart, go down the slide and you're on the beach. You know some people come to the shrine during the summer for their vacations instead of going to a hotel where you pay ten or fifteen dirhams a day. In the shrine a whole family pays fifteen or twenty dirhams a week or month. It's especially the people who live outside of the city and come from far away, the north, the south, all corners of Morocco. For them the shrine is ideal for vacations. The old people can pray and the young can go to the beach. In the summer I meet people from all over Morocco. It's as if I were in Mecca, but I'm in Salé! You must come and see it. We can go in the summer if you want, it's more pleasant. You don't have to come to pray, you can just come and look. I told you, when I go to the shrine it's not to pray. I never ask for anything. When I want something I'll ask God directly, but not the saint . . . he's a human being like I am.

This excerpt from an interview with a twenty-year-old maid, who works in a luxurious, modern part of Salé and lives in its *bidonville* section, suggests the great variety of experiences which take place in the sanctuary according to individual needs. Although they vary throughout the *Maghreb* (North Africa) from a humble pyramid of stones to a pretentious palace-like building,[2] all sanctuaries have one element in common: the saint's presence is supposed to be hosted there, because it is his tomb, a place he inhabited, or the site of an event in his life. The sanctuary testifies to the saint's welcomed presence in the community, but as an institution in a dynamic developing society it also reflects the society's economic and ideological contradictions.

Sanctuaries as Therapy

For women, the sanctuary offers a dramatic contrast to their subordinate position in a bureaucratic, patriarchal society where decision-making positions are held by men. In the courts and hospitals, women hold a classically powerless position, condemned to be subjects, receptacles of impersonal decisions, executors of orders given by males. In a public hospital, the doctor is the expert, the representative of the bureaucratic order, empowered by the written law to tell her what to do; the illiterate woman can only execute his orders. In the diagnosis process, she expresses her discomfort in awkward colloquial Arabic and realizes, because of the doctor's impatience and irritation, that she cannot provide him with the precise, technical information he needs. Moreover, the hospital is a strange, alien setting, a modern building full of enigmatic written signs on doors and corridors, white-robed, clean,

2. Emile Derminghem, "Les Edifices," in *Le Culte des saints dans l'Islam maghrébin* (Paris: Gallimard, 1954), p. 113.

and arrogant civil servants who speak French for all important communications and only use Arabic to issue elementary orders (come here, go there, take off your dress, etc.).

In comparison to the guardians who stand at the hospital's gates and in its offices, the saint's tomb is directly accessible to troubled persons. Holding the saint's symbolical drape or another object like a stone or a tree, the woman describes what ails her, and it is she who makes the diagnosis, suggests the solution or solutions which might suit her, and explains to the saint the one she prefers. Saints know no French and often no literate Arabic; the language of this supernatural world is colloquial dialects, Berber or Arabic, the only ones women master. The task of the saint is to help her reach her goal. She will give him a gift or a sacrifice only if he realizes her wishes, not before. With a doctor, she has to buy the prescription first and has no way of retaliating if the medicine does not have the proper effect. It is no wonder, then, that in spite of modern health services, women still go to the sanctuaries in swarms, before they go to the hospital, or simultaneously, or after. Saints give women vital help that modern public health services cannot give. They embody the refusal to accept arrogant expertise, to submit blindly to authority, to be treated as subordinate. This insistence on going to saints' tombs exemplifies the North African woman's traditional claim that she is active, can decide her needs for herself and do something about them, a claim that the Muslim patriarchal system denies her. Visits to and involvement with saints and sanctuaries are two of the rare options left to women to *be,* to shape their world and their lives. And this attempt at self-determination takes the form of an exclusively female collective endeavor.

In the sanctuaries, there are always more women than men. They speak and shout with loud voices as if they are the secure owners of the premises. Men, although allowed in, often have to shorten their *Ziara* (visit) because they are overwhelmed by the inquisitive and curious looks of ubiquitous female visitors. Women gather around each other at the saint's supposed tomb and feel directly in contact with a sacred source of power that reflects their own energies. Distressed and suffering, these women have a very important bond: the will to find a solution, to find a happier balance between themselves and their surroundings, their fate, the system that thwarts them. They know they are *wronged* (*Madluma*) by the system. Their desire to find an answer to their urgent needs is a desire to regain their rights. That other women are in exactly the same situation creates a therapeutic network of communication among them.

When a woman enters the sanctuary, she goes directly to the tomb, walking over the stretched feet of sitting women, the stretched bodies of sleeping women. If women have already cried and screamed, they often lie in a fetal position with their heads on the floor. The newly arrived woman will put her hand on the tomb, or on the drape over it, and will explain her problem either in a loud voice or silently. She might go into great detail about her son who failed his examination or was driven away from her by his bride. When describing an intimate fight with her husband, the woman will mimic what happened, name the actors, explain their gestures and attitudes. After she has expressed her needs, she will come to sit among the other women. Eventually, they will gather around her, ask her more details, and offer her the only expertise these women have: experience in suffering. Outraged by her situation and encouraged by this female community, the woman may fall on the floor and scream, twisting her body violently. Some women will rush to her, hold her, hug her, soothe her by talking to her about their own cases and problems. They will massage her forehead, cool her off with a drink of water, and replace on her head her displaced headgear or scarf. She recovers quickly, regains her composure, and leaves the scene to the next newcomer. Undeniably therapeutic, the sanctuary stimulates the energies of women against their discontent and allows them to bathe in an intrinsically female community of soothers, supporters, and advisors.

Sanctuaries as Antiestablishment Arenas

It is primarily as an informal women's association that the sanctuary must be viewed. It is not a religious space, a mistake which is often made. Most saint's sanctuaries are not mosques. With very few exceptions, they are not places where official orthodox Muslim prayer takes place. As Derminghem remarks, "En principe, la cubba n'est pas une mosquée, Mesjid, où l'on fait le soujoùd, la prosternation de la prière rituelle, çala, encore moins, la Jam', la mosquée cathédrale où se fait l'office du vendredi. On peut faire la dou'a, prière de demande et d'invocation facultative, mais non la sala, prière sacrementale devant un tombeau."[3] The institution of saints that is enacted in the sanctuary has an evident antiorthodox, antiestablishment component which has been the object of a prolific literature. But studies of the woman-saint relation have placed excessive emphasis on its magical aspect. Western scholars who investigated the institution were fascinated by the "paralogical" component of the "Moroccan personality structure" and the importance of magical thinking patterns in the still heavily agrarian Moroccan economy and paid little attention to what I would call the phenomenological aspect, namely, what the practitioners themselves derive from their involvement with the saint and the sanctuary.

Such practices have also been interpreted as evidence of the mystical

3. Ibid. "In principal, the *cubba* is not a mosque (*Mesjid*) where one does *soujoùd,* the prostration of ritual prayer (*çala*), even less so, the *Jam',* the cathedral mosque where Friday service is held. One can do the *dou'a,* prayer of supplication and optional invocation, but not the *sala,* sacramental prayer before a grave."

thinking of primitives as opposed to the secularity of the modern mind. As Mary Douglas points out,

> Secularization is often treated as a modern trend attributable to the growth of cities or to the prestige of science, or just to the breakdown of social forms. But we shall see that it is an age-old cosmological type, a product of a definable social experience, which need have nothing to do with urban life or modern science. Here it would seem that anthropology has failed to hold up the right reflecting mirror to contemporary man. The contrast of secular with religious has nothing whatever to do with the contrast of modern with traditional or primitive. The idea that primitive man is by nature deeply religious is nonsense. . . . The illusion that all primitives are pious, credulous and subject to the teaching of priests or magicians has probably done even more to impede our understanding of our civilization.[4]

Women, in particular, who are always the ones to be kept illiterate (and 97 percent of rural Moroccan women still are),[5] are described as simple-minded, superstitious creatures, incapable of sophisticated thinking, who indulge in esoteric mysticism. This view of women has gained even greater support with the advent of the development and nascent industrialization in Third World economies. If women in industrialized societies are granted some capacity for rational thinking, women in Third World societies are still described as enthralled in magical thinking, despite the fact that their societies are leaping into a modernity enraptured with rationality, technology, and environmental mastery.

Sainthood as an Alternative to Male-defined Femininity

Far from magical, a visit to a saint's tomb, an ongoing relation with a supernatural creature, can be a genuine attempt to mediate one's place in the material world. Interaction with the saint can represent an effort to experience reality fully: "Le sacré c'est le réel par excellence, à la fois puissance, efficience, source de vie et de fécondité. Le désir de l'homme religieux de vivre dans le sacré équivaut en fait à son désir de se situer dans la réalité objective, de ne pas se laisser paralyser par la réalité sans

4. Mary Douglas, *Natural Symbols: Exploration in Cosmology* (New York: Random House, Vintage Books, 1973), p. 36.

5. *Recensement général de la population et de l'habitat, 1971* (Rabat: Direction de la statistique, Ministère de Planification, 1971), 3:5. The illiteracy rate is evaluated to be 75 percent for rural women between the ages of ten and twenty-four and between 93 percent and 97 percent for older women.

fin des expériences purement subjectives, de vivre dans un monde réel et efficient, et non pas dans une illusion."[6]

At bottom, women in an unflinchingly patriarchal society seek through the saint's mediation a bigger share of power, of control. One area in which they seek almost total control is reproduction and sexuality, the central notions of any patriarchal system's definition of women, classical orthodox Islam included.[7] Women who are desperate to find husbands, women whose husbands have sexual problems, women who have lost their husband's love or their own reproductive capacities go to the saint to get help and find solutions. One of the important functions of sanctuaries is precisely their involvement with sexuality and fertility. Indeed, if power can be defined as "the chance of a person or a number of persons to realize their own will in a communal action, even against the resistance of others, who are participating in the action,"[8] then women's collaboration with saints is definitely a power operation. Excluded from ritualistic orthodox religion, women walking in processions around saints' tombs express their quest for power in the vast horizons of the sacred space, untouched, unspoiled by human authority and its hierarchies:

> Des jeunes filles pâles jettent dans la source des fleurs rouges, d'autres du sucre, des rayons de miel, pourque leur parole devienne douce, spirituelle, persuasive. Les femmes qui y lancent du musc rêvent de se faire aimer . . . nul ne s'y rend sans henné, sans benjoin. En brûlant son cierge vert ou rose, la vierge dit, "Maître de la source, allumes-moi mon cierge" ce qui veut dire "mariez-moi," ou encore "donnez-moi une santé brillante." La puissance à laquelle on s'adresses est capable de donner tous les biens de ce monde: vie, force, fortune, amour, enfants.[9]

Now this quest for power that underlies the woman-saint relation is

6. Mircea Eliade, *Le Sacré et le profane* (Paris: Gallimard, 1965), p. 27. "The sacred is the real *par excellence,* at one and the same time power, efficiency, source of life and fertility. The religious desire to live within the sacred is in fact equivalent to the desire to be in objective reality, not to be paralyzed by endless and purely subjective experience, but to live in a world which is real and efficient, and not illusory."

7. Fatima Mernissi, *Beyond the Veil* (Cambridge, Mass.: Schenkman Publishing Co., 1975), esp. the chapter entitled, "The Traditional Muslim View of Women and Their Place in the Social Order."

8. Max Weber, *From Max Weber, Essays in Sociology,* trans. and ed. with an introduction by H. Gerth and C. Wright Mills (New York: Oxford University Press, 1958), p. 180.

9. Desparmet, "Le Mal magique," in Derminghem, p. 44. "Pale young girls throw red flowers into the spring, others sugar or honeycombs, so that their voice may become sweet, spiritual, persuasive. The women who throw musk dream of being loved. . . . None goes to the spring without henna, without benjamin. While burning her green or red candle, the virgin says, 'Master of the spring, light my candle' which means 'marry me,' or else 'give me splendid health.' The power to which they speak is capable of granting them all the goods of the world: life, strength, fortune, love, children."

further confirmed by the fact that there are women saints who occupy a preeminent place and who specialize in solving problems of sexuality and reproduction.[10] They assume what Freud would certainly have called a phallic role and function. Some female saints go beyond the stage of penis envy and reverse traditional patriarchal relations: they are the ones who give penises to men suffering from sexual disturbances; such is the case of the Algerian female saint, Lalla Nfissa.[11] But this is not their only function. Unlike the emphasized passivity of women in the material, real world, supernatural women lead intensively active lives, perform all kinds of acts, from benign motherly protection to straightforward aggression, such as rape of men.[12] These women in the supernatural realm do not respect the traditional Muslim sexual division of labor which excludes women from power in religion and politics. In the supernatural realm, women may refuse to assume domestic roles and play active roles in both religion and politics.

In one of the most respected saint's biographies, the thirteenth-century *At-Tasawwuf Ila Rijal At-Tasawwuf,*[13] the biographer, Abu Yaqub At Tadili, makes no specific reference to the fact that some saints were women: they enjoy exactly the same rights and privileges and assume the same characteristics as male saints. At one point, a woman saint, Munia Bent Maymoun Ad-Dukali, says, "This year, hundreds of women saints visited this sanctuary." At another, a male insists that, "In Al Masamida [a region], there were twenty-seven saints who have the power to fly in the air, among whom fourteen are women."[14]

Female saints seem to fall into two categories, those who are saints because they were the sisters, wives, or daughters of a saint[15] and those who were saints in their own right.[16] Many of these saints have strikingly "unfeminine" personalities and interests. Imma Tiffelent, for example, literally fled her domestic condition: "Ne voulant pas se marier, Imma Tiffelent s'échappa sous forme de colombe et se fit prostituée dans la montagne. . . . Vingt-sept jeunes gens disparurent après l'avoir aimée.

10. Léon L'Africain, *Description de l'Afrique,* trans. from Italian by A. Epaulard Adrien (Paris: Maison Neuve, 1956), p. 216; and E. Doutté, *Magie et religion dans l'Afrique du Nord* (Alger: Typographia Adolphe Jourdan, 1908), chap. 1, p. 31.

11. Derminghem, p. 43.

12. Vincent Crapanzano, "The Transformation of the Eumenides: A Moroccan Example" (unpublished manuscript, Princeton University, 1974), and "Saints, Jinns and Dreams: An Essay on Moroccan Ethnopsychology" (unpublished manuscript, Princeton University, Department of Anthropology).

13. Abu Yaqub Yusuf Ibn Yahya At-Tadili, *At-Tasawwuf Ila Rijal At-Tasawwuf; vie de saints du sud Morocain des V, VI, VIIIème siècles de l'Hégire. Contribution à l'étude de l'histoire religieuse du Maroc,* ed. A. Faure (Rabat: Editions Techniques Nord Africaines, 1958). I will refer to this work as *Tasawaf* and cite the number of each saint's biography.

14. *Tasawaf,* no. 160, p. 312; no. 209, p. 397.

15. See *Tasawaf,* no. 240, p. 431; no. 7, p. 70; no. 25, p. 111; and Derminghem, Lalla Mimouna, p. 68; Lalla Aicha, p. 125, Mana Aicha, p. 107.

16. See *Tasawaf,* no. 160, p. 312; no. 209, p. 397; no. 207, p. 394; no. 210, p. 398; no. 167, p. 331.

Puis elle devint ascète, dans une hutte, au sommet de la montagne . . . déguenillée, hiruste, elle prêche la religion dans la vallée, revint à sa hutte, quitte même ses haillons, vit nue, prophétise. Il est interdit de toucher aux arbres autour de sa tombe, de tuer les oiseaux, de dénicher les oeufs de perdrix."[17] The same identical flight from patriarchal "womanhood" can be seen in Sida Zohra El Kouch, "qui fut aussi savante que belle, resista à Moulay Zidane, mourut vierge, et n'est visitée que par les femmes."[18] No less important, a prolific body of literature shows a number of female saints played important roles in the political arena.[19] One of the most famous is certainly the Berber saint Lalla Tagurrami, who played a strategic role in her region's history as a referee in conflicts between tribes and between tribes and the central authority.[20] Politically, she was so influential and successful that the king imprisoned her:

> Comme elle était parmi les plus belles jeunes filles du village, elle fut recherchée pour le mariage, mais refusa tous les prétendants. La réputation de sainte de la jeune fille en grandit et s'étendit au loin. Le sultan voulut connaître Lalla Aziza et la fit demander à Marrakech. Elle s'y rendit et continua dans la ville à se faire remarquer par sa piété et par le bien qu'elle faisait autour d'elle. Elle fut très honorée, mais son influence devint tellement grande que le sultan en prit ombrage et Lalla Aziza fut jetée en prison. Elle mourut empoisonnée.[21]

It is of course possible that her fate was devised by myth tellers to discourage other women from taking such paths.

Male Saints as Antiheroes

Male saints, on the other hand, were profoundly concerned with what we would call a housework issue: how to eat without exploiting

17. Trumelet, "Blida," and "Saints de l'Islam," as quoted in Derminghem, p. 53: "Not wanting to marry, Imma Tiffelant took the shape of a dove, escaped, and became a prostitute. . . .Twenty-seven young men disappeared after having loved her. Then she became an ascetic, in a hut, at the top of the mountain. . . . Ragged, unkempt, she preached religion in the valley, returned to her hut, shed even her rags, lived nude, and prophesied. It is forbidden to touch the trees around her grave, to kill the birds, to take the partridge eggs from the nest."

18. Derminghem, p. 49.

19. Jacques Berque, *Structures sociales du Haut Atlas* (Paris: Presses Universitaires de France, 1955), p. 296.

20. Ibid., pp. 281, 286.

21. Ibid., p. 290. "As she was among the most beautiful girls of the village, she was sought after for marriage, but refused all suitors. . . . Her reputation as a saint grew and extended far. The sultan wanted to meet Lalla Aziza and asked her to come to Marrakesh. Once there, she continued to distinguish herself by her piety and the good she did. She was very honored, but her influence became so great that the sultan took offense and had Lalla Aziza thrown into prison. She was poisoned and died."

somebody else's work. Most analyses of the saint's lives fail to emphasize their constant preoccupation with food and its preparation; that they walk on water, fly in the skies, are given more weight than their efforts not to exploit the traditional domestic labor force available—women. Around this question clustered all other issues, such as the repudiation of possessions, privileges, political power, and the condemnation of wars and violence, the very characteristics of a phallocratic system. Most saints fled urban centers and their sophisticated exploitative lives, tried hunting, fishing, gathering, and cooking for themselves.[22] Some fasted as often as they could[23] and trained themselves to eat very little; one went as far as to feed himself on one mouthful.[24] Still others had supernatural help which ground their own wheat or simply which gave them food.[25] They all tried to do without housework and to avoid food cooked by others,[26] and they also tried, to the community's dismay, to perform daily domestic chores themselves, such as taking the bread to the neighborhood oven.[27] One of the most famous of saints, Bou Yazza, went so far as to assume the appearance of a female domestic and to serve a woman for months.[28]

Some saints have families and children, some abstain and live in celibacy. But those who marry are unsuccessful fathers and husbands and live like embarrassed heads of families who can't provide properly for their dependents.[29] Others, especially elderly saints, did not hesitate to renounce their marital rights when these appeared to be totally opposed to the woman's happiness.[30] They definitely did not play the patriarcha role well. Among those who did not marry, one saint explained he was afraid to be unjust to his wife;[31] for him, apparently, marriage was an unjust institution to women. Another said he saw a beautiful woman walking down the street and thought he was in paradise; she was exactly like a *houri,* females provided to good Muslim believers in paradise.[32] Although he secluded himself because he was afraid females would turn him away from God,[33] he did not identify them with the devil, as classical Muslim ideology does, but with paradise, the most positive aspect of Muslim cosmogony.[34] Another saint fainted when he found himself

22. *Tasawaf,* no. 73, p. 186; no. 67, p. 170; no. 13, p. 88; no. 87, p. 217; no. 12, p. 86; no. 59, p. 162.
23. *Tasawaf,* no. 68, p. 76; no. 96, p. 228; no. 33, p. 124.
24. *Tasawaf,* no. 25, p. 111.
25. *Tasawaf,* no. 93, p. 223; no. 63, p. 171; no. 54, p. 156.
26. *Tasawaf,* no. 62, p. 166; no. 132, p. 184.
27. *Tasawaf,* no. 93, p. 224; no. 77, p. 197; no. 162, p. 321.
28. *Tasawaf,* no. 77, p. 200.
29. *Tasawaf,* no. 92, p. 222; no. 51, p. 152; no. 48, p. 144; no. 34, pp. 125–26.
30. *Tasawaf,* no. 99, p. 233; no. 56, p. 158.
31. *Tasawaf,* no. 45, p. 141.
32. *Koran,* Sourate 44, verses 53–54.
33. *Tasawaf,* no. 84, p. 214.
34. Abu Hasan Muslim, *Al-Jami' As-Sahih* (Beirut: Al Maktaba at Tijaria, n.d.), 8:130.

alone with a woman in a room,[35] an unmasculine gesture to say the very least. Indeed, all these fears are not those of a self-confident, patriarchal male.

Like the women who come to visit their sanctuaries, a large number of saints were of humble origin and were involved in manual or physical activities as shepherds, butchers, or doughnut makers.[36] Others had no jobs and lived off nature, eating wild fruits, roots, or fish. Some saints were learned men, even judges, who refused to use their knowledge to obtain influential positions and accumulate wealth, or even to teach,[37] and encouraged illiterates to be proud of their illiteracy. Like the women in the sanctuaries, however, many of them were illiterates. They reminded their communities, which respected them, of their illiteracy,[38] perhaps in order to demystify knowledge as a prerequisite for decision-making positions. Moulay Bou Azza made a point of not speaking literate or even colloquial Arabic.[39] Moulay Ábdallah Ou Said, for example, tried to practice a teaching method for the masses "without the intervention of written texts."[40] Although it shocked the learned mandarins, the illiterate female saint Lalla Mimouna constantly insisted she did not use the customary complicated Koranic verses in her prayers because she did not know them. "Mimouna knows God and God knows Mimouna"[41] was the prayer she invented. This resistance to hierarchical knowledge is a persistent characteristic of saints' lives and their battles, which finds sympathy with the oppressed of the new developing economies: the illiterates, who are predominantly women. It is, therefore, no wonder that in the disintegrating agrarian economies of the Maghreb, sanctuaries, among all institutions, are almost the only ones women go to spontaneously and feel at home in. The sanctuary offers a world where illiteracy does not prevent a human being from being a wholesome, thinking, and reasonable person.

* * *

The psychic and emotional value of women's experience in sanctuaries is uncontested and evident. Sanctuaries, which are the locus of antiestablishment, antipatriarchal mythical figures, provide women with a space where complaint and verbal vituperations against the system's injustices are allowed and encouraged. They give women the opportunity to develop critical views of their condition, to identify problems, and to try to find their solution. At the same time, women invest all of their

35. *Tasawaf,* no. 94, p. 224.

36. *Tasawaf,* no. 10, p. 79; no. 26, p. 115; no. 96, p. 228.

37. *Tasawaf,* no. 17, p. 95; no. 69, p. 178; no. 6, p. 69.

38. *Tasawaf,* no. 93, p. 223; no. 77, p. 197.

39. V. Loulignac, *Un Saint Berbère—Moulay Bou Azza; Histoire et légende* (Rabat: Hesperis, 1946), 31:29.

40. Jean Chaumel, *Histoire d'une tribu maraboutique de l'Anti-Atlas, le Aît Abdallah ou Said,* vol. 39, 1er et 2ème trimestre (Rabat: Hesperes, 1952), p. 206.

41. Derminghem, p. 69.

efforts and energies in trying to get a supernatural force to influence the oppressive structure on their behalf. This does not affect the formal power structure, the outside world. It has a collective therapeutic effect on the individual women visitors, but it does not enable them to carry their solidarity outside, to affect the system and shape it to suit their own needs. For these needs spring from their structural economic reliance on males and on the services they must give them in exchange: sex and reproduction. The saint in the sanctuary plays the role of the psychiatrist in the capitalist society, channeling discontent into the therapeutic processes and thus depriving it of its potential to combat the formal power structure. Saints, then, help women adjust to the oppression of the system. The waves of resentment die at the sanctuary's threshold. Nothing leaves with the woman except her belief that her contact with the saint triggered mechanisms which are going to affect the world, change it, and make it suit her conditions better. In this sense, sanctuaries are "happenings" where women's collective energies and combative forces are invested in alienating institutions which strive to absorb them, lower their explosive effect, neutralize them. Paradoxically, the arena where popular demonstrations against oppression, injustice, and inequality are most alive become, in developing economies, the best ally of unresponsive national bureaucracies. Encouragement of traditional saints' rituals by administrative authorities who oppose any trade unionist or political movement is a well-known tactic in Third World politics.

Department of Sociology
Mohammed V University
Rabat, Morocco

Women and Symbolic Systems

Women and the Hindu Tradition

Susan S. Wadley

Hindu Ideology and Women

The concept of the female in Hindu ideology presents an essential duality:[1] on the one hand, she is fertile, benevolent—the bestower; on the other, she is aggressive, malevolent—the destroyer. As a popular statement about the goddess suggests, "in times of prosperity she indeed is Lakṣmī, who bestows prosperity in the homes of men; and in times of misfortune, she herself becomes the goddess of misfortune, and brings about ruin."[2] In a similar vein, the name of the South Indian goddess Māriyammaṉ is made up of *māri,* death or rain or, according to folk

Because of space limitations, the Wellesley editorial committee could not print a longer version of this paper and abridged it.

1. Hinduism, as opposed to Christianity, Judaism, and Islam, lacks a single authoritative text; rather, it has thousands, produced over a 3,000-year period. In addition, within the geographic space of South Asia Hinduism assumes varied forms and often appears more diversified than unified. Thus any particular practice or belief may be contradicted elsewhere or denied by some Hindu. Clearly, not even the textually based and varied "great traditions" of Hinduism can be fully explored in a brief paper, and the "little traditions," or local practices that are not based on written texts, provide endless problems of interpretation and questions as to belief and practice.

2. Jagadisvarananda, *The Devī-māhātmyan or Shri Durgā Saptashatī* (Maylapore: Sri Ramakrishna Math, 1953), chap. 12, line 40, as quoted in Lawrence A. Babb, "Marriage and Malevolence: The Uses of Sexual Opposition in a Hindu Pantheon," *Ethnology* 9 (1970): 140.

etymology, "change," and *amman* "lady" or "mother;"[3] the goddess is the "changing lady," both death and life, destroyer and bestower.[4]

Two facets of femaleness reflect this duality and perhaps provide the cultural logic for it. The female is first of all *śakti,* Energy/Power, the energizing principle of the Universe; she is also *prakṛti,* Nature, the undifferentiated Matter of the Universe. In Hindu cosmology all beings emerge from *brahman,* the universal substratum which is "invisible inactive, beyond grasp, without qualifications, inconceivable indescribable,"[5] through the creative tension of cohesion (Viṣṇu) and disintegration (Śiva) that defines *śakti. Śakti* underlies both creation and divinity and is female. Although there would be no power or energy in the universe without the female, all beings have their share of *śakti,* a share with which they are endowed at birth but which they increase or decrease through later actions.[6] Nonetheless, the woman embodies *śakti,* the original Energy of the Universe.

Woman is also *prakṛti,* Nature, the active female counterpart of the Cosmic Person, *puruṣa,* the inactive or male aspect. But whereas *prakṛti* represents the undifferentiated matter of Nature, *puruṣa* provides the Spirit, which is a structured code. Thus *puruṣa* (Cosmic Person) is code (differentiated Spirit), as opposed to *prakṛti,* which is Nature (undifferentiated Matter). The union of Spirit and Matter, code and noncode inactive and active, leads to the creation of the world with all of its differentiated life forms; no life exists without both Matter and Spirit *prakṛti* and *puruṣa* (see fig. 1).

The unity of *puruṣa-prakṛti* underlies the notion of biological conception. The male contributes the hard substances—bones, nerves, and the structuring elements; the woman contributes the soft—flesh, skin blood, and the unstructured elements.[7] Put another way, woman is the

3. Brenda E. F. Beck, "Māryammaṉ: The Vacillating Goddess," mimeographed (Vancouver: University of British Columbia, 1971), p. 2.

4. Early Vedic literature (pre-600 B.C., brought by the Aryan migrators from the north) emphasizes the prosperity and benevolence of female figures. Later developments in Hindu literature introduce the dangerous image of females. This probably reflects an incorporation of Dravidian beliefs into the Aryan religious complex. The earliest available Dravidian literature (specifically, Tamil literature) refers frequently to dangerous female power, a theme not found until later in the Sanskrit literature of the Aryans (see George L. Hart III, "Women and the Sacred in Ancient Tamilnad," *Journal of Asian Studies* 32 [February 1973]: 233–50). The modern Hindu, however, does not know about these historical developments but only the dual image of femaleness as simultaneously bad and dangerous, good and fertile.

5. Māṇḍūkya Upanisad 1.7, quoted in Alain Danielou, *Hindu Polytheism* (New York Pantheon Books, 1964), p. 21.

6. McKim Marriott and Ronald B. Iden, "An Ethnosociology of South Asian Caste Systems" (paper read at the American Anthropological Association meeting, Toronto 1972).

7. See Ronald B. Inden and Ralph W. Nicholas, "A Cultural Analysis of Bengal Kinship" (paper presented at the Sixth Annual Conference on Bengal Studies, Oakland University, May 1970).

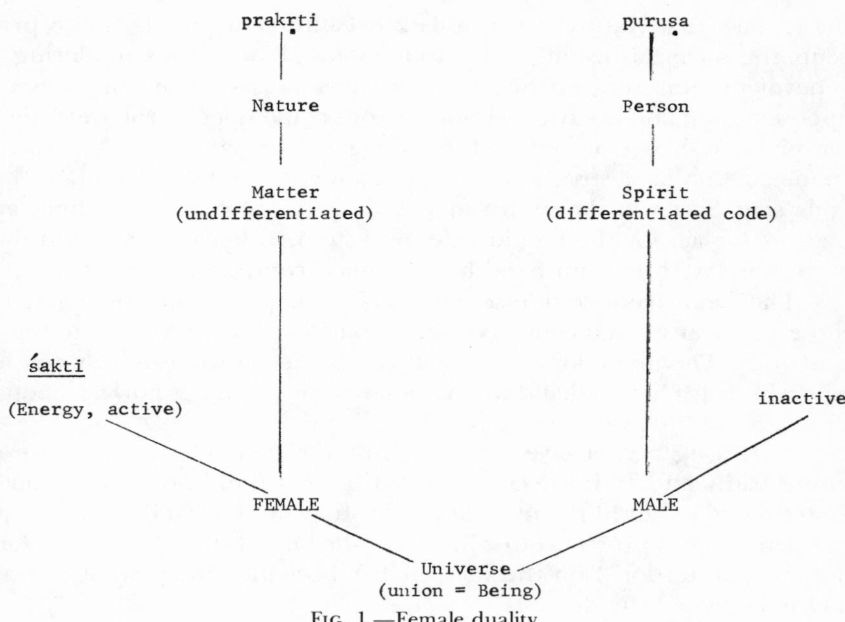

FIG. 1.—Female duality

field or earth into which man puts his seed: "By the sacred tradition the woman is declared to be the soil, the man is declared to be the seeds; the production of all corporeal beings (takes place) through the union of the soil with the seed."[8] And the *Laws of Manu* declare the seed to be the more important: "for the offspring of all created beings is marked by the characteristics of the seed."[9] The seed is the hard substance or structure as opposed to the soil, the soft substance or nonstructure. Women, then, automatically partake more of Nature than men, who symbolize Culture.[10]

Uncultured Power is dangerous, however: Thus the equation "Women = Power + Nature = Danger" represents one essential vision of femaleness in Hinduism. But, woman as the receptor of man's seed is also the benevolent, fertile bestower; like the closely conjoined images of cow and earth, she represents growth and prosperity. The source of this benevolence, as recent studies have suggested,[11] is that the male controls

8. G. Buhler, trans., *The Laws of Manu,* Sacred Books of the East, vol. 25 (Delhi: Motilal Banarsidass, 1964), 9. 33; p. 333. (i.e., chap. 9, verse 33, p. 333 of Buhler). *The Laws of Manu* were supposedly written by the first man, Manu. While not personally known to most Hindus, they do provide a corpus of belief, which is still prevalent.

9. Ibid., 35; p. 333.

10. Much of this argument is influenced by Sherry B. Ortner, "Is Female to Male as Nature Is to Culture?" in *Woman, Culture and Society,* ed. Michelle Zimbalist Rosaldo and Louise Lamphere (Stanford, Calif.: Stanford University Press, 1974).

11. See Babb and Beck.

the female; that Nature is controlled by Culture. A popular myth presents the male harnessing dangerous female Power, thus rendering it benevolent. Kālī, one of Śiva's many wives, was sent by the gods to oppose a giant and his army whom the gods could not control. Defeating the giant, Kālī performed such a savage killing dance that the earth trembled, and its destruction seemed imminent. Unable to stop her, the gods sent Śiva who lay down at her feet. About to step on him, an inexcusable act for the Hindu wife, Kālī stopped her rampage and the earth was saved. Her husband had regained control over her.[12]

The benevolent goddesses in the Hindu pantheon are precisely those who transferred control of their sexuality (Power/Nature) to their husbands. The mythology is replete with stories of the properly chaste wife who helps her husband win battles by giving him her power; among these are the following two myths:[13]

1. During a twelve-year war against the demons, the gods were losing badly and Indra decided to sacrifice his life. "Don't be afraid," Indrani said to her husband, "I am a faithful wife. I will tell you one way you can win and protect yourself." After she bound the *rakhī* (a bracelet, literally "protection") on the wrist of her husband, Indra went to war and defeated all the demons.

2. A demon named Jalandhar had a very beautiful and faithful wife named Branda. Because of the power of this faithfulness, the demon conquered the whole world. The god Viṣṇu changed a dead body into the shape of Jalandhar, gave it life, and thus deceived Branda into losing her faithfulness.

If control of her sexuality is transferred to men, the female is fertile and benevolent:

> Lakṣmī: The Goddess of Fortune, "She who springs forth from the body of all the gods has a thousand, indeed countless, arms. Her face is white, made from the light streaming from the lord of sleep (Śiva). Her arms, made of the substance of Viṣṇu, are deep blue: her round breasts made of *soma,* the sacrificial ambrosia, are white. . . . she wears a gaily colored lower garment, brilliant garlands, and a veil. . . . He who worships the Transcendent Divinity of Fortune becomes the lord of all the worlds."[14]

12. There are destructive and malevolent male deities in Hinduism, but they differ from female deities. Male deities and demons seem more logical in the trouble they cause and, unlike Kālī, are not carried away with the idea of killing. Guy Welbon and I suspect there exists a distinction of plotted (male) versus plotless (female) action. The logic (and Culture?) of the male dominates his actions; the nonlogic (and Nature?) of the female dominates hers.

13. These myths are excerpted from Susan S. Wadley, *Shakti: Power in the Conceptual Structure of Karimpur Religion,* University of Chicago Studies in Anthropology, Series in Social, Cultural and Linguistic Anthropology, no. 2 (Chicago: University of Chicago Department of Anthropology, 1975), pp. 131, 135.

14. Karapātrī, "Śri Bhagvati tattva" as quoted in Danielou, p. 262.

On the other hand, if a female controls her own sexuality she is potentially destructive and malevolent:

> Kālī: The Black One. "Bearing the strange skull topped staff, decorated with a garland of skulls, clad in a tiger's skin, she is appalling because of her emaciated flesh, gaping mouth, lolling tongue, deep-sunk reddish eyes. She fills the regions of the sky with roars. . . ."[15]

Hindu Role Models for Women

The dual character of the Hindu female, her *śakti* and *prakṛti,* allows us to understand the rules and role models for women in Hindu South Asia. These are laid down in Hindu lawbooks, collectively known as the *dharma-śāstras* (the Rules of Right Conduct). Written and oral mythology, in Sanskrit and in vernaculars, provides many examples of female behavior and its consequences and thus establishes explicit role models. Folklore yields yet other beliefs about female behavior which mesh with and reinforce social organization and structure.[16] In classical texts or folk traditions the dual character of the Hindu female reappears in the roles of wife (good, benevolent, dutiful, controlled) and mother (fertile, but dangerous, uncontrolled).

Classical Hindu laws focus almost exlusively on women as wives. Role models and norms for mothers, daughters, sisters, are more apt to appear in folklore and vernacular traditions. Furthermore, most written traditions emphasize women's behavior in relationship to men: wife/husband; mother/son; daughter/father; sister/brother. Role models for female behavior concerning other females (mother/daughter; sister/sister; mother-in-law/daughter-in-law; husband's sister/wife) are common themes in folklore and oral traditions but not in the more authoritative religious literature. The latter two relationships, which are of little concern to men in an essentially *purdah* society, do not represent important themes in the male-oriented and written literature of the Sanskrit tradition, but they surface in the popular oral traditions of women themselves.

The basic rules for women's behavior, as expressed in the *Laws of Manu,* ca. A.D. 200, stress the need to control women because of their evil character. "Because of their passion for men, their mutable temper, and their natural heartlessness, they become disloyal towards their husbands, however carefully they are guarded in this [world]. Knowing their disposition, which the Lord of creatures instilled in them at the creation,

15. Jagadisvarananda, chap. 7, lines 7–9 in Babb, p. 140.

16. See, for example, Susan S. Wadley, "Brothers, Husbands, and Sometimes Sons: Kinsmen in North Indian Ritual," *Eastern Anthropologist* 29, no. 2 (Spring 1976): 149–70.

[every] man should most strenuously exert himself to guard them."[17] Submission to male control is the dominant duty of women:

> Nothing must be done independently, even in her own house by a young girl, by a young woman, or even by an aged one.
>
> In childhood a female must be subject to her father, in youth to her husband, and when her lord is dead to her sons; a woman must never be independent. . . .
>
> Though destitute of virtue, . . . or good qualities, a husband must be constantly worshiped as a god by a faithful wife. . . .
>
> If she violates her duty towards her husband, a wife is disgraced in this world; (after death) she enters the womb of a jackal, and is tormented by diseases (as punishment) of her sin.
>
> She who controls her thoughts, words, and deeds, and never slights her lord, resides with her husband (in heaven after death), and is called a virtuous (wife).[18]

Later Sanskrit texts, vernacular writings, and oral traditions also define the ideal woman as the one who does not strive to break the bonds of control. The happiness or salvation of woman is a function of her faithful devotion to her husband. In the *Rāmāyana,* one of the most popular religious texts of India found in Sanskrit and most vernaculars, Sītā exemplifies the behavior of the proper Hindu wife, devotedly following her husband into exile for twelve years. Kidnapped by the evil Ravana, she proves her wifely virtue by placing herself on a lighted pyre. When she remains unscathed by the flames the gods shower her with flowers, and her husband finally and happily accepts her back into his household. This story is not only enacted yearly in villages and cities all over India; pictures of Sītā following her husband to the forest, kidnapped by Ravana, or on the pyre can be found in many homes, shops, and even government offices; famous cinema stars portray the tale in gargantuan film epics. For Sītā, symbol of the devoted wife, represents the ideal toward which all women should strive. Likewise, women who have committed *satī* (burning themselves) on their husbands' funeral pyres are acclaimed as goddesses and honored with shrines and rituals. Indeed, throughout North India women worship Savitrī, a goddess so devoted to her husband that she saves him from the god of death. She reveals the exemplary lengths to which a wife should go in aiding her husband.

Oral traditions essentially inculcate these norms, with one addition: the wife's desire for her husband and dismay at his absence. A minor theme in classical written literature, where devotion and dutifulness are

17. Buhler, 9. 2–16; pp. 327–30.
18. Ibid., 5. 147–65; pp. 195–97.

emphasized,[19] the longing for a husband's return and the mutual love between man and wife dominate the traditions created and perpetuated by women alone:

> One seed of wheat I will eat for one year,
> eat for one year,
> [But] I will not allow my husband to go.
> I will keep him before my eyes, [and] I
> will not allow my husband to go.[20]

Even in these female traditions, however, the husband's regard for and duties to his wife are only rarely discussed. And in the textual traditions passages stipulating that men should treat their women well are rare. "Women must be honoured by their fathers, brothers, husbands, and brothers-in-law who desire (their own welfare). . . . The houses on which female relations, not being duly honoured, pronounce a curse, perish completely, as if destroyed by magic. Hence, men who seek (their own) welfare should always honour women on holidays and festivals with (gifts of) ornaments, clothes, and (dainty) food."[21] Ideally then, women can use their power to destroy if they are ill-treated. But, the best wife (Sītā) will still worship her husband even when she is abused.

The wifely role is preeminent in Hinduism, the maternal only secondary. Thus, whereas mythology and law books provide endless models of the good wife, there are no prime examples of the good mother. And yet goddesses as mothers, rather than wives, are the village guardians, worshiped regularly for protection or aid, and feared. Moreover, a goddess is never called "Wife,"[22] a role of subordination, devotion, and dutifulness, but she is often called "Mother," the one who gives and loves but who must be obeyed, and sometimes rejects.[23] It is the mother, then, who is transformed into the mother goddess who is both the bestower and destroyer. As such, she does not represent proper or ideal behavior; rather, her danger is accepted because she is necessary. Indeed, the mother, more than the wife, represents impurity during childbirth and

19. There is one notable example of male/female love in the written traditions, the pairing of Radha and Krishna. In many parts of India, this pair is not believed to be married, and Radha is rarely recognized as an ideal woman.

20. S. L. Srivastava, *Folk Culture and Oral Tradition* (New Delhi: Abhinav Publications, 1974), p. 28.

21. Buhler, 3. 55–59; p. 85.

22. In one of the complications of this facet of motherhood, the goddesses who are said to have children are seldom called mother: rather it is the goddesses who do not have children per se (i.e., Durga, Kālī, Santoshi, Sitala) who are known as "Mother."

23. Susan S. Wadley, "Woman, Wife and Mother in the Ramayana" (unpublished paper).

the purifying milk after childbirth, another contradiction.[24] And mothers and the mother goddesses, in direct contrast to wives, are in control of their sexuality.

Over and beyond the duality that the mother represents, Hinduism also portrays women who are wholly malevolent. These figures, the ghosts of women who died in childbirth or witches, are, of course, the antithesis of the wife. If it is true, as Beck has suggested, that such women have lost control of their sexuality and cannot channel their actions to positive ends,[25] then women's roles in Hinduism assume the configuration as shown in figure 2. Although there are other female roles described within Hinduism—the daughter who obeys her father, the sister who is under her brother's protection as the essential link to her natal home, the husband's mother who is threatening, and the husband's sister who is an unreliable female—they are primarily to be found in women's oral traditions which reflect women's concern for their day-to-day welfare. In male-authored literature, however, which prescribes control and subordination of women, the wife even more than the mother dominates Hindu thought.

Women in Hindu Religious Practice

Women are active practitioners but have little religious authority in orthodox, textually sanctioned Hinduism. However, at the popular level they enjoy a prominent role as both specialists and nonspecialists. Of the five broader social classes that embrace thousands of castes in India—the four varna that originated in ancient times (Brahman, priest; Kshatriya, warrior; Vaishya, tradesman; Shudra, worker) and the Untouchable —only male members of the first three varna have access to the sacred texts of the Vedas, the earliest and most authoritative of Hindu

Wife	Mother	Ghost
Culture via Male control	Nature but in self control	Nature but out of control
Good	Good/bad	Bad
Subordinated	Worshipped	Appeased

FIG. 2.—The configuration of women's roles

24. I have not attempted to deal with the close relationship between female biology, pollution/purity, and perceptions of the female in Hinduism. Hindu mythology, however, does explicitly relate the low ritual status of women to (*a*) her monthly periods and (*b*) her ability to bear children. The woman's menses are "polluting," but not as "polluting" as childbirth.

25. See Beck.

scriptures.[26] Further restrictions dictate that only Brahman men can use the Vedas in rituals. Women, Shudras, and Untouchables[27] are not allowed to know, or sometimes even to hear, the Vedas. Women, therefore, have no less access to the sources of religious power than a great many men.

Fortunately, Hindu religious activity is not based solely on Vedic rituals. Today, the dominant form of ritual activity is *bhakti* or devotion to a deity. Stemming from the *Bhagavad Gītā* and gaining strength from an anti-Brahman, anti-Vedic movement starting about A.D. 700, *bhakti* and associated ritual forms such as *pūjā* (devotional ritual) do not require the services of a priest.[28] Women, then, can have direct access to the gods, and thus to salvation.

Nonetheless, men continue to be recognized as the legitimate religious specialists (see table 1).[29] They are the caretakers of temples and

Table 1

Religious Specialization in Hinduism

Specialist	Sex: Male	Sex: Female	Textually Sanctioned
Priest:			
Pandit	x(B)	(Wife)	+(not wife)
Purohit	x(B)	...	+
Pujārī	x	...	...
Actor as God	x(B)	...	?
Shaman	x	x	...
Exorcist	x	...	...
Client in Jajmani system	x	(Wife)	...
Yogi/Sadhu	x	Seldom	+
Personality cult leader	x	x	...
Davadasī	...	x	+(South India only)

NOTE.—(B) indicates must be Brahman; (wife) indicates plays role by virtue of wifehood.

26. Many people cannot name their varna, though Brahmans generally know theirs. Aside from religion, varna had little importance until recently when it regained popularity as a scheme for urban classification and for political purposes.

27. Untouchables, both men and women, are generally the most maligned members of Hindu society. Until recently, Untouchables could not enter many temples. Untouchability is outlawed in the Indian constitution but is still practiced in many parts of India.

28. The early *bhakti* movement was antitemple as well as anti-Brahman.

29. By the term "religious specialist" I mean (*a*) someone who is paid for religious/ritual services, and (*b*) someone who conveys religious instruction, is a guide in ritual practice, or performs rituals for others. People who provide essential ritual services (such as the flower grower or washerman) but not religious instruction or guidelines are not considered "religious specialists."

the ones to conduct life-cycle rites for families. In North India most priests must be Brahman males; for example, the *pandit* is the main temple priest and the *purohit* is the family priest who serves his patrons either daily or for major life-cycle rites.[30] The wives of Brahman priests can act as specialists for life-cycle rites or on other ritual occasions. Although they are often experts in oral tradition, and know the songs or stories associated with a particular rite or the unwritten rules for correct female ritual behavior, their role, unlike their husbands', has no scriptural sanction. Indeed, Brahman men dominate still other forms of public ritual. In the various religious folk operas and plays of India, the actors are usually male whether or not the deity they portray is male or female. The actor *is* in fact the deity and must be worshiped as a manifestation of the deity.

Less legitimate participants in public rituals are more likely to be non-Brahman males. In possession rituals, which are not textually sanctioned, exorcists and shamans, whose power comes from oral traditions and societal recognition, are non-Brahman and can even be female.[31] Moreover, the *jajmāni* system of inherited patron-client ties, which exists throughout most of South Asia, gives several of the clients ritual connections with their patrons. Thus the barber and his wife, who are necessary figures in most life-cycle rites—they cut hair, bathe the new infant or the groom—instruct and guide their patrons through the proper ritual forms. The midwife is another such ritual guide. None of these "specialists" has textual sanction; the instruction they provide is usually based on local traditions. Popular, nonclassical religious specialists in Hinduism can be either male of female; thus the "personality cult" leaders such as Guru Maharajji or The Mother. Female leaders of these movements occur regularly if less often than men and are sanctioned by society if not by textual tradition. Other such specialists are the sadhus and yogis. Some are only a presence in Hindu religious practice; others important lecturers and teachers. Occasionally, a woman will be a yogini. Although both male and female yogis are sanctioned by various textual traditions, they are removed from family ties and considered outside of the caste system and outside of society and its structure. All members of society can thus choose to be nonmembers.

Only one religious specialist, to my knowledge, was always female

30. *Pandit* is the astrologer who provides essential information and advice for marriages and births and who fixes auspicious dates for journeys and other undertakings. But *pandit* is also an honorific used for any Brahman male, including those who do not perform priestly functions. Today, however, astrologers are sometimes female—their ads appear in English-language newspapers or big hotels.

31. Exorcists and shamans come from any caste and from either sex, although female shamans are rarely mentioned in the literature and female exorcists may be nonexistent. Some authors have claimed that the shamans/exorcists (the two are often confused) are the non-Brahman counterparts of priests, but the situation in my view is vastly more complicated. For one thing, Brahman shamans are common.

—the *devadasī,* "votary of God." Textually sanctioned in South India,[32] the *davadasī* were nominally married to the god of the temple but allowed mates. Their offspring were legitimate: the girls were often dedicated to the temple; the boys might become professional musicians. Outlawed by the British, the institution of the *devadasī* fell into disrepute, although its dance traditions still exist with some descendants.

Clearly, then, Hindu women have considerable religious involvement, especially in folk practice, even though their role is not textually sanctioned. Indeed, women are essential to most yearly calendrical rituals and perform a large number of them alone in both rural and urban India.[33] In Karimpur, a North Indian village, women instigate and participate in twenty-one of the thirty-three annual rites.[34] Women also dominate nine of the twenty-one annual rites in the village Mohana, near Lucknow, and are apparently the sole participants in nine of the twenty-two festivals in the annual cycle of Rampur, a village north of Delhi.[35] The exact status of these rites of women—which are all based on *pūjā* (devotional ritual) rather than on Vedic fire sacrifices—has yet to be determined. However, most festivals easily identified as having no "great tradition" ties are women's festivals. And women's participation in and even domination of life-cycle rites is definitely part of the "little tradition."[36] In these cults and calendric rites women seek the protection of crucial kinsmen (especially husband, brother, and son) and the health and prosperity of the family as a whole; men's rites, on the other hand, focus on a good wheat crop, ridding the village of disease, and the like.[37]

It is, of course, not surprising to find this religious division of labor in the sexually segregated purdah society of traditional India.[38] Indeed, these practices are influenced by Hindu conceptions of the female. Although women have developed a vital, if subsidiary religious body of folk, local, or nontextual traditions, the notion that they are dangerous provides justification for not allowing them to be active participants in

32. See Ragini Devi, *Dance Dialects of India* (Delhi: Vikas Publications, 1972), pp. 45–50.

33. The evidence in the following discussion comes from rural North India; comparable evidence is lacking for most of the rest of India. Urban data comes from my personal experiences in Delhi and Agra.

34. See Wadley, "Brothers."

35. D. N. Majumdar, *Caste and Communication in an Indian Village* (Bombay: Asia Publishing House, 1958), pp. 252–76; Majumdar analyzes sexual participation for only the twenty-one rites I mention (see also Oscar Lewis, *Village Life in North India* [New York: Vintage Books, 1965], pp. 197–248). The evidence provided by these three villages suggests that there may be some variation in the festivals that are organized by females or males. This variation in local practice needs further investigation.

36. Men make fun of women's rites and generally tolerate them with condescension.

37. See Wadley, "Brothers." I would also like to thank William Houska for his insights into male-female orientations in North Indian rituals.

38. Hanna Papanek, "Purdah in Pakistan: Seclusion and Modern Occupations for Women," *Journal of Marriage and the Family* 33, no. 3 (August 1971): 517–30.

the most authoritative rites. Because of this segregation, religious practices draw women together and reinforce female solidarity. Moreover, many female rites relate to the dual roles of wives and mothers.

The Potential for Change

Although women are banned from the dominant sources of religious power and authority, India, a country which is 83 percent Hindu, has until recently been ruled by a woman. This disconcerting fact contradicts the image of the properly behaved wife. Indians see no such contradiction. A recently completed portrait of Mrs. Gandhi, in fact, depicts her as Durga,[39] a goddess who, like Kālī, has a vast potential for aggression and destruction. She does not remain under her husband's control and controls her own sexuality. Yet in contrast to Kālī, Durga is generally beneficent. Similarly, the Hindu villager is apt to describe the Prime Minister as *Devī,* the goddess. And in a poem dedicated to Indira Gandhi published in a popular English language magazine just after the Bangladesh War, we find these phrases: "Presiding deity of our country's fate" and "of noble grace and looks and yet defiant, thunder in her eyes."[40] Mrs. Gandhi is not Sītā of the *Rāmāyana,* the devoted wife who obeys her husband's every wish,[41] but the Mother, the goddess who epitomizes the dual character of the Hindu female. Thus Hindu conceptions of the female, in contrast to the American notion of the inherently passive woman, provide a meaningful avenue for active involvement in nonwifely roles.

Today, Indian women have access through schooling and mandatory learning of Sanskrit in many states to scriptures banned to them for the past 2,000 years. Moreover, the relaxation of purdah restrictions in some urban and rural areas allows women greater participation in public rituals. Practices such as *sātī,* bans on widow remarriage, and prepuberty marriage have already been outlawed. Divorce and abortion are legal, although social practice lags behind the law. Of course, many practices, based on Hindu orthopraxy, continue to impede women's secular status. Because of hypergamous marriages and dowries, both aspects of Brahmanical orthopraxy, daughters are still considered economic liabilities. A recent study suggests that Brahmanical practices contribute to a benign neglect of female children that results in juvenile female deaths;[42] a decreasing sex ratio—from 972 females per 1,000 males in

39. J. Anthony Lukas, "India Is as Indira Does," *New York Times Magazine* (April 4, 1976).

40. J. N. Dhamija, "The Rising Star," *Illustrated Weekly of India* (January 30, 1972).

41. Mrs. Gandhi does play on the image of the "proper Hindu woman," looks meek, covers her head, and displays mild manners on many public occasions.

42. Barbara D. Miller, "A Population Puzzle—Does the Desire for Sons in India Increase People . . . or Sons?" (unpublished paper read at the New York State Conference on Asian Studies, Albany, 1976).

1961 to 930 females per 1,000 males in 1971—confirms the fact that female mortality is high. And the Hindu desire for sons forces women into unwanted pregnancies and denies them control of their sexuality.

Many problems remain, but there is potential for further change. For Hinduism provides a conception of the world in which women are powerful and dangerous. Traditionally, this power and danger have been checked through religious laws which placed women under the control of men. Most Hindu women will probably continue to accept the Hindu conception of woman as dutiful wife. If women's ritual practices, which emphasize kinship and family relationships, have reinforced the role of woman as wife, those practices have also created possibilities for female solidarity and for alternative sources of religious power. More important, woman as mother in Hindu thought controls others and becomes the Hindu woman in control of herself. As such, she provides an alternative role to that of the dutiful wife, and a possibility for the future: "The fearful goddess (Candika), devoted to her devotees, reduces to ashes those who do not worship her and destroys their merits."[43] "For those who seek pleasure or those who seek liberation, the worship of the all-powerful Goddess is essential. She is the knowledge-of-the-Immensity; she is the mother of the universe, pervading the whole world."[44]

Department of Anthropology
Syracuse University
Syracuse, New York, U.S.A.

43. Devī Māhātmya, quoted in Danielou, p. 257.
44. Karapatri, "Śri Bhapavati tattva," ibid.

Migrants and Women Who Wait

Introduction

Lisa Peattie

There is no one single theme which emerges from this group of papers, unless it is the complexity of the trade-offs among which women construct their lives, as they and/or their men move in response to market opportunity.

The three papers on Africa concern women in societies in which male labor migration has long been a central feature of economic organization. Sibisi's paper deals with the Zulu women who wait back in the countryside while their men work in the cities. They endure, but, she suggests, certain illnesses associated with possession by alien spirits are a distinctive cultural reaction to the strains and tensions of the conditions under which they endure.

Sudarkasa points out that while in West Africa wage labor, a comparatively recent phenomenon, largely involves men, women have long been involved in a more ancient and still continuing migratory pattern for commercial purposes. These entrepreneurs, moving both north and south, into rural and urban areas, are as often as not Yoruba women who work to earn money "because they have financial responsibilities to their immediate and extended families that are independent of those of their husbands, fathers, or sons." One gets the picture of independent women who nevertheless remain married through long separations. A sort of subplot is the development of a different, more interdependent marital pattern among husbands and wives who have migrated together and have been thrust into commercial collaboration for lack of alternative ties.

Finally, the paper by Martha Mueller describes how women in

Lesotho who are fully integrated into the public life of the village, part of a strong female network which in effect runs things while the men are away working in South Africa, are still dependent on their men. Lesotho is itself a dependent economy; local employment is scarce; the major source of economic resources is jobs in South Africa. Women's resources are determined by the level of mine wages, their own men's access to these, and their claim on the men—not anything in the village power structure.

Elizabeth Jelin discusses a distinctively female kind of migration stream, that of young women from the rural areas into domestic service in the cities. She raises some issues concerning the role this plays in individual life careers, as perhaps an important means of adaptation to urban life, but more important to her are the issues it raises with respect to our understanding of the economics of the household. According to Jelin, "Housework and domestic production, differential participation in the labor force, the existence and use of paid domestic service, and the unequal division of labor between men and women in these tasks—all of these are interrelated phenomena that can be fully understood only if conceptualized as specific aspects of the organization of households."

The paper by Yolanda Moses looks at patterns of male dominance in relation to female economic contributions in working- and middle-class families on the island of Montserrat in the British West Indies. Moses started with the hypothesis that male dominance would be reduced proportionally as women's economic contribution to the household increased. She found, in fact, that the male was deemed the "head" of the family even when women earned as much and, in one case, where the man had been away for several years. She found, also, that men did not help women with the housework even if the women were also working outside the home.

But just as Jelin, looking at women in domestic service, opens up questions about the categories in which economic production is understood, this paper opens up questions about the categories in which male dominance is understood. A reader might well come to ask questions about the various arrangements of dependence/independence, subordination/equality which may characterize marriage, and the conditions under which one or another will prevail. In Montserrat "there has to be a head," and in the working class, where it is more than likely that women may earn more dependably than men, there are few marriages; to what extent is this because women, as Moses reports, see marriage as restrictive, and to what extent for other reasons? Looking at the contrast to the Yoruba case, one might ask, Under what conditions of female independence does marriage give way and under what conditions is it redefined in a more egalitarian mode? Further, one is led to reexamine subordination. Our cultural presuppositions make it easy for us to see power and potency in providing income, difficult for us to see it in providing housework. Women in Montserrat say that men are supposed to be "the head"—but they socialize boys to be "lazy" and irresponsible and as grown women they do the providing. Is this poor planning, or is it something else? Women who know that there have been times and social classes in which they have been systematically socialized for charming incompetence should recognize that when they see it coming round the other way.

The lesson from all this for social researchers, whether they are doing economics or social organization, is not to take the categories and the indicators for granted, because they are the most interesting part.

Department of Urban Studies and Planning
Massachusetts Institute of Technology
Cambridge, Massachusetts, U.S.A.

Migrants and Women Who Wait

Migration and Labor Force Participation of Latin American Women: The Domestic Servants in the Cities

Elizabeth Jelin

This paper deals with the migration of Latin American women from rural to urban areas and their occupational and domestic alternatives in the cities. Inquiry into the relationship between work (or economic participation) of women and family organization has been neglected in the Latin American social sciences, especially in studies focusing on the urban areas. Thus the ideas presented here are highly tentative, and my purpose is to suggest a framework for future research rather than an analytical scheme to cope with a mass of existing data. I will first discuss the main characteristics of rural-to-urban migration in the region, in order to place female migrants in the context of spatial relocation for the population as a whole. Then I will address questions about the productive role of migrant women in the cities, especially their role in domestic service. For the individual migrant, domestic service may be an important means of adaptation to urban life and the urban labor market, although there is some stigma attached to this kind of work. Within the labor market, domestic service has some specific features as regards both supply and demand. Finally, domestic service has a special place in the urban economy, sharing traits of domestic production for self-consumption while carrying a monetary payment and thus sharing some traits of wage work. In dealing with this last subject, the focus will necessarily have to shift to the household unit (or the family) where both the unpaid and the paid domestic production take place.

Urbanization and Internal Migration in Latin America

During the last few decades, the process of urbanization in Latin

American countries has been very rapid. In the region as a whole, the annual urbanization rate was 1.26 percent from 1920 to 1930 and 2.5 percent from 1950 to 1960.[1] This process was accomplished through a high rate of rural-to-urban migration, coupled with a relatively high rate of natural growth of the population. Furthermore, urban growth has been concentrated in one or a few urban centers in each country, with most growth in the largest cities, thus increasing the imbalance between the primary city and the rest of the country. Around 1960, between 60 and 100 percent of the urban population (defined as those living in places with 20,000 or more inhabitants) lived in cities with more than 100,000 inhabitants. In half of the countries this meant concentration in only one city, the capital.[2]

However, urbanization was the result not only of fast industrialization that was creating new occupational positions but also of rural economic crises, a very high rate of population growth in rural areas, and the attraction of city life. Thus industrialization did not keep pace with urbanization; migrants arriving in the cities faced difficulties in the labor market, and relatively high unemployment rates, "disguised" unemployment, and underemployment were the resulting consequences.

These facts have been the basis for many studies and interpretations of the Latin American reality.[3] During the 1960s, the prevalent interpretation stressed the fast growth of the service sector in the urban economy. According to several authors, migrants, faced with the scarcity of productive industrial jobs, flooded the service sector, encouraging "hypertertiarization" which accompanied "overurbanization." Residential, economic, social, and political marginality were seen as the inevitable consequences—and authors emphasized the difficulties in overcoming them, given capitalistic industrial-development patterns with capital-intensive technology.[4]

1. Juan C. Elizaga, "Migraciones interiores, migraciones y movilidad social, el proceso de urbanización: Evolución reciente y estado actual de los estudios," in *Conferencia Regional Latinoamericana de Población: Actas I,* edited by Susana Lerner y Raúl de la Peña (México: Colegio de México, 1972).

2. See ibid.; also, John D. Durand and C. A. Peláez, "Patterns of Urbanization in Latin America," in *The City in Newly Developing Countries: Readings on Urbanism and Urbanization,* ed. Gerald Breese (Englewood Cliffs, N.J.: Prentice-Hall, Inc., 1969).

3. The studies on this subject are summarized in Richard M. Morse, "Trends and Issues in Latin American Urban Research, 1965–1970," *Latin American Research Review* 6 (Spring 1971): 3–52, and 6 (Summer 1971): 19–75.

4. See esp. Fernando H. Cardoso and J. L. Reyna, "Industrialization, Occupational Structure, and Social Stratification in Latin America," in *Constructive Change in Latin America,* ed. Cole S. Blasier (Pittsburgh: University of Pittsburgh Press, 1968); José Nun, "Superproblación relativa, ejército industrial de reserva y masa marginal," *Revista latinoamericana de sociología* 5 (1969): 178–236; Wayne A. Cornelius, Jr., "The Political Sociology of Cityward Migration in Latin America: Toward Empirical Theory," in *Latin American Urban Research,* ed. Francine F. Rabinovitz and F. M. Trueblood (Beverly Hills, N.J.: Sage Publications, 1971), vol. 1; and the various papers included in *Migración y desarrollo: Consideraciones teóricas,* ed. Humberto Muñoz (Buenos Aires: Consejo Latinoamericano de Ciencias Sociales, 1972).

In recent years, however, both the theoretical and empirical bases of such statements on the nature of the urban economy and its relation to employment patterns and labor force participation of migrants have been challenged. The urban economy is not becoming increasingly sluggish in creating employment,[5] nor are migrants so prone to become unadjusted marginals because of the economy's inability to provide jobs for them.[6] It seems unjustified to equate "industrial" with productive and "service" with unproductive employment.[7] Yet even within the framework of these revisions, several issues still remain unexplained. Among these, migration and urban-employment patterns of women are a special problem, primarily because of the tremendous weight of domestic service as an occupational alternative for young females in cities of all sizes in the region. In facing this problem, commonsense preconceptions will have to be challenged, leading to a theoretical reconsideration of the links between family and work in urban settings.

In the first place, women migrate to cities more often than men. Elizaga reports migration rates by sex for the urban areas of seven Latin American countries and for seven important cities. In thirteen of the fourteen comparisons, migration rates for females are higher than for males, and in the remaining case there is no difference between sexes.[8] In-depth studies of specific cities illustrate this fact, although there are also diverse historical trends. Elizaga reports that the proportion of females among migrants to Santiago, Chile, from about 1940 to 1962 is high and growing;[9] for Mexico City, Cabrera shows that, although there are more female migrants than males, the difference has been decreasing with time;[10] for Buenos Aires, Recchini de Lattes concludes that there has been an important change in the migration patterns by sex: prior to 1915 foreign immigration, predominantly male, was prevalent, while after that time internal migration, predominantly female, gained importance.[11] One may ask why more women than men in the region migrate to the cities, when authors have continually stressed the importance of such Latin cultural traditions as machismo, a high degree of male control over women, and women's lack of autonomy outside the family. To answer this, one must analyze patterns of migration by age and

5. Joseph Ramos, "An Heterodoxical Interpretation of the Employment Problem in Latin America," *World Development* 2, no. 7 (1974): 47–58.

6. Jorge Balán, H. L. Browning, and E. Jelin, *Men in a Developing Society: Geographic and Social Mobility in Monterrey, Mexico* (Austin: University of Texas Press, 1973).

7. Paul I. Singer, *Economía política de urbanização* (São Paulo: Editora Brasiliense, 1973); Vilmar E. Faría, "Occupational Marginality, Employment and Poverty in Urban Brazil" (Ph.D. diss., Harvard University, 1976).

8. Juan C. Elizaga, *Migraciones a las áreas metropolitanas de América Latina* (Santiago: Centro Latinoamericano de Demografía, 1970), p. 21.

9. Ibid., pp. 33 ff.

10. Gustavo Cabrera, "Selectividad por edad y sexo de los migrantes en México," in Raúl de la Peña.

11. Zulma Recchini de Lattes, "Migraciones en Buenos Aires, 1895–1960," in ibid.

family position. Although it is not possible at this time to use a single source of standardized data for this purpose, some data can be presented here. About half of the migrants to Santiago living in the city in 1963 arrived at ages fifteen to twenty-nine (44 percent of the male migrants, 50.7 percent of the female migrants).[12] This study also shows that, of all migrants, male and female, arriving in the city at age fourteen or over, more than 50 percent came alone; approximately one-third of the migrants arrived as part of a family unit, as husband or wife, with or without children; around 7 percent of the female migrants arrived with children and no husband; finally, the rest were mostly dependent persons, including children and older dependents.[13]

No comparable data for other cities in Latin America are available at this time.[14] However, this lack of information should not deter us from drawing important conclusions regarding women migrants. Although the proportion in each category of the migratory group may vary from place to place, with regard to their productive activities there are two relevant classes of women migrants: young women arriving alone and, predominantly, looking for jobs and the ones arriving with their families who will devote their main effort to housework. No doubt both classes are numerically important in most cities. Analytically the qualitative difference between these two categories of women may at first appear important. However, the predominant tasks they perform are not that different: the former enter the urban labor force mainly as paid domestic servants, the latter perform unpaid domestic services for their own families.

Women's Work in the Cities

If so many young women come to the cities seeking a job, it must be because there is a demand for their labor. Actually labor force participation rates among migrants are higher than among the women native to the city. Available data show that in Santiago migrant women in all age groups have higher participation rates than natives. Furthermore, recent migrants (arriving during the ten years prior to the survey) show higher participation rates than earlier migrants. The difference is more striking among young women: 57 percent of recent migrants aged

12. Elizaga, *Migraciones a las áreas metropolitanas,* pp. 33–34.

13. Ibid., p. 86.

14. The Monterrey study included only male respondents, showing a considerably smaller proportion of men arriving alone—only 19 percent. However, straightforward comparisons are difficult, since in this study the migratory group was defined in such a way that at times it included persons not arriving together to the city. See Harley L. Browning and W. Feindt, "The Social and Economic Context of Migration to Monterrey, Mexico," in Rabinowitz and Trueblood (see n. 4 above).

fifteen to twenty-four were working at the time of the survey, while 35 percent of the earlier migrants and 30 percent of the natives in that age category did so.[15] The same pattern appears in a survey conducted in Belo Horizonte, Brazil, where 21 percent of the native women over ten years old and 35 percent of the recent migrants (arriving during the last year prior to the survey) were economically active.[16]

As could be expected, there is a wide difference in the employment profile of native and migrant women and, among the latter, between the recent and the earlier arrivals. Thus in Santiago the proportion of manual workers is highest among recent migrants, intermediate among earlier migrants, and lowest among natives. Furthermore, there is a sharp difference in the proportion employed as domestic servants: nearly two out of three recently employed migrants but only one in five earlier migrants and one in nine natives occupy such positions.[17] Data for the metropolitan area of Buenos Aires in 1970 show a similar pattern: among economically active females, 51.5 percent of the recent internal migrants and 62.6 percent of the recent migrants from neighboring countries work as domestic servants, while 35 percent of the earlier migrants and only 5 percent of the natives do so.[18] In Belo Horizonte, survey data for 1972 show that 73.1 percent of the economically active recent migrants and 44.8 percent of the natives work in personal services—a large proportion of these being jobs in domestic service.[19] Finally, an estimate for Lima, Peru, states that 30 percent of all female migrants to the city between 1956 and 1965, representing 62.5 percent of the economically active female migrants, entered domestic service upon arrival in the city.[20]

The results of these few studies on female employment and migratory status provide sufficient evidence to conclude that the native-migrant differences in the type of labor force participation of women are large and consistent across cities. Detailed studies have been made for the male labor force that include comparisons of the occupational standing of natives and migrants in the city. They have shown no clear pattern of differentials between male migrants and natives, with no dif-

15. Elizaga, *Migraciones a las áreas metropolitanas,* p. 148.

16. Thomas W. Merrick, "Informal Sector Employment in Brazil: A Case Study for Belo Horizonte," mimeographed (Belo Horizonte: Centro de Desenvolvimento, Planejamento Regional, 1974).

17. Elizaga, *Migraciones a las áreas metropolitanas,* p. 162.

18. The reported data are from unpublished special tabulations of the 1970 census sample. See Adriana Marshall, *Immigración, demanda de fuerza de trabajo y estructura ocupacional en el área metropolitana Argentina* (Buenos Aires: Facultad Latinoamericano de Ciencias Sociales, 1976).

19. Merrick.

20. Margo L. Smith, "Domestic Service as a Channel of Upward Mobility for the Lower-Class Woman: The Lima Case," in *Female and Male in Latin America: Essays,* ed. Ann Pescatello (Pittsburgh: University of Pittsburgh Press, 1973).

ferences in some cases and variations in opposite directions in others. But, as Muñoz and Oliveira state, as a conclusion to their bibliographical survey of the subject, "It is possible that important variations will emerge when studying the female population."[21] The scarce evidence presented here warrants the conclusion that the differences in the profiles of migrant and native women's occupations are considerably larger than those of the males and are more consistent across various cities and countries in Latin America.

It is well known that domestic service is a numerically important occupation for women in urban Latin America.[22] What we know now is that this occupation is predominantly filled by migrants to the cities and expecially by recent young migrants. As they grow older, many of them leave, either to become housewives or to move to other occupations. At the same time, the continuous influx of migrants replenishes the supply of young domestic servants for urban households. Although it is hard to offer precise estimates of the incidence of domestic service in the female urban labor force and the prevalence of recent migrants in that position, there is enough evidence to justify a more thorough discussion of the occupation, especially since, at the present time, only in Latin America are domestic servants such a numerically important category for women.[23]

Before approaching the topic of domestic servants in detail, however, it may be necessary to deal with the other important category of women migrants, those arriving in the city with their families, who will devote their efforts predominantly to housework. Information regarding the tasks performed by these women before and after migration is practically nil, and thus one can only speculate about the importance of their move to the city. Is there a systematic pattern of differences in the domestic activities performed in the rural areas of origin and in the cities? The extreme case that could be taken as a standard for comparison is that of a woman performing a wide range of subsistence activities in the area of origin, almost none of which can be reproduced in towns or cities.[24] If there are no alternative employment opportunities for such

21. Humberto Muñoz and Orlandina de Oliveira, "Notas acerca de la teoría de las migraciones: Aspectos sociológicos," in Muñoz (see n. 4 above), p. 21. See also Jorge Balán, "Migrant-Native Socioeconomic Differences in Latin American Cities: A Structural Analysis," *Latin American Research Review* 4 (Spring 1969): 3–29.

22. Nadia H. Youssef, *Women and Work in Developing Countries* (Berkeley: Institute of International Studies, 1974); Felicia R. Madeira and P. I. Singer, *Estrutura do emprego e traballo femenino no Brasil: 1920–1970,* caderno 13 (São Paulo: Centro Brasileiro de Análise e Planejamento [CEBRAP] 1973); and Elizabeth Jelin, "La bahiana en la fuerza de trabajo: Actividad doméstica, producción simple y trabajo asalariado en Salvador, Brasil," *Demografía y economía* 8, no. 3 (1974): 307–21.

23. Youssef.

24. Ester Boserup, *Woman's Role in Economic Development* (London: George Allen & Unwin, 1970).

a woman, she will enjoy "enforced leisure," which will be accompanied by a sharp decline in her family's standard of living, since her husband's income will never be sufficient to purchase all the goods and services previously produced at home.

Such extremes are not found in Latin American cities. Rural-urban differentials in the extent of cash transactions are not that large, and the variety of domestic subsistence activities that can be carried out in the cities is still considerable. Undoubtedly, the performance of domestic productive activities in urban areas is one adaptation of the low-income family to the low wages earned by the gainfully employed members of the household. In low-income families cleaning the house, taking care of the children, and preparing food are not the only domestic tasks urban women perform; they also make and mend clothes, raise animals and vegetables, collect fuel and water.[25] This range of activities may be narrower than that of peasant women, but if these activities are compared with the monetary value of the same goods and services purchased at market prices, the importance of domestic production in urban areas becomes unmistakable.[26]

Their specialization in housework allows these urban women to enlarge the scope of their activities in a different direction: sewing and mending clothes, washing and ironing, cleaning the house and taking care of children are services that can be sold in the marketplace. Housewives may engage in them for pay and thus derive some income from them. Since the tasks are practically the same ones performed at home for her family and can be performed on a part-time or irregular basis, they are added to the woman's responsibilities, without having to break the household routines or change the family organization. In a manner

25. Domestic tasks also may include the building of the house, but in this task the role of women is secondary. For a novel interpretation of these domestic activities in relationship to the dominant economic role, see Francisco de Oliveira, "A economía brasileira: Crítica a razao dualista," *Estudos CEBRAP* 2 (October 1972): 3–82.

26. Only recently has the subject of the economic value of housework been introduced systematically into the discussion about productive activities. One line of discussion has centered upon the issue of the role of housework in reproducing the labor force: see Wally Seccombe, "The Housewife and Her Labour under Capitalism," *New Left Review,* no. 83 (January–February 1974), pp. 3–21; Jean Gardiner, "Women's Domestic Labour," ibid., no. 89 (January–February 1975), pp. 47–58; Margaret Coulson, B. Magas, and H. Wainwright, "The Housewife and Her Labour under Capitalism: A Critique," ibid., pp. 59–71; and Wally Seccombe, "Domestic Labour—Reply to Critics," ibid., no 94 (November–December 1975), pp. 85–96. See also E. R. Weiss-Altaner, "Economía clásica, familia y actividad económica," mimeographed (México: Colegio de México, 1976). Another line has followed a more neoclassical path, centering attention upon the "opportunity costs" of various household and market activities of women: see Jacob Mincer, "Labor Force Participation of Married Women: A Study in Labor Supply," in *Aspects of Labor Economics,* ed. National Bureau of Economic Research (Princeton, N.J.: Princeton University Press, 1962); and various papers included in *Sex, Discrimination, and the Division of Labor,* ed. Cynthia B. Lloyd (New York: Columbia University Press, 1973).

analogous to that of the subsistence peasant who commercializes part of his/her production in order to earn some money—at times the part sold is a surplus; at other times, it means underconsumption for the peasant family in order to obtain some cash—the low-income housewife in a Latin American city can perform domestic tasks for others and thus earn money to supplement (and at times of unemployment to replace) the income of the gainfully employed members of the household.[27] The fluidity of the informal labor market for domestic servants allows for the existence of a number of women who can enter or leave part-time paid employment as a simple extension of their domestic subsistence tasks.[28]

The Domestic Servant in the City

The analysis of domestic service as an occupation in the urban labor market can now be approached from two perspectives: first, that of the domestic servant as an individual worker, her view of her job and her life cycle; second, the perspective of the urban labor market, focusing on the relationship between domestic service and other economic activities.

Job opportunities in domestic service offer rural women the possibility of moving to the city with a job and thus gaining autonomy away from their families of origin. It is quite likely that many rural families allow their daughters to move to the city just because there are jobs in domestic service available, jobs in which the basic subsistence needs of the young women, food and shelter, will be covered. Furthermore, parents may feel their daughters more secure, morally and psychologically more sheltered, if they live with families instead of having to fight the cold, impersonal labor market by themselves in the city. Thus, in part, the migration of young women to cities is encouraged by the existence of this occupational alternative.[29]

What is the importance of domestic service for the work career and, more generally, for the life cycle of the women involved? Few studies of domestic servants have taken into consideration the perceptions and orientations the women have toward their jobs. Margo Smith studied domestic service in Lima and attempted to show that "domestic service provides one of the few opportunities available to lower-class migrant

27. Jelin.

28. Larissa A. de Lomnitz, *Cómo sobreviven los marginados* (México: Siglo XXI, 1975). A different employment strategy for migrant women in families in Mexico City, namely, street vending, is studied by Lourdes Arizpe, *Indígenas en la ciudad de México: El caso de las "Marías"* (México: SepSetentas, 1975).

29. Of course the flow of rural-to-urban migrants does not depend solely on the job opportunities as domestic servants available in the cities. These opportunities are especially important in cases in which the economic role of females is relatively minor in the rural areas, and therefore transfer to the cities may mean engaging in a new activity without at the same time having to suffer a loss in the production of the family of origin. See Boserup.

women for upward socioeconomic mobility within the broad spectrum of the lower class."[30] Smith reports data from various studies, including her own, showing the regional, educational, and family background of domestic servants. She also constructs the typical career of the domestic servant:

> The typical servant's career follows a distinct pattern. The migrant woman destined to servitude spends the first few months following her arrival in Lima with relatives who have previously migrated to the capital. After this initial period of acculturation to the city, these relatives are instrumental in getting the young woman her first job as a servant, often with a lower-middle-class family living in a commercial neighborhood. . . . While receiving on-the-job training, the servant is likely to earn a low salary and receive few, if any, fringe benefits beyond room and board. After six months or a year, the servant moves on to a new job, in a better neighborhood. She usually augments her salary and begins to demand or command fringe benefits. . . . Each of the servant's jobs usually lasts from six months to two years, and it is not unlikely for a servant to have approximately six jobs during the course of her career. . . . Usually, by the age of twenty-four years, or after a seven-year career in domestic service, the servant drops out of the servant world to concentrate her efforts on a family of her own.[31]

Considerable variations are to be found in the career patterns within the city of Lima and many more if women in other cities are included in a comparison. For instance, in countries like Brazil or Argentina, the career of the domestic servant may include important residential moves, starting as a maid in a provincial city and moving then to the large metropolitan centers of São Paulo, Rio, or Buenos Aires. Salaries of domestic servants in São Paulo are probably three to five times higher than in the provincial city of Belo Horizonte, a city of more than 2 million itself. This "typical" career provides a good starting point for the discussion of the subject.

Smith contends that the passage through domestic service allows for upward mobility. Actually it is very hard to evaluate this hypothesis, given the lack of available empirical evidence. A complete test would have to compare the life cycle of women entering the urban labor market as domestic servants with that of women from a similar socioeconomic background who followed different paths: young women who did not migrate, those who entered other occupations, and those who never worked. Since this comparison cannot be made at present, only some tentative general statements will be made.

From the point of view of the work career, domestic service is in itself a dead-end occupation. It does not allow any major progress, train-

30. Smith (n. 20 above), p. 193.
31. Ibid., pp. 195–96.

ing, or change. As Smith shows, it may allow a person to obtain some formal training in other skills, permission to study being one of the most important "fringe benefits" mentioned. However, in most cases the skill acquired (the most common one is sewing) will not be one to be used in the labor market on leaving domestic service.

A good number of domestic servants are able to leave and enter other occupations, mostly in personal services, at times in industry. But the great majority of women will have as their desired goal marrying, forming their own families, and devoting themselves to housework (perhaps with the actual, although not particularly desired, possibility of having a domestic-service job on a part-time or irregular basis). However, domestic service is a very special occupation; it is a working arrangement that sets strong limits on the choices of the family life of the servant. Establishing a family always means having to abandon the present job itself and many times the occupation also. The conflict between family formation and work, so often discussed for women in general, has not been studied for domestic service, an occupation in which residence at the place of work and long hours create an extreme case of conflict.

Furthermore, a servant's goal of having her own family and thus becoming a housewife may be fostered (with considerable strains and frustrations) by her passage through the household of a higher-income family. For the young woman arriving in the city, entering a middle-stratum household instead of one in a periphery shantytown means having rapidly to become used to a variety of gadgets and habits of a life-style unknown to the migrant. Often the young woman does not know how to use a toilet or running hot water. In less extreme cases, elevators, electric appliances, telephones, and so on are novelties to which one has to become accustomed. Adaptation to these ways of life may include some psychosocial changes that are relatively unknown but important for the study of the servant's future: To what extent does servitude include a sense of idealization and identification with the employers rather than a sense of being exploited and at their mercy? To what extent does this identification hinder the development of a working-class identity, thus isolating the servant from interaction with other workers? What is the range of social interactions and relations that servants can establish in the city outside their jobs—given the long hours, the residential segregation, and the character of their identity? Are they not prone to developing much higher aspirations and expectations than other members of the working classes?

Domestic Service in the Urban Labor Market

In many senses, domestic service is not a job like others. The person is hired to provide some personal services, but not for a profit—the employer is not "doing business" when hiring a domestic servant. That is, the labor expended during the job is not producing any good or service that will enter the money-circulation process in that society. It is work performed for self-consumption, and in that sense domestic work is more comparable to housework performed by the members of the family without pay than to the work performed by a wage worker. Although it is work for "self-consumption," the self involved is not the worker herself but her employers, to whom only monetary links exist. It may be argued that in this respect it is not that different from the housework performed by the housewife, since in her case the services are also for others—the other members of the household unit. However, there are other links between the housewife and the members of her household, and that is not the case for the domestic servant.

In the second place, the fact that the work of the domestic servant is not a part of the production and circulation process in capitalist economies means that no parameters can fix the demand for domestic servants. As students of housework (and housewives themselves) know, there is no end to housework.[32] Time-budget studies show the enormous range in the amount of time spent in different domestic activities, varying according to family size, the technology employed for some tasks, the outside employment of the housewife, and so on.[33] Thus, if there is no end to housework, the demand for paid domestic servants has to be extremely elastic, although the income of the employing household (and secondarily its size) is an important determinant of that demand.

The existence of a constant, potentially unfulfilled demand for domestic service means that, even when the migrant has as a goal some other type of work, she knows that domestic service is always available as an alternative in the city. Thus, as Marshall has stated (for domestic service in the case of women and construction in the case of men in the city of Buenos Aires), "Employment opportunities and continuous flow of migrants stimulate each other: the former favor the continuity of the migratory flux, and the latter guarantees a comparatively cheap labor which, in turn, stimulates the demand for labor and the emergence of job opportunities in these sectors."[34]

For the economy and the employment structure, the performance of domestic tasks by means of paid domestic service has other consequences. First, the availability of an abundant and relatively cheap domestic service affects the quality of life of the middle and upper strata

32. Ann Oakley, *The Sociology of Housework* (New York: Pantheon Books, 1974).

33. See, among others, Martin Meissner, "Sur la division du travail et l'inégalité des sexes," *Sociologie du travail* 17 (October–December 1975): 329–50; and Arleen Leibowitz, "Women's Work in the Home," in Lloyd (see n. 26 above). There are no time-budget studies systematically comparing households with and without domestic service, nor am I aware of that type of study in Latin America.

34. Marshall (n. 18 above), pp. 44–45.

which can enjoy such services. If domestic servants were not available, personal services would have to be purchased from established enterprises (restaurants, laundry and dry-cleaning services, etc.) at considerably higher prices. Thus the use of domestic servants implies some savings for those who can afford them. However, as a source of savings for productive investments, the aggregate effects of domestic service are negligible, since the saved money is diverted more often to other consumption and luxury items than to investment. Therefore the existence of domestic servants may influence to some extent the demand for some luxury products and services. It may also mean a delay in the expansion of capitalistic personal-services enterprises, allowing alternative investments in more profitable and productive sectors.

Second, the availability of domestic service has some important consequences for the women in the households that can afford them. Although there is no end to housework, the availability of domestic help frees the housewife from many of her domestic chores. In the extreme case, domestic servants can take over the management and organization of the household almost entirely, the housewife only occasionally supervising their work. This means that it may be easier for middle-strata women to enter the labor force or remain in it after marriage and during child rearing without having to carry the full burden of a "double day." However, this effect should not be carried too far. Women's participation in the labor force (outside domestic service), in Latin America and elsewhere, is a complex issue in which numerous causes interact.[35] The availability of domestic service *may* encourage women to keep or take full-time jobs, but it may also encourage them to conduct a life of leisure and comfort unknown to women at comparable income levels in other countries where domestic service is considerably more expensive.[36]

Housework, Domestic Service, and Women's Work in the Context of the Household

Housework and domestic production, differential participation in the labor force, the existence and use of paid domestic service, and the unequal division of labor between men and women in these tasks—all of

35. See Boserup (n. 24 above); Youssef (n. 22 above); and the paper by T. Aldrich Finegan, Beth Niemi, and Solomon W. Polachek, in Lloyd (see n. 26 above).

36. In a cross-sectional study of the employment structure in sixteen Argentine cities in the late forties, I found some evidence of a positive relationship between the percentage of domestic servants and the rate of participation by women in other economic activities and a negative relationship between employment in domestic service and the percentage of the labor force employed in personal services carried out by enterprises (Elizabeth Jelin, "Estructura de empleo y tipo de organizaciones productivas: Los sectores obreros en las ciudades argentinas de la década del cuarenta," in *Estudios 17* [Buenos Aires: Centro de Investigaciones en Ciencias Sociales, 1975]).

these are interrelated phenomena that can be fully understood only if conceptualized as specific aspects of the organization of households. Households are the social units in charge of the tasks necessary for the reproduction of the members of society, both in the long-term perspective of giving birth and taking care of new members and in the short-term perspective of everyday survival of its active members. The organization of the household is so intertwined with the organization of production that one must approach its study from the perspective of the mechanisms of reproduction of the economic system.[37]

One can postulate that households develop a "strategy of survival," including differential participation in the world outside and the division of labor within the household. Even migration to the city should be seen not as an individual or isolated event but as part of the strategy of survival of the rural household. This strategy involves the management and organization of different resources: income and wealth, job opportunities for the members, possibilities of domestic production of goods and services, and networks of social relations. Of course these resources vary greatly among households of different social classes as well as within classes, according to the stage in the family life cycle. The next analytical step toward understanding women's migration, their position in the labor market and in domestic production, will have to focus on the survival strategy of the household and will have to relate the various dimensions of the problem to each other, looking at the alternatives available not to the individual but to the household group.

Centro de Estudios de Estado y Sociedad
Buenos Aires, Argentina

37. On these functions of households, see the references in n. 26 above. Lourdes Arizpe also takes this perspective in studying the household unit in the context of the productive cycle (*Parentesco y economía en una socieded nahua: Nican Pehua Zacatipan* [México: Instituto Nacional Indigenista, 1973]).

Female Status, the Family, and Male Dominance in a West Indian Community

Yolanda T. Moses

This article is a contribution to the study of the relationship between female economic contributions to the family and female status using data from the small, predominantly black island of Montserrat[1] in the British West Indies. Writers have argued that substantial economic contributions from women need not result in higher status, especially if existing cultural traditions define their activities as less prestigious than those of men.[2] My data support this claim. The status of employed women has less to do with economic contributions per se than with the presence or absence of males in the household and the degree to which women have internalized and perpetuate ideologies of male dominance, "a situation in which men have highly preferential access, although not always exclusive rights, to those activities to which society accords the highest value, and permits a measure of control over others."[3] Historically, such an ideology comes from British traditions, officially reflected in the law on Montserrat,[4] in which women are perceived as subordinate

1. Research, conducted over a thirteen-month period with forty-five employed women and their families, was sponsored by a fellowship from the Ford Foundation.

2. Beverly Chinas, *The Isthmus Zapotecs: Women's Roles in Cultural Context* (New York: Holt, Rinehart & Winston, 1973), p. 99; Phyllis Kaberry, *Women of the Grass Fields: A Study of the Economic Position of Women in Bambenda, British Cameroons* (London: Her Majesty's Stationery Office, 1952), p. 300; Peggy Sanday, "Toward a Theory of the Status of Women," *American Anthropologist* 75 (October 1973): 1682–1700. For a study of the United States, see Lois Hoffman, "Parental Power Relations and the Division of Household Tasks," in *The Employed Mother in America* (Chicago: Rand McNally & Co., 1963).

3. Ernestine Friedl, *Women and Men: An Anthropologist's View* (New York: Holt, Rinehart & Winston, 1975), p. 7.

4. See *Laws of Montserrat* (Montserrat: Government of Montserrat, 1962).

to men. Though laws have been modified in recent years to provide a more egalitarian view, older values are still inseparable from institutions and individual male-female role relations.

Montserrat also provides a chance to look at the status of women across class lines within the same society. The West Indies were, and are, a society based on class distinctions. Most work on the family or household in the West Indies has centered on the working class and especially the matrifocal family,[5] but I investigated middle-class and elite women as well as variants of the working-class family. The anthropological literature has noted that the middle-class family is patriarchal and that women are subordinate to men.[6] Working-class families, on the other hand, are thought to be female centered and men in the role of husband-father marginal.[7]

Looking at decision-making powers of employed working-class women within their own class context and then comparing them to the decision-making powers of the middle-class women, I have tried to provide more detailed structural-functional descriptions of female power.

My method was to analyze archival information such as surveys, government records, and interviews with government specialists (i.e., lawyers, educators, and administrators) and to use participant observation and comprehensive in-depth interviews with my sample of women and their families. I chose to do an intensive study of a small number of women for two reasons. First, there is a history of community surveys for the Caribbean area that have focused on household structure but not on the internal dynamics of these households, on male-female relations, or on information regarding people's attitudes and feelings about their roles.[8] The second and perhaps most important reason is that the nature of the data collected depended on the kind of rapport established with my informants. The interviews were conducted with employed women, that is, those who work for wages or a salary, married and single, with and without children and their partners where available (see table 1 for breakdown).

5. For more information on family studies in the Caribbean, see M. G. Smith, *West Indian Family Structure* (Seattle: University of Washington Press, 1962); R. T. Smith, "Culture and Social Structure in the Caribbean: Some Recent Work on Family Kinship Studies," in *Black Society in the New World,* ed. Richard Frucht (New York: Random House, 1971), pp. 251–72; and Sidney Mintz and William Davenport, "Working Papers in Caribbean Social Organization," *Social and Economic Studies,* vol. 10, no. 4 (1961).

6. Lloyd Braithewaite, "Social Stratification in Trinidad," *Social and Economic Studies,* vols. 2 and 3, nos. 2 and 3 (1953); and M. G. Smith, "The Plural Framework of Jamaican Society," in *Slaves, Free Men and Citizens,* ed. Lambros Comitas and David Lowenthal (Camden City, N.J.: Doubleday & Co., Anchor Books, 1972), pp. 174–93.

7. Judith Blake, *Family Structure in Jamaica* (New York: Free Press, 1961); Stuart Philpott, *West Indian Migration: The Montserrat Case* (New York: Athlone Free Press, 1973); and Nancy J. Pollock, "Women and the Division of Labor: A Jamaican Example," *American Anthropologist* 74, no. 2 (1972): 689–92.

8. Interview with the chief statistical officer for Montserrat, Richard Douthwaite, March 1973.

Money, Responsibility, Power, and Ideology

Domestic relationships often reveal much about sex roles in a society. For most married women at both economic levels, the husband is considered the head of the household and ultimate authority figure, even for those who make as much money as their husbands. One said, "In any *normal* family, there has to be a head. Somebody has to have final word and authority. I was always taught it was the man's place to be the head." In one case, where the husband was away from the island for several years and the wife was contributing about half of the income to the household, she would wait as much as two or three weeks to make decisions concerning routine purchases until she had gotten his permission by mail.

However, single women at both social and economic levels present a more varied picture of what "head of the household" means. Where there is no male present in the role of husband-father, the final authority figure in decision making is often determined by age, usually the deciding factor where female siblings and their children live with the mother. Two junior household members said, "My mother is the head. My sister

Table 1

A. Breakdown of Sample by Marital Status and Presence/Absence of Children

Marital Status	With Children	Without Children	Total
Married	11	0	11
Divorced/separated	4	1	5
Widowed	2	2	4
Single (never been married)	10	15	25
Total	27	18	45

B. Women with Children by Marital Status and Employment Ranking

Marital Status	Skilled*	Unskilled	Total
Married	11	0	11
Single†	4	6	10
Divorced	1	1	2
Separated	0	2	2
Widowed	0	2	2
Total	16	11	27

*Skilled women have training past primary level: including secondary (high) school, technical training, university training. Their jobs include teachers, nurses, social workers, clerical assistants, and beauticians. Unskilled women have six years or less of education and are employed in jobs such as domestic, store clerk, and farmer. On Montserrat skilled occupations are usually associated with middle-class status and unskilled occupations with working-class status.

†Single included only women who have never been married.

and me live with my mother. We live in her house. She takes care of all the children [five] while we work. She don't mind; she says she is too old to work anyway. She also tells us what food to buy, we bring it home to her and she cooks it." "We live in the house that my aunt gave to my sister. My mother watches the children while we work. We make the money. My mother spends it. She buys the food, and sometimes the clothes when we have money. She is a good mother. She loves children."

Skilled single women, whose education and income offset the age authority of a mother, can also be household heads. "I am considered the head of the household because I am the only person working. My mother is too old. She tells me to make most decisions since it is my money I am spending. She is really grateful that I support her. I always ask her what she wants to do even though I know the final decision is mine." Some households are egalitarian; decisions are made jointly, and the person who is available carries them out. This kind of household is usually composed of skilled siblings with roughly the same income. A sister, who had an egalitarian arrangement with her brother, said, "I took this apartment in Plymouth near my job. But I was not able to afford it by myself. My brother also had a job in Plymouth, so we decided to live together. We share expenses. We buy food together and he sometimes even looks after the baby when I go out. It is really nice having him here and we get along well. The only thing is I wish he would help cook more."

Owning property in the form of houses or land is a part of the local status structure. Many people who leave the island and go to Britain or the United States to work have their relatives buy land and have houses built on the island for them.[9] Most skilled married women confirm this, as they owned houses jointly with their husbands, but few of them decided or helped to decide to buy the house or have the house built. In most instances it was the husband's decision, made before he married. The women were all basically happy with the outcome. As one woman stated: "George already had the land before we got married. So we built here. Before the house was built we lived with his mother. I like the location and the neighbors. I like living a little away from the town, not too far, but just far enough." The wives of middle-class husbands derive satisfaction because houses symbolize middle-class status for both of them, and who makes the decision to buy or build one seems irrelevant. Skilled single women, on the other hand, usually fall into the category of renters, because it is too expensive to try to buy property or build a house as a single person. Married couples are pooling two incomes, while the single person is supporting herself and children, if any, on one

9. Richard Frucht ("A Caribbean Social Type: Neither 'Peasant' nor 'Proletarian,' " in *Black Society in the New World*) reports similar activity for the nearby island of Nevis. See also Nancy Foner (*Status and Power of Rural Jamaica* [New York: Teachers College Press, 1972], p. 211) for a study of such values in a rural Jamaican village.

salary. Most unskilled women do own property: small one- or two-room houses that have been in the family for at least two generations, inherited from a member of the family who has either left the island or died. Owning a home holds the same kind of value and prestige for unskilled women as it does for the skilled ones, but they seem to be more dependent on help from kin on the island or wherever they may live to secure their houses.

Skilled married women, except in one case, make less than one-half of the total household income. Though this group receives remittances, they give financial support to other relatives who are in need. Indeed, over a third of these couples have relatives living with them, while two-thirds of them give financial support to relatives who do not live in the household but on the island. I found among the husbands a deep sense of duty. "I take care of this old lady, she is not really related to me, but she was a good friend of my grandparents who raised me. I have known her for a long time. She has no one left to look after her, so I do. She must be about ninety years old now I guess. I take care of her because there is no one else to do it. I have an uncle who is a carpenter, he does a lot of odd jobs for me. I know that sometimes he doesn't do good work, but he *is* my uncle, and that's why I hire him." Because there is very little formalized support given to the needy, the care of the aged is still done mainly by the relatives.[10] Most middle-class people on Montserrat still have a strong sense of family duty, in part because they are what I call "the new middle class." That is, the majority are from working-class backgrounds but through education and income have become more affluent.

The consequences of this help to avoid a conflict between a Victorian British notion of sex roles (i.e., a woman's place is in the home) and the reality of the middle-class woman working outside the home. Ideally, though the male is to be provider and decision maker for the family, income from all sources is still needed. So, the working-class norm, that women must work to make a living, is still part of the value system of the middle class. This value will probably remain even after the middle class on Montserrat becomes firmly entrenched, because money will be needed from all working members in a household in order to maintain the new middle-class life-style. Moreover, women do not compete in traditionally male areas in the labor market, and they continue their role as nurturer in the home. Nor do the majority of men do increased housework or routine childcare activities as a result of their wives' employment. So, for the middle-class women, while education may confer social mobility, a good job, more income, and better housing when compared to working-class women, vis-à-vis her partner she is still

10. A social security system was started on the island in 1972, but it is still in its infancy and does not provide adequate support for the aged yet.

considered and considers herself subordinate to him. Plus, she is expected by society to marry, raise children, and be faithful to her husband, while he still enjoys the sexual and social double standards of the society.

Indeed, middle-class women internalize and manifest a male dominance ideology to a greater degree than the working-class women for several reasons. First, middle-class men are able to live up to their roles set forth by the ideology, that is, they are able to provide the major economic support for their families. Second, they are physically present in the household to make decisions and to see that women play their complementary roles in maintaining and perpetuating this ideology through early childhood socialization patterns as well as by acting as role models for their female children.

Single and divorced skilled women, in contrast to married skilled women, do not give much familial support. Instead, they must rely on friends and relatives to help them. One said, "My father gives me from $15.00 to $20.00 a week because I am always short of money. He comes to town about once a week and that's when I see him. My older brothers and sisters send him money from Canada, and I get it from him. The man who owns this building is a friend of my father, so he too keeps an eye on me. The people next door bring me vegetables because I don't have space or the time for a garden with my job and my baby."

The income of unskilled women is appreciably less than for all skilled women. One wonders how the little money is stretched to take care of the basic needs of its members. Yet, in the unskilled group, the women must provide 50 percent and more of the total household income. Among single women, remittances from relatives working abroad and the pooling of resources help ends meet. One informant who lives with her mother, her sisters, and their children said, "My cousins help us sometimes you know. But they don't have much. The children's grandmother she takes care of them sometime. I take them over to see my mother-in-law on Sunday." (She calls the mother of her children's father mother-in-law even though they are not married and she does not know where he is.) Single women who live alone with their children, separated, divorced, and widowed women also depend on their friends and relatives. One domestic said: "I get $25.00 a week from one of my daughters and $30.00 a week from the other. With the little money I make, my mother and me are able to get by. We have a garden, and my married sister here on Montserrat sometimes 'gives [to] the old lady.' "

Skilled married women usually make the routine purchases of small items such as food, dishes, appliances, and tools for the kitchen. But men decide on the larger, less frequently purchased items, such as radios, record players, or automobiles. Only in the area of buying furniture do women make major decisions. Most are quite satisfied with the arrangement. They frequently justify the husband's decision making in these areas by saying he is more "knowledgeable" about mechanical gadgets: "Lord, I don't know anything about record players. That's my husband's interest. So I let him buy whatever he wants. We did decide to buy the furniture together. I guess he really didn't care too much as long as it was nice." There is little conflict over these areas of involvement since both men and women have clear-cut ideas about what should be their areas of interest and expertise. Even single skilled women seek the help of "knowledgeable" males before they make the major purchase of a car.

Most skilled women feel that their working contributes very little to their decision-making power but rather to a good understanding between them and their partners: "I only make a little money. It surely doesn't decide what we do. My salary is too small. We decide together what is to be done." Another woman said, "I feel I could still help make decisions even if I wasn't working, my husband and I have a good understanding." Though the majority feel their economic contributions have little effect on their decision-making power, several also feel it is a definite advantage to work since that way they can buy what they want when they want. According to a head teacher of a primary school, "Well, I know I could buy something even if he didn't want me to. I can be very stubborn about things like that. This way, I don't have to depend upon him for everything."

Most skilled single women, in contrast, see themselves in the role of decision maker by necessity: "If I didn't work, I would be very dependent on other people. I don't like that idea." Yet a single woman who does live with her parents feels that her income from her occupation contributes nothing to her power in the household because her father is there and she is considered a daughter and not an adult: "I pay for rent at my father's house. He makes the big decisions in our family. Sometimes, he will ask my mother but not me."

Among the unskilled women in general, decision making about the purchase of goods is done on a much smaller scale. Working is necessary for survival. Basics, like food and clothing, are priorities. Luxury items usually come in the form of gifts from boyfriends or remittances from relatives.

As decision-making areas are grouped along sex lines, so are notions of what is "women's work" and what is "men's work" among middle-class families. Both women and men consider housework unsuitable for males. The cultural traditions of Montserrat dictate that women do housework. If they work outside of the home, in addition, that is fine, but they still must do the housework or have it done. Women and others (maids, helpers, or female relatives) overwhelmingly do cooking, cleaning, shopping, washing, and ironing. Husbands usually do repairs, yardwork, and gardening (see table 2). In two instances where gardening is the wives' task, the husbands are away from the island. In the two cases of the "wife and others" that included husbands and wives, couples like to garden and take turns doing it.

Table 2

Married Skilled Women: Household Tasks by Sex and Type of Task ($N=11$)

Tasks	Husband	Wife	Children	Other	Wife with Others
Cooking	. . .	3	. . .	. . .	8
Cleaning	. . .	2	. . .	7	2
Shopping	. . .	5	. . .	. . .	6
Washing	. . .	2	. . .	8	1
Ironing	. . .	2	. . .	9	. . .
Repairs	6	1	. . .	4	. . .
Lawn (yardwork)	6	. . .	. . .	3	2
Gardening	6	2	. . .	1	2

How do these women work and take care of a household? It is usually done smoothly and with little conflict of roles because middle-class couples can afford domestic help. This frees them from household chores to become employed, and men are not required to "help out." Men, in turn, have their duties, which do not overlap with their wives'. Single, skilled women either can afford to hire help or have a relative help for free. If their children are large enough, they, too, can do chores.

Unskilled women depend on friends and relatives for getting household tasks done. They cannot hire domestics (see table 3). Few of these women have repairs made, and when they do they are done by males—either a relative, a boyfriend, or, on rare occasions, a hired man. Repairs are expensive, and since the income level of the unskilled women is far below that of the skilled women, they are not considered a priority. Only roughly half of the women have yardwork to do. Having a

Table 3

All Unskilled Women by Household Tasks, Performance of Task by Sex, and Relationship to Informant ($N=11$)

Tasks	In-formant	Relative		Children		Friend		Informant and Relatives		Other
		F	M	F	M	F	M	F	M	
Cooking	5	2	. . .	. . .	. . .	. . .		4	. . .	. . .
Cleaning	5	1	. . .	. . .	. . .	. . .		4	. . .	. . .
Shopping	5	1	. . .	. . .	. . .	1		4	. . .	. . .
Washing	6	. . .	. . .	. . .	. . .	. . .		4	. . .	
Ironing	5	. . .	. . .	. . .	. . .	. . .		5	. . .	. . .
Repairs	0	. . .	1	. . .	. . .	. . .		. . .	. . .	1
Lawn (yardwork) . . .	2	. . .	1	1	. . .	. . .		. . .	. . .	1
Gardening	4	. . .	. . .	. . .	. . .	. . .		2	. . .	1

lawn assumes that one has both spare time and money to plant grass and shrubs. Unlike the skilled women, the unskilled women usually do their own gardening. Vegetable gardening is an essential part of many unskilled women's subsistence. So, if a male is not present, gardening cannot go undone the way repairs can.

Male children are not enlisted to ease the burden of the working unskilled woman. While talking to informants, I found that they themselves discourage male participation at an early age, cultivating a kind of relationship in which the boys are made to feel like pampered strangers in the household, catered to by mothers and sisters. The girls are trained to be hard workers, both inside and outside the home—responsible, dependable, tolerant, adept in domestic skills, and loyal to their kin group. Consequently, when the males grow up they will expect a similar kind of treatment from their wives or girlfriends, who will be trained to give it to them. A Monserration woman sums up the dichotomy of sex roles:

> Women do run the households. West Indian men don't like to do any work at all either. A lot of West Indian men like to drink. Those that do work to support their families usually do not make enough to support their drinking habits *and* their families. So women have to go to work too. Some of them who have no education or who can't get jobs as domestics go out and plant a garden or do farming to make ends meet. Not only do these women work all day, but they come home and cook for their families too. They have to do it to keep the family going. Women are used to supporting themselves, so they do it when the men are here and when the men are gone as well. They tell their daughters not to depend on men, but on themselves. They should tell the sons to have responsibilities, but they don't. It is the women who become responsible.

A vocal male nationalist also commented on the enormous responsibilities that women have: "Men here are basically lazy—they have it too easy. There is no stress placed upon production among men. So they do a nominal amount of work. As a result, women have worked out a system wherein they have to provide for children twenty-four hours a day. For men, this is not so. After work he comes home and relaxes." Another informant has a teenage daughter and a son in his early twenties. The daughter has a job as a clerk in a store in Plymouth, the capital town of Montserrat; the son is a "sweet man"[11] and does little work: "My son used to help me build the room on my house, but he is a 'sweet man' now. He don't have no money, but he won't work. When he comes home he gets his guitar and he sits and plays. I tell him that I want him to give

11. "Sweet man" refers to men who are lovers, men who love a lot of women and move on to the next: a kind of "ladies' man."

me money to buy food and things—and he gets mad and moves out; but I don't care."

In the cycle of socializing children, both male and female, we can observe the actual perpetuation of the conflict between the ideal and actual sex roles that children will take on as adults. Girls are taught strategies to insure their survival and maintenance whether males are present or not. Boys, on the other hand, are treated as guests. The main reason women say they do this is that it assures a mother her son's economic and emotional loyalty in her old age. Ideally, mothers believe their sons will have a good "position" (job) in life and that they will dote on an aged mother who may have no man of her own to depend on. Sisters do it because they say they need to have a man around to help them. But, due to the lack of economic alternatives these working-class men will have to face in life, they are not being socialized by their mothers to survive. Girls are actually being better equipped to survive, although it is still ideally believed and valued that men should be economically superior at providing and at decision making.

This kind of sex role training does in fact influence courtship and conjugal ties. Working-class women know they cannot always depend on males in the role of husband-father for economic and emotional support, so they take what they can get from their conflicted situation. They may form a series of "friending" relationships with men for sex, presents, and status. While a man may not be able to provide for a woman economically, her status in her circle of friends is enhanced if she can "hold a man" and keep him satisfied sexually.

Marriage is perceived by the majority of working-class women in my study as undesirable because it restricts their alternatives. If they married, they would have to be economically dependent upon and loyal to *one* man. While this may work for middle-class married women whose husbands have more steady jobs and incomes to help support a family, it would be a "dead end" for most young working-class women. They would not be able to form "friending" relationships with other men nor would they be able to expect a great deal of assistance from their kin groups.

Ideally, working-class women have the same value for males as middle-class women. They believe that men should take care of women and their children. But, in reality, working-class males in Monserrat have a difficult time finding employment. The alternative is, of course, migration to find jobs. Most of the men who migrate are forced to leave their families behind. Some of them send remittances to their families;[12] some do not. In their mates' absence, women must work. And, because there is no male present in the role of husband-father, she usually makes the decisions as head of the household. Whether men are absent or

12. See Philpott (n. 7 above).

sporadically employed, women tend to form and to maintain very strong bonds with their kin (usually female) as a source of reassurance as well as a ready source for financial assistance. This strong pull toward the kin group tends to make conjugal bonds weaker.[13] I am not suggesting that women do not form love relationships and sexual relationships with men but rather that these relationships are generally shorter and less binding than ties with their kin group. As a result, while the majority of women in the working class may ideally consider themselves subordinate to men (i.e., they may believe men are supposed to take care of them and make decisions for them), in reality, it is not true.

Here a tension between ideology and reality occurs. Both men and women are socialized to believe that men are superior, but one man cannot provide for a family because he has little or no political and economic control and no access to centers of power. A man may even be dependent upon his female kin for support. Working-class women can and do take care of themselves economically. (The frustration that stems from lack of access to political and economic power is also reported for working-class black males in the United States by Liebow and Hannerz, and from other areas of the West Indies by Wilson and Dirks.)[14] An argument that working-class women are not bound by the same social restrictions as middle-class women and therefore there is little sex role conflict between women and men at this level is not borne out completely. There is, in fact, conflict for several reasons: (1) both males and females are aware of the cultural ideal for the role of the male as provider and protector, but since males cannot live up to this expectation, women must assume this responsibility; (2) due to migration of the male labor force, both historical and contemporary, males are not often physically present to assume their roles and women have to take over; (3) last, and probably the most important, women are actually perpetuating the ideology that males should provide economically for their mothers and sisters while they are not preparing them to do so. Instead of teaching

13. For data on black women in the United States, see Joyce Aschenbrenner, *Lifelines: Black Families in Chicago* (New York: Holt, Rinehart & Winston, 1975); and Carol B. Stack, "Sex Role and Survival Strategies in an Urban Black Community," in *Women, Culture and Society,* ed. Michelle Zimbalist Rosaldo and Louise Lamphere (Stanford, Calif: Stanford University Press, 1974), pp. 113–28. For data on Navajo women, see Louise Lamphere, "Strategies, Cooperation and Conflict among Women in Domestic Groups," in ibid., pp. 97–112. See Chinas (n. 2 above) on women in Mexico. See also Nancie Solien Gonzalez, "Toward a Definition of Matrifocality," in *Afro-American Anthropology,* ed. Norman Whitten and John Szwed (New York: Free Press, 1970), pp. 231–43; Michael Young and Peter Willmont, *Family and Kinship in East London* (New York: Penguin Books, Pelican Books, 1962).

14. Elliot Liebow, *Talley's Corner* (Boston: Little, Brown & Co., 1967); Ulf Hannerz, *Soulside: Enquiries into Ghetto Culture and Community* (New York: Columbia University Press, 1969); Peter Wilson, "Caribbean Crews: Peer Groups and Male Society," *Caribbean Studies* 10, nos. 3–4 (1971): 18–34; and Robert Dirks, "Networks, Groups and Adaptation in an Afro-Caribbean Community," *Man* 7, no. 4 (1972): 568–85.

them responsibility, independence, and flexibility, the way they teach their girls, they are smothering them with attention. While they (mothers) are socializing females to take care of themselves, the males with whom they are to interact and ideally depend on as husband-fathers have not been taught those things. A cycle goes on. Both men and women learn contradictory ideal sex roles that they cannot fulfill.

Implications for Future Research

Some other approaches to the study of female economic contribution and decision making should now be undertaken. For example, studies of women's roles in politics and community affairs would tell us to what extent, cross-culturally, women participate in official and unofficial policymaking. Studies of kinship relationships and networks provide natural settings in which to study female status, as it is often through the kin group that women develop and maintain a sense of solidarity, continuity, and status.[15] The study of friendships would be another fruitful area of inquiry. With whom women associate is important, because it is one way of determining the degree of alternatives that women have in a culture and the degree to which the sexes are segregated socially.[16] But perhaps most important, the investigation of female status through religion and other symbolic systems such as myth and ritual provides insight into how and why ideologies such as male dominance are started, internalized, and perpetuated.

Department of Anthropology
California State Polytechnic University
Pomona, California, U.S.A.

15. Elizabeth Bott, *Family and Social Network,* 2d ed. (New York: Free Press, 1972); Gonzalez; Yolanda Murphy and Robert Murphy, *Women of the Forest* (New York: Columbia University Press, 1974); Stack (n. 13 above); Joyce A. Ladner, *Tomorrow's Tomorrow: The Black Woman* (New York: Doubleday & Co., 1971); and Aschenbrenner (n. 13 above).

16. See Bott.

Migrants and Women Who Wait

Women and Men, Power and Powerlessness in Lesotho

Martha Mueller

The problem this paper will address concerns the assumption made in recent literature on women that women's power and status are less than that of men in the same group, primarily as a result of less female participation in the public sphere.[1] Furthermore, it is assumed that low female public participation stems from male domination of and female exclusion from this sphere. This view presumes that valued resources—whatever their nature—are more plentiful in public than in private life. The argument I wish to make here is that village public life is not always an avenue through which effective strategies can be carried out. Social change can entail a devaluation of local resources so that participation as a "social adult" does not necessarily reap desired rewards. The differing natures of public spheres must be taken into account before assumptions as to the benefits of participation are made.

The thesis of this paper is that, while women in Lesotho, where my research was done, are fully integrated into the public life of the village, while their contributions to extradomestic relations are made explicit, while they are part of a strong female village network, they still perceive their role as wives to be far more important than their role as village members or Lesotho citizens. This perception stems from the realization that public participation offers few means by which a woman can change her life. Her husband's income is her primary vehicle for change. Her

1. Particularly Michelle Zimbalist Rosaldo, "Woman, Culture, and Society: A Theoretical Overview," and Peggy R. Sanday, "Female Status in the Public Domain," both in *Woman, Culture, and Society,* ed. Michelle Zimbalist Rosaldo and Louise Lamphere (Stanford, Calif.: Stanford University Press, 1975).

strategies, then, revolve around control of her immediate family. She is not excluded from a male-dominated public sphere; rather, she turns from it. My view is that the strategies open to women and men are determined primarily by Lesotho's relationship with South Africa. The former's extreme dependence—economic, social, political, and psychological—has created a situation in which valued objects and the means of attaining them are defined from without Lesotho. An analysis of male-female relations in Lesotho must be made in light of South Africa's exploitation of Lesotho as a labor reserve. Use of this broader framework demonstrates that the black-white distinction or conflict is a more powerful determinant of social relations than the male-female. Because a rural Mosotho's[2] choices are strictly delimited and defined by South African hegemony, male and female roles, strategies, and status cannot begin to be understood from within Lesotho itself. What emerges is a picture of the powerlessness of both Basotho men and women in relation to white South Africa.

This is not to say that there is not a pattern of female subordination in Lesotho or that this subordination cannot be found in indigenous patterns of behavior. It can, however, be more thoroughly understood with reference to the racial domination which prevails in South Africa than with reference to these indigenous male-female roles and behavior. Furthermore, it is difficult, perhaps impossible, to ascertain whether Basotho men or women suffer more from white domination. The different kinds of exploitation to which they are subject in many ways shape their relationship to each other. In southern Africa, as elsewhere, race is a more powerful factor than sex in the determination of social relations.

Rural Lesotho has strong political and economic links to both Maseru, the capital and only urban area of Lesotho, and the Republic of South Africa, which surrounds Lesotho and provides employment for 95 percent of Basotho cash earners.[3] These intra- and internation linkages have profound ramifications for rural women's power. Basotho men between the ages of eighteen and forty-five spend twelve to twenty-four months at a time working in the mines of South Africa, thereby leaving villages with a substantial numerical predominance of women. This migration, though it has increased in recent years, has been going on since the mid-nineteenth century. It is female rootedness

2. *Basotho* is used to refer to more than one person; *Mosotho* is the singular form of *Basotho; Sesotho* refers to the language spoken and the cultural heritage.

3. For a fascinating and complete account of the evolution of Lesotho from a country which made substantial profits from the export of its agricultural produce to an importer of basic foodstuffs, see Colin Murray, "Keeping House in Lesotho: A Study on the Impact of Oscillating Migration" (Ph.D. diss., Cambridge University, 1976). Michael Ward has stated that 95 percent of Lesotho's exports go to South Africa, sometimes for reexport, while 75–90 percent of its imports come from the Republic (Michael Ward, "Economic Independence for Lesotho?" *Journal of Modern African Studies* 5 [1967]: 363).

in rural life which allows women considerable power within a village. It is the extreme poverty of Lesotho which necessitates the extensive male participation in the South African economy. And it is the combination of large-scale migration, with the upward spiral in mine wages, the increasing inability of Lesotho to support herself agriculturally, and the authoritarian and potentially explosive political situation in Lesotho which depletes village life of vitality and valuable resources.

The village is not perceived by its residents as a locus for change or innovation; rather, it is seen as a "suburb" of South Africa. Life can be improved only when a man earns enough to modernize his home, educate his children, and perhaps save some of his earnings. These aspirations can be satisfied only by participation in a nonvillage-based, in fact a non-Lesotho-based, economy. Mutual aid and cooperation are patchwork efforts at best, to be partaken of only as long as one is poor and thus dependent enough to need them.

* * *

The research for this paper was carried out from June 1974 through November 1975,[4] during which time I lived in two villages: Ha Monyane, a village of 892 people in the southern part of Lesotho (the nearest town is four miles away and contains about 5,000 people), and Koali, a village of 264 people, fifteen miles from Maseru, a city of approximately 25,000 people.[5] Lesotho is a tiny country—11,716 square miles—and has 1.1 million inhabitants, the vast majority of whom are members of the Basotho tribe. At any given time, however, close to 40 percent of the working-age male population resides in the Republic of South Africa.

Within Lesotho, the Basotho are primarily engaged in agriculture. Sorghum and maize are the subsistence crops; while potatoes, beans, wheat, and peas are sometimes, though not often, grown as cash crops. No land is privately owned. Ideally fields are allocated by the chief to a man when he marries. Until recently each Mosotho had an average of three fields, and once allocated the fields were his for life.

Seahlolo (roughly, sharecropping) and *matsema* (work parties) are the forms of cooperation for clearing and plowing fields, planting and harvesting crops. *Seahlolo* takes place when two people, usually women and as often nonkin as kin, agree to cooperate in the production of a crop for a season. The crop will be divided between the two. The agreement lasts for only one season, though once one has found a suitable partner the cooperation often recurs for years. In general, it is the wife who makes

4. Fieldwork was supported by a grant from the American Association of University Women.

5. Village names are fictitious.

the arrangements and then informs her absent husband, by letter, of her decision. He rarely objects. *Seahlolo* is not engaged in enthusiastically. It involves, in a Mosotho's view, the loss of half of one's crop; but it is a necessity imposed on the woman unable to provide the seeds, oxen, and land for raising a crop.

When a woman wants her field cleared or her maize harvested, she can either notify friends or people in general that she is having a work party on a certain day, or she can pay people in cash or kind for their work. In the first case, it is her responsibility to provide a small-scale feast, for which she must have enough extra money or food. While men participate in the frequent work parties, it is always the women who organize them. In the second case, a woman will pay a small amount of money or a measure of grain for a certain amount of work. The payment is more often in kind than in cash.

While it is the women who organize *seahlolo* and *matsema,* few of them do the plowing. Sons or returned husbands are most often responsible for this. In terms of time spent and energy consumed, however, women are the primary cultivators and, aside from child care and domestic maintenance, spend most of their time in agricultural activity, which brings them into constant and necessary contact with other villagers. It does not, however, yield any cash. In fact it does not yield even adequate food for a family. Most women say that they have to purchase extra sorghum and maize to supplement what they grow.[6]

International migration removes the men from the process of agricultural production, yet because they do not go with their families to an urban center in Lesotho there is no increase there in the demand for agricultural goods; there is little market for cash crops; there is little impetus for any kind of agricultural revolution in the countryside. Per capita agricultural production decreases annually in Lesotho,[7] where the land is becoming increasingly poor because of extensive erosion each year. Population pressure has made it impossible for every married man to receive land. Twenty percent of the households in Ha Monyane and 11 percent in Koali are landless.

The only ongoing activity which involves a substantial number of people from each village is the communal garden. The one in Ha Monyane combines a garden begun in 1963 by a small group of women and a second begun in 1965, primarily by men. Now there are sixty-five garden members, only three of whom are men and only twenty of whom

6. For an analysis of the way in which migration reinforces the agricultural decline of Lesotho, see J. Williams, "Lesotho, Economic Implications of Migrant Labor," *South African Journal of Economics,* vol. 39 (June 1971).

7. In 1965, the average supply per person of maize, wheat, and sorghum grown in Lesotho was 295.5 kilograms. In 1970, it was 242.7 (see A. M. Monyake, "Lesotho: Land, Population and Food," in *Report of the National Population Symposium* [Maseru: Bureau of Statistics, 1974]).

are regularly active. The members of the garden meet weekly, at best, for only a few hours. Half the garden is a communal plot, cared for by all members. The money earned from selling the vegetables of this portion is used for seeds and for oil to help run the irrigation machine. The other half of the garden consists of individual plots. The money each woman earns from selling the vegetables for her plot is primarily used for small, daily necessities. There is not enough for saving or investment.

While it has always been difficult to maintain the enthusiasm and energy of garden members, the problem has worsened in recent years. Most of the blame is placed on "politics," a subject discussed in detail below. Apathy and lack of interest seem to be more prevalent than political antagonism, though it is very possible that the antagonism predisposes people to apathy.

Women are, then, the more active participants in village cooperative structures. The absence of the men has left them in charge of subsistence production, which is in turn carried out with the aid of others. The garden, besides yielding some money, is an arena in which women have learned to organize and work together toward a specified goal. In 1963 when the garden was first organized, a committee of men was selected to oversee the affairs of the women, who were expected to disagree among themselves and therefore be unable to administer the garden successfully. The men's committee no longer exists; yet when the work input of the garden falls to a dangerously low level, it is the authority of the chief, not of the executive committee members (all women), which brings the women back to work. This authority, however, is a function of the chief's position rather than his sex. His authority is also necessary to mobilize men or to terminate disputes among them. Nevertheless, the belief that women are spiteful, bad spirited, and jealous is often expressed by both women and men. Until twenty years ago, women settled disputes among themselves under the leadership of the chief's wife. This practice was terminated because settlement almost never occurred; the women did not respect each other or the chief's wife enough to stop fighting. At a certain point, they were brought under the authority of the chief's court. Only then would they obey.

The belief that women are more spiteful and less trustworthy than men may stem in part from the fact that the women live permanently in Ha Monyane and Koali, while the men only visit and retire there. Especially in a society in which there is such a wide gap between what is known to be possible for others (through exposure to the wealth of South Africa) and what is possible for Basotho, there are tensions generated which no villager can resolve.[8] Hence there are often conflicts, disputes, and general distrust among the women.

8. Sandra Wallman, *Take out Hunger: Two Case Studies of Rural Development in Basutoland* (London: Athlone Press, 1969).

The most frequently stated reason for intravillage conflict is "politics." "Before politics came, everything was fine in Ha Monyane." To summarize briefly, Lesotho became independent in 1966. At that time, the Basotho National party (BNP), a conservative and Catholic-based party, came into power. There was another election in 1970. When it became evident that the Basotho Congress party, a more radical, Pan-Africanist and Protestant-based party, was victorious, the prime minister declared the elections invalid and instituted a state of emergency. There was at this time substantial violent repression in various parts of the country. In 1974 there was an attempted coup which, though aborted, resulted in violence. Politics has bitterly divided people, though it is unclear whether the divisions at the village level rest on substantial policy differences. However, the acerbity of political divisions has rendered community self-help projects very difficult to effect. This bitterness, though it has subsided a good deal recently, reinforces the other processes which are devitalizing the public life of Basotho villagers.

Richard Weisfelder has asserted that the problems faced by the Lesotho government are in part caused by its profound dependence on South Africa.[9] Basotho political groups often accept labels placed on each other's ideologies and strategies by South African sources and blame each other for problems the solutions to which do not lie within Lesotho. The powerlessness has led to an ideological rigidity which has prevented the resolution of certain social conflicts. If, as Weisfelder maintains, all substantive decisions made by the government of Lesotho involve serious issues of foreign policy,[10] it is not difficult to comprehend a South African interest in and desire for some say—whether recognized or not—in these decisions.

Despite the crises of the political regime, the BNP has sought to establish village committees through which, ideally, the people speak to the government but which in fact are instruments of control. What is significant about these committees is that their membership is predominantly female. In Ha Monyane, eleven out of twelve of the members are women; in Koali, five out of five; while nine out of nine of the chief's advisers are men in the former village and four out of five in the latter. The reasons given for the fact that the chief's advisers are almost exclusively male is "Sesotho tradition." The reasons given for female predominance in the Village Development Committees (VDC) are that (1) the government, partially in response to female discontent, is insisting that women be granted status equal to that of men and (2) more women than men are members of the BNP. There is some truth to both assertions. A third village committee, the Land Allocation Committee (LAC),

9. Richard Weisfelder, *Defining National Purpose in Lesotho* (Athens: Ohio University Center for International Studies, 1969).

10. Richard Weisfelder, "Power Struggle in Lesotho," *Africa Report* 12 (January 1967): 7.

recently formed by the government and supposedly nonpolitical, serves to advise and limit the chief in his role as land allocator. The LAC is associated in the minds of village residents with his advisers, and thus most who are elected are men. However, the government appoints half the members and has seen fit to choose women at least as often as men. There is little resistance to or protest against women's entering these public decision-making roles.

So distrusted is the VDC because of its identification with the government that it cannot serve any innovative function within the village. The most active VDC members are in close touch with the political officials in the nearby town. They inform on and are informed of security risks in the area. A further responsibility of the VDC is to issue letters for men who wish to work as laborers on government projects. Party membership is specified in the letter, and it is important to be a member of the right party to secure one of these very scarce local jobs. A Mosotho woman once stated that the apartheid of politics in Lesotho is worse than the apartheid of race in South Africa.

While it is undeniable that the political situation in Lesotho is not conducive to any kind of genuine participation, it is the women who are participating in the more "modern" political structures, those of the nation; while the men are more active in chiefly village-based duties, which are slowly being eroded by the national government. The implications of these different kinds of participation for the question of women and power remains to be seen. It depends a good deal on the unpredictable course of national politics in Lesotho. Should an opportunity for effective participation emerge, women's experience and training in the management of the communal gardens, as well as their more limited experience in the VDC, will serve them well.[11]

Two facts about female power and status emerge in the examination of women's role in the public domain as VDC or garden-committee members. First, women are elected for offices according to the same criteria as men. They are chosen primarily on the basis of *kelello* or good sense, which to a Mosotho means the willingness to cooperate. There is little concern with clan, length of residence in the village, religion, wealth, or level of education when elections are held. Ability to lead well and peacefully is the most frequently cited quality necessary for any public duty. Second, wives have a status independent of that of their husbands, though this public status is less important to women than status derived from private wealth, which usually depends upon a husband's income. While some active women have husbands who serve or have served as advisers, many do not. At one point, informants were asked to rank residents of Ha Monyane according to their importance in

11. Pre-1970 days, when all political parties were active, witnessed extensive female actvity in the form of committee work and campaigning.

village life. Husbands and wives were not ranked together, nor were wives consistently placed higher or lower than their husbands. This was true with one exception. One young woman insisted that importance was determined by wealth and thus ranked according to that criterion. Husbands and wives were then placed together.

A necessary ingredient to any understanding of the power of the advisers, the VDC or the LAC, is the villagers' knowledge of them. Most people could name two advisers at best; few could name more than one or two members of the VDC, and often one committee was confused with another. One woman stated that she had no desire to be a member of any committee, since members are resented by the people they try to lead. In general, people were unaware of or uninterested in the membership and activities of these various groups. To a woman, each member of the VDC and the garden committee claimed that she did not want this position, that she assumed it only because she was elected and thus had no choice. An active member of the VDC asserted that, while her enthusiasm stemmed in part from her belief in the government, she was primarily concerned with obtaining a government scholarship for her daughter to attend teachers college. The secretary of the garden committee, a woman with an invalid husband, six school-age daughters, and one son at the mines, had worked devotedly for the garden. When an opportunity arose for her to work at the local general store and earn much-needed money, she left her job as secretary. No one objected. While the ideal of cooperation is espoused by everyone, it is understood to be a poor substitute for the ability to earn money.

Men and women have separate avenues by which they can earn money, the male avenue being by far the more lucrative. Women often sell fruit and vegetables from the gardens around their homes or raise and sell pigs and chickens. They also brew and sell beer or sell handicrafts. Occasionally they are able to sell some small portion of their crops. With a few exceptions, most women sell irregularly to their neighbors on a small-scale basis. The transactions usually take place when a woman has a special household or medical need. In Koali more women sell their handiwork and vegetables in Maseru, since there is more of a market there. A few were engaged in part-time domestic service. Buying is carried on as much as possible in town, and there are many and endless conversations comparing prices at various stores. Nevertheless, the village of Ha Monyane is able to support two general stores and Koali one. They are slightly more expensive than the stores in town, but far more convenient. When a purchase of more than few rands (R 1 = $1.15) is to be made, however, the time and energy for a trip to town, either by bus or on foot, are found. As more money comes in and as expensive purchases increase, more women are spending more of their money and hence more time in town. Within the village, men can earn a rand or so a day by plowing and by building houses or fences.

Often older men, retired from the mines, build in villages other than their own, but despite their skill they earn an irregular and scant livelihood. The demand for their services is fast rising, however, because of the rise in mine wages. A small number of men work installing water pipes and earn R 0.60 a day. It is regular, fairly long-term employment, and for men without cattle or construction skills it is the only kind of local employment available. Another job, related to the building trade and taken on by older men, is crushing stones, back-breaking, eye-damaging, and low-paying work (R 6 per 100 stones crushed).

For both men and women, local employment and locally generated income are insecure and scarce. Proximity to Maseru and, to a lesser degree, a town provides some employment or market for villagers, yet the bulk of female cash earning still takes place within the village. Men, on the other hand, have more of an intervillage economic network, especially in building. The house-building business has quadrupled in the last year, thus creating a large demand for that skill.[12] The road in the southern half of Lesotho will be paved next year—a project which will provide jobs for a number of men at R 1.50 a day. Since the wages in Lesotho cannot compare with those offered at the mines, most of the laborers will be older men or men at home on leave.

Women too profit from the influx of money, though their profit comes not so much from their own income as from their husbands'. While men sell services which have come to be much more in demand recently, the goods that women sell are not undergoing a similar rise in popularity. Women have regarded their own economic activity as patchwork, as a way of surviving those frequent small emergencies when no money is coming from the husband. The necessity for this kind of earning still exists, since men continue to bring the bulk of their earnings home with them rather than sending it home on a monthly basis. Most of this money goes to major purchases: home improvement, school fees, clothes, blankets, or livestock. Not a great deal more money is available for the goods which village women sell.

Women cannot live outside Lesotho, since South Africa will not permit non–South African Basotho women to enter for work, and living conditions at the mines preclude a man's bringing his wife with him. The average miner spends 35 percent of his working life in the mines, a total of approximately fifteen years away.[13] A Mosotho must, according to South African law, work in the mines rather than the urban areas, where pay is better and there is more freedom of choice as to living arrangements. He lives at the mine compound in a dormitory type of room with

12. Private communication from the manager of construction-material sales at the main store in a town near Ha Monyane.

13. M. McDowell, "Basotho Labour in South African Mines—an Empirical Study," mimeographed (Maseru Bureau of Statistics, October 1973).

five to nineteen other men. No women are allowed in the compound. His room, board, and health care are provided for him free of charge.[14]

A miner can receive his wages in three ways. First, he can be paid directly and thus be able to spend his earnings at his place of work. Second, there is a deferred-pay plan, by which a Mosotho must agree to put a certain percentage of his wages in the Lesotho National Bank. There his money will earn interest, and he will collect the money and interest upon his return home.[15] Third, a man may remit a certain portion of his wages home to his family while he continues to work at the mines.

Minimum wages increased by over 300 percent from June 1, 1972, to June 1, 1975, from R 0.50 to R 2.20 per day.[16] Deferred pay to Lesotho was R 2.5 million more in 1974 than in 1973, and remittance was R 1.5 million more. Though more is being remitted, the majority of men do not remit more frequently. Most remit between the fourth and seventh month of service. The R 1.5 million increase in remittance breaks down to a R 2–4 monthly increase per individual remitter, thus raising the average from approximately R 4.50 to R 7.[17] The miners are tending to spend more at the mines and to bring more home with them.

By holding on to most of his money through deferred pay, a miner retains primary control of the cash expenditure of his family. While his wife possesses considerable power in daily decisions, she needs his support for any major changes to be effected. If she wants to modernize her home or send a child to secondary school, she must obtain the money from her husband. She can, however, exert considerable influence over him in that she maintains his assets and builds his "nest egg" while he is absent. A Mosotho must return to Lesotho upon retirement from the

14. For an excellent and detailed study of a miner's life, see Francis Wilson, *Labour in the South African Gold Mines, 1911–1969* (Cambridge: Cambridge University Press, 1972).

15. The requirement that each Mosotho miner place a certain proportion of his wages in the Lesotho National Bank was instituted in 1975. Previously, a miner could defer his wages through his recruiting agency. The decision, announced by the Lesotho government with no previous consultation with any of the migrants, caused riots and unrest at the mines. Several Basotho were killed. Many were injured, and many more returned home until the trouble died down. The severity of the clashes was due to the fact that most of the miners are supporters of the opposition Congress party. They did not want their money placed in a bank where it might be used to increase the already extensive security forces in Lesotho.

16. *Financial Mail* (May 30, 1975).

17. This information was graciously provided for me by Michael Hobson, one of the managers of the Mine Labor Organization, the primary recruiting agency in Lesotho. To put these upward trends in perspective, some of Wilson's observations are important. In 1889, the ratio of average white cash earnings to black was approximately 7.5:1; in 1969, it was 20.1:1. Further, in real terms, black cash earnings in 1969 were no higher and possibly even lower than they had been in 1911. For whites, on the other hand, real cash earnings had increased by 70 percent (see Wilson).

mines, as there is absolutely no provision for unemployed Basotho in South Africa. The quality of the home that he returns to depends very much on the mutual effort of him and his wife. It is difficult for both men and women to end a marriage in Lesotho; the woman has almost no viable alternative means of self-support, and her natal family is most probably poor and dependent on the meager resources it can glean from its married sons.[18] Similarly, a man is denied fields if he is unmarried; and he has no one to tend his home, livestock, or children should his wife leave. This mutual dependence preserves a power balance between the husband and wife in the domestic or private domain.

Husbands and wives espouse similar goals, since they share both the desire for social security and the means of attaining it. Both want a "modern" home, a well-tended herd (though this is increasingly replaced by the desire for a bank account) and loyal—in terms of financial support—children. The conflict between man and wife centers on the woman's need for cash for daily family supplies versus the man's desire and need for entertainment at the mines. The living conditions at the mines and the distance of a man from his home only exacerbate this need. The substantial wage increases, then, do not necessarily relieve a woman's insecurity. Nevertheless, because the women are cut off from any profitable economic activity, their only access to the riches of South Africa, however limited, is as wives.[19]

The depletion of natural resources, the authoritarian political regime, and the increasing rewards which issue from labor migration combine to devitalize Basotho village life in which women are the primary participants. Women are the organizers of and participants in the cooperative activities surrounding agricultural production. They make most of the decisions concerning crop production, even more so now that more men are migrating for longer periods.[20] Yet the benefits derived from this kind of work are declining. Subsistence output, though still necessary for survival, is increasingly and necessarily being subsidized by cash purchases. Reliance on cash is increasing; reliance on crops, decreasing. While there exists a structure of cooperation and

18. The decline of the extended family, along with the increasing dependence of wives upon their husbands, results in near destitution for elderly people, particularly women since they live longer. Once a man marries, the demands of his own family are such that he gives very little support to his parents. Many parents feel that daughters rather than sons should be educated: "A son forgets, a daughter never does."

19. Young unmarried women and their mothers, however, see marriage as a trap in which a woman is forced to be dependent on her husband, who, "as soon as he marries you, begins to play with you" (i.e., he does not send enough money). For their daughters, mothers want an education and often a single life, since marriage still means many children. Poverty and lack of birth control often disallow extensive education and necessitate marriage.

20. In 1974, 68 percent of migrants exceeded one year in service, compared with 51 percent in 1973. Again, I am indebted to Hobson for this information.

reciprocity around consumption of crops, cash is regarded as the very private property of the one who earns it. It is to be jealously guarded and protected. With the growing reliance on cash, male work is assuming more importance; female, less; and women are isolated in the countryside with no access to wage-earning activities.

Aspirations are rising with the increased income derived from the mines. The long-term exposure of the Basotho to the lives of whites in South Africa and in Lesotho has definitively shaped the nature of these aspirations. Women know what a modern house should look like, how children should be dressed, how they themselves should be dressed. Fashion is determined by power, and power lies in the hands of white people. To achieve a good life is to live as much as possible like a white woman. The only way a Mosotho woman can begin to emulate a white woman is through her husband and the money he makes.

While a woman is exceedingly aware of her dependence on her husband and of his erratic and often less than adequate financial contribution to the family, she sees her primary loyalty as that of a wife. She does not tell anyone of her husband's arrival and departure for fear of a hex being put on him by another woman who is jealous of his job and the money he brings in. If she is one of the few wives who knows her husband's wages, she tells no one. Other husbands may lie about their wages or may spend them all on beer, but hers does not. Her problems as a wife are private ones. Women do not cooperate with each other as wives; they do not, as a group, try to protect their interests as wives. They perceive themselves as competitors with each other, though the prizes for which they compete are not ones over which they have power, not even through their husbands. A man's income is determined by the South African Chamber of Mines. He *may* earn more or less depending on his education, his age, his length of service, his health; but he too is powerless to determine the scope, nature, or rewards of his economic activity. Yet it is this activity which provides some escape from poverty for a Mosotho woman; it is this activity which provides access to "modernity" in one form or another. She does not find this access either through the cooperative structures of village life or the integrative structures of political life. While her power in these areas may grow as absence of husbands and other men increases in time and scale, it is a power within a context of increasing powerlessness. She knows it and acts accordingly.

The tragedy of Lesotho is that whatever security or power a Mosotho gains from the resources acquired in South Africa totally depends on South Africa's continuing need for Basotho labor. The mining interests in South Africa are increasingly nervous about their dependence on foreign labor, and their recent wage increases for migrant workers are only part of an apparently successful effort by the mining companies to recruit more South African Africans to work in the mines. Thus the security of Basotho men and women is in jeopardy.

The question of female power and/or powerlessness in Lesotho, then, cannot be answered through the public/private-domain paradigm. Basotho women, as has been demonstrated, are not confined to the private or domestic sphere. They are in many ways the "keepers of village life." The resources which can be acquired or controlled through this kind of activity are minimal, however. Resources of value lie outside Lesotho's borders, in a public domain open—if only minimally so—to participation by Basotho men only. Women gain access to these resources of value only through effective domestic management, that is, participation in the private domain. This kind of domestic activity, then, affords them greater reward than the public activity open to them. As I have tried to point out, this situation results in large part from the system of apartheid in South Africa. The crucial point is that the traditionally anthropological view of a village as a relatively self-contained unit is no longer adequate. This realization leads to some doubt as to the adequacy of the public/private paradigm in respect to answering the question of female power or powerlessness. Access to valued resources is the crux of the matter, and it is no longer possible to assume their existence in the public domain of village life.

Department of Politics
Brandeis University
Waltham, Massachusetts, U.S.A.

Migrants and Women Who Wait

How African Women Cope with Migrant Labor in South Africa

Harriet Sibisi

Poverty and enforced migratory labor among the indigenous peoples of South Africa are part of an ideology of apartheid. Hilda Bernstein and Liz Clark and Jane Ngobese stress the suffering of African women in apartheid South Africa.[1] My aim is not to add to what these writers have already said but to look at how such women cope and manage to survive in a family situation despite the enormous suffering with which they live.

In speaking about African women and migratory labor, we can divide women into three categories: those who live in the countryside while their menfolk work in the city; those who work in the city while their families are in the countryside; and finally those who, with their families, work in the city and live in the townships. Even the last category of women cannot truly be regarded as urban city dwellers, because their presence in the city is determined by the continued employment of the husband. Should he die, his widow and children must vacate the township house. Thus in practice every African in the township is a migrant of one category or another. This paper is about those women who live in the countryside while their husbands work in the city as migrant laborers.

The Zulu social system is organized on patrilineal lines; descent is through males organized into lineages—the most important group being a lineage segment whose members trace descent to a common grandfather. In order to perpetuate these lineages and maintain continuity

1. H. Bernstein, *For Their Triumphs and for Their Tears* (London: International Defense and Aid Fund, 1975); and L. Clarke and J. Ngobese, *Women without Men* (Durban, 1975).

while the men, the most important members of the corporate group, are away, women have devised various ways of coping with the men's absenteeism. For instance, young men now find it very difficult to meet and court young women. Courtship in my society is, by tradition, quite different from the Western manner of courtship. A Zulu young man makes no dates but, instead, surprises a young woman by waiting for her at a waterhole, on the road to a store, or wherever she is likely to be on her own, away from her parents. On these occasions, using the best phrases and oratory he can master, he tells her of his love for her. The woman responds by ignoring or deprecating him. To demonstrate his sincerity, he persists by trying to get further opportunities to speak to her and to win her heart. Only after several attempts, if it becomes obvious that all his efforts are futile, does he give up. Now that young men do not find time to pursue a girl in this way, their sisters often take over and woo other girls on their behalf, while the brothers always put in an appearance whenever they have an opportunity to return to the countryside. Thus a young woman finds herself acting the role of her brother while simultaneously seeking for herself a suitable husband, who is most of the time represented by his sister.

On marriage a woman joins her husband's family. Marriage in Zulu is not a contractual union between the spouses. A Zulu woman goes on a long journey (*enda*); a man receives her into his patrilineage (*thatha*), where she is expected to continue the descent line of her husband. She gradually becomes incorporated into her husband's group, and in her old age she is a full member. As an ancestress she is considered the mother of her descendants rather than a daughter of her parents in the spirit world. Conceptually she has indeed made a long journey—from her natal family to full membership in her family of procreation.

What is striking in traditional Zulu society is the rarity of broken marriages, despite long periods of separation because of migratory labor. For instance, among 263 married couples within 100 homesteads, there were only five cases of women with broken marriages. The concept of incorporation into a new social group and the value laid on the institution of marriage are crucial in understanding the stability of Zulu marriage. In addition, the fact that a wife has no rights over the children in cases of separation has far-reaching effects in maintaining marriages in spite of long periods of separation. I am not suggesting that the suffering caused by migratory labor be condoned because there are fewer broken marriages than one might expect but that the Zulu notions of marriage cushion the impact of migrant labor.

To understand this we must look briefly at some aspects of the institution of marriage from the woman's point of view. Marriage negotiations tend to stretch over a long period (one to ten years) because of poverty combined with the desire to marry according to traditional rules. Thus men work a long while to raise the funds equivalent to eleven cattle. In addition, the gifts exchanged periodically between the two families are becoming more elaborate and expensive. The result is a prolonged period of betrothal. Very often young women join their husbands' families before all the steps leading to marriage are completed or before the two families are ready to perform the wedding rites, such as slaughtering a special ox or cow provided by the bride's father at the bridegroom's home on the wedding day. If such a beast (*eyokwendisa*) has not been provided, the bride is not truly married. To bridge the gap, a goat is often sacrificed to appease the ancestors and to promise to perform the relevant rites in the future.

Table 1 illustrates the situation of "married" women in the survey I conducted in 1971 among the Nyuswa/Zulu of the Valley of a Thousand Hills. Without exception women who had not had a "complete wedding" in traditional terms did not consider themselves properly married, even in cases in which marriages had been registered in the magistrate's marriage registry office. Women who had only goat sacrifices on marriage or who had had no sacrifice performed at all usually attributed to the anger of the ancestors misfortunes such as sleeplessness at night, feelings of heaviness, or hearing voices whispering in their ears, "Who are you, what are you doing here?" They also reported frequent illness of their children, again as a result of the wrath of ancestors over failure to fulfill marriage rites. These states of mind and interpretations of the causes of illness suggest feelings of insecurity. The situation is aggravated by the fact that these women are living with the families of their husbands—husbands who most of the time are not there.

Although African women show resilience in coping with difficulties of political economics, some nevertheless break down from time to time. In order to understand how women in the countryside handle and contain extreme anxiety, depression, and mental breakdown, some basic cosmological concepts must first be explored. In Zululand we believe that both plant and animal life affect the environment. As countries may differ in flora and fauna, so people may fall ill in a foreign country because they are not adjusted to a strange ecology. Closely related to this

Table 1

Type of Marriage Obligation Fulfilled	*N* Women	%
Full marriage (essential sacrificial ox slaughtered)	166	63
Incomplete marriage (only a goat slaughtered)	45	18
Incomplete marriage (gift exchanges during marriage negotiation but no sacrifice)	42	17
No marriage (no negotiations started, but woman lives at man's home)	5	2
Total	258	100

concept is another, that when in motion both people and animals leave behind something of themselves and absorb something of the atmosphere in which they move. It is this essence left behind which is said to be tracked down by dogs following a criminal (*umkhondo*). Because both men and wild animals traverse strange countries, they may introduce foreign elements which pollute the atmosphere and countryside on their return to Zululand, thus endangering the lives of the local people. Because of these dangers, people are given prophylactic treatment from time to time to immunize them.

Zulu thought portrays the world as basically good but constantly threatened by evil which must be shut out or taken out. Evil is conceptualized among the Zulu as an entity that can be removed and discarded. This is well illustrated in the treatment of certain diseases known as "African diseases." These diseases are closely associated with Zulu morality and world view, both of which are believed to be understood by all Africans south of the Sahara but not by non-Africans. The diseases of this class are in sharp contrast to the "natural" class of diseases which have no cultural base, present themselves only in somatic symptoms, and are treated empirically by medicines believed to be potent and curative. African diseases, on the other hand, need not always manifest themselves in somatic symptoms—misfortunes may also be regarded as symptoms of illness. Medicines for such diseases have no effect outside the ritual context. Such symbolic medicines are characterized by their color—black, red, or white—and used sequentially. The black and red medicines are used to remove evil from the system, while white medicines are used to restore good health or good things of life.

Evil thus removed does not dissipate itself and must therefore be discarded in such a way that it does not harm other people. The best means of disposal is to cast such an evil on a scapegoat animal. Since it is not always possible to have enough animals upon which to cast evil, lesser evil is just thrown away. The dilemma here is how to throw away lesser evil without endangering the lives of other people in the community. Crossroads and highways are popular places for throwing away discarded evil, in the hope that, since these roads are used by strangers on long journeys, *they* will carry away the evil. This may seem unethical, but since strangers are themselves believed to be possible carriers of evil or foreign elements which may endanger the local people the equation becomes justified. This dilemma has been compounded by the disappearance of the Zulu kingdom—wherein through the institution of kingship the whole kingdom was purged at least once a year.

The Zulu believe that the Supreme Being or God (*Umvelinqangi*) lives up above (*ezulwini*) along with a goddess often referred to as the "Princess of the Sky" (*inkosazana yezulu*). The spirits of the deceased live down below and are often referred to as "those down below" (*abaphansi*).

Both deities are remote and rarely invoked; it is the ancestors who are more concerned with the day-to-day affairs of the living.

The World Below is divided into three sections—that of the unborn spirits, that of the recently deceased spirits, and that of the ancestors. When a woman conceives, the biological function is said to be in conjunction with the entry of a spirit from the section of the unborn into her body. Each baby during the first year of its life has a sacrifice (*imbeleko*) performed for it. By this sacrifice the baby is placed under the protection of its parents' ancestors. The child is given not only a social status by being made a child of a definite set of parents but also a ticket of passage which enables it to complete the cycle of life.[2] Thus, if a child dies before the first sacrifice is performed, the spirit returns to the section of the unborn; if the sacrifice has been performed, the spirit will be able to begin the process that will eventually enable it to join the ancestors.

The expectation or, rather, the ideal is that a person grows up to maturity, marries, has children, and dies of old age. Despite having had the first essential sacrifice, however, the deceased does not directly join the section of ancestral spirits. Soon after death the spirit is said to be lonely and unhappy "in a place of wilderness" (*endle*), "in an in-between state" (*esithubeni*). The duration of this isolation depends on the social status of the deceased. Ideally, at the end of this period a sacrifice is performed to integrate the spirit with the rest of the ancestoral spirits, which enables the spirit to be powerful—to bless or punish descendants.

* * *

This cosmology provides the background for a discussion of Zulu notions of spirit possession, some of which, I believe, covertly express levels of mental disturbance. In traditional spirit possession, the spirits said to take possession of a diviner (*isangoma*) are not the unborn or the recently deceased but those which have reached the desired state of spiritual being. Spirits in their completed state as ancestors return to this world through their daughters, not through their wives, mothers, or daughters-in-law. The diviner is possessed by spirits of her own descent group, and because divination is a woman's thing, if a man gets possessed, he becomes a transvestite, since he is playing the role of a daughter rather than that of a son. The spirits are believed to "ride" on the shoulders of the medium and to speak or whisper to her. She hears voices and in this way gets her clairvoyant powers. As a diviner she avoids unclean situations and uses white symbols to promote and emphasize her purity.

2. Through the first sacrifice an adoption of a child is effected; e.g., an illegitimate child of a daughter is placed under the protection of its mother's ancestors. Such a child then becomes the child of its maternal grandparents and calls them mother and father, while its biological mother becomes a sister to it.

At the turn of the century a new type of possession known as *indiki* was experienced in Natal and Zululand.[3] Bryant wrote about its outbreak in 1911 among the Zulu, and Junod reported the same thing among the Thonga in Mozambique in 1913.[4] Both reported it as a new form of spirit possession. It is still regarded as a new form of possession, closely associated with African industrial development. The *indiki* is believed to be the spirit of a deceased person, a spirit which has never been given the necessary sacrifice of integration with the body of other spirits. The people from countries north of South Africa who come to work in the mines often die at their place of work. Their families never know of their deaths and therefore perform none of the rituals necessary to place the spirits in their proper positions in the spirit world. These spirits wander about in desperation and become a menace to the local people by taking possession of them and causing illness. *Indiki* is therefore a male spirit (usually only one) which enters the patient and resides in the chest. The patient then becomes deranged, cries in a deep, bellowing voice, and speaks in a foreign tongue.

The treatment, always given by a diviner who was herself once possessed by *indiki,* involves about three months of initiation into the spirit cult. During this period of initiation, the treatment is calculated to exorcise the alien spirit and replace it with the ancestral male spirit, to protect the patient against future attacks. For this reason the *indiki* initiate uses red emetics to get the alien spirit out and white emetics to arouse her own ancestral spirit. These emetics are used on alternate days during the whole period of initiation. The notion of *indiki* has caused concern about the safety of infants in an environment which has been made dangerous by the presence of alien spirits. This has given rise to a new method of treating newborn infants, calculated to protect them against effects of alien spirits. The treatment, known as *igobongo* because the red and white medicines are prepared in two separate gourds (*amagobongo*), is meant to arouse the infant's male ancestor (to raise *indiki—ukukhiphula indiki*) to take special care of the infant until it passes through the dangerous stage of babyhood.

Neither Bryant nor Junod makes any mention of *ufufunyane.*[5] This suggests that *ufufunyane* is a much later concept. Indeed it is usually associated with the late 1920s and 1930s. A person with *ufufunyane* in its worst form usually behaves as a mentally deranged person would. She

3. The meaning of the term is not known. It is widely used in many language groups in Southern Africa where the same type of possession happens. Occasionally the term *amandawo* is used for *amandiki. Amandawo* seems to be a term related to the Ndjao people who live in Zimbambwe.

4. A. T. Bryant, *Olden Times of Zululand* (London: Longmans, 1929); and H. A. Jonod, *The Life of a South African Tribe* (Neuchâtel: Imprimerie Attinger, 1913), vol. 2.

5. The dictionary translation of *ufufunyane* is "rapidly spreading disease which causes delirium and insanity; type of brain disease, mania, hysteria" (C. M. Doke and B. W. Vilakazi, *Zulu-English Dictionary* [Johannesburg: Witwatersrand University Press, 1953]).

becomes hysterical and weeps aloud uncontrollably, throws herself on the ground, tears off her clothes, runs in a frenzy, and usually attempts to commit suicide. She reacts violently and aggressively to those who try to calm her. The patient is said to be possessed by a horde of spirits of different racial groups. Usually there will be thousands of Indians or whites and some hundreds of Sotho or Zulu spirits. Unlike the treatment for *indiki*, the treatment of *ufufunyane* may be given by any practitioner, that is, either a diviner (*isangoma*) or a male doctor (*iyanga*). When such spirits have been exorcised, they roam the countryside in small bands and attach themselves to people who are not sufficiently fortified against them. This is chance possession, and the attack is less violent or may manifest itself in some form of mild neurosis or mental confusion. *Ufufunyane* possession does not lead to cult membership or to any diagnostic or healing powers.

There is also an ailment among babies connected with *ufufunyane*. This is a condition of malformed placenta known as *ipleti* (a Zuluized form of the English word "plate"). It is said a normal placenta is shaped like a clenched fist, while a malformed placenta is flat and has the circumference of a dinner plate. The *ipleti* is said to have affected babies born in and since the late 1930s. Many elderly women claim that only the children they had in the late 1930s had *ipleti*, while those born before were carried in normal placentas. There are two causes of *ipleti*. If a mother suffers from *ufufunyane* even in a mild form, her baby will be born with *ipleti*. In addition, since the appearance of the notion of malformed placentas, midwives have buried discarded placentas along the main pathways, making it possible for any pregnant woman to step on one and get the condition of *ipleti*.

* * *

There are several things to learn from these different conceptualizations of spirit possession. One is that the notion of evil brought about in the cases of *indiki* and *ufufunyane* is thought of as a violation of the principle of patrilineage. A spirit that takes possession indiscriminately outside the patrilineal-descent principle is thus regarded as evil. The evilness inheres not so much in the spirit itself as in the confusion of categories. In other words, no spirits in their proper place have evil connotations. They only acquire evil connotations if and when they intrude. This intrusion is dramatically emphasized by the very nature of possession, when the alien spirit actually resides within and supersedes the identity and the personality of the patient, who becomes a husk that houses a spirit which speaks in its own voice from within her.

What is illuminating is that possession by alien spirits is associated with changing social circumstances. In the case of *indiki* possession, for instance, the development of the mines resulted in the recruitment of miners from alien cultures north of South Africa. These men came to work for long stretches of time without their families. The danger of intrusion into the family life of the indigenous peoples can be seen in this light as real, if we consider the probability of relationships developing between such alien men and the wives, sisters, and daughters of the Zulu men. Such unions constituted a threat to the stability of the society not only because of differences in culture but because miners were likely to return to their homes when their contracts expired, leaving their Zulu wives and children behind. In this way an element of disorder was introduced. It is significant that in treating *indiki* possession an attempt is made to replace the alien spirit with a male ancestor. This suggests rejection of the alien male and replacement with the native male.

Ufufunyane possession represents yet another dimension of social relations. As industries flourished, towns developed. This meant further intrusions of peoples from overseas, especially with the depression in Europe following World War I. With the increasing mobility and the intensified migratory-labor system, contacts between peoples of various racial groups grew. In addition, Zulus became a threat to one another as they competed for jobs, housing, land, and economic security. The feeling of insecurity grew, and both Indians and whites were seen as a formidable force bent on the disruption of equilibrium in Zulu society. I suggest that the thousands or millions of spirits of various races that are believed to possess an *ufufunyane* sufferer and to show their presence by violent aggression, hysteria, or suicidal tendencies indicate the social disorder which has led to many forms of deprivation for the indigenous peoples in an unequal society such as that of South Africa.

There is yet another important difference between the traditional and the new forms of spirit possession. In the former case, there are relatively few people who become diviners. Since diviners have to go through a long, drawn-out process, possession of this type is gradual. In the case of evil possession, it is sudden and may even assume a form of epidemic in a given area. This sudden and epidemic nature strongly points to the association of evil forms of spirit possession with stresses and strains experienced by people as a group at a particular time.

It would be naive to imagine that the possessed consider themselves as expressing the sociological notions above. However, the diviners' function is to understand the various types of illness, explain the new ones, and find relevant treatment. They have interpreted the manifestations of deviant behavior in such a way that it lends itself to sociological analysis. In examining and analyzing the interpretations of diviners, it is important to remember that there are good as well as evil types of spirit possession and that the diviners are possessed by good spirits. They may be considered to belong to the priestly class. Whereas in some societies a calling to the priesthood is reserved for men only, in other societies such a calling is reserved for women. Looked at in this light, diviners among the Zulu play a role which is set for them by the society for the benefit of the society. They are not primarily looking for outlets in an unequal, male-dominated society, as many anthropologists have suggested.[6]

To attain the status of a diviner, a candidate or neophyte goes through various phases of experience, including abstinence from various pleasures (e.g., drinking, smoking, sexual intercourse, eating certain foods), withdrawal from society, observance of silence, avoidance of unclean situations (such as contact with death), contemplation, and ecstatic singing and dancing. All these experiences are forms of asceticism calculated to achieve a desired contact with the sacred realm, part of a "priestly" behavior pattern.

In many ways similar to the possession of diviners is the temporary possession experienced by the faithful during worship in Zionist or Pentecostal sects. Possession in this category is not as continuous as in the other forms of possession. However, a prophet or prophetess in such sects may be thought of as being in continuous contact with the spirit, in which case the role is more or less identical with that of a diviner.

These traditional, morally acceptable spirit possessions are in sharp contrast to the evil, undesirable, unacceptable possession characterized by *ufufunyane*. In addition, there are the "in-between" forms of possession which may begin as evil and be developed into morally acceptable possession, like the *indiki* type. It must also be kept in mind that traditional possession is by an ancestoral spirit, while *indiki* and *ufufunyane* involve possession by alien spirits.

I. M. Lewis has argued that possession by capricious and evil spirits occurs especially among the weak and down trodden, and through such possession the lowly secure a measure of help and succor.[7] As an instance of this, Lewis cites cases of wives whose husbands provided them with good clothes and food because these items were demanded by the evil spirits possessing the wives. While Lewis's interpretation may apply to occasional instances, I find it difficult to accept as a central theme in explaining evil-spirit possession, partly because it suggests malingering, an attitude which is difficult to measure in a culture which regards the illness as genuine. In addition, the effects of evil spirits are seen by the Zulu as a threat to the whole community, necessitating elaborate and expensive prophylactic treatment for infants, who are believed to be especially in danger.

I therefore suggest that, since the notion of evil possession is a postcolonial concept associated with industrial expansion and migratory

6. M. Gluckman, "Moral Crises: Magical and Secular Solutions," in *The Allocation of Responsibility,* ed. M. Gluckman (Manchester: Manchester University Press, 1972); W. D. Hammond-Tooke, *Bhaca Society* (Cape Town: Oxford University Press, 1962); and S. G. Lee, "Spirit Possession among the Zulu," in *Spirit Mediumship and Society in Africa,* ed. J. Beattie and J. Middleton (New York: Africana Publishing Corp., 1969).

7. I. M. Lewis, *Ecstatic Religion* (Harmondsworth: Penguin Books, 1971).

labor, it may well be that the unsettling conditions of conquest and industrialization have brought about severe stress. I find it significant that most evil spirits are spirits of aliens—a point which indicates the sensitivity of the indigenous peoples to alien intrusions. Seen in this light, evil-spirit possession can be understood as an idiom used to indicate various forms of mental disturbance arising from new demands in a large-scale society.

The Zulu treat mentally disturbed people in such a way that they do not feel responsible for their condition; they are made to feel not that anything is wrong with their minds but that they are the victims of external forces—the intruding alien spirits—which must be removed. In this way, a patient gets the support, sympathy, and attention for which depressed people often long.

Because *ufufunyane* patients are believed to be susceptible to *ufufunyane* attacks even after recovery if provoked or annoyed, those around them take special care to avoid situations which might bring about recurrences. Whisson reports the same concept among the Luo of East Africa, where the patient, although pronounced fit, is treated with respect and consideration lest the dreaded affliction recur.[8] If we accept that spirit possessions of the *ufufunyane* type are symptoms of various forms of depression or nervous breakdown, such precautions become understandable, since people who have crossed the frontiers of mental balance become vulnerable in the face of stress. Thus the concept of evil-spirit possession among the Zulu is used as an idiom to handle the escalating proportions of psychoneurosis often associated with failure to cope with a changing way of life in colonial and postcolonial industrial society.

The infant ailments associated with evil-spirit possession have an expressive significance if we consider that in both situations the terms used are those referring to food containers. *Igobongo* means a dried, deseeded gourd or calabash, generally used to contain sour milk, the highly valued traditional Zulu staple (*amasi*). If a gourd is used for this purpose, it is referred to as *igula,* but if it is empty it is *igobongo. Igobongo* means essentially "emptiness."[9] *Ipleti* is used to refer to the mythical malformed placenta. The term used for a normal placenta is *umzanyana* (*umzali*—"parent"; *umzalinyana*—diminutive of *umzali,* therefore "little parent"; shortened form—*umzanyana.* The term is also used for a nurse girl who minds the baby while the mother attends to domestic chores). The placenta, as the Zulu see it, is a "little parent" that provides the fetus in the womb with the necessities for its growth. In contrast, the placenta in its supposedly malformed state is referred to as "just a

8. M. G. Whisson, "Some Aspects of Functional Disorders among the Kenya Luo," in *Magic, Faith, Healing,* ed. A. Kiev (New York: Free Press, 1966).

9. Indeed Doke and Vilakazi define *igobongo* as "hollow place or thing, empty container (as a calabash, hollow tree, hollow place beneath the ground, empty egg shell)."

plate"—an empty plate. Both *igobongo* and *ipleti* are used in a manner which suggests deprivation and starvation.

The Zulu practitioners interpreting mental disturbances as *ufufunyane* or *indiki* not only recognize them as derived from failure to cope with changing social conditions but also recognize how the disruptive social forces could threaten the very existence and continuity of Zulu society as a distinct entity.[10] Hence prophylactic mystical measures must be taken to reassure the people that their young are protected. This indicates an awareness of social problems and an attempt at containing and dealing with them to establish social equilibrium. The treatment is mainly in the hands of diviners, who compare favorably with Western-trained clinical psychologists and psychiatrists in their ability to observe and cope with the relationship between social conditions and various forms of mental disturbances. This brings to mind the saying "Wise women never sit and wail their woes but presently prevent the ways to wail."

Centre for International and Area Studies
University of London
London, England

10. The Zulu distinguish among different levels of mental disorder. For instance, a schizophrenic person is said to be constituted in this way (*uhlanya*) and not possessed by any spirits. An epileptic suffers from *isithuthwane,* an incurable condition. He or she is not possessed by spirits. Some people may suffer from a form of hysteria (*umhayizo*) whereby they weep aloud uncontrollably but are not necessarily possessed, if they do not show other symptoms of mental confusion.

Women and Migration in Contemporary West Africa

Niara Sudarkasa

For the past three-quarters of a century, intranational and international migration has been an especially prominent feature of sociocultural change on the African continent.[1] Given the overwhelming predominance of males in this process in the early part of the century, it is not surprising that most of the studies of migrants in Africa in general, and in West Africa in particular, have focused on men. One result has been the relative paucity of detailed information based on systematic research about women. Despite the virtual absence of full-fledged studies of female migration in West Africa, Caldwell's research on rural-urban migration in Ghana[2] and census data from various countries confirm the scattered observations of various scholars and other writers that there is a substantial female migrant population in most West African towns and cities. In the past twenty-five years, younger women have become a steadily increasing proportion of those migrating to the cities. In some areas it even appears that "the female propensity for rural-urban migration is rising faster than the male."[3] This "propensity" is, of course, a predictable response to actual and perceived opportunities for employ-

1. For a selected bibliography on migration in West Africa in particular and Africa in general, see the references cited in Niara Sudarkasa, "Commercial Migration in West Africa, with Special Reference to the Yaruba in Ghana" in *Migrants and Strangers in Africa,* ed. Niara Sudarkasa, *African Urban Notes,* series B, no. 1 (East Lansing: African Studies Center, Michigan State University, 1974).

2. J. C. Caldwell, "Determinants of Rural Urban Migration in Ghana," *Population Studies* 22, no. 3 (1968): 361–77; and J. C. Caldwell, *African Rural-Urban Migration* (Canberra: Australian National University Press, 1969).

3. Caldwell, "Determinants," p. 369.

ment, education, and/or marriage in the cities. West African women have been primarily involved in internal migration within their home countries. However, since early in this century, many of them, particularly traders, have been among the migrants who left their countries of origin to live and work in other West African nations.[4]

The present paper outlines the major patterns of female involvement in contemporary West African migration. It indicates some of the effects on the lives of women of their own migration and that of men. It notes the role of female migrants as innovators in the process of contemporary socioeconomic change and raises some questions as to the relationship this bears to the process of "development." Most of the illustrative data come from my studies of Yoruba migrants in Ghana.

Women and the Migratory Process in Twentieth-Century West Africa

Fundamentally, the reasons for vast twentieth-century West African migrations are to be found in the overall redirection, in colonial times, of economic activity *away from* the precolonial production and trade centers in the interior *toward* the coastal administrative, production, and commercial centers established or promoted by the colonial regimes.[5] By the imposition of taxes, the introduction of various goods and services that had to be purchased with European currencies, and the passage of compulsory labor laws, colonial governments virtually and literally forced people to move away from those areas which could not provide them with adequate cash incomes.

For most of West Africa, with the exception of Nigeria, the inland areas became virtual labor reserves for the coast.[6] Something of the magnitude of the resultant population shifts is indicated by Samir Amin's estimate that between 1920 and 1970 there was a net population transfer (including migrants and their offspring) of at least 4.8 million persons from the interior to the coast. This number represented about

4. Polly Hill, *Occupations of Migrants in Ghana,* Anthropological Papers, no. 42 (Ann Arbor: Museum of Anthropology, University of Michigan, 1970); Akin Mabogunje, *Regional Mobility and Resource Development in West Africa,* Keith Callard Lectures (Montreal: McGill–Queen's University Press, 1972); Sudarkasa, "Commerical Migration"; and Sudarkasa, "The Economic Status of the Yoruba in Ghana before 1970," *Nigerian Journal of Economic and Social Studies,* vol. 17, no. 1 (1975).

5. Jean Rouch, "Migrations au Ghana," *Journal de la Société des Africanistes* 26, nos. 1–2 (1956): 33–196; Elliott P. Skinner, "Labor Migration and Its Relationship to Sociocultural Change in Mossi Society," *Africa* 30, no. 4 (1960): 375–99; Hilda Kuper, ed., *Urbanization and Migration in West Africa* (Berkeley: University of California Press, 1965); Samir Amin, "Introduction" in *Modern Migrations in Western Africa,* ed. Samir Amin (Oxford: Oxford University Press, 1974); and Sudarkasa, "The Economic Status of the Yoruba."

6. Amin.

21 percent of the coastal population and 26 percent of the inland population of West Africa in 1970.[7] In Nigeria in the period between 1920 and 1970, millions of people migrated westward (to the Yoruba cities and towns), northward (to the Hausa towns and surrounds), and southward (to Lagos, Port Harcourt, and other coastal cities). Of course, to appreciate fully the magnitude of West African migration, one must add to the numbers of more or less permanent migrants the hundreds of thousands of seasonal migrants, originating primarily in Upper Volta, Mali, Guinea, and other parts of the Sahel, who were involved in annual or biennial circulatory patterns of migration from their homelands to work on plantations, in mines, and as unskilled laborers in various rural and urban areas in the coastal states.

In the late 1960s and early 1970s, the flow of international migration was reduced, though by no means totally diminished, by legal and economic moves taken against African aliens in various West African states.[8] The Ghanaian Aliens Compliance Order was particularly influential because of the large numbers of persons who were repatriated in its wake.[9] Yet in 1972, Amin could estimate an annual flow of 300,000 migrants through the West Africa region.[10] It is still too early to judge the impact that the fledgling Economic Community of West African States (ECOWAS) will have on the patterns of migration. However, one of its objectives is the free movement of persons among member states, and the success of the organization could lead to a new, substantial increase in international movement in the region.[11]

International labor migration in West Africa has been predominantly a male phenomenon. One survey of between 400,000 and 500,000 migrants to Ghana and the Ivory Coast in 1958–59 revealed that approximately 92 percent of the migrants were men.[12] Data from the 1960 census of Ghana, the country that received most of the migrants from the Sahel, also attest to the small size of the female component. These data show that there were four times as many adult males as adult females in the population of the Mossi, who were the largest group of migrant laborers in Ghana, having come there mainly from the Upper Volta. The Mossi population totaled 106,140 persons, of whom 79,910

7. Ibid.

8. W. T. S. Gould, "International Migration in Tropical Africa: A Bibliographical Review," in *International Migration in Tropical Africa,* ed. W. T. S. Gould, special issue of the *International Migration Review* 7, no. 3 (1974): 347–65; Margaret Piel, "The Expulsion of West African Aliens," *Journal of Modern African Studies* 9, no. 2 (1971): 205–29; and Margaret Piel, "Ghana's Aliens" in Gould, *International Migration.*

9. Piel, "Expulsion"; Piel, "Ghana's Aliens"; J. Adomako-Sarfoh, "The Effects of the Expulsion of Migrant Workers on Ghana's Economy, with Particular Reference to the Cocoa Industry," in Amin; and Sudarkasa, "Commercial Migration."

10. Amin, p. 74.

11. "What ECOWAS Says," *West Africa,* no. 3025 (June 16, 1975), p. 679.

12. Mabogunje, pp. 54–55.

were classified for census purposes as adults (i.e., aged fifteen and over).[13]

Although the Mossi women and other women from the "labor supplying" areas of West Africa can be said to have been involved in the labor migration process, they themselves were *not* labor migrants. Wage-earning opportunities, even in unskilled occupations, were generally unavailable to women. Hence, the female migrants who accompanied their laborer husbands or mates to Ghana, had, of necessity, to look to self-employment as a source of income if they were to have an income at all. Those among them who worked outside the home did so on their own account in farming, trade, crafts, and the service occupations. The 1960 Ghana census showed that 78 percent of the 15,720 Mossi women in Ghana did not engage in any type of income-earning activity. Of those earning incomes, 44 percent were engaged in agriculture (mainly as share-croppers rather than as wage laborers), 42 percent were traders, 11 percent prepared and sold cooked foods, millet beer, and so on, and 3 percent worked in other service occupations.[14]

In addition to labor migration, an older and equally significant migratory process is that of commercial migration, involving traders and independent craftspeople, who also tend to refer to themselves as traders. Whereas labor migration has characteristically flowed from the interior to the coast, commercial migration has tended to be multidirectional, with streams going north as well as south, criss-crossing the Sahel and the coast, and taking in rural as well as urban areas. Typically, commercial migration has involved much more long term sojourns abroad than has labor migration. In Ghana in 1968–69, I found that in a sample population of Yoruba traders, of whom 62 percent were under forty-five years of age, 92 percent had lived in Ghana five years or more; 89 percent of this population reported having lived there ten years or more; and 43 percent of these traders had been there twenty years or more. The tendency was for males and females to migrate to Ghana in their teens or early twenties and to remain there for most of their lives.

In both the precolonial period and contemporary times, commercial migration in West Africa has been dominated by a relatively small number of ethnic groups. The Hausa, Djoula, and Yoruba seem to have the longest histories of involvement in trans–West African trade. They are probably the most widely dispersed of the contemporary commercial migrants.[15] The Igbo (Ibo), who had well-developed internal trading

13. B. Gil, A. F. Aryee, and D. K. Ghansah, *Special Report E: Tribes in Ghana, Ghana Population Census of 1960* (Accra: Census Office, 1964), p. 66.

14. Ibid., p. C-46.

15. Mabogunje, pp. 58–65; Sudarkasa, "Commercial Migration"; Abner Cohen, *Custom and Politics in Urban Africa: A Study of Hausa Migrants in Yoruba Towns* (London: Routledge & Kegan Paul, 1969); Abner Cohen, "Cultural Strategies in the Organization of Trading Disporas," in *The Development of Indigenous Trade and Markets in West Africa,* ed. Claude Meillassoux (Oxford: Oxford University Press, 1971); Hill; Meillassoux.

networks in precolonial times but were not prominent in trans–West African trade, exemplify the groups who gained prominence as commercial migrants in the twentieth century.[16]

Women are conspicuous among the commercial migrants of West Africa. In the different migrant trading groups, however, there is considerable variation in the relative size of the male and female trading populations. Among Yoruba migrants, for example, women traders usually equal or outnumber male traders in terms of absolute numbers and in terms of percentage of their respective working populations. In Ghana in 1960, Yoruba women traders outnumbered their male counterparts by over 2,000. They also constituted a relatively greater proportion of the female working population than did male traders within the working male population. At the time of the census, 70 percent of the adult Yoruba female population was reported as being employed. Of these, 91 percent were traders and another 7 percent were self-employed in crafts and service occupations. By comparison, 48 percent of the working Yoruba males were traders and another 27 percent were employed "on their own account" in other occupations.[17]

On the other hand, among the Hausa the males are the internationally known traders. In Ghana at the time of the 1960 census, Hausa male traders and other self-employed workers outnumbered their female counterparts by three to one. In fact, most Hausa women, kept in seclusion in accordance with Muslim tradition, were not recorded in the census as being income generating.[18] It is possible, however, that they carried on in-house trade in a manner similar to that described by Hill for Hausa women in Nigeria.[19] Less than half (43 percent) of the adult Hausa women in Ghana in 1960 were recorded as being employed. Of those who were, 86 percent were traders and another 13 percent were self-employed in other occupations.[20]

In comparing the Yoruba and Hausa migrants groups, it is noteworthy that in terms of both absolute members and the ratio of females to males, Yoruba women outnumbered Hausa women in Ghana. This indicates the greater mobility of the Yoruba female population. Yoruba women constituted 44 percent of the adult Yoruba population in Ghana, Hausa women only 33 percent of their adult population. Other mobile female trading populations, as shown by my research on migrant populations in Ghana, include the Ewe of Togo, the Igbo of Nigeria, and

16. Sudarkasa, "Commercial Migrations."

17. The Yoruba population in Ghana in 1960 numbered 100,560. Adult Yoruba females numbered 25,110; adult Yoruba males numbered 32,000. There were 61,730 Hausa in Ghana in 1960, of whom 28,720 were adult males and 14,420 were adult females, according to Gil et al.

18. Approximately two-thirds of the Yoruba in Ghana in the 1960s were Muslims, but there was no tradition of wife seclusion among them.

19. Polly Hill, "Two Types of West African House Trade," in Meillassoux.

20. Gil et al.

various other ethnic groups from Southern Nigeria. In fact, Southern Nigerian women, including the Yoruba and the Igbo, appear to have been the largest group of female international migrants in West Africa.

Most of the millions of women involved in internal migration within the various countries would fall under the category of commercial migrants. The vast majority of women move from the rural areas to the cities. (This is the direction of most internal migration, although Mabogunje has demonstrated the importance of the "colonization" of rural areas as a process of mobility in Nigeria before 1950.)[21] Because they do not have the formal educational qualifications required for the types of wage employment open to women, many female rural-urban migrants have had to enter market trade or similar occupations. In the past two decades, however, more and more young women with some degree of formal education have been moving to the cities in the hope of obtaining jobs in the "modern sector." As often as not, these young women do not find the clerical, industrial, or technical jobs they seek, and they, too, have to turn to trading on their own account or with female relatives in order to eke out a living.

Various writers have made much of the incidence of prostitution among female urban migrants. As Gugler says, "they have attracted a disproportionate amount of attention and curiosity."[22] Kenneth Little's influential writings on women and the urbanizing process have been notable contributions to the creation of the stereotypic image of female migrants as actual or potential prostitutes.[23] Although female prostitution is one correlate of the large-scale migration of single or unattached males to the urban areas of West Africa, the existing discussion of prostitution simply underscores the need for better data on this subject. Moreover, it was my observation that only a small minority of female migrants and of local women in Kumas, where I lived while studying migrants in Ghana, relied on the sale of their sexual services as sources of income.

Selectivity Factors in Female Migration

Throughout this century most women involved in international migration left their homes after marriage rather than as single youths.

21. Akin Mabogunje, "Migration Policy and Regional Development in Nigeria," *Nigerian Journal of Economic and Social Studies* 12, no. 2 (1970): 243–62.

22. Josef Gugler, "The Impact of Labour Migration on Society and Economy in Sub-Saharan Africa: Empirical Findings and Theoretical Considerations," *African Social Research* 6 (1968): 463–86.

23. Kenneth Little, *West African Urbanization* (Cambridge: Cambridge University Press, 1965). For a critique of Little's book, see Roger Sanjek, "New Perspectives on West African Women," *Reviews in Anthropology* 3, no. 2 (March/April 1976): 115–34.

This contrasts with the pattern of first migrations for males, who usually undertake their first migration as unmarried youths in their twenties. I found this pattern to hold for Yoruba males who migrated to Ghana to trade.[24] However, Yoruba women who migrated to Ghana, like the Mossi women described by Skinner, normally came with their husbands or were sent for by their husbands.[25] Those who did not follow this pattern usually came as unmarried girls with their parents or other relatives.

Moreover, nearly all the women in the first generation of migrants were first wives or only wives of their husbands, or they were divorcees who had been first wives when they came to Ghana. Whereas nearly all Yoruba men born in Nigeria returned home for their first marriages or brought their first wives with them, those who married polygynously tended to take their second and subsequent wives from among the Yoruba divorcees or widows resident in Ghana or from among Yoruba women who were born in Ghana. Obviously the expense involved in marrying in Nigeria (either in person or by proxy) and bringing a wife to Ghana was the major reason why men did not usually go through that process more than once.

Within the pool of potential female migrants in the home town or village, previously unmarried women stood the best chance of migrating because they stood the best chance of becoming first wives. In addition, women who were junior wives of a potential migrant stood less of a chance of migrating with him than did his first wife. This seemed particularly to be the case when the first wife was still relatively young and of childbearing age. I knew a number of men who had left one wife behind in Nigeria while another traveled with them. In some cases, the wives left in Nigeria joined the family in Ghana; in other cases, these women divorced their absent husbands and married other men. The pattern of female migration after marriage seems to be characteristic of internal as well as international migration. Caldwell's data on Ghana suggest that most women moving to the cities were young brides or brides-to-be who were joining their fiances.[26] Moreover, half of the married male migrants in Caldwell's urban sample reported having been accompanied by their wives at the time of their migration, and two-thirds of the remainder later sent for their wives to join them.[27]

One reason why the pattern of female internal migration is more complex than that of international migration is the fact that where distances involved are relatively short, young girls are often taken to the city by relatives with whom they live and work until they reach marriageable age. In the period up to the 1960s, many of these young women

24. Sudarkasa, "Commercial Migration," p. 86.

25. Elliott P. Skinner, "Labour Migration among the Mossi of the Upper Volta," in Kuper, p. 75 (see n. 5 above).

26. Caldwell, "Determinants," p. 368 (see n. 2 above).

27. Caldwell, *Rural-Urban Migration,* pp. 126–27 (see n. 2 above).

then returned to their villages to get married, and often remained there at least until they had had one or two children. Next, depending on their husbands' occupational trajectories, they might move back to an urban area or remain in the rural area.[28] However, in the last decade or so, it has become increasingly common for young women who are brought to the city as girls to remain there up to and after marriage. It is my impression, based on observations in Nigeria in recent years, that these young women are marrying at a later age than their counterparts who used to return to the villages. These young female migrants, brought up in the cities, along with the young female school leavers migrating from the rural areas, are equalizing the sex ratio among single migrants under the age of twenty-five.

Caldwell's point that formal education is one of the most reliable determinants of migration from the rural areas to the city holds true for females as well as males.[29] Increasingly, young women who are literate in the European language of their country and who have attended school look to the intermediate-size towns or the large cities for employment opportunities. More and more of these young women regard themselves as overqualified academically and underqualified experientially for the types of work that women do in the rural areas.

Some young women (and young men) in the rural areas migrate to urban areas to serve as domestic help in the homes of relatives. In return, the relatives provide them with room and board and spending money. Usually they also pay for the young person's apprenticeship with a skilled craftsperson or arrange for their ward to attend some type of technical school. This type of migration from the rural areas is superficially reminiscent of the migration of young female domestic labor common in some Latin American countries (see Jelin's paper in this volume). However, in many respects the processes are different. In the first place, since the young African women go to live with relatives, they conceive of their move as one for the purpose of receiving an education, rather than as one for the purpose of working as domestics. Moreover, since in many cases there is salaried domestic help (often male) in the same homes with the young women (or men) from the rural areas, they can justify the view that they are relatives "lending a hand" rather than serving as domestics. Finally, if they do return to their villages, they do not normally go back with cash savings to turn over to their parents but rather with a skill (such as dressmaking) that they then use to earn a living.

When men and women are compared as to their ages at the time of

28. This was a phenomenon which I observed, for example, when I was conducting research in a small Yoruba town in Nigeria in the early 1960s (Sudarkasa, *Where Women Work: A Study of Yoruba Women in the Marketplace and in the Home* [Ann Arbor: Museum of Anthropology, University of Michigan, 1973]).

29. Caldwell, "Determinants."

their first migration, the findings are the same. Both sexes tend to move between the ages of fifteen and thirty, or they tend to be juveniles traveling with their parents or guardians. The main difference between male and female migrants in this respect is that most of the males in the fifteen-to-thirty age group are single, whereas most of the females in that category are married. In many areas, women still tend to be much younger than their husbands.[30] As I have indicated, this situation is changing as females gain parity with males in terms of education and occupational opportunities.

Of the women who migrate on their own, my research suggests that they are usually nearing fifty, widowed or divorced, with previous experience as a head of household. Gugler has observed that barren women often migrate on their own because "without children they are in a weak economic and social position."[31] Years ago, Nadel also noted that childless women often took up long-distance trade and, with it, prostitution.[32] He described some Nupe female migrants in Ibadan as well-known traders and equally well-known prostitutes.[33]

Given that women (and men) of various ethnic groups were differentially represented in migratory processes, the question might arise whether ethnicity per se operated as a selective factor. The data suggest that the differential participation of various ethnic groups in certain patterns of migration was primarily a function of the ways in which the colonial economic strategies influenced their communities. A careful study of Yoruba commercial migration reveals, for example, a difference in the magnitude of migration from towns and villages, depending on whether or not the particular localities fell outside the mainstream of colonial "development" in Nigeria.[34] Of course, the fact that Yoruba migrants chose to trade rather than to work as laborers, and the fact that Yoruba women were able to maintain relatively successful trading operations in a number of foreign environments, reflect their long experience in trade. However, cultural historical factors rather than ethnicity explain the patterns in question. Where ethnicity did play a role was in the organization of the migrant communities and, in the case of commercial migrants, in the establishment and maintenance of what Cohen has termed trading diasporas.[35]

30. Ibid., p. 368.

31. Gugler, p. 467.

32. S. F. Nadel, *A Black Byzantium* (Oxford: International African Institute, 1942).

33. I have no doubt that this picture I have suggested of the independent female migrant is likely to be drastically revised with the publication of the findings of some of the studies of female migrants recently completed or now in progress. I have in mind particularly the data from K. Okonjo's study of female migrants in Nigeria and from the very comprehensive study of migration in Nigeria undertaken under the direction of F. O. Okediji, in collaboration with J. Harrington and I. Osayimwese. Unfortunately, neither of these studies was available to me at the time of this writing.

34. Sudarkasa, "Economic Status" (see n. 4 above).

35. Cohen, "Cultural Strategies" (see n. 15 above).

Migration and Social Change

If one theme recurs in the literature on migration in contemporary Africa, it is that population mobility has been as much a catalyst as a consequence of social change. Scattered throughout the literature are discussions, for example, of the ways in which migration affects the husband-wife relationship, patterns of authority within the home communities, agricultural production cycles, and the host communities in which migrants form stranger communities. I want to illustrate the impact of migration on domestic patterns by citing one example from the data on Yoruba migrants in Ghana.

In their homelands, Yoruba women usually carry on their trade independently of their husbands.[36] When I conducted fieldwork in Western Nigeria in 1961 and 1962, I did not encounter a single case of a woman who traded jointly with her husband. Such cases undoubtedly existed, but they were exceptional. In Ghana, however, a number of males and females whom I interviewed reported that they were then engaged in or had previously been engaged in joint trading ventures with their spouses. This seemed to me to be directly related to the generally increased interdependence of spouses that resulted from their situation as migrants. Such interdependence developed because of (1) the way Yoruba women arrived in Ghana, and (2) the conditions under which most Yorubas lived in Ghana. As I have pointed out, almost all the Yoruba women who migrated to Ghana as adults came with their husbands or to join their husbands. Usually the man who was married polygynously brought only one of his wives to Ghana with him. Most migrants, even those who were polygynous, tended to live a de facto monogamous domestic life for years at a time. The economics of survival in Ghana was the major factor in limiting the number of women a migrant would marry and the number of wives he would bring with him to Ghana. The fact of living a de facto monogamous life would not necessarily have led to major changes in conjugal behavior had the couples been living in Nigeria in a traditional Yoruba compound. There husbands and wives had separate rooms and interacted on a day-to-day basis with the members of their respective sexes living in the compounds as much as with each other. In Ghanaian towns and villages, however, Yorubas usually rented rooms in compounds and many husbands and wives (and their dependents) shared the same room. The physical living arrangements had the effect of involving spouses in virtually every aspect of each other's lives.

Moreover, having migrated together and having to face life in a new society, those couples who did not have parents, siblings, or *close* relatives

36. Gloria Marshall [Niara Sudarkasa], "The Marketing of Farm Produce: Some Patterns of Trade among Women in Western Nigeria," *Proceedings of the 1962 Conference of the Nigerian Institute of Social and Economic Research* (Ibadan: Nigerian Institute of Social and Economic Research, 1963).

there (almost everyone had some relatives in Ghana) turned almost exclusively to each other as confidants. In this situation, husbands and wives had much more detailed knowledge of their respective financial situations than they necessarily would have had in Nigeria. Most domestic and business decisions were joint decisions. Furthermore, because in Ghana few migrants had a wide range of persons to turn to for assistance in raising trading capital, husbands and wives who were in serious financial straits often had no option but to pool their resources and work together. Interestingly, when such partnerships proved successful, very often the husband would give his wife a substantial sum of money to resume (or begin) trading on her own. They might even continue to deal in the same line of goods, but with the husband in his market stall and the wife in hers.[37]

The comparative data on Yoruba conjugal behavior in Nigeria and Ghana indicate that the presence of joint decision making and consultation and cooperation in the use of conjugal resources within African marriages do not always derive from "Westernization" or elite status, as one might assume to be the case.[38] These characteristics can emerge among non-Western-educated, lower-income, otherwise "traditional" marriage partners whose life-styles have been altered by the demands of existence in a new social environment.

Female Migration and Innovation in West Africa

Even though one can debate the question of whether it is appropriate to apply the term "development" to the socioeconomic changes that have taken place in West Africa (and other parts of the continent) in this century, the fact of the female migrant's contribution to these changes is undisputable. Through their occupational activities and their interpersonal relationships, female migrants have been one of the groups that have most consistently served to diffuse innovations throughout the West African region.[39]

The most obvious arena through which female migrants have contributed to change is the world of the marketplace. They have been responsible for most of the small-scale distribution of the overseas-manufactured goods imported into some parts of West Africa.[40] They

37. By separating the trading ventures, the husband and wife are in effect distributing the risk of failure (which is high in the type of market situation in which they operate). Should one of the businesses "go under," they would hopefully still have the other one to turn to.

38. Christine Oppong, *Marriage among a Matrilineal Elite* (Cambridge: Cambridge University Press, 1974).

39. Akin Mabogunje, "Migrants and Innovation in African Societies: Definition of a Research Field," in *Migrants and Strangers,* ed. Sudarkasa (see n. 1 above); Sudarkasa, "Commercial Migration."

40. Sudarkasa, "Economic Status."

have also been instrumental in moving commodities from one West African country to another, thereby making foodstuffs, textiles, housewares, medicinals, etc., available to consumers who would not otherwise have access to them.[41] In many instances, female commercial migrants have also helped to introduce new types of machinery, for example, pepper-grinding machines and flour mills, and to promote new techniques for getting tasks accomplished.

As important as their role in diffusing material innovations is the fact that female migrants have often been style setters and social interpreters for their sisters in rural areas. In their persons, female migrants have been perceived as the embodiment of the material and cultural offerings of the city or the foreign land. Like their male counterparts, returning female migrants often became objects for emulation for the young and sources of information for the old. For women in the rural areas, female migrants have been their eyes on the cities, and it is often as a result of their descriptions of city life that other women become enamoured of the prospect of migration.

Department of Anthropology
and
Center for Afroamerican and African Studies
University of Michigan
Ann Arbor, Michigan, U.S.A.

41. Ibid.

Politics and Institutions

Introduction

Jane S. Jaquette

The central problem of comparative politics, one of crucial concern in the study of comparative female political participation across national and cultural differences, is to identify appropriate categories which allow us, not only to measure such phenomena as male/female vote differentials in two or more settings, but also to compare them in some meaningful sense. Comparison implies two seemingly contradictory processes: measurement according to a single standard, and measurement in the light of different social, economic, symbolic, and even moral evaluations that may be applied to the same "behavior" in different cultural contexts. In addition, comparison always carries with it implicit or explicit value judgments. These may be desirable in the area of female political participation, where analysis is often intended to bring about change. It is here, however, that the questions of how to measure change and how to design appropriate strategies based on the data we have become most acute. Is the American experience, and particularly the American feminist experience, an appropriate basis for judgment? Are there viable alternatives?

The papers which follow have the clear advantage of having been written for an international conference by women who, in all but one case, are products of the cultures they are observing. In addition, they cover different levels of political participation. Pnina Lahav's paper deals with the legal status of women in Israel, the point of departure for all discussions of female participation. Lenore Manderson's historical study of the Kaum Ibu, the women's section of the United Malays National Organization, takes us one level further to the issue of women's roles in political party organization. Finally, Marysa Navarro's biography of Eva

Peron looks at a female charismatic leader—a political elite. These levels of analysis do not exhaust possibilities for research. Much comparative work needs to be done in the areas of women's political attitudes as part of mass publics and the sociological and psychological characteristics of women politicians—areas which are costly to research, but in which there are increasing data in the "center" or developed countries. And, in an age which is becoming increasingly bureaucratic in both the "center" and the "periphery," we must devote more attention to women as bureaucrats.

Beverly Chiñas's[1] matrix of social roles provides a useful perspective on what these papers can contribute. They focus on the link between the status of women (legal and attitudinal) and women's participation in formal public roles. They do not emphasize the way formal private roles may provide models for public activity in the political sphere (e.g., Chaney's notion of "supermadre" to explain a common female style of elite participation in Latin America),[2] nor do they look at the way informal roles, both public and private, influence the quality of female power and spill over into the public sphere. Without this context, meaningful comparisons are difficult. Nonetheless, these papers provide us with important data and some lines of analysis which are promising in working toward a comparative theory of political participation of women.

Lahav shows the weakness of the legalistic approach to sex equality, even when the Israeli Women's Equal Rights Law (1951) is viewed as having the limited goal of integrating women "in social and political areas now occupied by men" and not the radical goal of eliminating sex differences. She argues that the law has been ineffective because it is vague and because of the structure of the legal system. Religious beliefs play a particularly important role in the persistence of a marriage code and of protective legislation, both inconsistent with the equal rights law. Traditional religious groups do not want to lose political power or the religious core of Israeli national identity, and women believe protective legislation helps them "cope" in a man's world.

Yet Lahav's prescription, like her analysis, is legalistic: "Where do we find the time and energy to draft a suitable comprehensive statute to be enforced by the new courts?" However, the underlying problem is more basic, as Lahav implicitly recognizes when she notes that the "majority of persons do not consider the traditional pattern of sex roles as discrimination against women." There is no discussion of the process of attaining sex equality as a function of perceived opportunity costs for women.

In Manderson's analysis, traditional values working against female political participation break down in the presence of a powerful colonial

1. Beverly Chiñas, *The Isthmus Zapotecs* (New York: Holt, Rinehart & Winston, 1973).

2. Elsa Chaney, "Women in Latin American Politics: The Case of Peru and Chile," in *Female and Male in Latin America: Essays,* ed. Ann Pescatello (Pittsburgh: University of Pittsburgh Press, 1973).

"model" of behavior as an ideal, at least for urban elite behavior. In Malaya the Western model is considerably at odds with the requirement of both traditional values and Islam that women be confined to the private sphere. The adoption of the Western model as a high status life-style in the cities helps explain participation in this women's auxiliary. The political success of the Kaum Ibu in party affairs is attributed to its ability to get out the vote. The parallel between women as campaign activists and party workers who do not then go on to elective political careers can be drawn with studies in the United States[3] and Latin America.[4] Other important parallels are the roles which are granted during independence movements and times of war, but which are later withdrawn, and the problems of women's organizations themselves: the tendency to focus on internal disputes, and the setting of goals almost exclusively in areas of education and social welfare.

Navarro's review of the life of Eva Peron and her portrayal of Evita as a woman of independent political capabilities and of populist commitments is significant. Evita's political style—that only a woman could have adopted—illustrates some of the advantages of sex differences as a means to power for women. If, as many researchers now believe,[5] women can rarely be judged by others as worthy of "winning" in situations in which they compete directly with men—even in the United States—then a specifically female political role may be an appropriate strategy. This option may also explain why women succeed as political elites in "traditional" (i.e., nonegalitarian) societies. If individual women can overcome the general trend of socialization toward passivity in the public sphere so that they are *motivated* to succeed (and are not ground down by poverty), they will be *allowed* to do so, perhaps because they are not seen as competing directly with men.

As these papers take us through the various levels of female participation, we are forced to conclude, once again, that the higher the level, the lower the proportion of women. Sadder still, the increase of female participation as voters and party workers does not appear to lead, as many would hypothesize, to increases in the number of female elites. That, in the male jargon of our day, is the "bottom line."

Department of Political Science
Occidental College
Los Angeles, California, U.S.A.

3. E. Costantini and K. H. Craik. "Women as Politicians: The Social Background, Personality, and Political Careers of Women as Party Leaders," *Journal of Social Issues* 28: 217–36.

4. S. Harkess and P. Pinzon, "Women, the Vote and the Party in the Politics of the Colombian National Front," *Journal of Inter-American Studies and World Affairs* 17: 439–64.

5. See, e.g., Judith Stiehm, "Ideology and Participation" (paper given at the Western Political Science Association Meetings, Phoenix, Ariz., April 1977).

Politics and Institutions

Raising the Status of Women through Law: The Case of Israel

Pnina Lahav

Achieving social change, an ambitious task, requires meaningful changes in both social structure and group relations, norms, and roles. When we consider law as an instrument for altering traditional sex roles within the family, the magnitude of the undertaking is even greater. As the sociologist William J. Goode points out in a recent article on family disorganization, in general, there is little legal interference or regulation of the family system.[1] He suggests that "the relative autonomy of the family . . . expresses the fact that no one outside the family has any 'rights' in its deliberations and decisions." Therefore state interference occurs "only where (1) family members themselves initiate state action or (2) someone in the family is officially reported to be receiving inadequate physical care."[2] With this caveat, we can evaluate the contribution law can make toward raising the status of women in society. Goode also suggests that if the women's liberation movement gains momentum family relations will be transformed and many of the existing role patterns dissolved.[3] The law can help the group gain momentum, although it cannot create or replace it.

However, designing legislation to change sex roles raises many problems. The decision makers of particular societies should agree upon a uniform concept of sex equality: do they mean a complete dissolution of existing sex-role patterns (a radical concept), or do they want to elimi-

1. William J. Goode, "Family Disorganization," in *Contemporary Social Problems,* ed. Robert K. Merton and Robert Nisbet (New York: Harcourt Brace Jovanovich, Inc., 1971).

2. Ibid., p. 471

3. Ibid., p. 537.

nate legal barriers to the integration of women in social and political areas now occupied mostly by men (a progressive concept)? We must also estimate the weight and impact of external pressures relevant but not patently related to the issue of sex equality: if we conclude that a new family court should be established, can we cope with the resistance of religious courts and their supporters, whose power is directly attacked? Furthermore, if legislation concerning sex equality happens to be or is interpreted as being in direct conflict with a traditional value system, the threat of a national political or cultural crisis may become real. In developing societies, where national unity and cohesion rank high on the priority list, such a threat may cool the enthusiasm of the decision makers for sex equality. These factors are equally relevant in implementation of the law, which depends on the commitment and goodwill of the participants within the legal system and of the population itself.

The condition of women in Israel is far from satisfactory, though some encouraging signs have recently appeared, such as a special government commission to examine the status of women.[4] The same can be said of the relationship of the legal system and sex roles in Israeli society. The superstructure of the legal system does indeed provide for sex equality. However, its infrastructure is loaded with both sex-based discrimination and differentiation between persons, despite the fact that since 1974 some important legislation has been passed (the impact of which is still unclear),[5] and some major bills have been introduced in Parliament (the Knesset) to promote the status of women.[6]

This paper will inquire into the various factors which have affected and are likely to affect reception and implementation of sex equality in Israel in the future. My point of departure is the Women's Equal Rights Law of 1951, hereafter referred to as WERL.[7]

The Women's Equal Rights Law 1951

General Outline and Background

The Women's Equal Rights Law is composed of nine sections. It

4. See Pnina Lahav, "The Status of Women in Israel—Myth and Reality," *American Journal of Comparative Law* 22 (1974): 107, for my analysis of that condition. Recent studies reaching similar conclusions are: Rivka W. Bar-Yosef, "Household Management: An Organizational Model Applied to Comparative Family Research," *Human Relations* 26 (1973): 581; Dorit Padan-Eisenstark and Hellen Meir-Hechker, "Women in the Cooperative Settlement in an Ideological Trap," *Magamot* 21 (1975): 423; and Rivka W. Bar-Yosef and Zviah Levy, *The Conception of Feminine Roles among Seventeen-Year-Old Girls* (Jerusalem: Welfare and Research Institute, Hebrew University, 1976).

5. Spouses (property relations) Law 5733-1973. For text and comments, see Pinhas Shifman, "Property Relations between Spouses," *Israel Law Review* 11 (1976): 98.

6. The Bill for Basic Law: The Rights of Man 1973; The Bill for Basic Law: The Rights of Woman 1974.

7. Israel—Laws 5711–1951.

opens with a declaration that "with regard to any legal act, the same law shall apply to a woman and a man and any provision of law that discriminates against women shall be of no effect" (sec. 1). It proceeds to grant married women full competence in handling property (sec. 2); it grants women equal rights to custody of their children (sec. 3) and annuls discriminatory provisions of the Succession Act (sec. 4). Sections 5 and 6, respectively, provide that the new law shall not derogate from the laws applied to marriage and divorce and from laws "protecting women as women." These are the problematic sections upon which we shall elaborate in greater detail later. Section 7 allows litigants to opt for their religious laws, despite the existence of the new law, if all parties are consenting adults (above eighteen years of age). Section 8 makes the unilateral dissolution of marriage by the husband a criminal offense, unless a high court decision authorizes the divorce.[8]

The WERL is a product of a marathon parliamentary debate in the last days before the dissolution of the first Knesset. It was presented with two bills: one, proposed by the representative of a woman's organization (WIZO), was long, detailed, and comprehensive; it proposed a complete revolution in family law in Israel and was designed to erase any legal sanctioning of sex roles.[9] The second, presented by the government, resembled the present WERL.

During the debate, the Knesset was divided into three major groups: orthodox members of the religious party (part of the government coalition) who fiercely opposed the law, moderates (mostly members of Mapai, the ruling party),[10] and radicals (the one member of WIZO and members of the leftist parties). The moderates and radicals were united in their resolution to annul some of the more preposterous discriminatory provisions (secs. 2–5). Many of the moderates also favored civil regulation of marriage and divorce, but here they gave in to pressures from the religious bloc. The religious courts retained power over one of the most important areas of family law—matters of marriage and divorce. On the other hand, all three groups were agreed on section 6, retaining laws which "protect women as women." None of the participants in the debate questioned the propriety of legitimizing a privileged status for "women as women" or the actual effect a privileged status might have on the traditional pattern of sex roles.

In its concept of sex equality WERL was not revolutionary. Indeed, Rachel Cohen, the representative of the women's organization, accurately observed upon its reception that it was nothing more than a compilation of some (daring and positive, yet few) amendments to the preex-

8. For analysis, see Lahav, pp. 116–19.

9. The contents of this bill are described in *Divrei HaKnesset* (Parliamentary Records) 9 (1951): 2087–89.

10. At the time Mapai had forty-six seats in the Knesset, of which seven were occupied by women. The total number of women Parliament members was twelve (9.1 percent).

isting status of women.[11] A quarter of a century later, one can reliably assert that WERL did not significantly change the sociopolitical status of women in Israel. In my opinion, the two main components which were responsible for the failure of this law to fulfill the promises contained in its title and first section were sections 5 and 6, that is, the maintenance of religious jurisdiction over matters of marriage and divorce and the legitimation of a privileged status for women. Before examining the dynamics of these two legal phenomena more carefully, I would like to consider some general factors which affected the potentiality of this law to become an active instrument for social change.

WERL's General and Vague Quality

The WERL is too short, its provisions too general, and its terminology too vague. For example, the first section, providing for equal treatment of men and women with regard to "any legal act," says that a discriminatory law shall be of "no effect." It is not entirely clear what are "legal acts"; in other words, what is the extent of equal treatment granted by this section, which laws would fall under this category, or what is meant by "shall have no effect?" Does it mean that a court of law can declare them void, or does it simply mean that they are not to be obeyed?[12] Section 6 is no better. Nor is it clear which laws can be considered as discriminatory against women and which are designed to protect "women as women" (e.g., in their capacity as mothers).

If by social change we meant actual behavioral changes, and if we want the law to help us achieve social change,[13] then a vague and general statute is the wrong method. Normative vagueness and generality may be useful when a general framework is designed for society (such as a constitution), but not when actual changes in roles are required. One may argue that litigation can later supplement the law and fill it with meaning. However, it is doubtful whether transference of the burden to another institution (from the legislature to the courts) is likely to be effective. This is so for two major reasons: (1) the nature of judicial

11. *Divrei HaKnesset* 9 (1951): 2191. She also deliberately abstained from voting for the bill, on the grounds that it might "mislead the public to believe that the law gives equal rights to women."

12. One reason for the "no effect" formula was that a secular law cannot annul Divine Law but only order all courts to refrain from implementing it. In Loubinsky v. Tax Commissioner (C.A. 337/61 P.D. 16,403) it was claimed that the income tax statutory arrangement which provides for joint assessment of married couples' income was *ultra vires,* sec. 1 of WERL. The Supreme Court decided inter alia that WERL confers no power to invalidate statutes which were enacted *after* 1951.

13. I adopt Laurence Friedman and Jack Ladinsky's definition of social change: "Social change is any nonrepetitive alteration in the established modes of behavior in society," quoted in *Law and Change in Modern America,* ed. Joel B. Grossman and Mary H. Grossman (Pacific Palisades, Calif.: Goodyear Publishing Co., 1971), p. 3.

institutions, and (2) the superior capacity of a statute to serve an educational function.

The Nature of Judicial Institutions

The judicial approach to such an emotionally charged area as sex equality must be heavily affected by the attitudes of individual judges. To expect that they will fulfill the task of lawmaking in the area of sex equality assumes an enlightened attitude on their part which is by no means guaranteed, especially in a society where sex roles are deeply ingrained. In fact, one can more readily assume that, since judges are usually older people, they would tend to hold on to traditional arrangements, thereby obstructing the process of change or slowing it considerably. Moreover, judicial decisions are usually evolutionary in nature. First, they depend upon the volume of litigation. In Israel, the government, as well as the women's organizations, did not manifest any conscious effort to use WERL to its maximum capacity for promoting sex equality. Second, because the product of judicial lawmaking is to be found in diverse decisions, the effect on social change must be cumulative and incremental. Another weakness of courts in this context is their lack of an overall perspective of major policies. After all, judges are there to manage conflicts, not to design a master plan for sex equality.

The Superior Capacity of a Statute to Serve an Educational Function

There is no doubt that judicial decisions can play an educational role,[14] but this function can be effective only if (*a*) there is a clear principle or policy goal that they are implementing, and (*b*) they enjoy high credibility and high prestige in society. Hence, in developing societies, where the status of the court is not established, their educational role is likely to be negligible. But, even in societies such as Israel, where courts do enjoy prestige and the principle of sex equality is clearly part of the system,[15] the courts have failed to play a major educational role. My theory is that this is so because of the nature of the subject matter. The area of sex-based discrimination is emotionally charged and contains an indefinite number of biases and preconceptions. Understanding it requires keen sensitivity to manifestations of discrimination. Because judicial decisions attack the social set of values at random, they are not a good device to educate the population. In contrast, a comprehensive and detailed statute (in lieu of a vague and general one) contains the whole new concept of sex equality in one document. It is clearer in form and

14. Alexander M. Bickel, *The Least Dangerous Branch* (New York: Bobbs-Merrill Co., 1962), p. 26.

15. The principle appears in both Israel's Declaration of Independence of 1948 and in sec. 1 of WERL.

wide enough in scope to provide the reader with a solid idea of the expected change. It is also authoritative, especially in countries where the supremacy of the legislature is recognized, and makes the responsibility and commitment of the people's representatives clearer and more assertive. Since education is one of the most dominant components of social change, we should choose the legal device most efficient to play an educational role.

Politics also affected the potentiality of the WERL to become a useful device to achieve sex equality. As mentioned above, both the radical and the moderate blocks in the Knesset looked favorably upon the idea of secularizing marital relations. Within the framework of an ideal democratic process, this could suffice for guaranteeing the reception of a statute which would replace religious law with a modern secular law. However, the coalition government in Israel in 1951 consisted of both the religious party and Mapai, a collaboration that continued until recently. In order to maintain the participation of the religious party in the cabinet, the moderates (Mapai) had to compromise. The impact of such considerations on the value of sex equality is clear. Sex equality does not have enough weight and its advocates do not command enough muscle to prevent a political compromise in this area. In addition, the two areas where legislation could introduce a revolutionary concept—marital relations and the privileged status for women—were specifically excluded. We shall now proceed to evaluate their dynamics.

Sex Equality and Marital Relations: The Compatibility of Religious Law with Efforts to Improve the Status of Women

The Problem

Matters of marriage and divorce of persons affiliated with an organized religion are handled exclusively by religious courts, applying religious law.[16] This is not an original Israeli arrangement, but is inherited from the British mandatory regime, which inherited it from the Ottoman Empire.[17] Later, this arrangement was sanctioned and further institutionalized by original Israeli legislation.[18]

From the vantage point of sex equality, religious systems regulating personal relations have a major drawback: they are permeated with rules

16. Notice also that affiliation with religion in Israel is not a matter of choice. For a general discussion, see Amnon Rubinstein, "Law and Religion in Israel," *Israel Law Review* 2 (1966): 380.

17. Ibid., pp. 384–87.

18. E.g., Rabbinical Courts' Jurisdiction (Marriage and Divorce) Law 5713-1953; and Druze Religious Courts' Law 5723-1962.

and regulations designed to reinforce and promote sex roles. One example is the contents of the marriage contract in Jewish law (*Ketuba*) (although examples can be found in all religious systems operative in Israel). This contract provides for ten obligations of the husband toward his wife and four obligations of the wife toward her husband. For example, the husband should pay for his wife's maintenance, while she should provide household services.[19] The structure of the arrangement is such that the woman is sheltered from the outside world by her husband and in return she adequately runs the home. The obligations one has toward the other are not equal but rather based on clear gender differentiation.

The principal drawback is reinforced by the fact that the religious courts are relatively autonomous organs. Except for specific legal provisions imposed upon them by the secular legal system, they adhere to their own substantive and procedural law.[20] The system is also run exclusively by men, usually older men more likely to consider the social phenomenon of sex roles as preordained and morally right.

Within the entire legal system religious courts remain the sole stronghold of sex-based discrimination (as distinguished from enforcement of sex roles). Its most important manifestation is the status of men and women with regard to divorce. Within the Jewish system, marriage is based on a private contract; therefore, the rabbinical courts are devoid of authority to dissolve the marriage. Only the husband can grant his wife the divorce, upon her consent. Where the husband is unwilling to divorce, the positions of husband and wife gain a formidable difference: a reluctant wife cannot stand in her husband's way to remarry, once certain conditions provided by the law are met;[21] a recalcitrant husband can keep his wife in marital bond forever.[22]

Resistance Factors Operating against Change in the Prevailing System

How, then, could a moderate to progressive Israeli Parliament in

19. See, generally, Louis M. Epstein, *The Jewish Marriage Contract* (New York: Jewish Theological Seminary of America, 1927); and Benzion Shereshevski, *Family Law* (Jerusalem: Rubin Mass, 1967).

20. For a discussion, see M. Chigier, "The Rabbinical Courts in the State of Israel," *Israel Law Review* 2 (1967): 162–74. See also Izhak Englard, *Religious Law in the Israel Legal System* (Jerusalem: Harry Sacher Inst., 1975).

21. The husband can marry a second wife: "Section 2 of the Penal Law Amendment (Bigamy) Law 5719–1959, provides a special defence in the form of permission to marry a second wife before the marriage with the first has been legally terminated, which is granted by a final judgment of a rabbinical court with the approval of the two chief Rabbis of Israel" (Englard, p. 156).

22. If the court reaches a decision that the couple should divorce and the husband refuses to comply with this decision the court can order the imprisonment of the husband until his consent is given. However, this remedy has been sparsely used and did not prove its effectiveness. See Zeev W. Falk, *The Divorce Action by the Wife* (Jerusalem: Harry Sacher Inst., 1973) (in Hebrew).

1957 legitimize a system which is so clearly discriminatory? The answer to this question is relevant both to the understanding of the history of the women's struggle in Israel and for an evaluation of the resistance operating against sex equality there. We have noted above the significance of the role party politicking played in exempting marital relations from the general application of WERL. However, the reasons for this compromise go far beyond plain party politics. One can distinguish at least three interrelated factors which supported this arrangement:

1. *The position of divine law vis-à-vis secular law.*—The basic position of divine (religious) law is that "obedience to secular laws, in order to be permitted, must have justification in divine law."[23] At least in Jewish and Moslem law, "Divine law is . . . composed of . . . the Written Law as revealed through God's chosen prophet and, the Oral Law as developed on behalf of God . . . by his duly authorized agents." The written law is considered so sacred that "it is the invariable rule that no secular law can be allowed to oust . . . [it]." The oral law is open to change from within, but historically "[t]here came a time when . . . the gate of independent reasoning was closed" and changes were no longer acceptable.[24]

Within the Jewish system the *Halacha* (particularly the written law) pertaining to marital relations is thus not subject to change by secular law. Any attempt to change it will create a conflict between law and conscience and inevitably lead to "civil disobedience" by those adhering to the faith. Hence, the basic argument opposing change is that neither the personnel of the religious courts nor the religious population could conscientiously abide by laws annulling sex-based discrimination provided for by the divine law.

2. *Popular national attitudes toward civil marriage and divorce.*—Were the position of religious law toward secular change the only resistance factor, a relatively simple solution could be found: concurrent jurisdiction of religious and secular family courts could be established, thus maintaining the principle of freedom of religion while providing women with a secular system where sex equality is recognized.[25] However, at least in Israel, it so happens that religion is also a major component of nationality. "Judaism has, contrary to many other religions, hardly ever departed from the path of a mono-ethnic religion, which has strengthened the ethnic coherence among Jews both in actual practice

23. Haim H. Cohen, "Secularization of Divine Law," in *Jewish Law in Ancient and Modern Israel* (Jerusalem: Ktav Publishing House, 1971), p. 3.

24. Cohen, pp. 3 and 31, respectively. Divine Law can be changed through interpretation by the recognized religious authorities, but, as Justice Cohen points out, there is considerable resistance from within the religious establishment to do so.

25. Prof. Amnon Rubinstein suggests a law of civil marriage which takes into consideration religious interests in preventing adulterous marriages by making maximum concessions in the law of divorce (Rubinstein, "The Right to Marry," *Tel-Aviv University Law Review* 2 [1973]: 433, 453–58 [in Hebrew]).

and in intent."[26] Building upon this aspect of Israeli culture, the opposition to civil marriage and divorce advances the following arguments:

a) Israel is a melting pot for a wide variety of ethnic groups and cultures. Religion "has served as the main integrative factor preserving the unity of the dispersed."[27] An attack on this main bastion of religion would cause dissension and unrest and disrupt this integrating process, a particularly undesirable prospect in light of the geopolitical scene, where the nation is at war and lack of unity may impede its capacity for self-defense.

b) Establishment of civil marriage and divorce will go beyond mere disruption of the integrative process and encouragement of social disorganization. Secular law, so the opposition warns us, will lead to sharp polarization and even actual division between religious and nonreligious Jews. This is so because Jewish religion does not recognize a civil divorce granted to persons married in a religious ceremony. Hence, a woman married in a religious ceremony and divorced by a civil decree is considered married and forbidden to other men. Should she remarry in a civil ceremony and have children, they will be considered "bastards" (due to her sin) and forbidden to Jews. Consequently, the Jewish population in Israel will be sharply divided into two camps which cannot intermarry. More ominous yet, the religious population may—as a result of policy—refrain from intermarriage in order to further ensure prevention of the forbidden intermarriages.[28]

Within the Jewish majority, 25 to 30 percent of the population are religious observants (who fully adhere to the *Halacha*). In addition, "There is a very sizable sector of the population, primarily among the Oriental Jews, who consider themselves 'traditionals' to whom religious symbolism has a strong appeal, while their personal observance and their religious beliefs are rather restricted. Together these two groups make up well over 60 percent of the population."[29] It is widely assumed, but never empirically examined, that this majority prefers the religious system of marriage and divorce and shuns its civil alternative. This assumption should be read in conjunction with the already ascertained data concerning popular attitudes towards sex equality, which indicate that the majority of persons do not consider the traditional pattern of sex roles as discrimination against women.[30] Hence, an argument that

26. Emanuel Gutmann, "Religion and National Integration in Israel" (paper presented at the meeting of the International Political Science Association, Jerusalem, September 9–13, 1974), p. 4. Similarly, Muslim symbolism and thought play a considerable role in the stimulation of national sentiments among Arabs.

27. Lawrence M. Friedman, "Legal Culture and Social Change," in Grossman and Grossman (n. 13 above).

28. Izhak Englard, "The Relationship between Religion and State in Israel," in Cohen (n. 23 above), p. 187.

29. Gutmann, p. 17.

30. Lahav (n. 4 above), pp. 110–11.

religious systems inherently discriminate against women, and therefore should be changed, is not likely to rally popular sympathy and support.

3. *Resistance to changes in the power structure.*—Last, but not least, one has to understand the vested interest the religious bloc has in the religious courts. Beyond its adherence to the *Halacha,* the religious bloc sees the universal religious jurisdiction exercised by the religious courts as a powerful stronghold. Not only does it provide prestige and status, but it also provides the religious bloc with a unique opportunity to reach most persons in society, including a great percentage of the 40 percent who are neither religious nor traditionals. Establishment of concurrent civil jurisdiction in matters of marriage and divorce will further cut their power, status, and prestige. The religious bloc is likely to, and in fact does, manipulate the other resistance factors discussed above in order to diminish the threat of any conscious change.

To this battery of resistance factors one should add the concern about the family as an institution. The opposition to changes in family law that could eliminate legal recognition of sex roles also asserts that the liberation of women leads to destruction of the family, damages the children, and generates social disorganization. This argument is generally advocated by the nationalist political organizations and the religious bloc.[31] They warn us that a permission to attack the family unit (in its traditional form) would undermine national unity and cohesion, a value which they appreciate more than individual self-fulfillment.

These resistance factors are still alive and well in Israel. In fact, they may have even gained some power and support from the growing tide of nationalism. Of course, it does not follow that they are rational or that the ominous predictions concerning the social consequences of change are likely to occur in reality. Proponents of change point out that in a democratic society the freedom from religion of the minority (that 40 percent) is as important as the freedom to exercise religion by the majority, and that these two interests can be easily balanced through establishment of concurrent jurisdictions. Furthermore, concurrent jurisdiction operates in many countries and no clear indications of significant disruption have emerged. Similarly, there is no evidence that a concept of the family unit based on sex equality, once accepted by a society, will result in social disorganization.[32]

Easing the Burden: The Israeli Solutions

The opposition to direct changes led to the creation of other legal mechanisms which ease the burden and offset the discriminatory prac-

31. See, e.g., *Divrei HaKnesset* 9 (1951): 2090, 2166, 2174.

32. See Goode (n. 1 above) and Lenore J. Weitzman, "Legal Regulation of Marriage: Tradition and Change," *California Law Review* 62 (1974): 1169, for an interesting critique of the traditional concept of marriage.

tices of the religious systems. These solutions fall into three categories discussed below:

1. *Concurrent jurisdiction.*—This arrangement was one of the few achievements of WERL. Discriminatory religious norms in areas such as custody, married women's property, and inheritance were abolished and could be applied only if all parties involved were consenting adults.[33] However, the arrangement did not apply to matters of marriage and divorce.[34]

2. *Supervision by the High Court of Justice.*—The High Court of Justice, a secular institution, has authority to annul religious courts' decisions which either are *ultra vires* the religious court's jurisdiction or disregard secular norms imposed upon the religious courts.[35] Also, the High Court can perform an act which the religious courts refuse to perform, although they have the jurisdiction to do so.[36] The remedy, however, is again only partial since the High Court is banned from substantive intervention in matters of marriage and divorce.[37]

3. *Statutory recognition of the "reputed spouse."*—An increasingly growing number of statutes bestows legal rights and social privileges upon persons who share a household and family life but are not formally married. The Names Law, for example, provides that a child born to parents who are reputed spouses is entitled to acquire the father's name, regardless of the father's consent.[38] This method has considerably eased the plight of those who either are unqualified to marry by religious standards or are unwilling to be bound by the religious system, but no research has yet been done on the number of "qualified" persons who freely prefer it to religious marriage.

Appraisal of the Effectiveness of the Israeli Solutions and Some Reflections on the Possibility of Change

The common denominator of the Israeli solutions is their indirect

33. WERL (n. 7 above), sec. 7.

34. Ibid., sec. 5.

35. Sec. 7(b) (4) of the Courts Law 5717-1957 provides that the High Court is competent "to order religious courts to deal with a particular matter in accordance with their competence or to refrain from dealing or from continuing to deal with a particular matter otherwise than in accordance with their competence. . . ." For a discussion, see Englard, *Religious Law in the Israel Legal System,* pp. 142–68.

36. In Rodnitzki v. The Rabbinical Court of Appeal (H.C. J. 51/69 24 P.D. [1] 704) the High Court ordered the registration of a Cohen and a divorcee (prohibited to intermarry under religious law) as a married couple, after they had married in a private ceremony and the rabbinical courts failed to grant them a declaratory judgment that their marriage was only voidable but not void.

37. The remedy described in n. 25 applies only to persons who are prohibited to marry under religious law. For a general discussion, see G. Hausner, "The Rights of the Individual in Court," *Israel Law Review* 9 (1975): 477, 486–95.

38. For a general discussion, see Daniel Friedman, "The 'Unmarried Wife' in Israeli Law," *Israel Yearbook of Human Rights* 2 (1972): 287, and H. Shelah, "The Reputed Spouse," *Mishpatim* 6 (1975): 119 (in Hebrew).

quality: none collides directly with the problem of sex-based discrimination applied by the religious systems. As a result, the legal system recognizes both the principle of sex equality and the principle of sex-based discrimination. The principal question, to which I have no answer, is to what extent can the principle of sex equality flourish and meaningfully penetrate the legal and social culture when its rival is formally recognized by the state?

Beyond this basic question, the Israeli solutions have proved inadequate, as is evidenced by the constant call from the liberal bloc to abolish the exclusive jurisdiction of the religious courts.[39]

In the first place, the supervision by the High Court of Justice has proven to be inherently weak. The religious courts view themselves as autonomous and are extremely reluctant to accept secular supervision. Occasional vendettas between the two judicial systems have resulted in increased sensitivity of the religious courts to their autonomy[40] and, as a concomitant result, have led to stiffening of positions concerning the viability of old religious norms.[41] In addition to such heretofore insurmountable hardships, one must consider the viability of institutional supervision of this kind. Again, from the vantage point of sex equality, the goal is to introduce the principle to as wide a range of cases as is possible. Supervision by a higher court is bound to apply only to a small number of cases. There is even no guarantee that these cases would be the more serious ones, since litigation depends also upon the tactics of the parties, their financial resources, and their personal attitude to religious jurisdiction and norms. The majority of cases will be treated as before, undisturbed by possible reprimanding and guidelines coming from the High Court. This point is of extreme importance when we come to evaluate law as a device for social change, which, as the Israeli experience shows, cannot be brought about by mere legislation of norms. The institutions which apply the norms determine the degree of their penetration. If these institutions are not sympathetic to the goal of social change (sex equality), supervision by another (sympathetic) institution through litigation can do little to ameliorate the situation.

The solution of statutory recognition of the "reputed spouse" is better for purposes of bringing about social change, which it may encourage by providing people with a state-recognized alternative to religious marriages. I have already indicated that the potentiality of this alternative will have to be analyzed and evaluated empirically. As it is recognized today, however, this alternative suffers from several drawbacks. In the first place, the set of legal rights and privileges bestowed

39. Rubinstein, "The Right to Marry," and the Hausner Bill, designed to allow civil marriage among persons unqualified to marry under *Halacha (Divrei HaKnesset* 64 [1972]: 2996).

40. Englard, *Religious Law in the Israel Legal System,* p. 155.

41. See, e.g., the reluctance of the religious courts to find a religious solution to the women whose husbands refuse to grant them a divorce, described in Falk (n. 22 above).

upon the reputed spouse ends with the unilateral decision of one spouse to end their relationship; that is, there is no state interference with the stability or lack of stability of the union. Indeed, a private contract between the spouses may provide for maintenance and other arrangements concerning property, but the state-created legal rights (e.g., social security) expire upon the unilateral termination of the relationship.[42] Given this kind of arrangement, it is doubtful whether it is likely to appeal to the majority of people in Israel, where marriage as a status symbol and the stability of the union are also important values.

Broadening the concurrent jurisdiction to apply it to matters of marriage and divorce has several advantages: (1) it does not infringe upon the freedom of conscience and religion of people; (2) it is already accepted and operative in Israel's legal system; (3) it is likely, though not certain, to command less opposition from the religious courts, since a slice of their power shall be retained; and (4) the competition of other courts may encourage the religious establishment to modernize and humanize the religious law in order to broaden or maintain its appeal.

Beyond the resistance factors already discussed, this solution raises some substantive difficulties from the viewpoint of its effectiveness as an instrument of social change. The first difficulty revolves around its compatibility with sex equality. Unless the religious law is modernized, the litigants within the religious system will still be subjected to norms which enforce sex-based differentiation and discrimination. Thus, concurrent jurisdiction compels us to abandon our original goal of universal implementation of sex equality in society. The second difficulty with this solution is institutional. So far, the concurrent jurisdiction in personal matters has been conducted by the regular civil courts. This is in itself not particularly desirable, since it seems preferable to have a new, specialized family court where well-trained personnel, committed to a system free of sex roles, can handle the conflicts between the parties.

The next question is two-fold. First, where would we find the time and energy to draft a suitable comprehensive statute to be enforced by such new courts? Furthermore, how do we reconcile between the moderate-to-conservative legislators who are afraid that sex equality "ruins" the family and the radicals who feel that no trace of sex roles should be found in the law? This conflict is in itself potent enough to undermine meaningful change. The other side of this coin contains organizational difficulties which should not be underestimated. Establishing a new institution is not only an expensive step; it also requires trained personnel to administer it. Given the grim state of the economy in Israel, it is doubtful whether this plan stands a chance of appearing on the nation's agenda in the near future.

Another possible solution is changing the system from within—that is, encouraging the religious decision-makers to change the divine law

42. Friedman, "The 'Unmarried Wife' in Israeli Law," pp. 301–4.

and adapt it to modern concepts of sex equality. This solution is desirable not only because it is relatively inexpensive but because it may offset some of the more ferocious opposition to change. A change from within can capitalize on the traditional elements in Israeli culture in order to facilitate the penetration of sex equality. However, no step has been taken in this direction.

Sex Equality and Sex Roles: The Compatibility of Sex Equality with Maintenance of a Privileged Status for Women

Section 6 of WERL provides that the principle of legal equality declared in section 1 shall not affect laws designed to protect "women as women." This position was unanimously accepted by the Knesset when section 6 was submitted for voting.[43] The rationale for the creation of a privileged status for women is twofold and contains a built-in conflict. On the one hand, it is asserted that the status of women in society is so underprivileged that only the creation of sex-based social privileges can offset it and ensure equality. Proponents of this line of reasoning may strategically strive toward genuine sex equality and elimination of sex roles, but being pragmatists they think that tactically there should be an intermediate phase when a privileged status is ensured by law. On the other end of the spectrum stand those who think that some sex roles are natural (such as motherhood) and therefore should be recognized by the law. Proponents of this view do not share the radical concept of sex equality. For them, the policy contained in section 6 is a strategic not a tactical goal. The conflict between these two positions seems to be common to most societies, especially to developing societies where the social inferiority of women is more manifest. Social conditions may temporarily unite these two policies and blur the distinctions between them. Thus Israel of 1951 may well have been unprepared for a "radical" statutory arrangement, because of the mass of underprivileged, deeply religious, and traditional people who constituted the majority of the population. Under these circumstances, we can appreciate the conscious attempt to guarantee special social privileges to women only. The question is what price was paid for this policy and what fruits did it bear in terms of sex equality?

The policy of protecting women as women has led to conscious legitimization of sex roles. Israeli labor and social legislation assign the roles of postnatal care and child rearing to women, not to men.[44] Moreover, the presumption that women are more "fragile" than men is

43. *Divrei HaKnesset* 9 (1951): 2186.

44. See, e.g., the Employment of Women Law, which provides for a twelve-week leave for postnatal care for mothers only (excluding fathers who may wish to care for the newborn themselves) and the Severance Pay Law providing that a mother may resign within nine months after giving birth and be eligible for full severance pay.

also a part of the legal system. Two examples will suffice: women are generally prohibited from work at night; collective bargaining contracts provide for an earlier retirement age for women.[45] With hindsight, it is not easy to appraise the impact of this policy on the status of women —that is, to what extent has it improved the status of women and to what extent has it undermined progress? However, If we accept the proposition that the concept of sex roles generally hinders the free development of the personality and obstructs the participation of women in social endeavors, and if we accept as an indication of this proposition the generally inferior status of women in the Israeli labor force since 1951, then we must come to the conclusion that the policy contained in section 6 has been a barrier to sex equality, not an intermediary phase toward it.

The solution to this problem is simple: if we conclude that section 6 is not a useful device to advance women, then we can abolish it. The social rights and privileges of today can be transferred to a parent, leaving the option to exercise them to either mother or father. Similarly, all other regulative devices can be amended to provide optional possibilities to "persons" regardless of sex.

Would there be any resistance to such a solution? Yes, indeed. Women who are organized in the labor unions and their representatives at the top echelons of the political decision-making process strongly oppose any attempt to equalize the present system. Recently, a suggestion to equalize the retirement age was proposed. The women's labor unions have opposed it so strongly that the leadership of the *Histadrut* (the Federation of Labor) had to retract their acquiescence to it. Similarly, an effort to abolish the legislative prohibition of night work is obstructed by women Knesset members.[46]

In addition to this resistance which is particular to labor legislation, the variables discussed above which are related to traditional and religious elements in Israeli society are operative. The notions that the family unit in its traditional framework is a societal goal and that it affects positively national unity and cohesion militate against full and equal (as distinguished from partial) participation of women in public life and the labor force.

Again, it may prove futile to argue with those who consider sex stereotyping a part of nature. The only way to neutralize them is through election of more and more liberal persons to positions of power. A fear of losing material privileges is more difficult to deal with. One way of handling it is to let women maintain their privileges or opt for equality. However, such a solution has a pitfall: social attitudes may pressure women to exercise the option which is more in keeping with her sex role. Thus, we may find that the optional solution is still inade-

45. Article 16(a) of the Central Pension Fund of the Histadrut Workers.

46. This information is based on a discussion with Zohar Karty of the Ministry of Labor. Currently the ministry is conducting empirical research to assess the number of women who may be affected by a change in the present law.

quate for promoting sex equality. A better solution is to secure the privileges for those groups who have already joined the labor force, but to deny them to newcomers. Thus, women who are presently employed could exercise an option as to whether they wish to work night shifts, whereas newcomers would no longer have that option. This solution is neither elegant nor easy to implement from the organizational and administrative points of view, but it seems to be the only one which is capable of neutralizing the present opposition.

Whatever the solutions, the Israeli experience in this area can teach us an important lesson: legal devices to further the status of women may well turn into traps. The extra protection of women in 1951 created vested interests. The groups who enjoy them oppose change. Thus, the tactical step has proven a barrier for the long-term strategy.[47] It not only helps internalize and legitimize sex roles, but also makes change materially painful. Indeed, this development again demonstrates the immense difficulties to be encountered on the road to sex equality.

* * *

In their introduction to *Law and Change in Modern America,* Joel and Mary Grossman define social change by a continuum of three interrelated segments: rate, the time factor—how long it takes change to occur; the magnitude, the measurement of change—whether it is marginal or incremental, comprehensive, or revolutionary; the scope or type of change—the number of persons or groups in a society whose behavior norms change.[48] Applying this definition to Israel, we can conclude that law as a device of social change has done a very modest job. The rate of achieving sex equality is slow, the magnitude is less than comprehensive, and the scope is not approaching the level of societal mores; that is, the norm of sex equality is not widely penetrated within society. However, this is not a failure of law since the legalized concept of sex equality in Israel has always been ambivalent.

The prospects for future social change through legislation are not promising. This is so primarily because the majority of Israel's decision makers cannot free themselves of the traditional concept of sex roles.

The reform which has so far been proposed reflects either attachment to or compromise with the notion of sex roles. The proposed Bill for Basic Law: The Rights of Man contains the principle of equality regardless of sex (among other categories); yet, at least one version proposes to qualify this principle with a provision sheltering "women as women."[49] The Bill for Basic Law: The Rights of Women suggests that

47. It may still be considered as a meaningful and sufficient achievement for those who consider this type of sex equality as the long-term goal.

48. Grossman and Grossman (n. 13 above), p. 4.

49. Version (a) to section 2(b) (the section on equality), *Hatza'ot Hok* (Legislative Bills) 1085 (August 12, 1973).

the principle of equality shall not derogate from rights bestowed upon pregnant women or mothers to children.[50] The new law which legalizes abortion reflects a compromise arrangement, whereby abortion can be authorized by a committee of doctors and social workers under specific circumstances only.[51]

All the above means that, at least in Israel, law cannot be conceived of as the instrument of reform which will lead the camp to sex equality. In light of the Israeli experience, it may be advisable to see law as an instrument which can be moderately helpful but which still lags behind developing social standards. Within the framework of this conception of law, we have to concentrate more on social actuality and less on formal standards.

The implications of an approach to social reforms which emphasize the social actuality are that we have to devote our time and energy to supportive mechanisms. First and foremost, the educational system should be changed to prevent sex stereotyping from being hammered into children at an early date. The school system should also prolong the number of hours children spend at school, thereby making it easier for working mothers to undertake full-time jobs.[52] The bureaucracy can be combed carefully for sex-based discriminations, which will then be eliminated.[53] A similar practice can be applied to all public institutions and organs.

These are only a few of the supportive mechanisms which may help to bring about more equality. Many more will probably be recommended by Israel's governmental commission for the improvement of the status of women. Careful cultivation of sex equality in social actuality will soften some and eliminate other resistance factors, so vigorously opposing sex equality in contemporary Israel.

Faculty of Law
Hebrew University of Jerusalem
Jerusalem, Israel

50. A private bill presented to the Knesset by Shulamit Aloni.

51. The law was enacted on January 31, 1977 (*Sefer Ha-Hukim* 842). For a description and discussion, see Nitza Shapiro-Libai, "The Right to Abortion," *Israel Yearbook of Human Rights* 5 (1975): 120.

52. A plan to prolong the school day is presently facing heavy opposition: it is doubtful whether the government's budget can cover its costs; it needs personnel and facilities (e.g., dining rooms) which are not available. Moreover, the teachers' union (mostly women) opposes any attempt to prolong its working day.

53. Through conscientious application of WERL, sec. 1.

Politics and Institutions

The Shaping of the Kaum Ibu (Women's Section) of the United Malays National Organization

Lenore Manderson

The period prior to and immediately after independence in Malaya was one of rapid social change and political advantage, which provided Malay women as well as men with opportunities to participate in public life. This paper discusses the development of the Kaum Ibu (Women's Association) as an auxiliary of the United Malays National Organization (UMNO), the dominant party in Malaysian politics since the end of the Second World War. The paper suggests that the change of status of the Kaum Ibu from that of a group of relatively independent women's associations affiliated with the UMNO to a single adjunct of the parent party, with limited representation in its hierarchy, reflects the generally accepted view of the supportive role of women.

Traditional Roles of Malay women

Under both *adat* (custom) and Islam, a Malay woman is essentially without status until she has married and has borne children. Only after her childbearing years are over does she enjoy greater status and independence.[1] However, claims that "the wife does not even do the

This article is drawn from the author's Ph.D. dissertation, "The Development of the Kaum Ibu (Women's Section) of the United Malays National Organization, 1945–72" (Australian National University, 1977).

1. Peter J. Wilson, *A Malay Village and Malaysia: Social Values and Rural Development* (New Haven, Conn.: HRAF Press, 1967), p. 105.

shopping"[2] and that "man is the sole breadwinner"[3] belie the actual involvement of women in economic and social life.

Women were active in the traditional economy. Lewis, for example, notes that they were the rice growers in Negri Sembilian Minangkabau society.[4] This changed little while the Malays concentrated on subsistence farming. The 1947 census and its successors further attest to the importance of women in agriculture, although the returns, while including family workers without pay in the economically active sector of the labor force, still define as housewives the many women who do contribute to family welfare and income by tending vegetable gardens and fruit trees, running poultry, etc. Additionally, the importance of the home in traditional Malay culture,[5] where matters of village welfare were often discussed, suggests that the women of the household could have exercised significant influence in the decision making of the village.

Women of aristocratic birthright played less subtle roles in public life. For example, women succeeded to the throne in Aceh from 1641 to 1699[6] and in Patani from 1584 to circa 1688.[7] From the eighteenth century on, women ceased to be actively involved in government; however, many individual women exercised considerable political power through personal relationships.

From the Malay aristocracy came the women and men who became leaders in postwar politics and administration. The colonial education policy was a determining factor in their continuity. The majority of Malays who received formal education attended elementary vernacular schools, in keeping with their roles as peasant farmers and fishermen. Members of the aristocracy, however, received an English education, a prerequisite to entering the civil service and the exercise of some responsibility in the administration of the country.

The value of female education was discussed during the religious debates of the 1920s between the *kaum muda,* modernists influenced by the reformist teachings and pan-Islamic nationalism of universities in

2. Hashinah Roose, "Changes in the Position of Malay Women," in *Women in the New Asia,* ed. Barbara E. Ward (Paris: UNESCO, 1963), p. 200.

3. M. Swift, "Men and Women in Malay Society," ibid., p. 277.

4. Diane K. Lewis, "The Minangkabau Malay of Negri Sembilan: A Study of Sociocultural Change" (Ph.D. diss., Cornell University, 1962), p. 259 (see also Rosemary Firth, *Housekeeping among Malay Peasants,* 2d ed., in *Monographs on Social Anthropology,* no. 7 [London: Athlone Press, 1966]; and Michael Swift, *Malay Peasant Society in Jelebu,* ibid., no. 29 [London: Athlone Press, 1965]).

5. Wilson, p. 116.

6. Iljas Sutan Pamenan, *Rentjong Atjeh ditangan Wanita* (*Zaman Pemerintahan Radja2 Puteri diAtjeh*) (Djakarta: University of Djakarta [?], 1959).

7. A. Teeuw and D. K. Wyatt, *Hikayat Patani,* 2 vols. (The Hague: Martinus Nijhoff, 1970). The Kelantan dynasty, which succeeded the Patani dynasty, also had a queen, Raja Dewi, from 1707 to 1716.

the Middle East, and *kaum tua,* traditionalists who supported the traditional Malay elite and the court system of the Malay States. *Kaum muda* advocated greater freedom for women to receive an education, but they stressed religious training and based their appeals on the importance of a woman as the first educator of her children.[8]

If most Malay parents saw little point in educating their sons they could see even less in educating their daughters. After all, one did not need to be literate to work in the kitchen and the rice fields.[9] Few girls' schools were established, so most girls could only receive vernacular schooling if they enrolled at a boys' school—provided there was room for them—with a female teacher being assigned to the school only where the enrollment of girls was large enough to justify a needlework class. The failure of the British to provide an alternative to such coeducation compounded parents' fears that their daughters would simply learn to write love letters, and served as an additional discouragement. Thus the number of educated Malay girls remained small. However, among Malay aristocrats an educated daughter also enhanced her father's status and assured her family of favorable marriage prospects,[10] and thus daughters as well as sons from this class often did receive an English education. The first Malay woman to so benefit was Cik Sofiah binte Abdullah, who was enrolled at the Bukit Nanas Convent in 1907. She, as Mrs. Majeed, was prominent in public life some decades later, as were many others who took advantage of the available English education.

The Rise of Women's Associations and the Birth of the Kaum Ibu

Women's associations before World War II, such as the YWCA and the Girl Guides, followed the interests and activities of similar organizations in Britain. Often they were founded by the wives of British administrators or by women of the local elite in contact with the British. Local "Ladies' Associations" similarly differed little in function from women's social and philanthropic associations in the West, on which they tended to be modeled.

Though such organizations included some Malay women, a few specifically Malay women's organizations had also been established. Hajjah Zain, who became the second leader of the women's section of

8. See, for example, Marina Merican, "Sayed Shaikh Al-Hadi dan Pendapat2nya mengenai Kemajuan Kaum Perempuan" (academic exercise, B.A. Honors Malay Studies, University of Malaya, 1969), and Khalidah Adibah binte Haji Amin, "Ahmad Luthfi on the Education and Freedom of Women" (academic exercise, B.A. Honors Malay Studies, University of Malaya, 1957).

9. Caroline R. Gerhold, "Factors Relating to Educational Opportunities for Women Residents of the Malay Peninsula" (Ph.D. diss, Cornell University, 1971).

10. Ibid., p. 72.

UMNO, had founded the Malay Women Teachers' Union in 1929.[11] The Kesatuan Melayu Singapura had an active women's section by 1940, when it sent representatives to the Second Pan-Malayan Congress. In 1940, too, Azizah binte Jaafar, sister of the political leader Datuk Onn bin Jaafar, sponsored the Malay Ladies' Association in Johore. It undertook social welfare work during the war years as well as holding literacy, cooking, and sewing classes.[12]

The immediate postwar period saw a mushrooming of associations for women of all races, as well as the specifically established Malay political associations of the late 1930s. Most were not provoked by specific government action, the exception being the Women's Service League established in October 1946 by the wife of the governor, Lady Gent, to "clean up the mess made by the men of the nations."[13] Its voluntary welfare and social-educational functions were continued by the Women's Institutes, founded in 1952 by Lady Templer and sponsored by the government. The institutes' leadership also came from upper-class women, such as the wives and daughters of federal administrators, district officers, and assistant district officers.

The membership of most women's organizations, both political and nonpolitical, was predominantly from one race—Malay, Chinese, or Indian. For example, one of the earliest women's organizations founded after the war was the Women's Union, a branch of which was established in Johore Bahru in December 1945. It had a predominantly Chinese membership but was concerned for all women, as indicated by resolutions passed at its conference, held in Kuala Lumpur in February 1946, which inter alia called for the representation of women on the Selangor Religious Advisory Council, the establishment of creches, the elimination of prostitution, and the establishment of schools for free education for women.

Malay women beyond the peninsula had established social and welfare associations, but on the peninsula the organizations, though concerned with such matters, were often expressly political; for example, Free Indonesia Union (Women's Branch),[14] the Malay Women's Eman-

11. Asiah binte Abu Samah, "Emancipation of Malay Women (1945–57)" (academic exercise, B.A. Honors History, University of Malaya, 1960), p. 6.

12. T. H. Silcock and Ungku Abdul Aziz, "Nationalism in Malaya," in *Asian Nationalism and the West,* ed. William L. Holland (New York; Macmillan Co., 1953), p. 308. For accounts of the beginnings of nationalism and political organization, see also Mohammad Yunus Hamidi, *Sejarah Pergerakan Politik Melayu Semenanjong* (Kuala Lumpur: Purtaka Antara, 1961); W. R. Roff, *The Origins of Malay Nationalism* (Singapore: University of Malaya Press, 1967), and "The Persatuan Melayu Selangor: An Early Malay Political Association," *Journal of Southeast Asian History* 9, no. 1 (March 1960): 117–46; and Radin Soenarno, "Malay Nationalism, 1900–1945," *Journal of Southeast Asian History* 1, no. 1 (March 1960): 1–28.

13. *Straits Times* (October 11, 1946).

14. *Majlis* (December 17, 26, 27, 1946).

cipation Association,[15] and AWAS (Angkatan Wanita Sedar), the women's section of the Malay Nationalist Party, successor of the Kesatuan Melayu Muda (known during the war years as Kesatuan Rakyat Indonesia Semenanjong). Active for about two years, AWAS was created as a separate section to "arouse in Malay women the consciousness of the equal rights they have with men, to free them from the old bonds of tradition and to 'socialize' them."[16]

Most significant, though, were the Malay women's associations and leagues (*kumpulan kaum ibu*) which appeared from early 1946 in support of the Malay associations. The Kaum Ibu, sometimes established without the knowledge of the male leaders and maintaining more or less autonomous status,[17] undertook to raise funds to support protests against the Malayan Union proposals as well as to rally together women to protest publicly. On her return to Malaya, Britain had announced her future plans for the country, which provoked a dramatic surge of political activity by educated middle-class Malays with strong rural support. Essentially, Britain proposed to separate Singapore from the peninsular states and settlements and to prepare the way for self-government for the peninsula by introducing a unitary government, replacing the powers of the Sultans with British jurisdiction and establishing a common Malayan citizenship which gave all those permanently domiciled in Malaya equal citizenship rights. These proposals undermined rights of the traditional elite that had been previously accepted and protected and placed the Malays on an equal and therefore vulnerable political footing with the economically advantaged Chinese and Indian immigrant communities.

A *kumpulan kaum ibu* was established in Batu Pahat in support of the Pergerakan Melayu Semenanjong (Peninsular Malay Movement) shortly after its inauguration, with branches in neighboring villages, by the wife of the leader Datuk Onn. His sister, Azizah binte Jaafar, established a similar association in Johore Bahru. By December 1946 Kaum Ibu organizations had been established in Persatuan, Selangor, Ipoh, Taiping, Larut and Metang, Kelantan, Kuala Langat, Kuala Krai, Ulu Langat, Lower Perak, Kajang, Klang, and Kuala Kubu; and Saberkas, a left-wing party affiliated with UMNO, had an active women's section. Early in 1947 a similar association was founded in Dungun.

Malay women played a vital role in demonstrations against the Malayan Union. Miller describes them as "the most remarkable feature of the period": "They were challenging, dominant, vehement in their

15. This association supported the radical nationalist element of postwar politics and participated in anti-Federation meetings.

16. Ahmad Boestaman, leader of the youth movement of the MNP, API (Angkatan Permuda Insaf), in an interview with Asiah binte Abu Samah (Asiah, p. 13).

17. For example, see Datin Onn's interview in *Buku Cenderamata Jubli Perak Wanita UMNO Malaysia* (Kuala Lampur: United Malays National Organization, 1974), p. 37.

emergence from meek quiet roles in the kampongs, the rice fields, the kitchens and the nurseries. . . . Sir Theodore [Adams] said later, 'Seven speeches delivered by Malay women rank with anything I have heard in Malaya since my arrival as a cadet in 1908. They seem a forecast of the great assistance which women will bring to the future welfare of the whole country. A revolution has come about!' "[18] The women who took their dissatisfaction and concern to the streets provided striking evidence to the visiting Parliamentary Mission of the real and general Malay opposition to the Malayan Union proposals. The proposals were subsequently abandoned, and following consultation with members of all communities, but particularly with UMNO, the Federation of Malaya came into being on February 1, 1948.

From the outset women also were involved in both the establishment of UMNO and in encouraging others to play an active role in public life. Women delegates attended the March Pan-Malayan Congress at which Cik Zahara Tamin expressed Kaum Ibu support of the protest against the Malayan Union proposals and entreated the men to extend equal rights to Malay women. Shortly after, Cik Maznah of the Taiping Kaum Ibu called on Malay women to "take an active part in the reconstruction and rehabilitation of the country" and "not to lag behind our sisters in other communities."[19] The editorial of the *Straits Times* of May 18, 1946, noted with interest the presence of Malay women at the two-day conference held to discuss the formation of UMNO. Their presence was seen as a "remarkable indication of a new spirit and consciousness among the Malays," although one of the women attending the conference, Cik Saleha binte Mohamed Ali, honorary secretary of the Selangor Malay Women's Association, had only a few days earlier prophetically expressed her doubt that women would soon become directly involved in politics: "We are more interested in education and social welfare, but I have no doubt that eventually we will get down to politics. We still have a lot to learn about politics."[20]

The concept of a single Malay women's association, with the general aims and objectives of UMNO, was first introduced for discussion at the 1946 UMNO General Assembly by Cik Puteh Mariah binte Ibrahim Rashid of the Persatuan Melayu Perak, Cik Zainab binte Abdul Rahman of the Persatuan Melayu Seberang Prai, and Cik Saleha binte Mohamed Ali of the Persatuan Melayu Selangor. Following these discussions, a Kaum Ibu office was established within UMNO headquarters. At a party meeting later that year it was decided to appoint to this office Cik Puteh Mariah, then president of the Ipoh Women's Branch of the Persatuan Melayu Perak and wife of the UMNO Officer-in-Charge of Politics. She accepted the position on January 4, 1947.

18. Harry Miller, *Prince and Premier* (London: George Harrap & Co., 1959), p. 80.
19. *Straits Times* (March 25, 1946).
20. Ibid. (May 14, 1946).

The first separate women's conference was held as part of the UMNO General Assembly on September 1, 1947, and was attended by seventeen delegates representing twelve women's associations affiliated with UMNO, whose membership totaled some 20,000 women. The major purpose of the conference was to discuss the most effective organization at state and national levels for these organizations. At the time, each state had several small independent women's associations, which effectively prevented the Kaum Ibu from having a voice in the UMNO Assembly. Cik Puteh stressed the need for women to find a means to cooperate to improve conditions (affecting the status of women) and to increase the usefulness of the women's organizations: "We must unite if we are not to be defeated in the struggle for our national existence. The time for parochialism is past."[21] Thus it was decided at the conference that the Kaum Ibu associations should confederate into single united state organizations affiliated with UMNO. Representatives at the conference were then directed by Cik Puteh to ask their individual organizations to become part of UMNO. At the same time, liaison/information officers were appointed in each state to assist the Kaum Ibu Officer-in-Charge with her work.

Matters other than organization were also discussed, including the problems of easy divorce and arranged marriages, the need for Malay women to be employed in the Department of Welfare to help their own people, and the provision of UMNO scholarships to enable Malay girls to further their education. The Persatuan Melayu Perlis became the first to propose, unsuccessfully, a change of name from *Kaum Ibu dan putri* (literally, mothers and girls) to *kaum perempuan* (women).

One month later the UMNO Executive Committee met in Ipoh and effected certain organizational changes. It was now to consist of four inner committees as follows: (1) the president and the Departments of Political Affairs, Publicity, and Women and Social Welfare; (2) the secretary-general and the Departments of Religious Affairs, Education, and Youth; (3) the Secretary for Legal Affairs and the Departments of Economics, Labor, and Trade and Industries; (4) the Secretary for Financial Affairs. Cik Puteh's office within the UMNO organization was expanded and upgraded from Officer-in-Charge, Kaum Ibu, to Secretary, Department of Women and Social Welfare. Six months later, at the Tenth General Assembly, a new constitution was introduced, providing for direct individual membership with UMNO instead of membership through affiliated organizations.

Two hundred women delegates and observers attended the women's conference of the UMNO General Assembly at Arau on May 27, 1949, at which motions dealing with divorce, religion, education, and the representation of women in Parliament were discussed. Three

21. Ibid. (September 2, 1947).

months later more than 200 women attended the women's session of the Twelfth UMNO General Assembly at Butterworth. There the system of independently affiliated Kuam Ibu organizations was replaced by a single auxiliary of the party for women, to be known as the Pergerakan Kaum Ibu UMNO (UMNO women's movement). This was also the first Kaum Ibu meeting since UMNO had been formed into divisions, and because of this Datuk Onn, in his opening address, reassured the women that they would have the right to elect their own representatives: "The voice of the Kaum Ibu will be as that of the men—the voice of both will determine the shape of the administration of the country."[22]

Kaum Ibu as an Auxiliary of the United Malays National Organization

The organization of the Kaum Ibu, like that of UMNO Youth, paralleled the structure of the parent body, with a branch office (*cawangan*) at the grass-roots level; a division (*bahagian*), regarded as most important by the party; and a state committee, composed of the divisional leaders of the Kaum Ibu, which distributed information and acted as liaison between the divisions and the national Kaum Ibu. From early 1959 Kaum Ibu also had its own full-time secretary, located in the UMNO national secretariat, to undertake the functions relating to the section previously handled by the UMNO secretary-general.

The supreme decision-making body of the Kaum Ibu was the annual assembly attended by representatives from the divisions. However, power effectively lay in the hands of the Kaum Ibu National Executive Committee, elected by the assembly. Provision was also made for women to attend the UMNO General Assembly. At one held at the end of December 1955 a revised constitution was adopted which provided for more effective control of the party. Both UMNO Pemuda (Youth) and the Kaum Ibu were to have more say in the assembly, but henceforth they were to be strictly supervised by the UMNO Central Executive Committee. The UMNO Youth was granted twenty-four seats in the assembly, instead of the former two, while Kaum Ibu was allocated one seat for every 750 members. At the 1960 assembly the UMNO constitutional decision of 1955 was reversed, and the youth and women's sections were each allotted only three seats in the assembly.

In the central UMNO organization the Pergerakan Kaum Ibu was initially represented by the Ketua Kaum Ibu (national leader), but from 1951 on she was assisted by four committee members whom she had the power to appoint. The five of them constituted the Jawatan Penasehat Hal-Ehwal Kaum Perempuan (advisory committee on matters relating to

22. *Malay Mail* (August 26, 1949).

women). Among the first four appointments was one man. This committee continued with slight variations. Two Kaum Ibu members represented the section on the National Executive Committee of the party. Other national committees occasionally included one or two women. The Selection committee for election candidates had one Kaum Ibu member, and despite repeated requests by the section their representation on this committee was not increased.

A few motions in the early 1950s suggest some dissatisfaction with the degree to which women were included in party decision making and in the structure of the organization. For example, in 1953 at the UMNO General Assembly held in Malacca a resolution called for the establishment of an independent women's league to have direct dealings with UMNO headquarters. A later modified resolution called for Kaum Ibu branches to be responsible to the Kaum Ibu division and not to the UMNO branch.[23] Despite such motions, the representation of women in the parent body never reflected the number of women who were members of UMNO, or even their contribution to the party accredited by its male leaders.[24]

However, Kaum Ibu members were concerned more with the internal organization of their section than with its relationship with the parent body, and organizational moves were to strengthen Kaum Ibu itself. In 1954, for example, it was proposed that a special organizing committee be established to meet at least once every three months; in 1956 Kaum Ibu leaders from twenty-three divisions met to discuss plans to streamline the section. Kaum Ibu members frequently drew attention to the lack of women on public bodies and constantly called for the preselection of women candidates, but there does not appear to have been any sustained effort to redress the severe underrepresentation of women within the party.

Although the effect of the subservient and supportive status of women assumed both by men and women themselves cannot be underestimated, a partial explanation of this acquiescence may lie in the membership and leadership of the section. National leadership during this period was fairly unstable. In 1949 Puteh Mariah led the movement. In August 1950 she was succeeded by Hajjah Zain Binte Suleiman. Due to Hajjah Zain's ill health, the Raja Perempuan Perlis Tengku Budriah

23. Early in 1956 a change was introduced with regard to the payment of fees (*yuran*). Kaum Ibu branches were now to pay fees directly to their particular Kaum Ibu division rather than to the UMNO branch, except where there was no Kaum Ibu division, in which case the fees were forwarded direct to national UMNO through the UMNO State Committee.

24. For example, the secretary-general of UMNO in 1952, Encik Zulkifli bin Mohamed Hashim, praised Kaum Ibu: "It has been a very good year for UMNO, which owes so much to its women members for their loyal support, services and progress in the fields of social welfare, education and politics. By the determination and diligent efforts to improve their social participation in civics and politics, the women have turned out to be the backbone of UMNO " (*Straits Times* [January 7, 1953]).

(later Queen of Malaya) acted in the position for three months until the end of 1953, when she was succeeded by Khatijah Sidek. Khatijah's period in office was marred by several controversies, culminating in her dismissal from the party in November 1956. The Central Executive Committee then appointed Fatimah binte Haji Hashim as the new ketua, a position she held by election until 1972. Such fluctuations were not evident among the larger leadership group. These women, active at national, state, and division levels as office bearers and committee members, were a small and constant group, holding office for many years with little challenge. Those who held key leadership positions were for the most part urban women, often the daughters or wives of political activitists from the aristocracy and the English-educated elite. Most women who held office at the division and branch levels were again often urban or suburban dwellers who had received vernacular or religious education. While almost all of them were married and with children, the majority were also in paid employment, particularly as teachers in Malay schools, in adult education classes, or as religious teachers. Significantly, most women leaders had family members —parents, siblings, or spouses—active in UMNO, again often in leadership positions or, alternatively, in the public eye through their position within the administration. The ability of the urban leaders to undertake such positions was facilitated by their socioeconomic status, since they were able to employ domestic help and so were released from domestic duties to pursue a career or to be involved in associational activities.

Most women in leadership positions were relatively young, in their early to mid-twenties at the time of joining UMNO and first holding office. However, despite increasingly frequent pleas to younger and educated women to join the section, the majority of women comprising the mass membership were married, middle-aged, village women whose time was devoted largely to subsistence activities. They were often illiterate, their occupation described as *ahli rumah, kerja rumah* or *kerja kampong* (housework or rural work). Thus most Kaum Ibu members had neither the time, education, nor opportunity to lobby persistently for party changes.

As education became increasingly available and as attitudes of Malay parents changed toward their daughters' education, so too did the number of educated women increase in the Kaum Ibu. However, their number remained insignificant, and the suspicion with which they were often regarded by older village women militated against their undertaking forceful leadership within the organization.

The Role of Kaum Ibu during Elections

While Kaum Ibu's aims, as expressed in the UMNO constitution, were both political and social, activities of the branches usually centered around the latter, making the Kaum Ibu little different from the non-political Women's Institutes. Adult education literacy classes and classes in cooking, sewing, and religion were held for members; help was given to families who were victims of fire, flood, or personal tragedy. The sick were visited, wedding feasts were prepared, and occasionally cooperatives were established. Concerts, fun fairs, and sales of goods made by members were held to raise funds for use by the branches. These activities were a continual source of pride for the Kaum Ibu, and their educational and voluntary welfare activities were particularly praised by national leaders.

The major political activity which involved village members was concentrated around election time. The party's need for mass support to insure its role in government was reflected in the Kaum Ibu's care to maintain its grass-roots membership and to establish new branches and divisions in any area where there was not yet one established. Yet membership of the Kaum Ibu, originally part of the general Malay reaction to the Malayan Union, tended to decline as immediate nationalist goals were attained. This became a perpetual problem. As early as 1947 Kaum Ibu leaders were expressing concern at the falling membership. For example, Cik Puteh Mariah, Officer-in-Charge, Kaum Ibu, brought to the attention of the secretary-general of UMNO in June of that year the depleted membership of Klang Kaum Ibu, which its leaders attributed to the restriction on women making speeches at political rallies. The leader of UMNO, Datuk Onn, was skeptical that the progress of the organization did depend on this factor and suggested that the group organize its own functions and that Cik Puteh personally visit the Klang group. The 1947 assembly, recognizing the importance of liaison between national and local Kaum Ibu organizations, discussed the possibility of appointing assistant Kaum Ibu officers in each state and requested that Cik Puteh visit all locations where associations had already been set up.

To ensure the consolidation of old and the establishment of new branches, Siti Rahmah binte Haji Kassim was appointed as Assistant Information Officer (Women) in 1950, in which capacity she spent much of her time traveling from one district to another addressing established groups and encouraging women in areas where Kaum Ibu had not yet been established[25]. Such personal contact was an important means of motivation, as evidenced by the number of new branches established in the wake of visits by other leaders. For example, the secretary-general of UMNO, in a letter to Tengku Abdul Rahman prior to the latter's visit in Pahang Selatan Division, requested, "If you could find a day or two I

25. She was appointed on May 1, 1950. On December 1, 1951, she left UMNO to join the Independence of Malaya Party, but the following year rejoined UMNO and was approached to accept her old position. This was rejected by the UMNO Executive Committee. By 1955, however, she had reestablished herself as state leader of Negri Sembilan Kaum Ibu, and in 1958 was deputy leader for South Malaya.

would like you to come down to give some more inspiration to the women folk. I have just opened up two women's branches—Kuantan and Pekan, they are now working very hard, perhaps to compete with their opposite sex."[26]

At election time Kaum Ibu members were drawn into campaigning. Small working groups within each electorate moved from house to house, distributing polling cards and party manifestos, discussing voting procedure and candidates with those they found at home (usually women and old men), and insuring that the people in the villages were not ignorant and would participate in the voting. Kaum Ibu made lists of voters in the areas for which they were responsible, and on election day their task was to see that all registered voters, regardless of party affiliation, did exercise their right of franchise. Theoretically, preelection campaigning should have been nondiscriminatory, but in fact known supporters of the opposition were avoided.[27]

This grass-roots activity was essential to insure the election of the UMNO-MCA-MIC Alliance. Voting was not compulsory, and the right to vote was contingent on a citizen's registration. The rate of registration was low, and poll turnout even lower, during early polls. Electoral apathy was apparent in the first election held in Singapore in 1948. This was also the case on the peninsula. In the municipal elections in Kuala Lumpur in 1953, for example, less than one-twelfth of the potential electorate, 2 percent of the population, was registered. Yet despite their confusion and unfamiliarity with voting, Malay women had already shown their willingness to participate in this process:

> The most striking feature of the 1952 election . . . was the way women of Malay turned up at the polls. In the six Federation towns of Penang, Kuala Lumpur, Malacca, Batu Pahat, Muar and Johore Bahru, and in Singapore, they went in their thousands to choose their representatives to the three municipalities, three town councils and city council. In Penang, despite the rain, the women cast their votes on the way to do the day's marketing. In Johore Bahru, they defied their husbands and exercised their rights as citizens to have a say in the running of their towns. . . ."[28]

At the time of the first federal elections, although several local gov-

26. UMNO/SG-115/53/7 (October 11, 1953), Files of the Setiausaha Agung UMNO, 1947–63.

27. A letter to the secretary-general of UMNO, May 6 1955, suggests that at times Kaum Ibu were not requested to door knock opposition areas: "Kaum Ibu in every division and branch have been requested to undertake the task of giving information, by going to the houses of UMNO members and supporters and explaining the Alliance symbol, so that they will know how to vote." The alliance was initially formed between the UMNO and MCA (Malayan Chinese Association) to fight the Kuala Lumpur local government elections and was later extended to include the MIC (Malayan Indian Congress).

28. *Straits Times* (December 7, 1952).

ernment and some state elections had already been held, the majority of rural (Malay) dwellers had had no experience of elections. Despite this, over 84 percent of the potential Malay electorate registered, and a similar percentage of the registered electorate cast their vote—of whom half were women. Among the Chinese, half as many women as men voted; among Indians, the ratio of women to men was one to four. The high registration rate and turnout at polling booths among Malays was largely due to the campaign work of the Kaum Ibu, whose presence was noted on polling day:

> UMNO women, as usual, stood out among the voters [in Penang]. . . . apart from the eagerness of UMNO women, there was no excitement [Province Wellesley]. Polling in Malacca was very keen, especially among Malay women, both young and old. . . . [in Perlis] women, as expected, easily outnumbered men. . . . Hundreds of Malay women waited on the roadside for Alliance cars to take them to the polling stations [Trengganu]. . . . UMNO women played a big part in the Alliance campaign. In the fishing village of Kuala Kedah, Kaum Ibu members came out by their hundreds and formed long queues at the polling stations. . . . At Bakri [near Muar, Johore] by noon eighty per cent of the women on the electoral roll had cast their vote. . . .[29]

Again in 1959 women stood out on election day: "Women of all races led the roads to the polling stations . . . as in the 1955 elections, Malay women left their kitchens and their children and with market baskets in their hands, became the most conspicuous figures in the queues that formed at polling stations everywhere."[30]

National and state leaders of UMNO supported the grass-roots activity of Kaum Ibu at election time by traveling the countryside, speaking at rallies, and attending meetings. In the preelection period of 1955 the then leader of the Kaum Ibu, Khatijah Sidek, emerged as an ardent campaigner for the Alliance and its concern for Malay rights. She was aided in her election campaign by Cik Rahimah binte Abdul Rahman who, early in 1959, was appointed as the first full-time secretary of the Kaum Ibu. At the time of her appointment Cik Rahimah stressed the importance of the women's vote in previous elections and the need for UMNO to ensure that Malay women, 80 percent of whom, she was sure, supported the party, would vote for the Alliance at the time of the elections: "I am determined to see that these women, who have been instrumental for the Alliance success in 1955, will vote for the Alliance once again this year."[31]

Cik Rahimah toured the country to establish the support of Malay

29. Ibid. (July 28, 1955).
30. Ibid. (August 20, 1959).
31. Ibid. (March 9, 1959).

women for the Alliance, stressing in her campaign the role of women in independent Malaya, the achievement of the Alliance in the short time it had been in office, and urging women to indicate their confidence through their vote. While Alliance votes were significantly lower during the 1959 election, the party nevertheless secured over 70 percent of the seats in the federal legislature.[32]

The significance of the campaign work undertaken by the Kaum Ibu was not lost on parties opposed to the Alliance. Datuk Onn, former leader of UMNO and then secretary-general of the Party Negara, indicated after that party's resounding defeat in the 1955 election that the possibility of a political comeback depended to a large extent on his ability to win over women voters.[33] To that end, one of his major tasks was the reorganization, strengthening, and expansion of the women's section, Putri Negara. The Parti Islam Samalaya (PAS—Pan-Malayan Islamic Party) similarly recognized the important role of Kaum Ibu: ". . . our women's section is still behind that of the opposition parties, particularly the UMNO. Therefore it is imperative for us to make an immediate effort to rectify our backwardness. . . . The duty of the members of the women's section during the elections will be to explain things to the voters, particularly through house-to-house canvassing, until they are able to attract the women folk in each constituency to support PMIP candidates."[34]

Women in Elected Government–the Test of Strength

Instances of general political interest by the Kaum Ibu were reflected in the resolutions presented at annual assemblies. Motions on education and the provision of scholarships for women, the inclusion of women in the Shariah (religious) Court, prostitution, marriage and divorce, and social welfare, as well as on the participation of women in civic and political life, were fuel for a future show of strength by the Kaum Ibu. However, motions calling for changes that would affect the status of women were usually passed by the assembly and then forgotten; there is little evidence of further action to ensure the implementation or follow-through of such motions. As already noted, Kaum Ibu did not press its requests for increased representation within the party machine;

32. In 1955 the Alliance polled over 79 percent of the votes, securing fifty-one of the fifty-two legislative seats. In 1959 it polled over 51 percent of the votes and won seventy-four of the 104 seats.

33. *Straits Times* (August 10, 1955).

34. K. J. Ratnam and R. S. Milne, *The Malayan Parliamentary Election of 1964* (Singapore: University of Malaya Press, 1967), p. 167, citing the "Communication from the Chairman of the Central Election Committee to all State Commissioners and Branch Secretaries" (PMIP).

only on the issue of the participation of women in government did Kaum Ibu test its strength.

From the days of the Malayan Union women had been included in political discussions. On May 28, 1946, for example, women as well as men met with the Sultans and representatives of the British government to discuss the Union scheme and the alternative Federation proposals.[35] When the Federation Agreement was signed in January 1948 some women had already been accepted into public office. Two years earlier, for example, the Selangor Ladies' Association had called for women representatives on the Advisory Council then being established and had submitted a petition to this effect. In August 1946 it was decided that one of the sixteen members of the proposed Penang Advisory Council be a woman, and two months later Cheah Inn Kiong was appointed. On January 13, 1948, a significant advance was made with the appointment of two women, Cik Azizah binte Jaafer and Hajjah Zain binte Suleiman, to the Johore State Council as unofficial members. Thus it was with precedence that Cik Puteh Mariah, who had attended the deliberations of the working committee for the Federation agreement, was appointed to both the Perak State and the Federal Legislative Councils. Even more encouraging was that she was not alone: Mrs. B. H. Oon of Penang, the Federation's only practicing woman lawyer, was also appointed to the Federal Legislative Council.

Cik Puteh was confident of the role of women under the new federal government: "The new Federation will give Malay women the opportunity of taking a prominent and full part in State matters and this should lead to improved social and educational welfare among the Malays."[36] However, Kaum Ibu members were not complacent over these appointments. Addressing the second annual general meeting of the Selangor Kaum Ibu, its leader, Cik Halimahton binte Abdul Majid, declared:

> We of the Kaum Ibu are not at all satisfied with the present state of affairs. It is now up to us to push ourselves forward and work with greater zeal to gain recognition from the authorities. . . .
>
> We are all proud to claim that we shared heavy and great responsibilities in the successful struggle against the Malayan Union. . . .
>
> But although we took our full share in the struggle, we, the Kaum Ibu of Selangor, . . . have been left out of several matters of importance. . . .

In the discussions preceding the framing of the Selangor State

35. *Straits Times* (May 26, 1946).
36. Ibid. (January 22, 1948).

> Constitution, only the men were invited to attend while no offer was made to the Kaum Ibu to participate in them. . . .
>
> In the choice of members to sit on the State Legislative Council, not one seat has been offered to the Kaum Ibu. In other states, such as Johore and Perak, members of the Kaum Ibu have been appointed Councillors, but here it looks as if not one of the members of the Kaum Ibu is considered fit enough to occupy such a position. . . .[37]

Not until March 1951 was the first woman appointed to the Selangor State Council; in the intervening period Negri Sembilan and Perak State Councils and the Federal Legislative Council had gained new women members.

Despite Islamic doubts about the correctness of the participation of women in politics, raised in 1952 by the Supreme Committee of *ulamas* at Al-Azhar University, Cairo, and subsequently by *ulamas* of the All-Malaya Muslim Missionary Society in Singapore, Malay women sought to contest elections shortly after their introduction in 1951. From 1952 some Malay women had contested and had been successful in both local government and state council elections, and the Kaum Ibu had begun to apply pressure to have women fielded in the federal elections. Initially, there was some internal opposition. At the 1954 assembly, for example, Kedah and Perlis Kaum Ibu opposed a resolution which called for the allocation of five seats to Kaum Ibu, on the grounds that women were not yet ready to enter national politics. Most women, however, supported the motion. Aishah Ghani, speaking to the resolution, reminded UMNO of the appeals that had been made to the women to work closely with the men to attain independence: "This appeal can be put into deeds if there are women Federal Councillors among us. The time has come for UMNO women to take a more active part in Malayan politics."[38] In response Tengku Abdul Rahman, leader of UMNO from 1951, applauded the decision but cautioned the Kaum Ibu that their candidates must know English, since the deliberations of the Council were in that language. The Malay daily, *Utusan Melayu,* questioned this criterion for nomination in an editorial and, stating that it believed that UMNO could field several women candidates, urged the party to press for the immediate introduction of Malay as the sole language of the Council.[39]

At the concluding ceremony of the assembly the question of women contesting the elections was revived, with a threat by the Kaum Ibu to boycott the elections if they were not allowed to stand as candidates, for "we are fed up with being merely voters every time."[40] In response to this,

37. *Malay Mail* (March 22, 1948).
38. *Straits Times* (October 16, 1954).
39. *Utusan Melayu* (November 1, 1954).
40. *Straits Times* (October 18, 1954).

an amendment on behalf of the central committee was passed: UMNO women would be allowed to contest the elections "if the executive committee of the UMNO-MCA considers them fit." Despite the nomination of several women for preselection, only one woman, Cik Halimahton binte Abdul Majid, gained it. She was elected in the Ulu Selangor constituency.

Kaum Ibu's second test of strength occurred shortly after Cik Halimahton's particular and UMNO's general electoral success, when Kaum Ibu again threatened a boycott, this time of the imminent state elections. The new cause for dissatisfaction was the failure of Tengku Abdul Rahman to nominate the leader of the Kaum Ibu to one of the five reserve seats in the new Federal Legislative Council. The Tengku refused to concede to the demands of the section on the grounds that he had not promised earlier to nominate a woman to the reserve seats but only that there would be a woman councillor—which there was, Cik Halimahton having been elected. Moreover, the Tengku argued, the leader, Khatijah Sidek, would not have been the right person to sit on the council, since she was still under a bond of good conduct which he and the Minister of Lands and Mines, Dr. Ismail, had executed after her release from detention in Johore under the emergency regulations.

The Kedah state elections, held soon after the federal elections of 1955, brought another sweeping victory for the Alliance and for two more Kaum Ibu women. Three days later, following representation by the Kaum Ibu, it was announced that more women would be fielded in town and municipal elections in the Federation: "We have asked our branches to tell women that they should start from town or municipal councils and work their way up. The Alliance policy is to increase women's representation in councils as a recognition of their great contribution in the recent Federal elections."[41] A qualification was made to this statement: the Alliance was finding it difficult to get capable women to stand as candidates, and to ameliorate this situation it was proposed to pick and train UMNO, MCA, and MIC women leaders.

In June 1959 there was further tension between the Kaum Ibu and UMNO over the choice of Alliance candidates for the second parliamentary elections, caused by reported insistence by the Penang Kaum Ibu that one of their members be named as candidate. Following denial of this by the Penang Divisional Secretary, it was reported that two women would probably be fielded: Puan Dasimah Dasir and Puan Che Bee Noor. When the candidates were announced, however, no women from Penang were included, but the section took no further action.

* * *

It was only after the reestablishment of the colonial government and

41. Ibid. (August 17, 1955).

the announcement of the Malayan Union proposals that most Malays were drawn into a political world beyond the confines of the village. The Malays had become increasingly aware of their economic disadvantage compared with the immigrant communities and recognized their vulnerability in a political system, as proposed in the union proposals, which would not guarantee the rights of the *bumiputra* (sons of the soil) and which would undermine the previously sacrosanct privileges and duties of the sultans. Incensed, village women and men, led by members of the traditional aristocracy and the educated elite, took to the streets. Marches protesting colonial government policy, fiery rallies, and stirring speeches marked the beginning of a new period of Malayan history.

When the Federation of Malaya came into being in 1948 several political parties had been founded, one of which was the United Malays National Organization, a conservative communal party with mass grassroots support. This party was to emerge as the leading party in national politics. Among the women's associations founded during the same period, a number concerned more with the well-being of the Malays in general than with the status of women specifically had affiliated with UMNO. In 1949 these associations amalgamated as the Pergerakan Kaum Ibu, an auxiliary of the party. Kaum Ibu was not the only women's section to participate in national politics, but its mass membership and its role in political life made it the most significant during the postwar period.

The day-to-day activities of the Kaum Ibu were not markedly different from those of nonpolitical associations. Political courses and seminars were occasionally held for its members, but its activities centered on the interests of women as wives and mothers. Only around election time were most Kaum Ibu drawn into concentrated political activity. Their role at this time was crucial—both because they were undertaking a basic political education of the majority of people for whom involvement in government was quite foreign and because UMNO was dependent on the work of its women's section to canvass votes to insure its return to office.

While UMNO members recognized the necessity of the work of the section at election time, little effort was made to encourage women to participate in the broader political sphere. Women were neither given equitable representation within the party nor encouraged to seek political office at local, state, or federal level. Kaum Ibu had hoped that the amalgamation of the associations as an auxiliary would provide a strong platform from which it could voice its opinion. A platform was provided, but the subordinate status of the section to the party proper, its limited representation within the party machine, and the interests of the majority of its membership determined its greater attention to social rather than political activities and its inability to rally the support necessary to force the issue of its members participating more fully in public life.

The ancillary status of the section reflected and reinforced those social attitudes which already allowed women a role outside the home, provided it was in a field of traditional female interest or was supportive of the role of men. The participation of members of the section in areas of activity dominated by men, such as seeking political office, was largely the result of party concessions to the section's demands for reasons of expediency: to insure the continued goodwill toward and support of the party by the section. But Kaum Ibu's general acceptance of its status within the party and national politics illustrates the entrenchment of social attitudes regarding the role of women and attests that participation in the public sphere without reassessment of those attitudes does not effect a changed role.

Department of Asian Civilizations
Australian National University
Canberra, Australia

Politics and Institutions

The Case of Eva Perón

Marysa Navarro

In 1946, when Doña María Eva Duarte de Perón began to take an active part in Argentine politics, First Ladies were expected to remain in the background, running a few charities and attending an occasional ceremonial function. Voting in national elections was restricted to male adults, which remained true until 1951. Except for a small number of activists engaged in the Socialist and Communist parties, women generally showed little concern for politics. However, three years later, she had become both Eva Perón, Argentina's widely known First Lady, and "Evita," the charismatic *abanderada de los descamisados,* the standard-bearer of the shirtless ones.[1] By the time she died, on July 26, 1952, she was undoubtedly the second most powerful political figure in Argentina, though she held neither an elected post nor an official position in Perón's government. In the following pages, I will attempt to examine what personal and structural factors allowed her to acquire that power, what was its nature, and, finally, what were its limits.

Evita was born on May 7, 1919, in Los Toldos, a hamlet of Buenos Aires province. (Throughout the paper, I will use the name "Evita," by which she was known politically.) Like her three sisters and her brother, she was the illegitimate child of Juan Duarte, a local *estanciero* ("landowner") who abandoned their mother when Evita was three years old. She attended school first in Los Toldos, then in Junín, a railroad town

1. The term *descamisado* first appeared on October 17, 1945. It was used pejoratively to describe Perón's supporters as they gathered in the Plaza de Mayo, the central square of Buenos Aires, demanding his freedom. The *Peronistas* adopted it to identify themselves by December 1945.

also in Buenos Aires province, where the family moved in 1930. She was a below-average student, uninterested in school work, and in 1935, after completing her primary education, at the age of fifteen she went to Buenos Aires to become an actress. Living in cheap and dirty *pensiones,* hungry and cold in winter, she made the theater rounds, never playing a better role than a maid or a silent character that disappeared too soon from the stage. In the meantime, she tried to break into films and here again only got small parts. Success did come at last, not from the stage or films but through the radio. In 1939, she headed her own soap-opera company, and when she gave up acting in October 1945, she was under contract with the top radio station in Buenos Aires and had two daily prime-time shows.[2]

Evita may have had an exceptional goal in mind when she left Junín, but her background of poverty and her first years in Buenos Aires were not very different from those of thousands of men and women who also moved to Argentina's capital throughout the 1930s. According to Gino Germani, "during the 1935–1947 decade, the proportion of Argentines born in the provinces that settled in Buenos Aires' metropolitan area was equivalent to almost 40% of the total population growth of these provinces."[3] Unable to earn a living in the countryside because of the crisis that crippled agriculture since the world depression, they went to the city hoping to find work in its numerous factories. Argentine industry, forced to produce substitutes for European manufactured goods, was expanding at a rapid pace. Throughout the thirties, factories mushroomed and increased their output, reaching new peaks after World War II.[4] While Argentina was undergoing such profound changes, the government was in the hands of a conservative landed oligarchy that managed to remain in power by rigging elections. Working and living conditions for the new urban masses were therefore understandably poor, and despite the efforts of a small, divided, weak, and bureaucratic labor movement they continued unchanged until June 4, 1943, when a bloodless military coup put an end to the landed oligarchy's rule.

Colonel Juan Domingo Perón began to emerge as a controversial figure among the group of officers that came to power on June 4 shortly

2. There is no reliable biography of Evita. The various works that have been written about her are diatribes or eulogies based on gossip, rumors, or ideological prejudices. See, for example, María Flores, *The Woman with the Whip: Eva Perón* (Garden City, N.Y.: Doubleday & Co., 1952); Fleur Cowles, *Bloody Precedent* (New York: Random House, 1952); Américo Ghioldi, *El mito de Eva Perón* (Montevideo, 1952); Francisco A. Costanzo, *Evita alma inspiradora de la justicia social en América* (Buenos Aires, 1948); and Erminda Duarte, *Mi hermana Evita* (Buenos Aires: Ediciones "Centro de Estudios Eva Perón," 1972).

3. Gino Germani, *Política y sociedad en una época en transición* (Buenos Aires: Paidós, 1962), p. 230.

4. See Carlos F. Díaz Alejandro, *An Interpretation of Argentine Economic Growth since 1930* (New Haven, Conn.: Yale University Press, 1967); Guido Di Tella and Manuel Zymelman, *Las etapas del desarrollo argentino* (Buenos Aires: Eudeba, 1967).

after he took over the department of Labor. Defining the role of the state as an arbiter between labor and management, he directed his office to terminate previous antilabor practices and to implement existing legislation. He then transformed the department into a secretariat with ministerial rank and proceeded to draft new laws, create labor boards, improve working conditions for rural and urban workers, expand the social security system, and in general pursue a policy that raised the standard of living of workers and employees. A good listener, energetic and efficient, he gradually gained the trust of some important labor leaders. However, since his policies also found strong resistance among certain unions led by Communists and Socialists, he did not achieve his objectives without some degree of violence.[5]

Evita met Perón in February 1944 during a fund-raising festival for the victims of an earthquake. He was a forty-eight-year-old widower. She was twenty-four, dark haired, and, despite her large brown eyes, not particularly beautiful. Two months after their first meeting, they were living together—a situation socially unacceptable for an Argentine woman at that time, especially if the man was a public figure and did not treat her like a mistress. Indeed, as Perón introduced Evita to his friends, went out with her, and actually behaved as if she were his wife, "the colonel's mistress" became a favorite topic of conversation in Buenos Aires salons.

Moreover, he included her in his political life. His heavy schedule generally ended with a round of daily meetings with politicians and fellow officers in his apartment. Contrary to what women were expected to do in such circumstances, Evita was usually present.[6] She did not leave after serving coffee but sat and listened. It is not possible to ascertain whether she remained because she wanted to or because Perón urged her to do so. In these meetings as well as through her conversations with Perón, Evita discovered a very different world from her own. She found herself sharing and defending his ideas. In June 1944, she began to do a daily radio program of political propaganda in which she extolled the benefits that the Secretariat of Labor had brought to the workers.

Evita's transformation paralleled the changes taking place in Perón during this same period. Both his support among the rural and urban working-class and middle-class sectors and his influence in the military government were growing steadily. On February 26, 1944, when General Edelmiro J. Farrell became president, Perón took over the Ministry

5. See George I. Blanksten, *Perón's Argentina* (Chicago: University of Chicago Press, 1953); Juan José Real, *30 años de historia Argentina* (Buenos Aires: Actualidad, 1962); Samuel I. Bailey, *Labor, Nationalism and Politics in Argentina* (New Brunswick, N.J.: Rutgers University Press, 1967); and Ruben Rotondaro, *Realidad y cambio en el sindicalismo* (Buenos Aires: Editorial Pleamar, 1971).

6. Statement by Arturo Jauretche, quoted in Otelo Borroni and Roberto Vacca, *La vida de Eva Perón* (Buenos Aires: Editorial Galerna, 1970), p. 85.

of War, and that same year he rose to the vice-presidency. However, his labor secretariat policies had continued to provoke very strong resistance, and by early 1945 he had succeeded in uniting all political parties against him.[7] From the extreme Left to the conservative Right, they denounced him as a Nazi and a dangerous demagogue. As the months went by, the opposition mounted a campaign against Farrell and redoubled its attacks on "the colonel." Perón sought to strengthen his gains by pronouncing increasingly radical speeches, but to no avail. In October 1945, a group of military officers forced a confrontation with him. He finally agreed to resign from his three government posts on October 9, but not without making a speech in front of the Secretariat of Labor that angered his opponents and eventually led to his arrest and confinement on the island of Martín García. While Farrell tried to rebuild his cabinet, which had resigned en masse, and while the opposition celebrated Perón's political demise, his supporters saw his jailing as a threat to the benefits they had obtained since 1943. With the help of some of Perón's collaborators in the secretariat, they began to organize demonstrations. On October 15, the sugar workers of Tucumán declared a general strike. The following day, as the General Confederation of Labor (CGT) debated whether or not to follow suit, groups of workers in several cities took to the streets. On October 17 in Buenos Aires, men and women marched from the outskirts of town to the Plaza de Mayo, stayed all day long to demand Perón's release, and did not leave until he spoke to them from the balcony of the Casa Rosada close to midnight.[8]

Contrary to what has been stated repeatedly both in Peronist and anti-Peronist works, Evita did not play a major role in the events of October 17.[9] After Perón was arrested, afraid for his life and her own, she left their apartment and slept at friends' homes. In the daytime, she tried desperately but unsuccessfully to get a writ of habeas corpus for his release. They were reunited on the night of October 17, after he addressed the delirious crowds in the Plaza de Mayo. Six days later, in a quiet civil ceremony, Perón married Evita.

After she married Perón, Evita became even more of a fascinating fixation for the Argentinian upper classes. According to most sources, her lower-class origin, illegitimacy, supposedly stormy love life before 1944, and notorious affair with Perón created an unsurmountable barrier between her and them once he was elected president in February

7. See Félix Luna, *El 45. Crónica de un año decisivo* (Buenos Aires: Editorial Sudamericana, 1972); Alberto Ciria, *Partidos y poder en la Argentina moderna (1930–1946)* (Buenos Aires: Editorial Jorge Alvarez, 1968).

8. For the best account of the October 17 events, see Luna.

9. See Bailey, p. 89; Robert J. Alexander, *The Perón Era* (New York: Columbia University Press, 1951), p. 104; Arthur P. Whitaker, *Argentina* (Englewood Cliffs, N.J.: Prentice-Hall, Inc., 1964), p. 118. For an opposing view, see Luna, p. 340, and Cipriano Ryes, *Yo hice el 17 de octubre* (Buenos Aires, 1973), p. 246.

1946. Resentful and ambitious, the sources say, since the oligarchy refused to forget her past and snubbed her, she decided to get enough power to avenge herself. The only proof generally offered for this theory is her purported attempt to be named honorary president of the Sociedad de Beneficencia de la Capital, a position traditionally reserved for the First Lady. When the matrons of the Sociedad ignored her overtures, Evita's spite was so great that she demanded the takeover of the institution by the government and then proceeded to set up her own charitable foundation, the Fundación Eva Perón.[10]

In her memoirs, Evita ridicules such an interpretation. She explains that she had the choice of being like any other Argentine First Lady or of doing something entirely different.

> As for the hostility of the oligarchy, I can only smile.
>
> And I wonder: why would the oligarchy have been able to reject me?
>
> Because of my humble origin? Because of my artistic career?
>
> But has that class of person ever bothered about these things here—or in any part of the world—when it was a case of the wife of a President?
>
> The oligarchy has never been hostile to anyone who could be useful to it. Power and money were never bad antecedents to a genuine oligarch.
>
> The truth is different. I, who had learned from Perón to choose unusual paths, did not wish to follow the old pattern of wife of the President.[11]

Evita's decision was by no means as simple or as unilateral as she would like us to think, and it is hard to believe that upper-class opposition to her, particularly strong after the presidential campaign, would have disappeared easily had she chosen a less irritating path. On the whole, her statement might be questioned as a rationalization a posteriori. Yet certain facts tend to indicate that, in essence, it is more credible than most traditional interpretations of her behavior. In the case of the Sociedad de Beneficencia, for example, there is little doubt that it was taken over for reasons other than her anger, that is, poor working conditions for its employees and low salaries. As a state-financed institution, it had already undergone some degree of reorganization in 1943, before Evita met Perón. Denunciations of bad working conditions had been presented in Congress since 1939.[12] Finally, the request for the government investiga-

10. See Flores, and Cowles (n. 2 above).

11. Eva Perón, *My Mission in Life,* trans. Ethel Cherry (New York: Vantage Press, 1953), p. 60.

12. Congreso Nacional, *Diario de Sesiones de la Cámara de Diputados* (Buenos Aires: Imprenta del Congreso Nacional, 1939), p. 444.

tion that led to the intervention began in the Senate in July 1946, at a time when she lacked the means to influence such a move.

Whenever authors evaluate Evita's background as a barrier she could not overcome, and present it, together with her resentment and her ambition as an explanation of her extraordinary political career, they make several assumptions. (1) She had remained untouched by the politicization and polarization that had divided Argentines since 1943. (2) She had lived with Perón for two years, at a time when his personality underwent a profound transformation, but somehow she had not been affected by that relationship. (3) She wished nothing better than to forget her past. (4) Her main goal was to become what the oligarchy had said a First Lady should be. (5) Driven either by her resentments, her hatreds, or her "insatiable ambition," her actions after 1946 were the direct result of her willpower and Perón's acquiesence.[13]

It is true that after 1946, Evita never mentioned her premarital relationship with Perón and concealed her illegitimacy. Indeed, before she married Perón, she obtained a false birth certificate stating the name of her father. But even as an actress, Evita did not hide the facts that she came from a poor family and that she had started to work very young.[14] There is no indication that she desired to forget all of her past. Moreover, it would have been difficult for her to become a ceremonial figurehead and be involved in old-fashioned charitable work at a time when Perón's election was acclaimed by his supporters as the end of an era dominated by the oligarchy and his inauguration as the beginning of a new society in which social justice would reign; poverty would be wiped out; and to be a worker, a *descamisado,* would become honorable.

In this atmosphere, Evita could hardly have sought to identify herself with the ladies of the Sociedad de Beneficencia. She may not have had a precise idea of her own role as First Lady, but it could not be what Argentines were accustomed to. She had indicated that much by her actions during the presidential campaign—she accompanied her husband in all his trips through the provinces, listened to his speeches, and even addressed a women's rally in the Luna Park stadium. In fact, a few days after Perón's inauguration, she had already begun to define a new model of First Lady by meeting with labor leaders three times a week in an office of the Post Office building, visiting factories and labor unions on her own, and by standing beside Perón every time he presided at a public gathering.

Furthermore, by that time Evita had realized that she was bound to Perón's supporters with ties she could not possibly break. As a result of the workers' massive demonstrations, in October 1945, "the colonel's mistress," "that woman" so despised and criticized, had become overnight the respectable wife of the most important political figure in

13. Flores (n. 2 above).

14. Interview with Evita published in a trade magazine, *Radiolandia* (April 7, 1945).

Argentina. Like a movie heroine or a character in her soap operas, she found herself metamorphosed by her marriage. Whatever her past may have been, she was now Perón's wife. As she would explain on countless occasions in her inimitable style, once again love had triumphed, and in this case, it had overcome the worst obstacles thanks to the men and women, the *descamisados,* who demanded Perón's release. When she had lost all hope of seeing the man she loved, the *descamisados* brought him back to her. On October 17, she therefore contracted with them an immense "debt of gratitude" which could only be repaid by loving them as they had loved Perón and dedicating her life to them.[15]

By themselves, Evita's personal reasons for wanting to "pay her debt" to the *descamisados* and to Perón or wishing to be a different First Lady do not explain how she gained access to the political structure or the role she eventually performed in Perón's government. Neither is it sufficient to recognize that she ultimately could do so because he did not put a stop to her activities in the initial stage and later on legitimized them. Considering his relationship with Evita prior to 1946, his behavior is not really surprising. The question, therefore, is not why he did it but rather what were the structural factors that permitted Evita to play her political role.

At this point we must return once again to October 17, 1945, a date that shaped the following thirty years of Argentine history. The consequences were felt immediately insofar as the workers' mobilization ended a twelve-day-long crisis, allowed Perón to become a presidential candidate, and changed Farrell's regime into a caretaker government. But perhaps more important, it also brought forth a new type of political relationship. Built gradually by Perón after he took over the Secretariat of Labor, the charismatic relationship between "the leader" and the *descamisados* that revealed itself on October 17 neither destroyed existing institutions nor replaced them partially but superimposed itself upon them once he became president. His election was the culmination of the bid for power begun in 1943 and the ratification of the mandate of October 17.

Yet Perón's position in February 1946 was far from secure. Although he had obtained 52 percent of the votes and could count on a favorable Congress, he faced a number of problems. The already acute polarization that had characterized the political process since 1943 was accentuated even more by the bitterly fought presidential campaign in which almost all political parties joined in an anti-Perón front, the Unión Democrática. He entered the campaign without a solid organization. His supporters were divided into two major groups, united mainly by Perón: the Unión Cívica Radical (Junta Reorganizadora), a small offshoot of the old Unión Cívica Radical, and the Partido Laborista, a party organized

15. See, for example, *Democracia* (January 12, 1947), and Evita's last October 17 speech, also in *Democracia* (October 18, 1951).

by labor leaders right after October 17. Of the two, the Partido Laborista was undoubtedly the more important and the more dangerous for Perón because he did not control it. The October crisis had proved that labor was the social basis of his power and his leadership. Therefore, if he was to retain them, he could not allow his charismatic relationship with the *descamisados* to deteriorate. On the other hand, as president, Perón could no longer play the role of social agitator he had performed as secretary of labor, nor could he continue to receive workers' delegations, listen patiently to their complaints, and help them to solve their internal conflicts or their confrontations with management. The limitations imposed by Perón's new presidential functions threatened his leadership of the *descamisados.*

His situation was particularly troublesome because, among other reasons, the labor movement was undergoing a vast process of expansion. In 1941, the CGT had a membership of 441,412; in 1945 it rose to 528,538; in 1948 1,532,925, reaching 2,256,580 by 1954.[16] Furthermore, there were growing signs of dissatisfaction among labor. Workers continued to strike for higher wages and better working conditions, even in the openly Peronist unions such as the one that declared the general strike on October 15. The composition of the labor movement was also changing rapidly. In 1941, only 33 percent of the CGT membership belonged to the industrial sector, while in 1948 the number had gone up to 52 percent.[17] Perón's control of the CGT was shaky. Its performance during the October crisis had not been entirely satisfactory: after a heated debate, the central committee voted to strike on the 18th, without mentioning his name.[18] Finally, in May 1946, when he decided to dissolve the Partido Laborista to form a more pliable organization, the Partido Perónista, some labor leaders openly resisted his orders. Others obeyed them but continued to oppose the growing identification of their movement with him.

If Perón was to maintain and strengthen his labor support, he needed a strong minister of labor, especially at a time when the ministry was unprepared to meet the demands of an expanding and aggressive labor movement. He could not appoint to the ministry a person who could use it to build his own political power—as he had done under Farrell. That is probably why he bypassed all the officers who had worked with him in the secretariat from 1943 to 1945 and named instead José María Freire, an obscure labor leader. But the workers continued to flock to Perón, looking for his advice or his help as they had

16. Louise Doyon, "El crecimiento sindical bajo el peronismo," *Desarrollo Económico* 15 (April–June 1975): 158.

17. Louise Doyon, unpublished manuscript, based on research for a Ph.D. dissertation on the Argentine labor movement.

18. See the minutes of the CGT meeting in *Pasado y Presente,* nos. 2 and 3 (July and December 1973).

done while he was only secretary of labor. They were turned back until Evita began to meet with them in her office of the Post Office building.

In September 1946, Evita abandoned her Post Office headquarters and moved to the ministry of labor itself. Her presence in the old secretariat confirmed what had gradually evolved in the previous months and what the *descamisados* already knew: all contact with Perón was to be channeled through his wife, his personal representative in the ministry. Perón never announced officially that Evita was his liaison with labor. In another example of his pragmatism, he let it be known by her move, after she had worked long enough for him to see positive results: workers accepted dealing with her and she proved to be quite efficient.

Perón's decision to rely on Evita for maintaining his personal contact with labor legitimized the activities she had been carrying out since his inauguration and altered their political value significantly. From then on she began to act as the extension of Perón, his substitute, his "shadow," as she described herself in her autobiography.[19] Evita's presence in the ministry indicated to the workers that, despite his presidential functions, Perón had not ceased to be secretary of labor. His wife, the person who was closest to him, would perform some of his duties and also keep him informed of the needs and problems that the *descamisados* might have. She therefore could summon ministry of labor functionaries to give advice to a delegation on how to organize a union, help workers to force the compliance of a labor law, or back their requests for additional funds to build a clinic. She also began to represent Perón at union rallies. She would arrive accompanied by the presidential military aide, but while he remained silent, she spoke to the workers in the name of Perón. She acted as his delegate in ceremonies marking the signing of new labor contracts and once again made speeches in his name. Indeed, as early as 1946, one of Evita's main activities was to address the *descamisados.* The content of her speeches in this period indicates that her task was to impress upon them the continuity between 1943–45 and the present. Perón was always "the colonel," not the president. She also reminded her audiences how badly Argentine workers had lived before 1943, what "the colonel" had accomplished for them through the secretariat, and how his enemies had wanted to destroy him but how the *descamisados* had saved him on October 17.

Evita's experience as an actress proved to be an enormous asset in her work. Although unsure of herself at first, she showed none of the inhibitions and self-consciousness that might have paralyzed another woman in her place. In fact, she plunged into her life as First Lady as if it were a role, like the ones she had performed on the stage and in films.[20] Her keen eye for theatrical effects was particularly useful in molding her

19. Perón, p. 43.
20. Ibid.

public image, and she was most careful of her hair, by then bleached blonde; her jewels; extravagant hats; and elegant clothes. Although she knew that the oligarchy criticized that image, she sensed that the *descamisados* approved of it, and indeed they looked at her with a strong feeling of self-satisfaction and pride. Furthermore, at a time when the radio first became a powerful means of communication in Argentina, Evita found herself in possession of a very special talent. Having worked for so long in soap operas, she was comfortable in front of a microphone.

Because of that talent and the wildly enthusiastic responses it elicited, from 1946 to 1952 Evita acted as an indefatigable one-woman ministry of propaganda for Perón. The style of her public speeches reflected unmistakably the political role she played in Perón's government. Whereas he was "the leader" who elaborated the doctrine, explained it, and led the road toward social justice, she was the rabble-rouser who whipped up emotions; urged the *descamisados* to "offer their lives to Perón" as they had done on October 17; professed an undying love for Perón, the workers, and the poor; and lashed out violent diatribes against the oligarchy and other enemies of "the people." She never passed up the opportunity to make a speech, even when she had to interrupt most of her activities because of her illness. Too weak to carry on her heavy load in the ministry of labor, she still had the strength to do broadcasts from the presidential residence.[21] Her highly emotional style may have been an expression of her passionate temperament, but it also reflected to a large extent the years she had played women who proclaimed their love or suffered because of it in her soap operas. The adaptation of her radio style and vocabulary to politics was facilitated by her year-long program of political propaganda, "Hacia un futuro mejor." The scripts of this program were written by the authors of her radio shows, and at least one of these persons continued to write speeches for Evita throughout 1947.

Her social origin, which created so much resistance among the upper class, turned out to be another asset. When she spoke at CGT rallies or in her meetings with workers, she never failed to remind them that she was born poor, a *descamisada* too, and that she could therefore understand their problems and their concerns.

In the initial stage of Evita's political career, being a woman and being married to Perón proved to be crucial factors. She did not represent a threat to him or to his relationship with the *descamisados* precisely because she was a woman. Furthermore, as his wife, she was part of him, an extension of him, and since all her actions appeared endorsed by him, from the very first moment, she had a substantial latitude to exert her influence. She strengthened her position by asserting her power to

21. Evita recorded her last 1951 presidential campaign speech just before being taken to the hospital to be operated on for cancer.

influence decisions and by contributing to the Peronization of labor unions. Her activities in the ministry of labor were the basis of the political power she accumulated from 1948 onward. In so doing she defined a new identity for herself. She gradually made herself into the indispensable link between Perón and the *descamisados,* the only means to reach him outside normal channels, or, as she would call herself, the intermediary between the leader and the *descamisados,* "the bridge between Perón and the people." While he remained "the undisputed Leader," by 1950 she had become "the standard-bearer" and even "the plenipotentiary" of the *descamisados.* Her titles reflected her own relationship with labor, as charismatic as his own, but subservient to his. She was Perón's complement, but to the workers she was also their leader.

By 1948, having gotten rid of the old, independent-minded labor leaders, Perón had also tightened his control of the CGT; the Partido Peronista was firmly in his hands, and he no longer had to worry about dissidents in Congress. The following year, he even managed to reform the Constitution so as to allow his reelection in 1951. As Perón pursued his policy of income redistribution and consolidated his power, Evita's position also became stronger.

Her power became visible after 1948 when she ruled over the Fundación Eva Perón (1950). She organized her own party, the Partido Peronista Femenino (1949), whose officials she named personally and whose candidates in 1951 she designated herself. Among additional sources of her power and influence was her ability to name people to jobs of all ranks. The nature of Evita's power is perhaps best explained by the Fundación Eva Perón, her own private social aid foundation, whose funds she controlled exclusively and whose explicit objectives were to complement the social goals of Perón's government. Though part of the political structure in an informal way and consequently outside institutional limitations, in order to implement its objectives, which in certain areas such as health, education, and welfare overlapped with the policies of various ministries, Evita very frequently interfered with the plans designed by government officials.

There are no indications that Evita ever attempted to undermine Perón's power for her own purposes. Even at the height of her influence, there were no signs of rivalry or competition between them. She understood very clearly that she had become "Evita" because of him. As she explains in the preface of her autobiography, when she met Perón she was a humble sparrow and he was a mighty condor.

> If it weren't for him who lowered himself to me and taught me how to fly in a different way, I would have never known what is a condor and I would have never contemplated the marvelous and magnificent immensity of my people.
>
> That is why neither my life nor my heart belong to me and

> nothing of what I am or have is mine. Everything I am, everything I have, everything I think and everything I feel belongs to Perón.
>
> But I do not forget and will never forget that I was a sparrow and that I am still one. If I fly high it is because of him. If I walk among the mountain tops, it is because of him. If I sometimes almost touch the sky with my wings, it is because of him. If I see clearly what my people are and I love my people and I feel the love of my people caressing my name, it is because of him.[22]

Her power and her leadership depended on his. Her influence, though far reaching, was not unlimited, because she was accountable to him. Perón rarely used his prerogative to restrict her, because he consistently benefited from Evita's power. Therefore, within the limits that only he could establish, she was free and did as she pleased—as long as Perón's own power was enhanced. Perhaps the best example of the relationship between his ultimate authority and her freedom of action was the issue of her candidacy to the vice-presidency. Although she wanted it and allowed the Partido Peronista Femenino and the CGT to stage a massive demonstration for the proclamation of the Perón-Perón ticket, when he opposed it, she retreated and refused to accept the nomination.

Evita died on July 26, 1952, at the height of her power, but when Argentina was entering a period of serious economic difficulties. As Perón's economic troubles increased, his policy of income redistribution slowed down and his isolation from the *descamisados* deepened. Though he tried for a time to substitute for her in all her activities—her social work, the presidency of the Partido Peronista Femenino, and her daily meetings with workers' delegations and the CGT—he had neither the time, the patience, nor the energy to do it. Though in 1946 he could transfer power to her, her power was not transferable to anyone, least of all him.

Department of History
Dartmouth College
Hanover, New Hampshire, U.S.A.

22. Perón (n. 11 above).

Women, Education, and Labor Force Participation

Introduction

Cynthia Nelson

The fundamental conceptual link between the essays by de Miranda and Clignet is that economic development goes along with improved levels of education and training. Paradoxically, however, the upgrading of the labor force during the process of economic development is likely to threaten or constrain female participation. In different but related ways the two essays address this paradox by analyzing women's education and participation in the labor force in the developing societies of two major regions of the world: Brazil and West Africa. Specifically, they question the commonly held assumption of a positive correlation among "education," "women's labor force participation," and "development" by focusing on the concrete social, cultural, and historical factors which influence the level and form of labor and education of women in these two regions. Both essays demonstrate empirically that neither in Brazil nor in the Cameroun or Ivory Coast does economic development necessarily mean high levels of women's labor force participation nor participation at the same level of equality with men.

However, it is where these essays differ that provides their more interesting and valuable contribution. For these essays represent excellent examples of the various kinds of questions posed, the differential emphasis given to "determining factors," and the conclusions reached when one approaches a similar problem from the different theoretical perspectives of Marxist analysis (de Miranda) or structural/cultural analysis (Clignet). Now de Miranda describes Brazil in a process of "dependent capitalist development" which tends toward the *marginalization of workers* of both sexes, although it affects women more than men.

Clignet, on the other hand, discusses the growing complexity of societal and cultural "modernizing structures" in the Cameroun and Ivory Coast which shape the current *pattern of sexual differentiation* in urban education and employment. Both authors are concerned with the interplay of education and women's employment on development, but de Miranda places more emphasis on class structure in an analysis of female economic roles in Brazil over the past thirty years; Clignet places more emphasis on cultural models of sex roles, ethnic stereotyping, and perceived occupation alternatives. Thus table 7 in Clignet's essay emphasizes how sexual and ethnic stereotypes interact with one another in influencing the fate of various types of wage earners, while table 9 of de Miranda's essay stresses how women of different social classes have different occupational opportunities.[1] Each author conceptualizes the principle of inequality quite differently, although they implicitly agree that women's participation at the same level of equality with men is a sine qua non for development.[2]

Both essays stress the significance of the colonial experience on the changing status of the indigenous female populations. For de Miranda, the colonial impact in Brazil led to the adoption of a particular model of development (dependent capitalism). She analyzes the transformations of the Brazilian women's labor force through a historical description of female economic roles under colonization. In the Cameroun and the Ivory Coast the colonial impact, according to Clignet, created divergent cultural models and stereotypes that compete with their local counterparts in shaping current patterns of sexual differentiation. Differences in the particular colonial policies of the three countries affect the role played by women in the labor force.

Despite conceptual differences, both authors agree that as development increases women are concentrated in the tertiary sector. Clignet points out, however, that notwithstanding their shorter history of educational development, women in the Ivory Coast are proportionately more numerous in the tertiary sector than their Cameroun counterparts. De Miranda's data lead her to conclude that schooling is the most important factor that contributes to an increase in women's labor force participation. Indeed, both authors conclude paradoxically that economic development does not necessarily lead to higher levels of women's participation in the labor market. For de Miranda it is not the

1. Attention should be drawn to Gunnar Myrdal's cautionary note that "educational statistics are probably even less satisfactory than statistics in almost every other field pertinent to underdevelopment" (*The Challenge of World Poverty* [New York: Vintage Books, 1970], p. 164).

2. Space does not allow for a critique of that unexamined assumption; however, see Cynthia Nelson and Virginia Olesen, "Veil of Illusion: Critique of the Concept Equality in Western Feminist Thought," in *Catalyst, Critiques of Feminism* (special issue), ed. Cynthia Nelson and Virginia Olesen (May 1977).

process of industrialization per se that creates underemployment and marginalization but a type of industrialization based on and controlled by international, monopolistic finance capital and advanced technology with no prior fundamental changes in the economic structure. For Clignet, the growing complexity of societal structures does not automatically imply a corresponding increase in the number of alternative choices made available to female adults.

This conclusion seems all the more paradoxical when we read the results of a recent Organization for Economic Co-operation and Development report showing a female labor surge. The impact of the 1973–75 recession was less serious on women than men, according to Ken McLennan of Britain, head of the Social Affairs Division: "One reason for the surge of women into the ranks of workers might be that *service industries* which so heavily employ females *are expanding,* while agriculture and industry at the moment are not. But underlying this is a social economic change of the last ten to fifteen years—women now are behaving more like men as having a *commitment to work.* There has been a fundamental change in the behavior of women toward working."[3] Employment in the modern sector, then, requires not only formal training, but also a certain attitude which may best be described as the capacity to work regularly and attentively. Realistic and relevant research must analyze the distributional spread of education among districts, social classes, and the two sexes, and emphasize what is taught, with what intention, in what spirit, and with what effect. The contributions of de Miranda and Clignet are steps in that direction.

Department of Sociology, Anthropology, and Psychology
American University in Cairo
Cairo, Egypt

3. *Egyptian Gazette* (February 4, 1977).

WOMEN, EDUCATION, AND LABOR FORCE PARTICIPATION

Social Change and Sexual Differentiation in the Cameroun and the Ivory Coast

Remi Clignet

Differences in research on male and female social activities reveal the preoccupations of social scientists with their own societies rather than the reality they intend to change.[1] Even though modernization requires an assessment of the changes characterizing the behaviors most relevant to development, notably with regard to the roles of women whose socialization functions are essential, in most societies the task is still not done.

Changes in the status of women may be evaluated by reference to two distinctive hypotheses. First, the extent and form of sexual inequalities may depend primarily upon the complexity of social structures and hence upon the growth of schools, cities, and modern enterprises. The major task, then, is to identify the form and magnitude of the association between patterns of sexual differentiation and the growing complexity and differentiation of basic institutions.

But sexual inequalities may also depend upon past and present cultural models and stereotypes. In Africa, the traditional prescriptions and proscriptions regarding female roles were not initially uniform.

1. Aaron Cicourel, *Theory and Method in a Study of Argentine Fertility* (New York: John Wiley & Sons, 1974). As a case in point, few female British anthropologists who have worked in Africa have been particularly interested in the role played by African women in domestic as well as in larger structures. To be sure, ethnic rather than sexual status is often a most crucial determinant of the research which is possible as suggested by E. Smith Bowen in her novel, *Return to Laughter* (New York: Doubleday & Co., 1964). But even if this is so, it is regrettable to see that research is influenced by the constraints of the fieldwork rather than by the urgency of the problems to be solved.

Further, if the status of women varies with the extent of modernization in the ethnic groups studied, it may also be influenced by models and stereotypes inherited from former colonizers. Indeed, such models continue to affect contemporary African societies.

This paper will explore the independence and the complementarity of these two hypotheses as they apply to the Ivory Coast and the Cameroun. Are overall similarities between the two countries associated with concomitant variations in the patterns of sexual differentiation at work in educational, residential, and occupational environments? Alternatively, do current and historical differences between these two countries affect the differential distribution of economic and social opportunities between the two sexes?[2]

The Cameroun and the Ivory Coast: An Overview

There are significant contrasts in the original ethnic structures of the two countries. Although the majority of Camerounian ethnic groups share a Bantu origin, their familial structures have evolved distinctively because their past migratory experiences differ. Familial groups are almost all characterized by a patrilineal type of descent, but their autonomy varies with the environment and hence with modes of subsistence. In the southern part of the country, kin groups and lineages have a higher political and religious significance than in the north, where political and religious activities develop across familial lines.[3]

Ethnic diversity is more marked in the Ivory Coast. Local ethnic groups differ from one another in their rules of descent. East of the Bandama River peoples are matrilineal, while west of that river they are patrilineal. As one moves from the south to the north of the country there are also significant contrasts in modes of subsistence and hence in patterns of interaction between familial units. Settlements are generally larger and more internally differentiated in the east than in the west, and in the north than in the south.

These variations in types of descent and political complexity are uniformly associated with parallel contrasts in the status of women. Among matrilineal peoples, a man acquires few rights over his wife or wives; bride-price is therefore limited, as is the incidence of polygyny.[4] A

2. Thus such a comparison involves the tests of contingency generalization and of specification (see Robert Marsh, *Comparative Sociology* [New York: Harcourt & Brace, 1969], pp. 39–41). Later in this article, the importance of diachronic as opposed to synchronic factors becomes apparent.

3. Victor Levine, *The Cameroun Federal Republic* (Ithaca, N.Y.: Cornell University Press, 1971).

4. Remi Clignet, *Many Wives, Many Powers* (Evanston, Ill.: Northwestern University Press, 1970), pp. 356–59.

husband's rights tend to be greater among patrilineal societies, which are also characterized by higher bride-prices and more frequent polygynous arrangements. Among such societies, however, the rights that a male acquires over his bride, and hence the value of the bride-price as well as the frequency of plural marriage, tend to vary with the complexity of economic and political arrangements.[5] In 1958, as measured by the ratio of married women to married men, polygyny ranged in the Ivory Coast from 127:100 in the matrilineal area of Abengourou to 154:100 in the patrilineal region of Man and Daloa. Similarly, in 1962, the frequency of polygyny in Cameroun varied from a minimum of 120:100 to a maximum of 169:100, as a direct function of the political and economic complexity of the various regions. Variations in the incidence of plural marriage are also associated with contrasts in the roles of co-wives, who may alternatively be treated as sources or as symbols of wealth. Similarly, polygyny may enable them to enjoy more domestic independence, or it may intensify their subservience toward their husbands.[6]

Because of these interethnic differences in the distribution and organization of polygynous households and in the status of women, changes in the interaction between the sexes are unlikely to be uniform. New life-styles involve more often a transformation than a rejection of preexisting patterns of interaction.[7] But if this is the case, should the processes underlying the emergence of new life-styles be more complex in the Ivory Coast than in the Cameroun, because the former is more ethnically diverse?

While new patterns of sexual differentiation depend upon the initial diversity of the forms of familial organization, they vary also with the colonial experiences of individual countries. Although the eastern part of the Cameroun and the Ivory Coast were both exposed to French colonization, there were contrasts in the colonial policies adopted in the two territories. Ivory Coast was a colony, but Cameroun was only a "mandate," and after World War II, a "trusteeship," and this limited the strategies colonial authorities could use to impose their will. Correspondingly, educational development occurred earlier and was more diverse in the Cameroun, where mission schools are more numerous and where the diffusion of Islam is more marked.[8] Similarly, there is a greater disperson of urban centers in the Cameroun. Thus, Camerounian elites

5. Lloyd Fallers, "Some Determinants of Marriage Stability in Busoga: A Reformation of Gluckman's Hypothesis," *Africa* 27 (1957): 106–21.

6. Clignet, pp. 211–12.

7. Remi Clignet, "Distributions et functions de la polygamie en milieu africain," *Psychopathologie Africaine* 11 (1971): 151–77.

8. In fact, the development of modern schools in North Cameroun leads boys to attend both Koramie and European schools, while an increasing number of girls attend only the former. In this sense, social change leads to a feminization of the Islamic world (see Renaud Santerre, *Pedagogie Musulmane d' Afrique Noire* [Montreal: Presses de l' Université de Montreal, 1973]).

were and continue to be more numerous and more diversified than their Ivory Coast counterparts.[9]

Contrast in the colonial experiences of the two countries should be accompanied by contrasts in the changes of status experienced by local women. Does the greater differentiation of Camerounian elites imply greater variation in women's participation in modernizing structures? Do variations in the importance of missions in the two countries affect female enrollments within local public and private educational institutions and the curriculum to which women are exposed? Does the greater number and size of cities in Cameroun create more economic opportunities for urbanized women?

To summarize, if changes in the status of women reflect both the weight of external stimuli (measured by the multifaceted aspects of colonial legacies) and the relative vulnerability of existing cultural models to such stimuli, there should be convergences as well as divergences in the changing levels and forms of participation of Camerounian and Ivory Coast women in modernizing structures.

The Participation of Women in Educational Structures

In general, the sex ratio of student populations varies with the size of overall enrollments.[10] Right after independence, primary school students were not only more numerous in the Cameroun than in the Ivory Coast (59 percent against 44 percent of school-aged children), but the Cameroun sex ratio was also smaller (181 boys:100 girls as compared to 204 boys:100 girls). Within the two countries parallel differences could be observed across regions: in 1964 Camerounian overall enrollment rates ranged between 11 percent in the Benoue area and 77 percent in the Wouri region, while the ratio of male to female students varied from 4.5:1 to 1.3:1 in these two cases. Similarly, in the Ivory Coast overall enrollments varied between 15 percent for the Korhogo department and 75 percent for the entire southeast, while the relevant ratios went from 2.9:1 in the first case to 2:1 in the second.[11]

Although educational development stands as a necessary condition for an increase in female enrollments, its role in this regard is not sufficient. Overall high enrollments do not uniformly imply the presence of additional female students. In the Cameroun, 94 percent of school-aged children living in the Mungo and the Nyong-and-Kelle area attend schools; yet the proportion of female to male students rises from

9. Aristide Zolberg, *One Party Government in the Ivory Coast* (Princeton, N.J.: Princeton University Press, 1964), pp. 65, 275, 278.

10. Remi Clignet, *Liberty and Equality in the Educational Process* (New York: John Wiley & Sons, 1974), pp. 232–35.

11. Louis Roussel, *Côte d' Ivoire Population: 1965* (Paris: Sedes, 1966), p. 92.

33 percent to 67 percent between these two regions. Similarly, in the Ivory Coast in 1963, the city of Abidjan had a slightly lower enrollment rate than the rural department of Aboisso (67 vs. 73 percent), but the proportion of female to male students dropped from 71 percent to 65 percent between these two cases. Female educational enrollments are also affected by the economic and social roles expected of adult women. The greater the number of *perceived* occupational alternatives available to women (as is often the case in cities), the greater the incentives that parents have to send their daughters to primary school.

Because of our concern for the modernization of female roles, it is essential also to determine whether the differentiation of these schools into a complex number of tracks and cycles, each with distinctive educational and occupational rewards, accentuates, confirms, or erodes existing patterns of sexual differentiation.[12] At the apex of the hierarchy, academic studies prepare students for the baccalaureate and hence for universities. This particular type of institution has a longer history, and therefore tends to be more egalitarian, in the Cameroun than in the Ivory Coast (see table 1). The picture changes, however, when we compare male and female enrollments across various academic cycles. In the Cameroun, there are proportionately more girls than boys attending short academic cycles; in the Ivory Coast, the pattern is reversed. Camerounian educational authorities seem to have a more definite view of the occupational roles most "suitable" to women, whose relatively large numbers in short-cycle academic institutions suggest that a majority is expected to enter middle-range clerical positions in the modern economic sector. Contrasts between the two countries may reflect their differential educational and occupational growths. Insofar as the number of Camerounian girls entering postprimary schools has been

Table 1

Enrollment in Postprimary Streams and Cycles per Sex:
Cameroun and Ivory Coast, 1970–71

	Cameroun		Ivory Coast	
	N	Sex Ratio*	*N*	Sex Ratio*
Long academic	26,832	300.4	46,293	333.5
Short academic	23,678	263.7	18,935	563.5
Long technical	2,419	226.9	1,072	428.1
Short technical†	5,487	168.9	324	332.1

Sources:—*Annuaire statistique du ministere de l'education nationale, 1970–1971,* for Cameroun; *Enquete sur les possibilities d'education de formation et d'emploi offertes aux femmes en Côte d'Ivoire* (UNESCO, 1974), for the Ivory Coast.
*Measured in terms of number of male students over number of female students ×100.
†Commercial studies only.

12. Remi Clignet and Phillip Foster, *The Fortunate Few* (Evanston, Ill.: Northwestern University Press, 1966), pp. 42 ff.

larger for a longer time, their ethnic and socio-economic origin tends to be more diverse. This diversity influences the way their abilities and aspirations are processed by the educational environment.

As might be expected, contrasts in the history and characteristics of female enrollments in the two countries are associated with differences in individual educational trajectories. Thus, declines in relative female enrollment by years of studies are sharper in the Cameroun than in the Ivory Coast (see table 2). Even though their background is more diverse, Camerounian girls, like their Ivory Coast counterparts, originate from a more modernized family environment more often than their male counterparts. Because disparities between abilities and aspirations are more frequent among girls entering secondary institutions than among boys, girls more frequently repeat the early grades.[13] In addition, they are obliged more frequently to change track, cycle, or type of school.

The career of girls in academic streams also depends upon the different functions of private and public educational institutions. Thus, certain private schools may compete with the public sector to attract the most talented students, regardless of their sex, whereas other private, notably religious, institutions aim above all at providing girls with an appropriate cognitive and moral education. Not only does the small private sector of the Ivory Coast attract a proportionately larger number of girls, but in addition, the number of its students who repeat their classes is larger than in the Cameroun (see table 3). Competition between Camerounian public and private schools probably leads mission schools to eliminate rapidly those students most prone to lower their track rec-

Table 2

Percentage Female to Male Students in the Differing Cycles of the Ivory Coast and Cameroun Academic System by Year of Studies and Ownership Status of School, 1970–71

	Cameroun			Ivory Coast		
	Public	Private	Total	Public	Private	Total
1st year	39	46	44	29	42	33
2d year	36	41	39	27	35	29
3d year	30	37	34	20	34	23
4th year	28	32	31	18	28	20
5th year	28	17	22	22	13	21
6th year	28	15	21	28	10	25
7th year	19	19	19	23	13	22
Long	35	31	33	28	37	31
Short	27	43	38	18	6	17
Total	32	37	35	24	35	25
N	18,175	32,335	50,510	49,739	15,489	65,228

Sources.—See table 1.

13. Clignet, *Liberty and Equality.*

Table 3

Percentage of Academic Students Repeating Their Grade, by Educational Sector, Year of Study, and Sex, 1970–71

	Cameroun				Ivory Coast			
	Public		Private		Public		Private	
	Male	Female	Male	Female	Male	Female	Male	Female
1st year	8.0	12.0	7.0	8.0	8.0	15.0	7.0	10.0
2d year	13.0	10.0	7.0	9.0	10.0	9.0	9.0	10.0
3d year	11.0	10.0	11.0	14.0	12.0	12.0	12.0	18.0
4th year	16.0	18.0	19.0	21.0	12.0	14.0	23.0	13.0
5th year	15.0	18.0	7.0	8.0	10.0	13.0	6.0	5.0
6th year	23.0	25.0	13.0	15.0	10.0	6.0	3.0	0.0
Terminal	31.0	34.0	16.0	12.0	9.0	7.0	7.0	23.0

Sources.—See table 1.

ord. Conversely, in the Ivory Coast the function of the terminal classes of private schools is primarily to prevent the downward mobility of the least talented but most modernized segments of the female student population.

Similar differences characterize the patterns of sexual differentiation in the technical schools of the two countries. Because of the initially sharper rate of economic development in the Cameroun, local vocational and technical schools there have developed earlier and with different modes of recruitment than in the Ivory Coast. Thus, in the Cameroun, more girls are in long technical streams than in academic tracks, whereas the pattern is reversed in the Ivory Coast (see table 4). In both countries, however, the distribution of girls among the branches of technical postprimary education reflects European sexual stereotypes. In the Ivory Coast as in the Cameroun, girls are oriented toward becoming seamstresses, beauticians, and home economists. In commerical fields, they are concentrated in typing rather than accounting, and they are more often found in short than long cycles of technical studies (see table 5).

Finally, despite the longer history of educational development in the Cameroun, women there are not proportionately more numerous in universities than their Ivory Coast counterparts (the ratio of male to female university students is 13:1 in the first case, but only 11:1 in the second one). In this sense, early stages of educational growth are not necessarily associated with a commensurate decline in patterns of sexual differentiation.

To summarize, the first "fortunate few" women in a colonized population enter postprimary institutions at a later date than their male counterparts and are usually drawn from narrowly defined ethnic and socioeconomic strata. As educational development proceeds, schools at-

Table 4

Female Enrollment in the Academic and Technical Public Streams of Cameroun and the Ivory Coast, 1965–70

	Cameroun				Ivory Coast			
	Technical		Academic		Technical		Academic	
	N	% Girls	*N*	% Girls	*N*	% Girls	*N*	% Girls
1965–66	7,324	32	26,308	21	4,457	21	20,454	17
1966–67	8,186	36	28,632	22	3,756	24	23,879	18
1967–68	9,685	35	33,448	23	3,896	24	28,617	22
1968–69	11,272	38	37,237	24	3,438	28	34,666	22
1969–70	13,698	39	43,339	25	4,838	21	40,441	25

SOURCES.—See table 1.

Table 5

Female Enrollment in Technical Institutions by Skill and Stream in the Cameroun (Male to Female Students)

Skill	Overall	Top*
Secretary	141	233
Accounting	455	1,000
Insurance	417	...
Banking	111	90
Typing	61	35
Clerical	238	525
Chemist	525	1,428
Medical secretary	141	147
Others	182	1,000

Source.—See table 1.

*Depending on the skills involved, to reach the top takes four to six years.

tract male and female students from a wider spectrum of the socioeconomic and ethnic continuum and in this sense, educational development implies greater equality. However, educational development is also associated with an accentuated institutionalization of educational and occupational hierarchies. In turn, this institutionalization induces increased divergences in the academic trajectories of the two sexes, both through the influence of informal patterns of socialization and through the mechanisms of selection used by educational authorities. Thus, in the Ivory Coast, sexual differentiation in the educational system continues either to provide women with access to the top of the ladder or deprive them of any form of postprimary schooling. In contast, Camerounian women have more chances to acquire postprimary training but are more often enrolled in the least rewarding tracks and cycles of the system.

Urbanization and Sexual Differentiation

Both structural and cultural factors affect female participation in urban environments and hence in the modern sector of the economy. While this participation depends on the growth of cities, the relationship between city size and sex ratio of its adult population is nonetheless variable. Although Abidjan almost tripled in size between 1955 and 1963 from 120,000 to 330,000 inhabitants, the local adult ratio of men to women only declined from 160:100 to 136:100. In the Cameroun, the population of Douala doubled between 1956 and 1964 from 115,000 to 250,000 inhabitants, but its sex ratio decreased from 134 men:100 women to 119:100. Although in 1964 Yaoude, the capital city, was half as populated as Douala, its ratio of men to women was 124:100, almost the same as that observed in the larger Douala. The relationship between the growth of cities and their male-female ratios depends upon ethnic factors. Even though Abidjan is the same distance from the matrilineal Baoula and the patrilineal Bete hinterlands, the adult sex ratio is 77:100 for the first group but 132:100 for the second. In Douala, the sex ratio of adult residents varies similarly between a minimal of 76:100 for the segmented Douala peoples and a maximum of 165:100 for the socially integrated Bamileka. In short, the ratio of men to women of the various peoples present in an urban center reflects a complex set of interactions between: (1) the distance of place of origin from the city; (2) the length of time during which migrations have taken place; (3) the overall number of migrants already present in the urban centers; (4) the economic status achieved by such migrants; (5) the economic role performed by women in their places of origin; and (6) the autonomy they enjoy in their communities of origin.

Declines in the sex ratios of urban populations are usually associated with changing marriage patterns. In Abidjan, such decreases have been associated between 1955 and 1963 with a decline in the proportion of the male population which was single (from 53 to 50 percent) but also with an increase in the proportion of women who are unmarried (from 13 to 18 percent). In Douala, the trends have been similar. These increases in the proportion of single females affect the number and type of women seeking jobs.

In the same way, the pressures that married women exert on urban labor markets vary with the organization of their households. Thus urbanization modifies the economic functions of polygyny.[14] In Abidjan, 19 percent of monogamous women were in the urban labor force in 1963 as compared to 5 percent of senior co-wives and 4 percent of their junior counterparts. In Douala, the relevant figures in 1964 were 13, 19, and 12 percent, respectively. In addition, the persistence of polygynous arrangements in urban areas frequently induces the creation of multiple residences, and certain co-wives perform rural activities while others enter the urban job market.

Finally, the chances that women have to participate in the urban market varies with the structure of local households. In Abidjan only 6 percent of heads of households are female, as opposed to 29 percent in Douala and 15 percent in Yaounde (see table 6). Thus, the different educational and urban development of the two countries is associated with differences in the relative independence of their urbanized female residents. Regardless of inter- and intracity constrasts in the characteris-

14. In fact, many African surveys suggest that the assumptions of Goode (William Goode, *World Revolution and Family Patterns* [New York: Free Press, 1963]) regarding the diffusion of the type of nuclear family found in industrial countries are valid for only a tiny segment of local elites.

Table 6

Female University Enrollment in Cameroun and the Ivory Coast by Type of Studies (% of All Students)

	Cameroun	France	Ivory Coast
Faculty of Law	4	29	3
Faculty of Social Science and Fine Arts	14	63	20
Faculty of Sciences	7	32	6
Faculty of Medicine and Pharmacy	12	33	7
Ecole normale superieure	14	n.a.	6
Total	8	42	8

SOURCES.—For France, 1961–62 data derived from P. Bourdieu and J. C. Passeron, *Les Heritiers* (Paris: Editions de Minuit, 1970); for Cameroun and Ivory Coast, see table 1.

tics of female heads of households, such households uniformly shelter fewer adults than those with male heads. Further, to the extent that there is a correlation between the sex of "hosts" and "guests," women are less likely to find supportive structures in the cities; in that sense, they enjoy fewer opportunities.

Employment and Sexual Differentiation

For a long time, planners have adhered to models of development inspired by neoclassical theories. In the context of such models, the differential participation of men and women in the modern sectors of the local economy should reflect their different levels of education and hence their uneven productivity. Once educated women enter the modern labor market, however, they should do as well as their male counterparts. However, modern labor markets may be differentiated internally so that employers distinguish among various occupations and use different hiring, promotion, and salary policies for each.[15] Segmentation of the labor market may reflect the stereotypes attached to the *job seekers* rather than those attached to the *jobs* themselves. If this is so, there should be contrasts not only in the distribution of male and female workers across occupations and branches of activity but also in the rewards earned for the same type of employment.

There are sharp contrasts in the levels of female employment prevailing in the Ivory Coast and the Cameroun (see table 7). Camerounian women not only have a more frequent access to the modern labor market, but are also entering different occupations. First, they are more frequently employed than their Ivory Coast counterparts in primary concerns, notably in plantations. During the initial phases of colonization, French authorities imported a large number of alien male unskilled

15. Michael Carter and Martin Carny, *Theories of Labor Market and Workers' Productivity* (Menlo Park, Calif.: Portola Institute, 1973).

Table 7

Distribution of Gainfully Employed Women across the Major Sectors in the Cameroun and Ivory Coast Economy

	Cameroun		Ivory Coast	
	% of Women in Each Sector	Sex Ratio by Sector*	% of Women in Each Sector	Sex Ratio by Sector*
Primary	40.0	1,330	4.2	33,233
Secondary	21.0	4,800	27.7	8,225
Tertiary	39.0	1,330	67.9	3,125
Total	100.0	2,400	99.8	6,165
N	1,348	...	5,031	...

SOURCES.—For Cameroun, *Enquete Emploi, 1965,* raw data collected under the supervision of J. Chammont by the Camerounian government and analyzed by Remi Clignet; for Ivory Coast, see table 1.
*Number of men per 100 women.

agricultural laborers to work on the Ivory Coast plantations, but were unable to do so in the Cameroun. This initial contrast continues to affect the role of Camerounian and Ivory Coast women in agriculture: in the Cameroun, a large number of unattached or married women migrate to European-owned plantations (notably banana plantations) before growing their own cash crops. In the Ivory Coast, the participation of women in agricultural activities as independent producers or as wage earners is a more recent and limited phenomenon.

In the two other sectors, the level of female participation is primarily influenced by patterns of urban development, by the nature of the industrial activities started by expatriates, and by the stereotypes held in their countries of origin about the requirements for special jobs. Thus, in both the Ivory Coast and the Cameroun, women are particularly numerous in textile or tobacco firms because of the historical role that European women themselves have played in those industries. In both the Cameroun and the Ivory Coast, women are most frequently found in the tertiary sector, a pattern that can be observed also on the French metropolitan scene.[16] However, the local women's chances to fill the most rewarding occupational roles in this sector depend upon their success in competing against both local men and expatriate women. In the Ivory Coast, for example, no less than 41 percent of expatriate women in the tertiary sector hold supervisory or executive positions, as compared to only 14 percent of their local counterparts.[17] Although we do not have comparable figures for the Cameroun, it is plausible to assert that, because the local European population is significantly less numerous, the competition between Camerounians and foreigners is more limited.

16. Evelyne Sullerot, *Les Française au travail* (Paris: Hachette, 1973).

17. UNESCO, *Enquete sur les possibilities d'education de formation et d'emploi offertes aux femmes en Côte d'Ivoire* (Paris: UNESCO, 1974).

Since urban occupations are the most differentiated, it is essential to compare the occupational status of male and female residents. In their early phases, processes of urbanization are associated with an accentuation of educational differences between the sexes and hence of the difference characterizing their job opportunities. Between 1955 and 1963, literacy increased in Abidjan from 23 percent to 36 percent among adult males but only from 5 to 9 percent for adult females. During the same period in Douala, literacy went up from 40 to 60 percent among adult males but only from 15 to 25 percent for their female counterparts.

The differential increases in the levels of education acquired by adult women living in Abidjan and Douala are associated with differences in their respective levels of participation in the urban labor force. In 1963, only 11 percent of the adult female residents of Abidjan were gainfully employed, as compared to 28 percent of their counterparts in Douala.[18] Women in Douala are proportionately more numerous in agriculture and in various service activities than their Abidjan counterparts, who are more frequently found in the nonmanual jobs of the modern sector (see table 8). Despite these differences, however, the effects of educational development on the patterns of employment of educated women in the two cities are similar. Among women over thirty years of age, the level of participation in the labor force increases with level of education. Conversely, among their younger counterparts such a relationship tends to be curvilinear; both women with no education and those with a postprimary education are the most likely to find jobs. In short, the occupational rewards that women derive from formal education cannot remain stable over time.

Table 8

Occupational Status of Adult Male and Female Residents of Abidjan and Douala (%)

	Abidjan		Douala	
	Men	Women	Men	Women
Agriculture and fishing	5.0	1.0	5.2	12.9
Trading	13.0	47.0	14.7	40.7
Artisans	4.0	14.0	6.6	12.1
Services	9.0	18.0	1.2	25.6
Modern nonmanual	16.0	17.0	19.8	5.0
Modern manual	53.0	3.0	52.5	3.7
Total	100.0	100.0	100.0	100.0
N	69,070	7,600	44,919	14,030

SOURCES.—For Abidjan, *Etude socio-economique de la zone urbaine d'Abidjan* (Paris: SEMA, 1964): for Douala, raw materials of the 1964 census—analysis conducted by R. Clignet and J. Sween.

18. These data are derived from *Etude socio economique de la zone urbaine d' Abidjan, 1964* (Paris: Société d'Etudes et de Mathematiques Appliques, 1967) and from the data of the raw census materials of Douala (1964) analyzed by R. Clignet and J. Sween.

Our last task is to examine the differential rewards men and women derive from their education within a single branch of the economy. In both the Cameroun and the Ivory Coast, banking absorbs the highest proportion of women (12 percent). In the Cameroun, the only place for which we have relevant data, men and women do not enter the same occupational roles.[19] While one-half of Camerounian female bank workers are employed as typists, two-thirds of their male counterparts are engaged in general clerical activities (accounting, bank teller, etc.).[20] In addition, the men and women engaged in these two types of jobs do not have the same educational background. Among general clerical workers 41 percent of the men have a postprimary education, as compared to 14 percent of the women, while the figures among typists are 14 percent for males, but 33 percent for females. As typing becomes stereotyped as a "feminine" occupation, it attracts women with increasingly higher levels of formal qualifications but includes men with lower educational status.[21]

Occupational careers, however, depend less upon tasks than upon skill levels. Differences between male and female bank wage earners in this regard are insignificant and they correspond in fact to the slightly lower educational and occupational qualifications (seniority) of the latter (see table 9). Most important, while an increase in educational attainment is uniformly associated with an increase in skill level, the distribution of skill level within each educational category is always more homogeneous in the case of female than of male wage earners. In this sense, employers are more prone to stick to the rules and to apply universalistic and impersonal criteria in the case of their female than of their male labor force.

As a matter of fact, the same pattern tends to obtain as far as income is concerned. There are greater variations among male than female

19. Dolores Koenig, "Occupational Recruitment and Sexual Stereotyping in a Developing Country: The Case of Cameroun," mimeographed (Evanston, Ill.: Northwestern University).

20. This division reflects conflicts between ethnic and sexual stereotypes. Initially, in the banks of the public sector, women tended to be preferred to males for the operations involving the sorting of bank notes because such operations were performed by women in metropolitan France. This solution was quickly abandoned, however, because French managers could not communicate in an appropriate manner with the local female labor force and did not like the idea of using the services of interpreters. Yet, they returned later to that solution because they were afraid of the potential larcenies that male employees would be tempted to commit. If males and particularly African males are deemed to become "thieves" easily, local women as their metropolitan counterparts are more "honest because they suffer from a lack of imagination."

21. Female typists with a postprimary education earned an average annual income of 305,300 CFA, while the annual income of their male counterparts was only 255,000 CFA. Similarly, 6 percent of these women, who started their career as typists, enjoyed some sort of upward mobility over the years as opposed to less than 1 percent of their male counterparts.

Table 9

Mean Skill Level and Income (in 1,000 CFA) of Camerounian Bank Male and Female Wage Earners by Vocational Training and Sex

Vocational Training	Skill Level				Income			
	Men		Women		Men		Women	
	Mean	S.D.	Mean	S.D.	Mean	S.D.	Mean	S.D.
None	3.21 (*N* = 207)	1.62	3.41 (*N* = 27)	1.28	480.4	421.7	441.0	543.5
Private vocational training	3.04 (*N* = 78)	1.01	2.82 (*N* = 22)	0.91	381.9	384.7	283.7	153.0*
Training in large-scale organizations	3.38 (*N* = 219)	1.18	3.33 (*N* = 21)	0.43	401.2	255.8	357.0	90.7
Traditional sector training	3.60 (*N* = 166)	1.41	3.13 (*N* = 24)	1.20*	481.9	480.9	308.6	175.0*

SOURCE.—Dolores Koenig, "Occupational Recruitment and Sexual Stereotyping in a Developing Country: The Case of Cameroun," mimeographed (Evanston, Ill.: Northwestern University). Her data are derived from *Enquete Emploi, 1965,* conducted by the Camerounian government.

NOTE.—Male-Female pairs were tested for significant differences.

*$P < .05$.

workers with similarly low educational levels. Symmetrically, if at the upper end of the educational continuum, some male individuals earn over a million CFA per year against none of their female counterparts, none of the women with a postprimary education earns less than 200,000 CFA a year, but some of their male colleagues do. In brief, the careers of female bank employees are both less risky and less rewarded than those of male employees in the same branch of activity.

Yet, differences in the relationships between the qualifications and the social as well as economic rewards of men and women may reflect above all the differing attitudes of the particular employers to which the two categories of workers are attached. Over half of the women in the sample are employed by government-owned concerns, compared to only 18 percent of the men. Even though our data are limited to only one branch of activity, they suggest that in the Cameroun, as in many other developed and developing countries, public services tend to be the first to adopt innovative practices in hiring females. The question remains to ascertain the time lag between such changes in the private as opposed to the public sector. It also remains necessary to determine whether our findings might be generalized to all types of employment and whether the attitudes and practices of various branches of the public sector are the same.

* * *

The growing complexity of societal structures is associated with changes in patterns of sexual differentiation. Because Cameroun has experienced educational development prior to the Ivory Coast, there is a sharper contrast in the academic careers of the two sexes in Cameroun. Similarly, because the historical roots of Douala are deeper than those of Abidjan, the women of Douala more often enjoy economic and social independence, although they have fewer occupational choices.

Indeed, social change exerts both positive and negative effects on the status of women. My observations in this regard are not original. Scholars of North African countries have also shown why the early stages of urban growth are associated with increasing constraints imposed on females.[22] Thus the association between social change and patterns of sexual differentiation may be curvilinear rather than linear. As an example, if educated women have additional chances to find employment during early stages of educational development, this may cease to be the case when their formal schooling is viewed as serving primarily matrimonial functions.[23]

22. Germaine Tillion, *Le Harem et les cousins* (Paris: Plon, 1965).

23. Pierre Bourdieu and Jean Claude Passeron, "La comparabilité des systèmes d'enseignement," in *Education, Development, et Democratie,* ed. Robert Castel and Jean Claude Passeron (Paris: Mouton, 1969), pp. 25–26.

The interaction between social change and patterns of sexual differentiation is not necessarily universal either. Because of the distinctions between matrilineal and patrilineal descent groups in the Ivory Coast, the effects of urbanization and education on the interaction between the sexes continues to be culturally specific. Similarly, contrasts between the colonial experiences of the Ivory Coast and the Cameroun are associated with differences in the choices and constraints confronting local women as a result of social change.

Finally, structural and cultural factors lead to differentiation within the female populations themselves. At the domestic level, there are increasingly rigid but diverse boundaries between monogamous and polygynous life styles. Within polygynous households, differences in the roles of co-wives with distinctive matrimonial ranks are accentuated. Similarly, outside the family, social change induces a greater diversity in the occupational trajectories of various types of women and in the available rewards. Such observations parallel the view of Fanon, who complained that the concept of Negritude is antirevolutionary, because it obfuscates the specific forms of racist exploitation occurring in distinctive historical and social contexts.[24] Similarly, the achievement of sexual equality raises different problems within and without family units, and in differing cultural contexts.[25]

Department of Sociology
Northwestern University
Evanston, Illinois, U.S.A.

24. Franz Fanon, *Les Damnes de la terre* (Paris: Maspero, 1961).

25. Albert Memmi, *The Dominated Man* (New York: Frederick A. Praeger, Inc., 1968), pp. 141–51.

Women, Education, and Labor Force Participation

Women's Labor Force Participation in a Developing Society: The Case of Brazil

Glaura Vasques de Miranda

In any society, female labor force participation is contingent on both cultural and economic conditions. During the process of dependent capitalist development, rising levels of unemployment and underemployment may be expected to occur simultaneously and to affect women's participation in the labor force more than men's. This phenomenon, while reinforced by the traditional domestic roles women are expected to perform, depends on the capacity of the productive system to absorb the excess labor. In Brazil, a society where violent economic development is occurring in a context of capitalism and dependency,[1] female labor has traditionally been used in special crisis situations as a means of reducing the costs of production and as seasonal labor, especially in commercial agricultural production.[2] Since the female's wage is considered complementary to the male's, women receive lower wages than men for similar work.[3] Because of their passivity in the labor relation, which prevents them from improving their bar-

The author is grateful to Shery K. Girling for her comments in the first draft of this paper, and to the Ford Foundation, CNRH, and FIBGE for their support in the present research.

1. F. Henrique Cardoso, *Dependency Revised,* Hackett Memorial Lecture (Austin: Institute of Latin American Studies, 1973).

2. Because of a lack of manpower for the construction in 1973, women in Brasilia were used as a substitute for unskilled labor. As soon as the situation normalized, however, women were fired.

3. In all Brazilian regions women have a mean salary which is three times lower than that of men (see G. V. Miranda, "The Brazilian Woman: A Case of Earnings Discrimination," *Lacdes Newsletter,* vol. 2, no. 3 [June 1973]).

gaining position, women's wage labor is particularly suitable to capitalists.[4]

The evolution of women's labor force participation in Brazil, according to Madeira and Singer, has occurred in different phases.[5] At the beginning of industrialization, when agriculture is still a major source of employment and commerce or manufacturing is limited to domestic circles, women are well integrated in the work force because their work can be easily reconciled with domestic responsibilities.[6] During the second phase, however, economic development reduces women's participation in productive activities. As the structure of the rural economy becomes more capitalized and commercialized, men take the place of women on large farms and the total number of both male and female workers decreases. Moreover, when industrialization occurs women lose their central role in handicrafts production, which had the family as the central productive unit. As the family ceases to be the economic center, the domestic and economic functions are divided between sexes, and this leads to the economic independence of men and the economic dependence of women.[7] The removal of women from home to factories creates objective obstacles (the need to take care of domestic tasks) and subjective ones as well (prejudices against women's labor outside the home).[8] Technological change—the introduction of different tools and mechanization—tends to encourage male labor rather than female.[9] Even when they are employed in specialized occupations outside the home, women tend to fill the lower ranks, receive lower wages, and have fewer opportunities for training and promotion than men. The movement to urban centers does not necessarily mean improvement in the social condition of migrants, but to the contrary economic marginalization in an environment which cannot absorb their labor at all or can

4. Marianne Schmink, "Dependent Development and the Division of Labor by Sex: Venezuela" (paper presented in the Fifth National Meeting of the Latin American Studies Association, San Francisco, November 1974).

5. F. R. Madeira and P. Singer, "Structure of Female Participation and Work in Brazil, 1920–1970," *Journal of Interamerican Studies and World Affairs,* vol. 17, no. 4 (November 1975).

6. Adolfo Gurrieri et al., *Estudios sobre la juventud marginal latinoamericana* (Mexico: Siglo Veintuno Editores, 1971).

7. Heleieth I. B. Saffioti, *A mulher na sociedade de classes: Mito e realidade* (São Paulo: Livraria Quatro Artes Editoria, 1969).

8. Madeira and Singer.

9. In Carmen Diana Deere's opinion, "New techniques based primarily on know how, such as application of fertilizer or the use of improved seed varieties, obviously do not carry an inherent sex designation for utilization. But to a certain degree, the acceptance and use of improved agricultural methods do depend on education. And unequal education for the sexes, with primarily boys sent to school or boys remaining longer in school than girls, creates an ever widening gap between the sexes" ("The Division of Labor by Sex in Agriculture: Peasant Women's Subsistence Production on the Minifundios" [Ph.D. research essay, University of California, Berkeley, 1975]).

absorb it only at low levels of productivity and low wages.[10] And it is women who are usually employed in the very low productivity occupations. Thus women, more than men, are concentrated in the tertiary sector.[11] Dependent capitalist economic development does not, then, improve the level of women's labor force participation, nor does it mean equal participation with men.

The Case of Brazil: 1940–70

From 1940 to 1970 the total labor force participation compared to the total adult population (persons ten years old or more) dropped slightly in Brazil (see table 1).[12] There was little expansion in the female labor force participation during this period (.04), which was not able to compensate for the reduction within the male labor force (.09). Male employment grew 22 percent from 1940 to 1950, and 96 percent in toto from 1940 to 1970, while female employment fell 10 percent from 1940 to 1950, but increased 120 percent in toto from 1940 to 1970 (see table 2). The ratio of employed men to women has varied in the period 1940–70. In 1950, there was an increase in the ratio (5.8:1), but after that there was a declining trend. In 1970 there were 3.8 men in the labor force for each woman. More specifically, there was a reduction in the proportion of men to women in the primary and tertiary sectors, but in the secondary sector the proportion increased during this period of

Table 1

Ratio of Labor Force Participation over the Total Population Ten Years of Age or More

	1940	1950	1960	1970
Total	.51	.47	.46	.45
Men	.83	.81	.77	.72
Women	.19	.14	.16	.18

Source.—*Tabulações Avanqdas do Censo Demográfico: Resultados Comparativos,* table 5, p. 29.

10. See Anibal D. Quijano, "Dependencia, cambio social y urbanización in Latino America," in *Latino America: Ensaios de interpretacion sociologico-politicas,* ed. F. H. Cardoso and F. H. Weffort (Santiago: Editorial Universitaria, 1970).

11. Traditionally the labor market is divided into three sectors: primary, secondary, and tertiary. The primary sector comprises not only agrarian activities but extractive activities as well. But because women are concentrated almost exclusively in agricultural activities I am using the terms primary and agriculture interchangeably.

12. There are several reasons for this reduction: the prohibiting of employment for persons under fourteen years old; the expansion of the education, especially in urban centers; and changes in social security legislation and retirement plans, which lead to the retirement of older persons.

Table 2

Evolution of Labor Force Participation by Economic Sectors and Sex (in Millions)

Economic sectors	1940		1950		1970	
	Men	Women	Men	Women	Men	Women
Primary	8.416	1.311	9.496	.758	11.836	1.258
	(100)	(100)	(113)	(58)	(141)	(96)
Secondary	1.220	.298	1.955	.392	4.660	.636
	(100)	(100)	(160)	(132)	(382)	(214)
Tertiary	2.231	1.180	3.141	1.340	6.348	4.110
	(100)	(100)	(141)	(114)	(285)	(348)
Total	11.959	2.800	14.610	2.508	23.392	6.165
	(100)	(100)	(122)	(90)	(196)	(220)

Source.—Demographic Census of Brazilian Population, 1940, 1950, and 1970.
Note.—Numbers in parenthesis are indexes of growth.

rapid industrialization. Industrial development does not, then, necessarily lead to higher participation of women in secondary activities; rather it would seem to push women out of handicraft production.

As table 2 further suggests, there was a decrease in the number of women employed in agriculture from 1940 to 1950 and a 13 percent increase in the number of men. Indeed, whereas in 1940, 47 percent of all women workers were concentrated in the primary sector, in 1970 that figure declined to 20 percent. Some authors attribute the reduction of women in agriculture to the different criteria used to classify women's labor in rural areas in different censuses, especially that of 1940.[13] Those who consider the data correct argue that women's participation in the labor force depends on reconciling domestic and economic activities and that in the family type of rural productive organization this reconciliation was possible.[14] However, with the growth of both large- and small-scale holdings,[15] the domestic agricultural production of women becomes marginal and they are not absorbed in machine-intensive large-scale modern agricultural production.

In 1940, similar percentages of men and women workers, 10 percent and 11 percent, respectively, were employed in the secondary sector (see table 3). In 1950, the percentage of women increased relative to that of men (16 percent to 13 percent) because a large proportion of industrialized manufacturing, such as textiles, was considered "female work."

13. See Manoel A. Costa, *Aspectos demográficos da populacao economicamente ativa* (Rio de Janeiro: IPEA, 1968).

14. In "Algunos aspectos del la actividade económica de la mujer in Latino America" (Santiago de Chile: CELADE, 1963), Pesephus van den Boomen tested the hypothesis that so long as the countries are predominantly rural a higher women's participation could be expected. However, the census data did not allow him to prove his hypothesis.

15. Madeira and Singer showed that the number of both extremes of landholdings increased during this century.

Table 3

Relative Distribution of the Labor Force, by Economic Sector and Sex (%)

Year and Sex	Economic Sector: Primary	Secondary	Tertiary
1940:			
Men	70	10	20
Women	47	11	43
1950:			
Men	65	13	22
Women	30	16	54
1970:			
Men	51	20	29
Women	20	10	70

Source.—Demographic Census of Brazilian Population, 1940, 1950, and 1970.

After 1950, however, industrial development expanded into other areas, and by 1970 more men than women (20 percent to 10 percent) were employed in the secondary sector.

A Regional Analysis by Sector

The process of development does not affect all regions of a country such as Brazil in a homogenous way. Thus female labor force participation rates vary considerably according to the stage of development of a particular region (see table 4). While the most developed region (South-

Table 4

Women's Participation in the Labor Force Compared with Female Population Ten Years of Age or More, by Region

Stage of Development and Region	1940	1950	1970
Developed:			
Southeast B	21.2	19.4	22.8
Intermediate:			
Subtotal	16.4	11.2	17.2
South	19.1	13.5	19.4
Southeast A	15.0	10.2	15.6
Middle-West	11.8	4.8	13.6
Underdeveloped:			
Subtotal	20.3	11.5	16.1
North	21.5	11.3	14.2
Northeast	20.1	11.6	16.3

Source.—Demographic Census of Brazilian Population, 1940, 1950, and 1970.

east B) shows the highest level of participation in all three census years, the intermediate region had the lowest level of participation in 1940, and the middle level in 1970 (17.2). The underdeveloped region, which had levels almost similar to the most developed region in 1940, could not sustain that rate of participation in 1970. Within the broad category of intermediate development, the Southeast A and the Middle-West regions showed lower levels of participation in the three census years, which indicates a slow rate of industrial development, as compared with the South. The Middle-West had a very large percentage increase in 1970 over 1950 (8.8 percent), because of the move of the federal capital to Brasilia, but it still has the lowest rate of participation (13.6 percent).

Women's employment in the agricultural sector is inversely related to regional development (see table 5). Whereas in 1940, 33 percent of the women in the developed region were in rural labor, in the intermediate region 50 percent of them were, and in the less developed, 55 percent. Regional variations in the forms of agrarian production and patterns of landholdings always existed in Brazil. For example, in the sugar plantations of the Northeast, peasants worked for the landowner in exchange for plots of land which they cultivated for personal consumption. This type of *latifundia* system has persisted in the less developed regions, where agricultural technology is almost primitive.[16] In these areas, therefore, there is a high percentage of women in agriculture. In the Southeast and South, where commercial agriculture such as coffee plantations dominated, women had fewer opportunities to work

Table 5

Percentage of Female Labor Force Participation, by Economic Sector, Region, and Census Year

Stage of Regional Development and Census Year	Economic Sector		
	Primary	Secondary	Tertiary
Development:			
1940	33	14	53
1950	18	24	59
1970	5	17	78
Intermediate:			
1940	50	7	44
1950	33	10	58
1970	24	6	70
Underdeveloped:			
1940	55	11	35
1950	43	11	46
1970	36	7	57

SOURCE.—Demographic Census of Brazilian Population, 1940, 1950, and 1970.

16. Juarez R. Brandao Lopes, "Capitalist Development and Agrarian Structure in Brazil" (paper presented at the International Conference on Sociology of Urban and Regional Development, Sicilia, April 1976), p. 4.

as permanent laborers; they were used mainly as a seasonal labor supply. However, they could continue subsistence farming on the plots received by the *colonos.* At a later stage, when the agriculture of the region became even more capitalized and commercialized, there was a drastic proletarianization of the labor force, and *moradores* and *colonos* were replaced by pure wage earners who were given no land.[17] Although mechanization reduced employment for all workers, the change continues to affect women more than men: "Beginning in 1966/68 mass dismissals of permanent workers of the fazendas took place, all over the regions; these displaced ex-colonos formed new rural barrios or settled in the periphery of towns where gang-labor could be recruited for the temporary jobs in the plantations of the region, being transported by trucks from one place to another, just when and where labor was needed. A purer rural proletariat than the *colono* had made its appearance and an industrial reserve army, in the strict sense of the term, had been formed."[18] A typical case of underemployment, and an extreme case of exploitation of the labor force, these workers have no fixed jobs and are paid by intermediaries, who literally "auction" them. But women have fewer opportunities to find this wage labor, and the few who do work are even more exploited than men, since the intermediaries subtract a larger amount from their wages.[19] Moreover, and as often happens in the development process in large holdings which tend to become more specialized in commercial production, men take the place of women.[20]

The secondary sector concentrates in the already more developed regions, and thus intensifies the uneven development of Brazil. In 1940 the largest concentration of female labor within the industrial sector (14 percent) occurred in the developed region of Brazil. The larger percentage in the less developed regions (11 percent), as compared with the intermediate regions (7 percent), seems to indicate that industrial development does not always lead to higher female participation in the labor force. Now in the second stage of development, according to Singer,[21] the vast majority of productive units of the secondary sector are made up of handicrafts workshops, many of which simultaneously produce and repair goods. Many women did this work at home in combination with domestic tasks or were employed through the putting-out system of the textile industry in the Northeast. Thus a less developed region could exhibit higher levels of female labor force participation.

In the tertiary sector, a complex of very diversified activities, we can

17. Ibid., p. 1.

18. Ibid., pp. 7–8.

19. See Verena Martinez Allier, "As mulheres do caminhão de turma," *Debate e critica,* no. 5 (March 1975).

20. Madeira and Singer.

21. See P. Singer, "Força de trabalho e emprego no Brasil: 1920/69," *Cadernos de pesquisa,* no. 3 (São Paulo: CEBRAP, 1970).

distinguish between productive activities and consumption activities (production services, collective consumption, and private consumption).[22] This criterion allows us to evaluate the proportion of women employed in the lower productivity subsectors. Between 1940 and 1970 there was an increase in all the categories included in table 6. As development occurs, women's labor tends to concentrate in the category of personal services, which resembles women's traditional activities in the home. In the other categories it is possible to observe some increase in women's labor force participation, especially in collective consumption and professional activities in the developed regions.[23] This increase is probably due to the expansion of the educational system, which employs a large number of women as primary school teachers, and the expansion of civil service activities, especially in bureaucratic services, where women are willing to work for lower salaries and are generally more stable employees than men.

The Conditions of Women of Different Social Classes

Although it is clear that economic development does not necessarily mean higher levels of women's participation in the labor force, it is not clear how this process specifically affects women of different social classes. A comparison between two distinct groups of women—married women from fifteen to sixty-five years of age living with their husbands, and single women in the same age group living with their parents—reveals significant differences as to the effect of development on different social groups (see table 7). This subset of women in the labor force that represents 75 percent of the two groups constitutes a female population fifteen to sixty-five years of age. Three subsets are missing: women separated from their husbands and widows, who represent 3.4 percent and 8.8 percent of the total population, respectively, and single women living by themselves, who represent 39.4 percent of all single women. The level of participation of the subsets excluded (40 percent) is higher than the subsets included in this study (14.6 percent) because most women who live by themselves must work. Using disaggregated census data on our sample we can analyze such variables as region of the coun-

22. Singer. Production services comprise occupations in commerce of goods, real estate, stocks, credit, etc., transportation, communication, and storage. Consumption is subdivided into private and collective consumption services. The latter include public administration, social activities, education, health, and social security. Private consumption, on the other hand, is also subdivided into personal services and professional services.

23. This increase in the liberal professions is assumed to be largely positive for the improvement of women's social status, while an increase in activities of personal services is assumed to be negative, since this category represents marginal occupations such as domestic service.

Table 6

Percentage of Female Labor Force Participation in the Tertiary Economic Sector, by Region and Year

Stage of Development and Year	Productive	Collective Consumption	Private Consumption		Others	Total
			Professional	Personal Services		
Developed:						
1940	4.1	7.5	0.5	40.3	0.4	52.8
1950	6.7	12.9	0.8	37.9	0.3	58.6
1970	11.3	18.8	1.6	43.5	2.8	78.0
Intermediate:						
1940	2.0	5.7	0.3	35.1	0.4	43.5
1950	4.7	12.3	0.5	39.6	0.4	57.5
1970	7.0	21.0	0.9	39.0	2.4	70.3
Underdeveloped:						
1940	1.7	2.7	0.2	29.7	0.4	34.7
1950	3.8	7.8	0.4	33.4	0.3	45.7
1970	5.9	15.6	0.4	32.2	2.7	56.8
Brazil:						
1940	2.5	5.0	0.3	34.4	0.4	42.6
1950	5.2	11.1	0.6	36.9	0.3	54.1
1970	8.3	18.7	1.0	38.9	2.6	69.5

SOURCE.—Demographic Census of Brazilian Population, 1940, 1950, and 1970.

Table 7

Labor Force Participation Rates, by Levels of Schooling and Marital Status

Level of Schooling	Married Women, Husband Present		Single Women Living with Parents	
	Labor Force (%)	Population (%)	Labor Force (%)	Population (%)
Illiterates	6.35	39.57	19.71	19.82
Elementary incomplete	7.20	32.01	23.96	29.23
Elementary complete	12.08	21.93	29.66	36.08
Lower secondary	21.44	2.97	24.35	8.94
Higher secondary	49.38	2.88	64.69	4.22
University incomplete	54.25	0.13	43.44	1.08
University complete	65.82	0.51	77.17	0.63
All levels	9.93	100.00	27.48	100.00

Source.—Demographic Census of Brazilian Population, 1970, data aggregated by author.

try, level of schooling, age, occupation, and socioeconomic status (SES) (see table 8).

As table 8 suggests, the rates of labor force participation increase with the level of schooling for both single and married women. Among illiterates only 6.4 percent of married women and 19.7 percent of single women work, as compared to 65.8 percent of married and 77.2 percent of single women with university education. Participation differences by marital status are larger in the lower levels of schooling; in the higher levels, differences tend to diminish, perhaps because married women have domestic help for household and child-care activities. Low SES women earn low salaries which do not cover the costs for the unpaid work they do in the home; only when the salary covers this cost can these women enter the labor market. Since less than 1 percent of women had completed university studies in 1970, the proportional rise in participation among these women has not affected the overall women's labor force participation. Indeed, the opportunities for higher education are not great in Brazil; very few women (6.5 percent married and 14.8 percent single) have attended more than elementary school.

Schooling is clearly related to socioeconomic status. Higher levels of parents' schooling, higher family income, and higher occupational attainment all favor schooling attainment (see table 9). While married women of low SES have only 2.2 years of schooling, women of higher social class have 10.7 years of schooling. The difference is less accentuated for single women, because they are younger than married women (twenty-one versus thirty-five years old, mean age) and have thus had more opportunities to profit from the considerable expansion of the Brazilian educational system in the past few years.

If education leads women to higher levels of participation, and edu-

Table 8

Distribution of Some Occupations of Women in 1970, by Marital Status and Socioeconomic Status

Occupation	Married Women, Husband Present				Single Women Living with Parents			
	Socioeconomic Status (%)			Mean Years of Schooling	Socioeconomic Status (%)			Mean Years of Schooling
	Low	Middle	High		Low	Middle	High	
Farm laborer	33.75	1.86	0.03	1.42	28.68	6.25	...	2.27
Domestic maid	9.45	1.66	0.03	1.87	2.13	1.07	0.60	3.28
Industrial worker	17.51	11.65	0.97	3.19	14.09	8.89	2.21	4.03
Others	24.81	19.64	14.26	3.91	30.46	18.78	16.02	4.21
Commerical worker	3.15	5.86	1.52	4.20	6.07	9.17	1.98	5.34
Personal services	0.63	2.60	0.10	4.58	0.92	1.38	0.27	5.15
Nurses	1.51	4.06	1.81	5.83	1.49	1.82	0.23	5.65
Clerical worker	1.64	15.38	15.97	7.79	8.13	24.66	34.01	7.92
Elementary teacher	6.80	31.96	38.17	9.14	6.96	23.08	29.59	9.43
Secondary teacher	0.63	4.26	17.04	11.42	0.78	3.56	10.91	11.94
Professional worker	0.13	1.07	10.10	13.71	0.28	1.34	4.19	13.28

SOURCE.—Demographic Census of Brazilian Population, 1970, data aggregated by author.

Table 9

Labor Force Participation by Marital Status and Socioeconomic Status

Marital Status and Socioeconomic Status	Labor Force (%)	Mean Years of Schooling	Mean Age	Population (%)
Married women, husband present:				
Low	7.94	2.24	35.17	78.29
Middle	15.02	5.54	34.07	18.92
High	30.99	10.72	35.76	2.80
Single women, living with parents:				
Low	28.18	4.28	20.84	78.68
Middle	25.30	7.67	20.89	18.85
High	21.73	9.77	21.24	2.47

SOURCE.—Demographic Census of Brazilian Population, 1970, data aggregated by author.

cation depends on socioeconomic status, then labor force participation is also affected by socioeconomic status, through education. As table 9 demonstrates, women of higher SES are four times more likely to work than women of lower SES. Over and beyond higher levels of schooling, women of higher SES have better opportunities to find jobs because of their social contacts. Although married women of low SES should theoretically be more inclined to work, since they probably need to complement their husband's low salary, the fact remains that their level of participation is 7.9 percent lower than women of the other classes. It is possible that these women have difficulty finding jobs compatible with their domestic responsibilities. By comparison, more lower SES single women work than higher ones, again because of their extended schooling.

Table 8 shows that women of different social classes have different occupational opportunities. Here, the pattern for married and single women differs in only a few cases. Farm laborers, industrial workers, domestic servants, and women in "other" occupations are predominantly from lower SES. Commercial workers, personal services workers, and nurses are typically from middle SES, while elementary teachers and professional workers are predominantly from higher SES. Elementary teaching continues to be a predominantly female activity for women of middle and higher social classes, married or not. Elementary teachers include 38 percent of all married women of higher SES who work, as compared to 16 percent in clinical work. The number of single women who are primary teachers has been declining; only 30 percent of women of higher SES are so employed. Overall, however, many women continue to work as primary teachers, despite low salaries, because of short hours, job stability, legislative protection, long vacations, and because it has been traditionally considered appropriate for women.

Industrialization increases bureaucratic and clerical activities for women. However, these occupations remain predominantly limited to single women of higher (34 percent) and middle SES (25 percent). Among married women the percentage of clerical workers is smaller than in the corresponding SES group of single women. This reflects discrimination in the labor market against married women; some Brazilian banks, for example, hire younger females only on condition that they agree in writing to resign when they marry.

Domestic service ranks high among the occupations of married women of lower SES (9.45 percent) and low among those of single women. Of course if all women were considered in the sample, the number of domestic servants might have risen considerably. These occupations are growing in the cities, because of a lack of alternative employment opportunities for women. Indeed, many single women who need housing as well as money might resort to this activity. A possible consequence of the marginalization of female labor in Brazil is that the level of unemployment among urban women remains disguised.

For Brazil, then, economic development has not led to higher levels of women's participation in the labor market. The process of dependent capitalist development is responsible not only for a lower level of women's participation in agriculture, but also for a lower level of absorption in urban development. However, it is not industrialization per se that creates underemployment and marginalization, but an industrial finance capital and advanced technology (intensive in capital), which does not permit fundamental changes in the economic structure. In Brazil, this situation is aggravated by the concentration of industrial activities in a few regions. Unequal regional development generates different female participation rates in economic activity, because regions are in different stages of development.

When agriculture was the center of economic activity, the labor force participation of both males and females was high. In this sector the female labor force continues to be high in underdeveloped areas, because the type of agricultural production favors women's activity. However, when agriculture becomes more capitalized and commercialized, the total labor participation in this sector is reduced, and the opportunities for women to work outside the home become limited. Thus, female employment in agriculture is inversely related to regional development.

Reduction in the level of participation was not limited to agriculture, however. In the secondary sector, women's labor did not expand at the same rate of total employment. The maintenance of a similar level of participation in the two extreme years of our analysis is due to the substitution of manufacture production for handicraft production. Where industrial manufacture has displaced handicrafts, women are pushed out of handicrafts without being reabsorbed into industry. Thus a visible reduction takes place in female participation in the secondary sector.

Finally, female employment in the tertiary sector increased considerably with the expansion of productive and collective services in urban centers. However, a significant part of this expansion is occurring in occupations which are extensions of women's activities at home. The growth of occupations such as domestic service confirms once again that capitalist development does not always improve women's position in the wage labor market, especially that of lower-class women.

The analysis of labor force participation in 1970 by social class helps to explain the lower absorption of women in the wage labor market. Although married women are less likely to work than single women, more schooling increases labor force participation of both married and unmarried women. However, since the majority of Brazilian women have less than four years of schooling, schooling may be said to obstruct female employment. It continues to be a privilege of few women, the women of high SES.

Dependent capitalist economic development, therefore, does not necessarily increase employment in the primary and secondary sectors of the labor market, where lower class women have the educational requirements to work as wage laborers, And these same women did not benefit from the expansion of the educational system. In all probability, expansion of educational opportunities to women of all classes in a later stage of economic development will lead to an increase in job requirements. Thus these women will continue to have relatively poor opportunities in the wage labor market, unless changes in the very process of economic development begin to facilitate the incorporation of women into the labor force.

School of Education
Federal University of Minas Gerias
Belo Horizonte, Brazil

Methodology and Data Collection

Introduction

Nadia H. Youssef

Current studies on the comparative status of women in developing countries raise a question that is central to the subject of methodology and data collection: Do the empirical dimensions selected to measure status actually represent operational indicators of female position and status? Such a question confronts two interrelated problems: the *definitional* issue of what constitutes "high" or "low" status for women in a given social setting, and the validity of available data on which conclusions about the comparative status of women are reached. Translated into operational terms, we must address ourselves to the following questions: (*a*) What do we still need to know to evaluate the status of women and the progress of women's participation in society; (*b*) How can we combine different categories of available information about different social settings to generate new insights into the position and status of women in the social structure?

The major problem that the methodologist has to contend with is that the comparative status of women as a subject matter has been stripped of its theoretical guidelines. The ethnocentric evolutionary model, which has traditionally associated the equalization of the sexes with industrial-economic development and northwestern European culture and which has been used as a yardstick for comparing the status of women in the non-Western world, has been recently challenged. We have had to confront some of the contradictions between the "ideology" of egalitarianism and the empirical "reality" of a highly competitive industrial system in which men have denied equal access to women because they threaten to compete for educational, occupational, and income opportunities. Another challenge to the evolutionary notion of progress, which linked industrialization and Westernization with female emancipation, is that modernization may well have an adverse—rather than salutory—impact upon the status of women. The flow of Western cultural values and industrial technology into certain non-Western settings may indeed have restructured sex roles in such a way as to "depress" the traditional status of women and push them toward complete dependency on men.

Because of such conflicting findings, the current search for a new theoretical orientation seeks to find the golden mean between evolutionary economic determinism, on the one hand, and absolute cultural relativism, on the other. The repercussions of this theoretical vacuum on methodology are enormous, however. Social scientists and historians have become sensitized to the enormous problem of devising a direct multidimensional measurement of female status and of ascertaining which empirical dimensions do actually represent operational indicators of women's status in different parts of the world. An integral part of this questioning also involves caution and reserve toward the use of published secondary data because of the obvious idiosyncracies in definition and internal methods of collection. More important yet, social scientists now feel the imperative need to interpret social quantification according to the qualitative meanings attached to behavioral patterns in different sociocultural contexts.

Two important papers have been selected for the section on methodology. The first, by Ximena Bunster B., entitled "Talking Pictures: Field Method and Visual Mode," makes a contribution to our understanding of the subjective definition of a situation from the point of view of the women themselves. The second, by Mary Chamie, entitled "Sexuality and Birth Control Decisions among Lebanese Couples," tackles a topic on which virtually no systematic information exists.

In her research, Bunster B. and her interdisciplinary team maximized the use of still photography combined with structured open-ended interviewing as a new method of researching and communicating with functionally illiterate proletarian working mothers in Lima, Peru. This study shows that the talking-picture approach as a field method can yield a sophisticated understanding of how the marginally employed proletarian woman structures, perceives, evaluates, and assigns meaning to her work and family and to the public domain in which she is or is not involved. In Chamie's research, the linkage of fertility control decisions to the intimate details of a couple's sexual relationships through structured/open-ended interviews is not new. What is unique, however, is the accomplishment of this feat in a Middle Eastern social setting. For although we suspect that sexual activity, responsiveness, assertiveness, and compatibility are frequent and popular topics of discussion at female gatherings in Middle Eastern society, there is virtually no research on the subject of female sexuality in the Arab world. Chamie is also to be congratulated for rejecting the established tradition of linking Middle Eastern behavior to religious ideologies and for focusing instead on structural factors to explain social behavior and social reality.

International Center for Research on Women
Washington, D.C., U.S.A.

Methodology and Data Collection

Talking Pictures: Field Method and Visual Mode

Ximena Bunster B.

The aim of this paper is to discuss the use of still photography, or "talking pictures," combined with open-ended interviewing, as a research strategy. Using it, the interdisciplinary team of which I was a part studied 200 proletarian working mothers in Lima, Peru.[1] Some were illiterate, but bilingual (Quechua and Spanish). Others, who had resided in the city all their lives, had a rudimentary education equivalent to the completion of the first three grades of primary education. They were street vendors, factory workers, domestic servants, and market sellers with fixed stalls in the main markets.

One of our main goals was to analyze the adjustments that these women, marginal to the occupational structure, had made in order to survive within an underdeveloped, dependent capitalist structure. Such a "mode of production has enormous repercussions in shaping the ways in which the marginally employed view and experience their many worlds. Ultimately consciousness reflects existence."[2] Because of this, we wanted the women to formulate their conventional, explicit, and conscious rules of behavior as workers, mothers, and members of unions; to

1. The research team included an anthropologist, Ximena Bunster B.; a political scientist, Elsa Chaney; a psychologist, Carmen Pimente; a social psychologist, Gabriela Vilalobos; a sociologist, Hilda Mercado; and a psychologist who was also a professional photographer, Ellan Young. In addition, we are greatly indebted to Jeanine Anderson, anthropologist and research assistant in our study, who tested the interview kit critically and contributed creatively toward its standardization as a research tool. All of the photographs printed here were taken by Ellan Young.

2. Heleieth Iara B. Saffioti, personal communication with the author. For an important theoretical contribution to women's studies, see Saffioti, *A mulher na sociedade de classes: Mito e realidade* (São Paulo: Quatro Artes, 1969).

state their values, objectives in life, and aspirations. We also desired to tap an inner world of feelings, values, and significance. Relying solely on verbal communication, through interviewing, is not the best way of understanding the subjectivity of informants who may have difficulty with language. Using photography in the social sciences is, of course, not new. We were influenced by Margaret Mead, among others; by her courses at Columbia University on methods and problems in anthropology; and by her pioneering publications.[3] She has stressed that the best camera recording is made by the individual who combines training in photography or filmmaking and anthropology.[4] Though we share her general views, our approach, as we evolved the talking-pictures technique, was interdisciplinary and collaborative, which entailed its own methods.

Development of the Photo-Interview

We first investigated to see whether the subjects of the study were familiar with photographs, a luxury for the bulk of the population of the countries in the process of development. But in spite of its high costs, poor people in Latin America try to record the important events of their life cycle, of that of their family, and sometimes of that of the neighborhood or community to which they belong. In towns and cities photos of first communion, baptism, or marriage may protrude, extravagantly framed, from otherwise bare walls in slum dwellings, and carefully packed photographs of a child's wake and funeral may be kept under key with such other important documents as a marriage license.

Proletarian families are also familiar with movies and television. Sets were found operating in the most dilapidated houses, a phenomenon common to large cities of Latin America. Families may lack the bare essentials of food and clothing, but will become indebted for years to buy a TV. The most watched programs are soap operas produced in Mexico, Venezuela, Argentina, and Peru. The plots invariably deal with a female heroine of the working class, most often a domestic servant, who achieves upward mobility through sex. She is usually seduced by an upper-middle-class student or an upper-class man and gives birth to a child. Through self-denial, hard work, and refusal to settle down with a man from her class, she wins the child's father over and eventually marries him. This is the happy ending, though getting him to the altar sometimes take a lifetime.

Working-class women also devour *foto-novelas,* a weekly magazine whose content is made up of plots of novels, the equivalent of the "true

3. Margaret Mead, "Anthropology and the Camera," in *The Encyclopedia of Photography,* ed. Willard D. Morgan (New York: Greystone Press, 1963), 1:166–84.

4. Margaret Mead, "Visual Anthropology in a Discipline of Words," in *Principles of Visual Anthropology,* ed. Paul Hockings (The Hague: Mouton Publishers, 1975).

confessions" story or the dime novel for the English-speaking public. The novels are presented through the photographic arrangement of scenes illustrating different chapters or sequences. Technically, there is no readable literature in the magazine, with the exception of very short captions printed in large white letters over the corners of the photographs to interpret what is going on, in case the photo is ambiguous. The dialogue of the main characters and the conversation of the minor actors are also printed in this fashion.

However, for women and their families who had recently migrated into the city from the highlands or from jungle areas, photographs were a novelty. Their inclusion in the photo-interview posed added problems and introduced added variables within the expected range of cultural and idiosyncratic interpretations. This was especially true of some of the street vendors, or *ambulantes,* who peddle their goods inside and outside the markets and on the main streets of Lima, attired in Indian dress. For example, we took a Polaroid picture of an *ambulante* who was selling prepared food outside a market. The photo portrayed her leaning against a wheel cart and evading the strong sun by wearing a beautiful, wide-rimmed straw hat. We handed her the photograph and told her she could keep it as a *recuerdo,* or souvenir. She thanked us but politely refused to accept the fact that the woman in the photograph was she. She crossed the street to a friend of hers, another street vendor, who reinforced our statement. Matching her sense of self with the image of the straw-hatted woman staring back at her from the picture was such a forceful revelation that she burst out with manifestations of childish glee. For about half an hour she abandoned her selling post at her cart and did the rounds in the market place, showing her co-workers the photograph and giggling uncontrollably.

In general, we utilized a Polaroid camera to catch the interest of the female workers in our study; to engage fully the ones who were more knowledgeable of their environment and willing to help us; to open communications and to assure trust in us. Latin American Indians and the rest of the mixed urban proletarian population are wary of tourists snapping shots of them; they feel cheated and used because they never see the end result of the action of the prowler with the camera. For this reason we offered Polaroid photographs as gifts in exchange for their collaboration. The film is developed in a matter of minutes in front of the interested party, who could then take the photo of self home as a token of reciprocity. As John Collier has said, "the feedback opportunity of photography, the only kind of ethnographic note-making that can reasonably be returned to the native, provides a situation which often gratifies and feeds the ego enthusiasm of informants to still further involvement in the study."[5]

5. John Collier, Jr., *Visual Anthropology: Photography as a Research Method* (New York: Holt, Rinehart & Winston, 1967), p. 13.

During the first phase of photographing, we followed Collier's recommendations closely. We shot pictures of the total environment of our four basic occupational roles—street vendors, market women with fixed stalls, domestic servants or maids, factory workers (see figs. 1, 2, and 3). We recorded overviews of markets, factories, and private homes belonging to the city's different social classes. The team's photographer/psychologist and anthropologist combed the streets of Lima for three weeks in order to choose salient aspects of the panoramic vistas and to become familiar with the complexity of the specific places we would select for study. To interest women, we explained that we were

FIG. 1.—Credit for all photographs, Ellan Young

FIG. 2

FIG. 3

investigating working mothers in the city to commemorate International Women's Year, whose celebration in 1975 coincided with the Peruvian Woman's year officially proclaimed by the military government.

During the second phase of photographing, we had the full collaboration of key informants, about twenty-five women from the four occupational groups under study. They allowed the photographer and the anthropologist to follow them around during daily, weekly, and monthly work and domestic routines. Ideally, we would have taught the key informants how to use the camera and then made their shots part of the photo-interview kit. Sol Worth and John Adair, in a pioneer experiment, instructed seven chosen native collaborators.[6] We gave up the idea for many reasons. The Navajo, though living on reservations, form part of a large national culture which exposes them to the technology of film, whereas our working mothers belong to a developing society in which cameras are luxuries and the process of picture taking is surrounded by the aura of high complexity, if not magic. On-going communication between researcher and informant will, because of the informant's knowledge of her/his culture, keep the researcher "from being carried away." Informants not only help to determine the emic dimension of a phenomenon, but they check, correct, and modify the components in a set of photographs that will later serve to illustrate a whole category of events.

6. Sol Worth and John Adair, *Through Navajo Eyes* (Bloomington: Indiana University Press, 1975). Worth's paper, "Margaret Mead and the Shift from 'Visual Anthropology' to the 'Anthropology of Visual Communication' " (presented at Margaret Mead Symposium AAAS Meetings, Boston, February 20, 1976), is also relevant to the methods we used in Peru.

When the photographs were developed, we took them back to our key informants for the first elicitation meetings. During them we chose the most appropriate pictures to be included in the final photo-interview kit. We kept in mind Collier's assessment of the photograph as a focus on which the interviewee may center her/his attention. As such, it promotes empathy between interviewer and interviewee and provides a fluid and fruitful context for understanding and data gathering. We also asked our informants to aid us in a tentative arrangement of scenes under researcher-defined categories. For example, which photographs would an informant pick to show the kinds of machines operated by men and by women in a factory?

The photo-interview kit was assembled with 120 photographs chosen out of over the 3,000 that were shot. They were pasted in a large album, designed for the study. The format, though bulky, was a versatile interviewing tool. It could be opened on the grass; we talked to many maids while they were taking care of children in parks. It could also be accommodated over crates and piles of vegetables in markets. The pictures were then combined with a structured, but open-ended questionnaire.

The whole photo-interview was then given to a group of key informants who had not collaborated in the previous stages of its construction. They were asked to read the photographs, to respond to the questions, and to react by criticizing the interview. Only after testing did we go to the groups of working mothers selected for the study. During the first experimental photo-interview sessions with informants, we became aware of the fact that, not only did they enjoy talking pictures, but they were eager to do well during the two-to-three-hour structured dialogue. They asked such questions as, "How did I do?" or made such statements as, "I liked our conversation very much; it is the first time that I talked about my life as a worker and as a mother."

A decision was then made to focus on these extraprogrammatic segments of conversation to aid in assessing both the informant's evaluation of the photo-interview and the interviewer's experience. Questions were appended to each long interview. The informant was asked: (1) What did you think of our talking pictures? Do you think these photographs illustrate accurately the everyday life of a worker like you? (2) Would you add other photographs to the album? Which ones? (3) Which photos in the album did you like the most and why? Not like and why? (4) What did you think of me [the interviewer]? The researcher also observed the subject and her general reactions to the event. (See the Appendix for an outline of the organization of the photo-interview itself.)

Patterned statements about the world of the subjects of our study emerged as we pulled together the responses of the 200 women. Of the pictures included in the family set, all the informants selected the same one as their favorite: a scene portraying a working woman at home, sitting at the table with her husband and her five daughters (fig. 4). She is laughing and looking fondly across the table at her toddler. The other girls are involved with the father, who is leafing through a magazine. Empty dishes and cups are scattered on the table. The recurrent evaluation of the family scene by all the informants was: "It is a beautiful photograph because the family is together"; "they are having fun together"; or "they have time to share each other's company." Most working mothers never have the chance nor the time to enjoy their families; factory workers have to comply with work shifts stipulated by the management, which contribute to atomizing further their already fragmented family interactions. Market women–street vendors and those with fixed stalls have to get up at three in the morning to start their day buying wholesale, usually taking infants with them and leaving toddlers and older children at home to fend for themselves. Domestic servants are the most alienated of all. When hired young—sometimes at the age of ten—they are cut off from their families of orientation. When they grow older and become mothers themselves, their slavelike seclusion in the homes of their employers impoverishes the nature, the quality, and the frequency of healthy and happy family relationships.

Two other photographs in the family set were chosen unanimously. One shows another family, a pregnant mother, her husband, and four children. The mother is putting the baby to bed and the father is supervising the homework of the older ones (fig. 5). This family scene was praised because "the family was together and everybody was doing something in the company of other members of the family." The other photo portrays a young couple strolling in a park with their small son (fig. 6).

Fig. 4

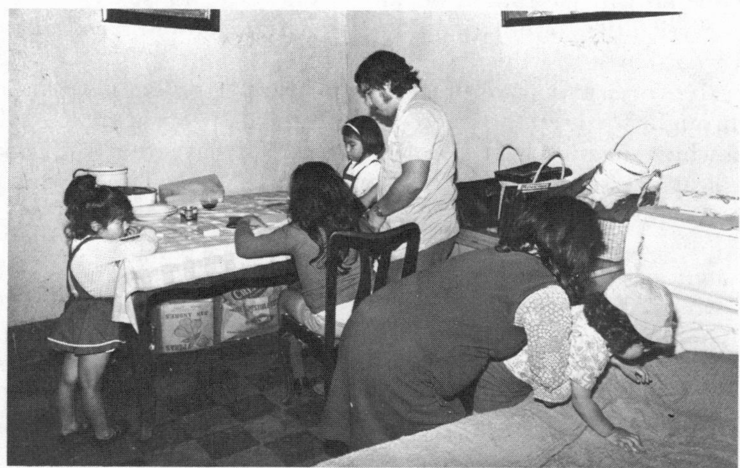

Fig. 5

Fig. 6

The bodies of the parents are harmoniously linked to the child's. The activity of the parents with the young son was perceived as an unattainable ideal situation, for most women never had the time to go on an outing solely for relaxation, and all of them would like their husbands or *compañeros* to share more of their free time with their sons and daughters, something they seldom do, as the men go off by themselves. The members of the research team naively yet purposely included with the rest of the family interaction scenes one of a man sitting in a comfortable sofa, all by himself, watching TV. We expected the informants to read the photograph as one of an "uncooperative father" (watching news and film while his wife continued working around the house). However, the replies carried the connotation that it was wonderful to have something (the TV) at home to while away the time.

Both manifestations of upward mobility and conflict-laden attitudes were brought forth by the photographs of the different types of dwellings in which the bulk of the proletarian mothers live in urban Lima: (1) the typical one- or two-room thatched house without roof which is a common sight in the shanty towns, or *barrios jovenes,* that encircle Lima; and (2) the one-story brick house and the half-finished two-story home of the more prosperous families (see fig. 7). Though around two-thirds of the women in the sample would instantaneously relate to the photographs and talk about their living conditions and their migration into the capital city as they pointed to the different type of houses in the *barriadas* where they had first arrived, the upwardly mobile women would set themselves apart from the scenes. These women, most with fixed stalls in the markets of the more affluent neighborhoods and a step away from the rest of the still trapped population within the context of the marginal pole of the national economic system, came up with patterned "market-stall occupational responses" opposed to the ones of domestic servants, market peddlers, and factory workers. They felt that their houses, compared to the ones in the album, were so much more *decente,* decent, of good quality; "certainly their neighborhoods were so much nicer," as they had managed to buy homes in *urbanizaciones,* middle-class houses in residential areas. In spite of such differences in outlook, it was possible to conclude that the one material thing that all the proletarian mothers dream of is to own a house, no matter how small. The majority of them were going through great financial stress at the time of the study to attain this generalized and strongly felt need.

FIG. 7

The value attached to the economic role of children emerged from the pictorial analysis of working mothers photographed alongside their working children (figs. 8 and 9). Child labor is not perceived as parental exploitation, but necessary for the survival of the whole family. Eight- to twelve-year-olds of either sex become so skillful at selling, handling money, preparing and marketing food, and performing domestic services that their income or salary becomes an essential part of the whole family's financial pool. Sometimes they make more than their mothers—usually the ones selling in markets. In many of the cases the women interviewed had children who had sporadically assumed the role

FIG. 8

FIG. 9

of worker and family provider, transforming the mother (when ill or giving birth to another child) or both parents into their dependents. The economic roles of children were also looked upon as part of the socialization process in the proletarian urban context. "Children have to start working early in life; it's the only way in which they can learn their obligations as members of a family." "Boys and girls have to keep their minds engaged in something, otherwise they roam free on the street; work keeps them out of mischief." "When our children work we all eat better and lead a better life."

After the women had talked about the pictures, they were asked, "After having lived all these years, with all the good, regular, and bad things that life has in store for us, what choice would you make if you had the chance—would you like to be born as a man or as a woman?" Over two-thirds of the women interviewed openly confessed that they would have rather been born male. Caught in the subuniverse of the marginally employed and unable to rise because of lack of education and a rigid class system, most of the proletarian mothers expressed themselves thus: "I would like to be a man, because if he is educated he can go in and out of important places and earn more, because men were born to accomplish more." "I would like to be born again as a man, they only have one thing to worry about—to bring money home—and that's all; women have to look after the children, cook, wash, and work outside the home." Clearly, the culturally patterned male and female roles, with their pertinent ideology, operate against the working proletarian mother. She has been socialized to accept the shared cultural belief in the inferiority of women as compared to men, itself a sine qua non for the perpetuation of the machismo concept.

Yet the most revealing photographs, for all of the working women studied, were the ones illustrating the most significant events in a woman's reproductive cycle: pregnancy, childbirth, and motherhood (see figs. 10 and 11). Scenes depicting a couple dating on a bench in a park were the most evocative in bringing forth their remembrances and past love experiences. Marriage and raising a family were clearly perceived as manifestations of love and sacrifice. Photos portraying pregnant women extracted detailed accounts of the way in which they viewed their bodies and themselves, and a picture representing a factory woman breast-feeding her child was rated the most beautiful of all. These photographs were able to stir up their hidden emotions better than any others. For nearly all proletarian working mothers, the experience of childbirth and motherhood—in spite of their economic situation—is the most meaningful experience of their lives, and the only one they can really claim as their own. It brings them, apparently, the only real feeling of fulfillment, a sense of sheer being, tenderness, and joy.

The data also indicate a lack of political awareness and of proletarian consciousness. Working mothers do not have the institutional

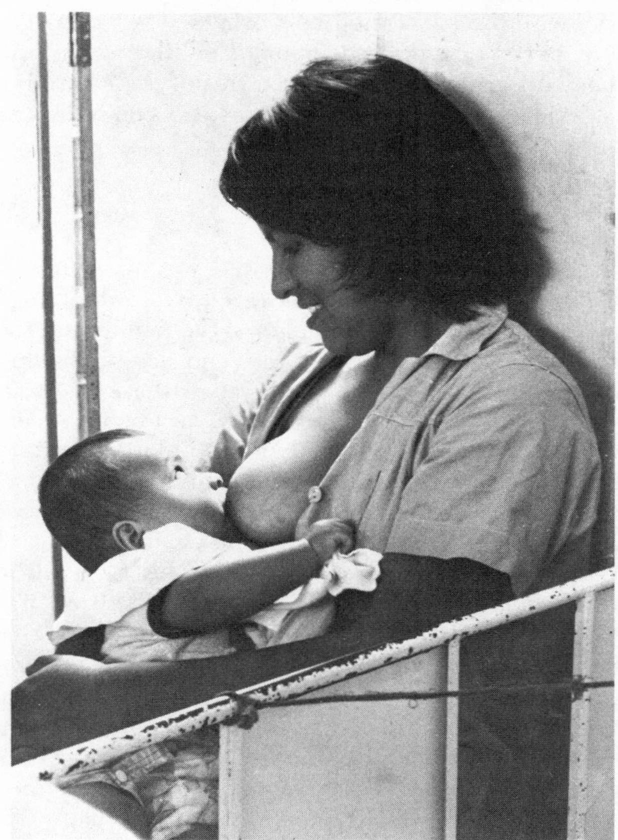

FIG. 10

FIG. 11

framework that would help them develop a sense of class consciousness and solidarity with the lot of their co-workers. They participate neither in unions nor in political parties—banned by the present military government. They understand mobility in terms of their own life and occupational history instead of in terms of their socioeconomic position in the society at large.

* * *

We tried to understand the patterned ways in which proletarian women—in our case the Peruvian—saw, felt, labeled, and experienced their many worlds: work, private domain of the family, and those institutions in their society to which they have no access, "including those sectors which produce the symbols and values that endow activity with cultural meaning."[7] We doubt the existence of a better means—for the purposes of a study such as ours—than the talking-pictures technique for establishing communication. Meaningful photographs had a cathartic effect on the women of our sample. They were often moved to tears and strong outbursts of emotion. Again and again, we heard such statements as, "I have seen my life before my eyes and I cry for my sorrows and for the hard life of the working mothers like myself." This was especially true of maids and market women who lead an extremely tough existence. Experiencing the photographs, they released and discovered hidden dimensions of the ways in which they structure and conceptualize their life cycle. As researchers, we were invariably overwhelmed by their suffering. The constant reaching out to them during critical moments of the interview gave us added insights into their lives and exposed us to hitherto stifled dimensions of their battered existence.

We strongly recommend the use of a photo-interview technique for other studies in Latin America as well as other nations in the process of development. It is adaptable for the study of working women in any region—rural or urban—and in any nation. However, any study of the specific problems of women in the labor force must be done within an analytic context of the socioeconomic structure of the nation to which they belong.

Appendix

The Organization of the Photo-Interview

The talking pictures kit consists of three general sets. Though overlapping, they can be used independently. They were:

7. For an elucidating article on the subject, see Constance Sutton, "The Power to Define: Women, Culture and Consciousness," in *Alienation: Contemporary Perspectives,* ed. R. S. Bryce-Laporte and C. Thomas (New York: Prager Publishers, in press).

I. Labor Set

This sequence of photographs is intended to help the working mother focus her attention on a pictorial exhibit of her work environment. It serves as a stimulus for interviewing, a tool for projection, and a means of establishing rapport at the beginning of the interview. Its subsets include:

Panoramic vistas.—The outside physical culture, surroundings, and personnel of markets, factories, and private homes, as well as the complexity of their interior and relevant aspects of their material inventories.

Types of work.—Different aspects or activities within an occupation with detailed photographs portraying maids hiring themselves for a job, cooking, cleaning, laundering, and looking after children; street vendors engaged in the sale of assorted merchandise, with the visually explicit difference in ranking by economic capacity.

Daily routine.—A detailed photographic arrangement, with a different set for each occupational group, displaying a typical daily work routine. Factory workers start the day at the entrance of the factory, punch the clock, work, and put an end to their routine while eating prepared food on the street, bought from local vendors. Market women open their stalls in the market, unload trucks with foodstuffs, snatch a bite while selling to their customers, and doze exhausted during the early afternoon over piles of vegetables while nursing their babies over the counter.

Services.—A sequence of photographs illustrating the kinds of services offered to working mothers in an ideal factory setup, such as medical care and day care. Designed to find out if they are part of women's life and to probe into their perception and evaluation of them. For the market women, to whom the majority of these services were not available, scenes showing the lack of these facilities, such as a toddler sleeping in a cardboard box on the street with toys scattered around.

Political participation through unions.—Scenes of women marching with flags, factory women on strike, belligerent women arguing against two men in uniform wearing helmets during a public demonstration, and a full view of the building of the Ministry of Labor where workers file their complaints against their employers—basic for the sifting of the women's views on the nature and frequency of their union participation.

Interpersonal relationships in work.—The work milieu of the factory worker, the market woman, and the domestic servant, intended as stimuli for the projection of the proletarian mother's preferential attitudes to different styles of interpersonal relations in work. For example, *ambulantes* were exposed to photographs representing a vendor working alone selling fruit in one of the main streets of Lima; two *ambulante* women working together; a woman selling yarn from a bicycle cart with her husband and children; a prepared-food ambulatory vendor peddling her goods and chatting with another male *ambulante.* Other photographs render occupational situations in which women were in a position of authority, such as supervisor at a factory, or were under an authority figure male or female.

Socialization.—A cluster of photos of children of both sexes working alongside adults—included only in the photo-interview of the market women. Designed in this context to investigate attitudes about children working and the value of their economic roles. Photos feature a woman selling inside her market stall aided by a young boy; three generations of female artisans—a grandmother, daughter, and young grandchild carving gourds in their shop; mothers being helped by their children in uniform at their work post in the market; street vendors shouting their goods while aided by their offspring. Sequence also utilized to flash back and focus on the interviewee's childhood.

Evaluation of occupations and level of aspirations.—Pictures of twelve different occupations embodied by women of all ages and ethnic groups aimed at investigating how informants ranked them and which seemed suited for daughters. They included: market woman with fixed stall, peasant woman handling a hoe, artisan, schoolteacher, seamstress, nurse, salesgirl, secretary, and hairdresser.

II. Family Set

These photographs were designed to illustrate the average proletarian mother's family life and to help us learn about the significance and meaning that the women placed on the family. Among its subsets were:

House styles.—A careful photographic record of the different types of dwellings and neighborhoods in the urban context, the aim to generate data on the housing situation; the value, if any, placed on home ownership; and information relevant to the Peruvian setting, such as whether they had been involved in land invasions to secure a plot of land on which to build their home.

Attitudes, values, and feelings on critical stages of the woman's reproductive cycle and ideas about their bodies and about themselves.—Intended to probe into the feelings of the working mothers about male-female interpersonal relationships, sex, pregnancy, childbirth, and motherhood. Shots of young single women, couples on park benches (the patterned style of dating), a pregnant woman alone, a pregnant woman with a child, and a nursing mother.

The typical domestic routine.—To discover the perception and evaluation of the dual role as mothers and marginally employed workers. Photos of mothers putting children to bed, cooking for them, and washing on the street.

Working mother's interpersonal relationships with husband or "compañero" (mate in consensual union) and children.—Revolving around the activities of family members, the man in the house helping the working mother in house chores or else not collaborating. To elicit attitudes and feelings relevant to the way proletarian mothers structure family relations and roles and their rationale for the allotment of responsibilities within the territory of the home, decision making about children's activities, punishments, and rewards (which one of the parents does it under what circumstances), the husband's ideas about the mother working outside the home, and the mother's perception of the same problem. Pictures here included a father playing with a child in a park, and a father alone.

Sequence of children alone at home while mother is away at work.—Photographs emphasize the loneliness of a little girl in a house, children playing by themselves, and scene of a large group of male children tampering with an old bicycle in a slum.

Activities of children in collaborative work with mother at home and at work.—Snapshots of young female children cooking with adult utensils, and of a child studying alone, to inquire into beliefs sustained by the working mothers about child domestic help.

III. Participation Set

Under this third broad category of observation and analysis were grouped photos aimed at learning whether the women had been exposed to political institutions and processes at the national and union level; whether they were aware of what political participation entails; whether they were familiar with the voter registration card; to elicit their views on military service for women; and to get their ideas about women's groups and associations and their attitudes about women in key positions in power structure. For example, the photos included a female judge at a professional meeting addressing a group of men. Two particular subsets were:

Religious behavior.—Pictures designed to help understand when, how, and why working women would resort to the sacred world for the solution to their problems, for example, a woman kneeling and praying before the entrance of an easily recognizable Lima church; a portrait of San Martin de Porres, a favorite patron saint.

Migration.—Three photos—an Indian woman tending a flock of sheep amidst the scenery of the Peruvian highlands, young women buying bus tickets at the station, and a young mother on the street with a toddler and suitcases—presented to learn about attitudes, feelings, and experiences on migrating to the city.

Institute of Latin American Studies
University of Texas at Austin
Austin, Texas, U.S.A.

Methodology and Data Collection

Sexuality and Birth Control Decisions among Lebanese Couples

Mary Chamie

My work on marital sexuality and birth control is derived from a larger study of marital relations and birth control decisions among Lebanese couples. I am focusing my discussion on sexuality primarily because of its hypothesized importance as a sensitive indicator of marital compatibility as well as the degree of intimacy in a marital relationship. In addition, I am concentrating on this topic because of the limited information on female sexuality in general and the virtual absence of such information for Middle Eastern women in particular.

We expect sexual behavior to vary widely among Lebanese women as well as to be an important differentiator of their birth control decisions. The sexual factors I deem pertinent to a couple's marital relationship and ultimately to the decisions to use birth control are: (*a*) wife's sexual responsiveness, reflected in her personal interpretation of her sexual feelings and her current orgasmic frequency; (*b*) wife's sexual assertiveness, indicated both by the frequency of her initiation and by refusal of coitus with her husband; (*c*) the couple's current level of sexual activity, that is, coital frequency; (*d*) the wife's perception of reasons for

I am deeply indebted to Dr. Adnan Mroueh, director of the University Hospital Family Planning Clinics and assistant professor of obstetrics and gynecology at the American University of Beirut in Lebanon, for his considerable guidance and inspiration throughout the entire research project. In addition, Hasmig L. Goenjian, May Magdelene Huxley, Salam Ali Nasser, Mary Deeb, and Elham Sabre contributed substantially during their employment as research assistants in the project at the American University of Beirut. Drs. Joseph Chamie, Jason Finkle, Ruth Simmons, and Thomas Poffenberger of the University of Michigan were helpful with their criticisms of an earlier version of this paper. The author takes full responsibility for the errors and shortcomings of this report.

sexual relations within marriage; and (*e*) the couple's overall marital-sexual compatibility, which includes the wife's perception of her sexual suitability with her husband and their current marital stability.

Sexual relations may be interpreted by men and women to be prohibitive or permissive, pleasurable or uncomfortable. These different feelings toward sexuality contribute to the general marital environment within which birth control decisions are made. A wife's infrequent initiation of sexual relations, her perception of coitus as a marital requirement rather than an act which offers personal or mutual pleasure, and her absence of orgasmic experience indicate the lack of an egalitarian relationship within the marriage. When coitus is viewed as solely for the husband's pleasure, it is likely to be viewed as his responsibility as well.[1] Sexual inequality of any severity may leave the wife feeling that she is not personally accountable for what happens during coitus. Under such circumstances, neither the husband nor wife may consider her to be the appropriate person to make birth control decisions. Not until the wife's fear of another pregnancy substantially overcomes the prohibitive influence of the sexual relationship may she be able either to consider or use a definitive birth control method such as female sterilization.

Couples who are nonegalitarian in their sexual behavior may view themselves as compatible and sexually suited to each other. Still, it is likely that their birth control decisions will be affected by male dominance. For example, even though they may eventually decide to use highly effective methods of birth control, the marital climate is likely to hinder significantly the process of decision making. Both sexual inequality and incompatibility are expected to influence birth control decisions by: (1) lessening the degree of discussion about intimate matters, diminishing the probability that birth control use will be a joint decision; and (2) lengthening the time which it takes for an effective device to be considered, deterring the use of such methods until the later stages of a woman's reproductive cycle.

Various researchers have hypothesized the importance of a couple's sexual relationship to birth control decisions.[2] Empirical investigations, however, are rare. Noteworthy exceptions are Chesser's study of English women, which found sexual satisfaction positively associated with current birth control use, and Rainwater's investigation of American couples, which studied the relations between sexuality, the marital relation-

1. For a theoretical framework that considers the power structure of the marriage as part of the overall explanation to fertility decision making, see N. K. Namboodiri, "The Integrative Potential of a Fertility Model: An Analytic Test," *Population Studies* 26 (November 1972): 465–85.

2. For an overview of these hypotheses, see C. B. Bakker and C. R. Dightman, "Psychological Factors in Fertility Control," *Fertility and Sterility* 15 (September–October 1974): 559–67. Also see E. Pohlman, *The Psychology of Birth Planning* (Cambridge, Mass.: Schenkman Publishing Co., 1969); and L. Rainwater, *Family Design: Marital Sexuality, Family Size, and Contraception* (Chicago: Aldine Publishing Co., 1965).

ship, and contraceptive behavior.[3] The extent of variation in marital relations regarding sexual behavior and contraceptive use among Middle Eastern couples has not yet been empirically documented. Discrepancies between expected and actual behavior, though believed to be considerable, are not currently known. For example, though numerous attempts have been made to distinguish between Muslim and Christian behavior in marriage and sexuality as they relate to fertility, there is little evidence which goes beyond speculation.[4]

Theoretical discussions about Islam itself have been inconsistent. While Muslim women are often characterized as oppressed and subordinate to men and required at all times to display modesty, Islam is frequently described as encouraging an active sexual life, with little contraceptive use, and an abundance of children among its followers.[5] In contrast to the above viewpoint, Mernissi has argued that Islamic theology may be considered as potentially a more positive approach to sexuality and fertility than is Christianity.[6] She contends that Islam regards sex as an instinct, which does not in itself connote good or evil. This source of energy, when successfully utilized and properly controlled, may be beneficial to society as a source of inspiration and need not be procreative. With such a positive approach to sexuality, the use of contraception is not likely to create excessive guilt and anxiety among Muslim couples.[7]

A fundamental problem with religious ideological explanations for expected sexual, marital, and contraceptive behavior is that they assume religious ideology to be equally powerful in its influence across all subgroups, irrespective of the subgroup's current levels of development. Structural factors such as the educational and occupational status of women may strongly influence Middle Eastern families' behavior regardless of their particular religious affiliation. For example, based upon

3. Eustace Chesser, *The Sexual, Marital and Family Relationships of the English Woman* (New York: Roy Publishers, 1957); L. Rainwater, assisted by Karol K. Weinstein, *And the Poor Get Children* (Chicago: Quadrangle Books, 1960); Rainwater, *Family Design.*

4. For example, see H. S. Karmi, "The Family and Its Development in Islam," *Birth Right* 7, no. 1 (1972): 11–17; A. H. As-Salih, "Islam's View of the Family in a Developing Society," ibid., pp. 18–25; and I. Nazer, ed., *Islam and Family Planning* (Beirut: International Planned Parenthood Federation, 1974).

5. J. I. Clarke, introduction to *Population of the Middle East and North Africa,* ed. J. I. Clarke and W. B. Fisher (London: University of London Press, 1972), p. 24. See also D. Kirk, "Factors Affecting Moslem Natality," in *Proceedings of the World Population Conference, Belgrade, 1965* (New York: United Nations, 1967).

6. Fatima Mernissi, *Beyond the Veil, Male-Female Dynamics in a Modern Muslim Society* (New York: John Wiley & Sons, 1975).

7. Bullough offers a slightly different interpretation of Islamic ideology and sexuality. He suggests that the teachings of the prophet Mohammed regard the sexual drive as essentially good, which opposes Mernissi's view of sexuality as neutral energy. Both Mernissi and Bullough, however, believe that Islamic theology holds a potentially more positive approach to sexuality than does Christian ideology (see Vern Bullough, *Sexual Variance in Society and History* [New York: John Wiley & Sons, 1976]).

the results of a survey of Sunni Muslims in several rural and urban areas of Lebanon, Prothro and Diab suggest that the following factors influence the continuing evolution of the Arab family: "In the first place there has been since independence, a continuing Western influence. . . . A second important factor has been the spread of egalitarian ideology in the pursuit of political objectives. . . . Arab political leaders have adopted the views of the nineteenth and early twentieth century writers that improvement in the status of women is both necessary and compatible with Islam. . . . It can be inferred from the preceding remarks that the rate of change has varied and will vary from one group to another, and our data show that this indeed has been the case."[8]

This study breaks from the tradition of linking Middle Eastern sexual behavior, marital patterns, and fertility to religious ideologies and attempts to link them instead to such factors as the educational attainment of Arab women. Sexual inequality and incompatibility, for example, are likely to be more critically disruptive to the decision-making processes of women who are poorly educated or who have low rates of participation in activities outside the home.[9] This is because women who do not receive cooperation and information from their husbands or from the immediate family about sexual and reproductive matters and who are primarily confined to their home environment have few alternative sources of contraceptive information and advice.

In contrast, highly educated women and those in occupations outside the home environment are more likely to identify sources of information that do not depend upon the husband's explicit participation; they may practice contraception without the husband's approval or knowledge; they may gain access to information from outside friends, private physicians, family planning clinics, or from books and newspapers. In addition, they may proceed to influence or attempt to modify their husbands' current opinions about birth control use. Women with higher educational attainment are also more likely to be sexually responsive and assertive than are their less educated counterparts because they are more likely to view sexuality as their domain as well as that of their husbands. Therefore, these women should feel more qualified to make contraceptive decisions or at least to participate in the decision-making process than would poorly educated women, regardless of their sexual compatibility with their spouses.

The Study

The data in our study are based upon the responses of Middle

8. Edwin Prothro and Lutfy N. Diab, *Changing Family Patterns in the Arab East* (Beirut: American University of Beirut, 1974).

9. See Rainwater, *Family Design.*

Eastern women who used the facilities of the University Hospital Family Planning Program of the American University of Beirut in Lebanon (hereafter the AUH/FP program). The program has, for several years, provided basic family planning services to the diverse groups of women entering its clinics. The family planning clinics offer women a range of birth control devices such as conventional methods, the oral pill, and intrauterine device (IUD) at no cost or for a nominal fee. In addition, the AUH/FP program maintains the only sterilization clinic in Lebanon. Women are operated upon and return home within the same day. This outpatient procedure is possible because of recently developed surgical techniques, which allow tubal ligations to be done while the patient is under local anesthesia and with minimal surgical cutting (culdoscopic and laparoscopic techniques). Like other clinic services, tubal ligation is done either free of charge or for a nominal fee.

Between December 1971 and May 1974, 450 women visited the sterilization clinic and requested the tubal ligation operation. Three hundred of them returned with their husbands' required signatures and were operated on. For one reason or another, 150 women did not return for their scheduled operations. The primary concern of this research project is to examine the process by which these women decided to either accept or reject female sterilization. In order to assess fully whether the particular decision-making process used for sterilization is different from other birth control decision-making processes, we interviewed a separate group of women who did not attend the sterilization clinic. Instead, these women attended a family planning clinic and chose either the IUD or the oral pill to limit their family sizes.

This study, then, focuses upon three general types of women: (1) the IUD/pill users, women who attended the university hospital family planning clinic in 1974, who stated they never wanted to be pregnant again and chose less permanent methods of birth control which did not require the husband's signature of approval; (2) tubal ligation users, all those who attended the separate and autonomous sterilization clinic for a tubal ligation between December 1971 and May 1974; and (3) tubal ligation nonreturnees, women who attended the sterilization clinic during the same time period for consultation but did not return for the operation. In total, 530 women were interviewed: 102 family planning clinic attenders (102 IUD/pill users) and 428 sterilization clinic attenders (298 tubal ligation users and 130 tubal ligation nonreturnees). During 1974, 257 of these women were interviewed in their homes throughout Lebanon; the rest were interviewed at the clinic.

Although all three groups said they never wanted another pregnancy, their birth control behavior was very different. The family planning clinic attenders either used the IUD or pill, both proven to be highly effective contraceptive methods. The sterilization clinic attenders were using a number of birth control methods, which varied considerably in effectiveness. In contrast to tubal ligation users, over half of the tubal ligation nonreturnees were not well protected from further pregnancies; 38 percent were using highly unreliable contraceptive methods and 19 percent used no method at all. Some of the nonreturnees had gained access to the IUD, pill, and tubal ligation outside the AUH/FP clinic system. Thirty-eight percent of them were using either the IUD or pill; 5 percent had gone to private physicians for a tubal ligation rather than returning to the sterilization clinic for their scheduled operations.

The instrument used to interview our respondents was written in colloquial Lebanese Arabic, which differs substantially from classical Arabic. Considerable effort was invested in the construction of questions to assure that they were in the familiar, colloquial form. The interview as a whole was adjusted so that it was more culturally appropriate for Middle Eastern women. For example, many of the political, economic, and familial questions were phrased in such a way that they would relate more directly to the respondents' roles as wives and mothers. The directness of the questions and the degree of intimacy attained during the discussion about marriage and sexuality gave even highly educated and occupationally oriented women the opportunity to express their opinions without feeling restricted to any prescribed social role.

The primary concern of the questionnaire was contraceptive decision making, which no doubt allowed most women to view the questions about sexuality as appropriate rather than as attempts to pry into their private lives. The organization of the questionnaire also helped to assure the women that there was a legitimate purpose for inquiring about their sexual behavior. For example, sensitive marital and sexual questions immediately followed a series of medical questions concerning birth control symptomatology. Response rates to both general and potentially sensitive questions about marriage and sexuality were close to 100 percent. This, coupled with the general warmth and sincerity of the Lebanese women and the candor of their answers, particularly when discussing marriage and sexuality, encourages our trust in the validity of the data.

The interviewers, all Lebanese women, wrote down the respondents' answers as closely as possible. Because of the exploratory nature of this survey and our desire to document the ways in which Lebanese women express themselves concerning intimate matters, the interviewers were discouraged from translating colloquial Arabic expressions immediately into English equivalents. Group sessions of interviewers, translators, and coders later took place on a regular basis in order to resolve any questions of proper translations for Arabic colloquialisms. Open-ended questions were used extensively to insure that the responses to the closed-ended questions were reasonably valid.[10]

10. A forthcoming report by this author will discuss in detail the problems and subtleties associated with research about women, sexuality, and birth control with particular reference to the Middle East.

Demographic and Educational Summary

A comparison of the women in our study to the 1971 National Fertility and Family Planning Survey of Married Lebanese women between the ages of fifteen and forty-nine indicates that sterilization clinic attenders were older, somewhat less educated, had been married longer, were of higher parity (i.e., had more pregnancies), and maintained a much higher sex ratio of living children (i.e., more boys to girls) than did married Lebanese women of reproductive age in general (see table 1). Family planning clinic attenders, in contrast, were more educated and somewhat younger than the national average. Although generally they had been married for similar periods of time, they were of higher parity than the respondents to the national fertility survey. The sex ratio of living children for family planning clinic attenders indicates a ratio closer to unity, similar to the 1971 Lebanese national average. We found few notable demographic or socioeconomic differences between tubal ligation users and nonreturnees.[11]

Table 1

Demographic and Educational Comparison of Family Planning Clinic Attenders, Sterilization Clinic Attenders, and All Married Lebanese Women between the Ages of Fifteen and Forty-Nine

Characteristics	Family Planning Clinic Attenders (IUD/Pill Users)	Sterilization Clinic Attenders for Tubal Ligation: Users	Sterilization Clinic Attenders for Tubal Ligation: Nonreturnees	All Married Lebanese Women Ages 15–49
Age (in years)	32.8	35.2	35.6	34.2
Proportion who never attended formal schooling (%)	19	47	45	40
Desired number of living children	3.7	3.7	4.1	4.0
Mean number of living children	5.3	6.6	6.7	4.4
Sex ratio of living children	1.03	1.26	1.20	1.08
Mean marital duration (years)	13.7	16.6	17.0	13.9

SOURCE.—Statistics on all married Lebanese women ages fifteen through forty-nine are taken from the National Fertility and Family Planning Survey of Lebanon, 1971, which is analyzed in Joseph Chamie, "Religious Fertility Differentials in Lebanon (Ph.D. diss., University of Michigan, 1976).

11. For a more detailed analysis of the socioeconomic and demographic differences among the groups, refer to Adnan Mroueh and Mary Chamie, "Social and Psychological Correlates and Determinants of Female Sterilization in Lebanon, 1974," in *New Advances in Sterilization,* ed. Marily Schima and Ira Lubell (New York: Association for Voluntary Sterilization, Inc., 1976).

Variations in Sexual Behavior and Factors Related to Birth Control Decisions

The majority of women in our study described themselves as living in reasonably stable and sexually active marriages. For example, 88.6 percent stated that they participated in coitus at least once or twice per week, 88.9 percent achieved orgasms at least a few times, and 84.4 percent said that they were at least reasonably sexually suited with their husbands. Since much is lost in the categorization of the responses and owing to the originality of the subject matter, the analysis will be supplemented with some of the respondents' comments.

Greater marital stability and sexual suitability with the husband were more often reported by IUD/pill and tubal ligation users than by tubal ligation nonreturnees (see table 2). In conjunction with these two broad

Table 2

Frequency of Separation from Husband, Coital Frequency, and Sexual Suitability of the Couple by Type of Birth Control Decision Made for Couples Who Wanted No Additional Children, Lebanon 1974
(%)

	Birth Control Decision Made		
	Family Planning Clinic Attender (IUD/Pill User)	Sterilization Clinic Attender for Tubal Ligation	
Responses Given by the Women	(*N* = 102)	User (*N* = 298)	Nonreturnee (*N* = 130)
Separation from husband:			
No separation over the previous 5 years	78	79	62
In and out, intermittent separation	4	4	5
Separated for 1 month or more	18	17	33
Total	100	100	100
Frequency of coitus:			
3–7 times per week	35	28	17
1–2 times per week	54	61	68
A few times per month or less	11	11	15
Total	100	100	100
Sexual suitability of the couple:			
Very well suited	61	68	50
Fairly well suited	27	20	24
Poorly suited	12	12	25
Refused to say	0	*	1
Total	100	100	100

*Less than 1 percent.

indicators of the marital-sexual compatibility of the couple, we also found that the frequency of coitus was substantially lower for tubal ligation nonreturnees than for the other two groups.[12] It should be kept in mind, however, that all three groups were sexually active and therefore candidates for further pregnancies.

With respect to the respondents' perceived reasons for sexual relations, 20 percent of the IUD/pill users, 28 percent of the tubal ligation users, and 34 percent of the tubal ligation nonreturnees perceived coitus as mainly relevant to the man's role in marriage and for his pleasure, a marital duty, or as primarily a strategy to keep the husband at home (see table 3).

> Because it is a sexual need for the man. When this liquid comes out of his body, he relaxes.
>
> A man has the authority over the woman. Whatever he asks she should do.

Table 3

Wife's Interpretation of the Value of Sexual Relations by Type of Birth Control Decision Made for Couples Who Wanted No Additional Children, Lebanon 1974 (%)

	Birth Control Decision Made		
	Family Planning Clinic Attender	Sterilization Clinic Attender for Tubal Ligation	
Reasons Given by the Women for Sexual Relations	(IUD/Pill User) (*N* = 102)	User (*N* = 298)	Nonreturnee (*N* = 130)
Childbearing is the only reason	2	2	1
To please the husband; his instinct, his need; to keep the man from going outside for sexual relations	16	24	30
It is a marital requirement	4	4	4
For pleasure, enjoyment, fun, variety, entertainment	46	42	47
It is natural, human, a lust, a desire that a couple has which creates a relationship, love	32	26	18
Other reasons, but cannot or will not describe them	0	2	0
Total	100	100	100

12. Because we have selected a universe of sterilization clinic attenders and a quota sample of IUD/pill users, statistical tests of significance are not strictly appropriate. However, distributional differences are important and shall be acknowledged during the discussion of the groups.

> Life on earth is for the enjoyment of the man.
>
> Her feeling is from the man's feeling.
>
> Marital life demands it.

Similar proportions of women in all three groups viewed coitus as a form of marital pleasure for both husbands and wives to partake in, or as mutually gratifying.

> So that both of them will be pleased. Parents eat sour grapes; the children feel the effect.
>
> It is a pastime for both of us. We don't go to the movies, nor do we have a TV.
>
> For (both) their pleasure. In order to be happy . . . and a woman is not just a cat, making love for kittens only.

A greater proportion of IUD/pill and tubal ligation users perceived intercourse to be "lustful," a passionate act which is part of love, or one important way of relating "intimately" with another person than did tubal ligation nonreturnees.

> It is the lust of life . . . the best thing in life . . . not for having children.
>
> Your intimacy . . . this is the thing that links a man to his wife.

A small percentage in all three groups felt that coitus was solely for childbearing purposes.

> God created the earth this way. The universe (population) has to grow in this fashion.

Tubal ligation nonreturnees, therefore, were more often found among those who viewed sexual relations as for the husband's pleasure—less often in groups who viewed coitus as part of an active expression of a couple's relationship. Also, this same group of women, as opposed to IUD/pill and tubal ligation users, exhibited striking contrasts in marital stability, sexual suitability, and coital frequency with their husbands. Such regular reporting of sexual incompatibility and lower rates of coitus are likely symptoms of a broader problem which permeates the entire marital relationship, that is, greater dominance of the husband within the marriage and a lesser degree of joint discussion about intimate concerns.

Orgasmic frequency is thought to be one important indication of the degree of personal gratification available from the respondent's sexual relations with her husband. It also suggests her current level of sexual responsiveness. Questions about their orgasmic experiences indicate that differences were more apparent in the extremes of the rates of orgasmic frequency for the three groups (see table 4). The proportion who reported never having experienced an orgasm was 7 percent for the IUD/pill users, 10 percent for tubal ligation users, and 16 percent for tubal ligation nonreturnees. Women who reported never having had an orgasm were generally cognizant that orgasms were an expected outcome of intercourse, although there were a few who were unaware that such an experience even existed.

> I have six children and never knew that the woman was supposed to feel something!

> I don't know why I never reach an orgasm. Neither with my first husband, nor my second. He wants to take me to a doctor, but I refuse.

Small proportions of the three groups of women who experienced orgasms were reluctant to describe them, suggesting that shyness to discuss the event with interviewers was not a critical factor in the explanation of their differences. Of those women who reported orgasmic experience, the stated degree of pleasure and intensity was similar for all three groups. Negative feelings were infrequent. The most common negative feeling was one of "suffocation," often described as a heavy feeling in the neck and chest. Second to a feeling of suffocation were feelings of pleasure and guilt or nervousness. In this situation, orgasms were described as strange, queer, or embarrassing as well as pleasurable.

> Pleasure . . . sometimes my body gets numb, at other times . . . I have a feeling of suffocation and nervousness.

All three groups included similar proportions of women who described an orgasm as a happy, pleasant experience. In addition, considerably more IUD/pill users and tubal ligation users reported trembling, rapid heart beats, and uterine contractions than did tubal ligation nonreturnees.

> I become very active and strong . . . just like a piece of steel.

> My body trembles, and I enjoy it very much.

> A kind of feeling that is difficult to describe . . . a lust and pleasure and a rise in temperature . . . then a feeling of relaxation.

Table 4

Wife's Personal Description of Her Orgasmic Experience and Orgasmic Frequency by Type of Birth Control Decision Made, for Women Who Want No Additional Children, Lebanon 1974 (%)

	Birth Control Decision Made		
	Family Planning Clinic Attender (IUD/Pill User)	Sterilization Clinic Attender for Tubal Ligation	
Responses Given by the Women	(N = 102)	User (N = 298)	Nonreturnee (N = 130)
Personal description of orgasmic experience:			
Doesn't experience orgasm	7	10	16
Negative experience: suffocation, anxiety, body gets cold, gets annoyed by something else being in her body, backache	7	7	5
Ambivalence: a strange, pleasant feeling (refers to it as though it is unusual, or strange, queer sensation, enjoys it but feels ashamed or embarrassed afterward)	4	3	4
Intermediate response: enjoyment, feels happy, loose, relaxed, satisfied, light headed, pleasurable	23	37	26
Strong response: body becomes numb, nerves are completely "feelingless"	30	14	23
Body trembles with excitement, rapid heart beat, uterus throbs ("All my body moves and I feel a lust, and pleasure.")	17	13	8
I feel it like a man, strong feelings like the man's	0	1	1
Other response: is orgasmic but cannot or will not describe	11	14	14
Refuses to say whether she is or is not orgasmic	1	1	3
Total	100	100	100
Orgasmic frequency of the wife:			
Never experiences/inapplicable	8	11	19
Hardly ever	26	19	20
Sometimes	37	44	45
Almost always	29	25	16
Refused to say how often	0	1	0
Total	100	100	100

A final category, which we kept separate because of lack of comparability with orgasmic descriptions offered by women in Western cultures, was a feeling of "numbness," or completely "feelingless" experiences described by 22.3 percent of the women who were orgasmic.

> Numbness of the whole body . . . the most beautiful thing God granted human beings in intercourse.

> First there is a numbness in my body . . . I get relaxed . . . I'll have a tendency (urge) for intercourse, and when I reach an orgasm I'm happy. My body is tired, then relaxed, I can move no more, and am very happy.

A minority of women in each of the three groups claimed to have ever initiated coitus with their husbands, and the proportions did not differ greatly across the three groups: 14 percent of the IUD/pill users, 17 percent of the tubal ligation users, and 16 percent of the nonreturnees. Nor did the proportion refusing coitus when not in the mood differ greatly across the three groups. One noteworthy comparison, however, is the proportion who "almost always" refused sexual relations because they were not in the mood: 20 percent of the IUD/pill users, 19 percent of the tubal ligation nonreturnees, and 12 percent of the tubal ligation users.

A wife's refusal of coitus for fear of pregnancy is one indication of her degree of confidence in the couple's ability to contracept successfully as well as of her fear of further pregnancies. As hypothesized, tubal ligation users were highest on the scale of having ever refused coitus during the previous five years for fear of pregnancy, followed by the IUD/pill users and then the tubal ligation nonreturnees: 68, 61, and 56 percent, respectively.

In sum, the IUD/pill and tubal ligation users were relatively similar with respect to their marital sexual behavior. The differences between these two groups of effective birth control users seem more a consequence of socioeconomic and demographic considerations: the IUD/pill users' relative youthfulness, their lower parity and lower proportion of living sons to living daughters, and higher educational levels. IUD/pill users also reported less fear of pregnancy than did the tubal ligation users. Possibly with increasing age, and if further unexpected births were to take place, the IUD/pill users might ultimately opt for a more definitive method of birth control, such as tubal ligation. It seems reasonable that likely candidates for female sterilization would be women who have a fairly strong fear of pregnancy but who derive considerable sexual gratification from their marriage. Comparisons of tubal ligation users and nonreturnees indicate important differences in their sexual behavior with their husbands as well as minor socioeconomic and demographic differences. Not only did nonreturnees indicate that they were less closely bonded to their husbands by sexual gratification, but they also more frequently said they were sexually incompatible with their spouses and generally lacked strong fears of further pregnancies, even though most were using either unreliable or no contraceptive techniques at the time they were interviewed.

Social Status, Sexuality, and Birth Control Decisions

We now discuss the manner in which social status appears to moderate the relationship between marital sexuality and birth control. These results are preliminary. We plan to investigate these relationships further while controlling for social status and utilizing more sophisticated statistical techniques.[13]

The effect of wife's age on the sexual variables was similar for all three groups of women. For instance, tubal ligation nonreturnees who were nineteen through twenty-nine, thirty through thirty-four, and thirty-five through thirty-nine years of age reported lower rates of coital frequency than did IUD/pill and tubal ligation users who were in the same age categories. We were unable to determine whether this was so for women who were forty years and older, because the number of cases in this age group was too few among the IUD/pill users for adequate comparison (see fig. 1), but it is noteworthy that for all three groups, low rates of coital frequency were highest for women in the thirty-five to thirty-nine age category. Orgasmic frequency also appears to be somewhat related to age. For all three groups of women, reports of being inorgasmic increased with age. For example, among tubal ligation nonreturnees, the proportion who were inorgasmic in the age category nineteen through twenty-nine was 7 percent; at ages forty to fifty-one, it was 39 percent. The difference by age was much less for tubal ligation users; 11 percent of the women who were between the ages of nineteen and twenty-nine and 13 percent between the ages of forty and fifty-one reported being inorgasmic. In general, age did not seem to play any major role with respect to the hypothesized relationship between sexual behavior and types of birth control decisions made.

Educational attainment is a reasonably established indicator of the socioeconomic and developmental level of women. As was anticipated, responses to many of the questions varied markedly by wife's level of educational attainment. For example, women at higher levels of education reported the initiation of coitus more frequently than did women at lower levels (see fig. 2). Such behavior suggests both a more egalitarian

13. Due to the fact that there were small numbers of rural respondents for the IUD/pill users and the nonreturnees, we were unable to investigate properly the relationship between urban-rural status and the sexual variables for the three groups. In addition, wife's occupation was not included in the analysis, because the overwhelming majority of the respondents were housewives.

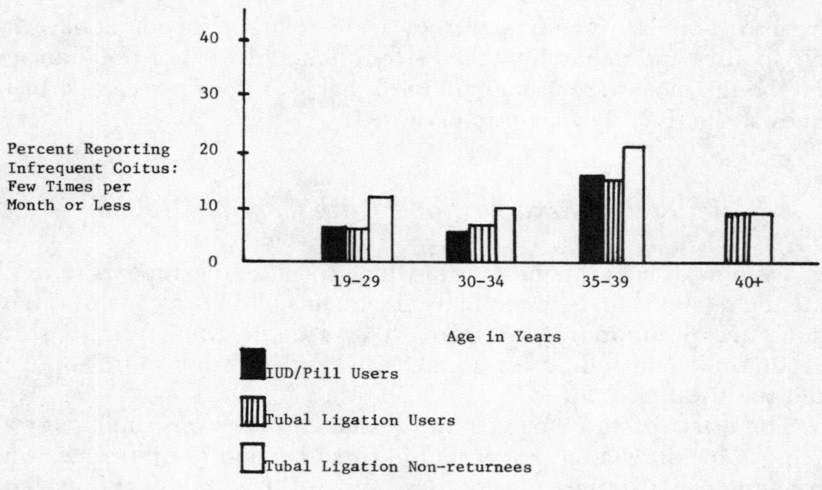

FIG. 1.—Proportion who reported infrequent coital activity, according to age by type of birth control decision made, for women who wanted no additional children (Lebanon, 1974).

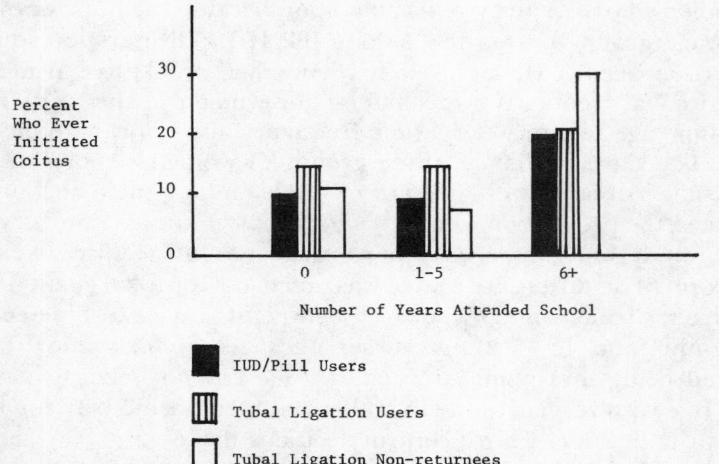

FIG. 2.—Proportion who initiated coitus during the previous five years, according to educational status by type of birth control decision made, for women who wanted no additional children (Lebanon, 1974).

sexual relationship between the husband and wife and the expected increase in sexual assertiveness among women at higher levels of education. Higher educational attainment also substantially decreases the variation in sexual behavior across the three birth control groups. For example, among women who had never attended school, reports of orgasmic frequency were significantly lower for tubal ligation non-returnees than for the two other groups. Among those who had six or more years of schooling, the proportion who reported being frequently orgasmic converged for the three groups (see fig. 3).

A second illustration of a convergence pattern by education is the refusal of coitus for fear of pregnancy (see fig. 3). In this case, the variable is somewhat more difficult to interpret because the direction of the responses differed, indicating that increased educational attainment was not associated with a general increase in the fear of pregnancy across all three birth control groups. Rather, for nonreturnees, a positive association with educational attainment was evident, whereas for tubal ligation users, a slightly negative association was found. This means that for tubal ligation users, higher educational levels were associated with somewhat less refusal of coitus for fear of pregnancy, whereas the opposite was so for nonreturnees. Most likely, very strong fears of pregnancy influenced higher-educated tubal ligation nonreturnees to utilize private physicians or clinics for their selection of birth control methods. Perhaps they perceived private medical facilities to be more reliable sources of information and service than those available at the sterilization or the family planning clinic.

Support for this hypothesis may be found when we observe current birth control use of the nonreturnees according to their educational attainment. For example, among nonreturnees who had never attended school and among those who had attended school for one to five years, the proportions currently not using any birth control method were 24.6 and 22.5 percent, respectively. In contrast, among the nonreturnees who had attended school for six or more years, the proportion currently not using birth control was 6.1 percent. The proportion of tubal ligation nonreturnees who utilized private physicians for their tubal ligation rather than the sterilization clinic also increased according to the number of years of schooling. Therefore, for nonreturnees, educational attainment was strongly and positively associated with birth control and the use of highly effective methods. It would therefore seem that at least for the more highly educated nonreturnees, not coming back to the sterilization clinic for scheduled operations reflected primarily a choice of other effective alternatives. In contrast, nonreturnees who were poorly educated generally lacked both sufficient marital sexual compatibility with their husbands to foster mutual discussion and solutions to their reproductive problems and adequate alternative sources of birth control information.

Finally, we grouped our respondents into five major religious sects: three Muslim (Sunni, Shi'a, and Druze) and two Christian (Catholic and non-Catholic). Christian and Muslim sects in Lebanon differ substantially in their socioeconomic and fertility levels. The effects of religion upon fertility and fertility control in Lebanon, however, are dependent upon the educational levels of the religious sects.[14] The educational

14. Joseph Chamie, "Religious Fertility Differentials: Lebanon, 1971," *Population Studies,* vol. 31, no. 2 (1977).

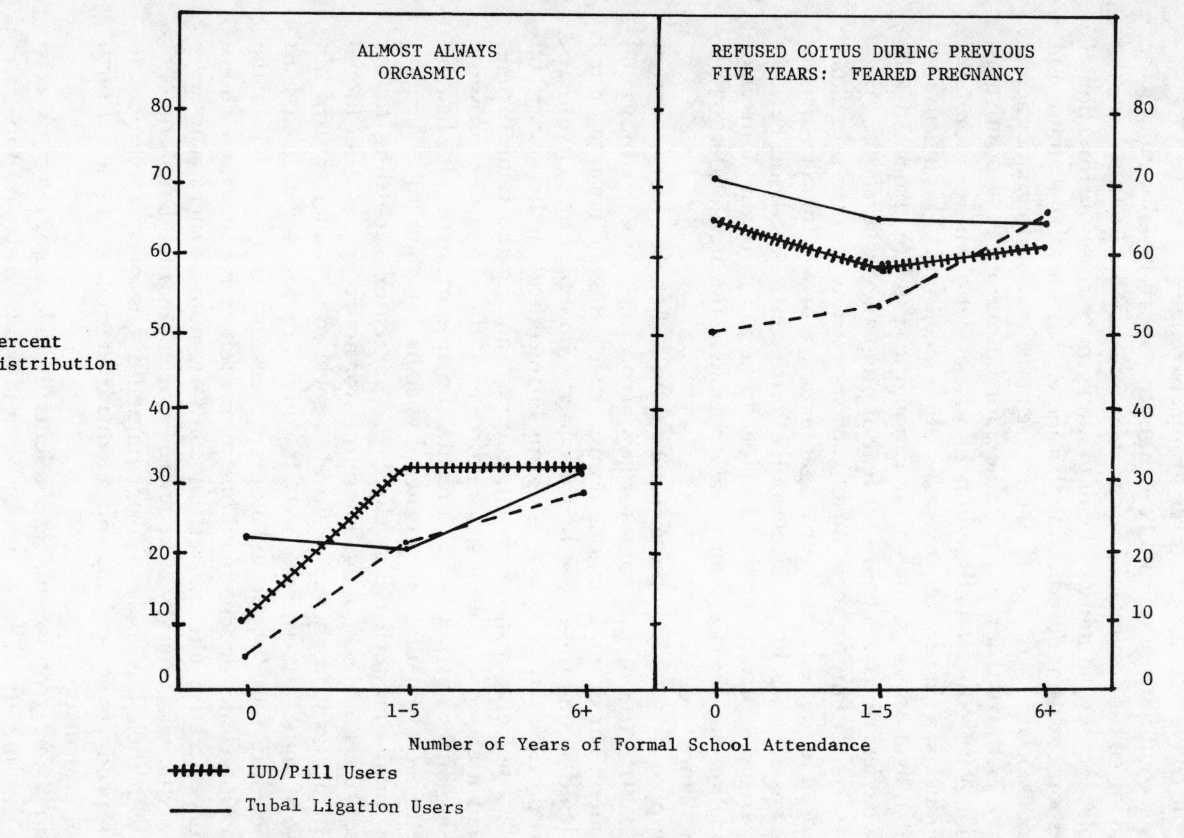

FIG. 3.—Proportion who were almost always orgasmic and who refused coitus for fear of pregnancy, by type of birth control decision made and educational status, for women who wanted no additional children (Lebanon, 1974).

levels of the women in our study varied significantly by religious sect. The non-Catholic Christians and Druze Muslims, for example, reported a mean number of 5.43 and 5.07 years of schooling, respectively. Catholic Christians and Sunni Muslims were intermediate, with 4.57 and 3.79 years of school attendance, respectively. Shi'a Muslim women were least educated, reporting a mean of 1.54 years of schooling. Such variation in educational attainment among religious groups precludes anything but very preliminary reporting of the relationship among religious affiliation, sexual behavior, and birth control use until adequate controls can be instituted for educational status.

Without proper controls for education, the religious sects vary significantly with respect to the relationship between sexuality and birth control behavior. For example, tubal ligation nonreturnees who were Sunni Muslim most often said they were poorly sexually suited to their husbands (35 percent), followed by the Shi'a (33 percent), the non-Catholics (5 percent), and Catholics (5 percent).[15] In contrast, among the tubal ligation users, the difference in the proportions among the religious sects was substantially less. For example, 18 percent of the Shi'a, 10 percent of the Sunni and non-Catholic women, and 6 percent of the Catholics rated themselves as poorly sexually suited to their husbands. The relationship between sexual suitability and birth control behavior, therefore, is not consistent by religious sects. For the Sunni and Shi'a Muslims, sexual suitability differentiated their birth control decisions, whereas for the two Christian groups it did not.

Other researchers have suggested that differences in marital sexual behavior should influence contraceptive decision making. The findings of this report offer some empirical support for this proposition and provide insight into the relationship between sexuality and birth control decisions among Lebanese couples. Although sexuality does not act upon birth control behavior in isolation from other aspects of marriage, we found sexual compatibility, responsiveness, and, to a lesser extent, equality to be associated with the use of more effective or permanent birth control methods.

The wife's educational attainment was positively associated with the wife's sexual responsiveness, assertiveness, and compatibility with her husband. Women who were more educated generally initiated sexual relations more often, were more frequently orgasmic, participated in coitus more frequently, and reported fewer separations from their husbands than did women with less schooling. This suggests that there are important social structural dimensions other than religious affiliation which need to be included in any analysis of sexuality and birth control

15. Rates for Druze are very tentative because there are too few cases for sufficient comparison across the three groups. However, their general trend is reported in the text.

behavior. In addition, we found that at higher levels of educational attainment, the patterns of behavior for the three groups of women were similar. Sexual behavior appears to be less critical in the explanation of birth control decisions among higher-educated women because, irrespective of their current sexual relations with their spouse, numerous options are available to them other than simple dependency upon the husband and the marriage for solutions to reproductive and sexual problems.

These observations, I hope, will encourage others to expand their investigation of Middle Eastern marital, sexual, and birth control behavior to include the influence of social structure, even when studying a couple's most intimate and personal concerns.

Amman, Jordan

Implications

Reflections on the Conference on Women and Development: Introduction

Michelle McAlpin

Most of this volume represents what went on in the planned sector of the Wellesley Conference on Women and Development, inside a traditional academic framework of presentation and discussion of research papers. But these papers show only one facet of the conference. Women from many parts of the world gathered, their expectations as varied as their home countries. Inevitably these differing expectations brought participants into conflict with each other and with the planners. These conflicts—deep, real, and difficult—ranged over all aspects of research on women in less-developed countries. Who should do the research? How should it be disseminated? How policy oriented should it be? What theoretical frameworks that now exist, if any, are useful? How should research on women in developed countries be related to it? What are the biases of Western-trained researchers? What research is most needed in the future?

The five short essays in this section address some of the questions that arose from the clash of our diverse expectations. They were written by individual participants at the request of the Editorial Committee. They are not intended to be a comprehensive history of the conference, but, rather, we hope that they may transmit some of the excitement of the event, some of the awareness gained from meeting together, and a sense of the opinions of persons from the major geographical regions of the world.

Department of Economics
Tufts University
Medford, Massachusetts, U.S.A.

Reflections on the Conference on Women and Development: I

Bolanle Awe

> It is obvious that feminist issues exist in South Africa but the Black women would have to work out their own priorities according to their experience and the future society which they wish to see. [ZANELE DHALAMINI]

One thing that became clear at the Conference on Women and Development in Wellesley, as well as the other activities that marked the International Women's Year in Mexico, is that many of our assumptions about the universality of female interest and objectives are questionable. Apart from the distinctions of class, occupation, environment, etc., the position of women differs nationally and, even more significantly, from Third World to developed countries. The problems of women, therefore, have to be examined within many contexts and with an awareness of differences.

To devote a conference to women and development and to raise questions that have policy implications for the full participation of women in the development process was a good idea. The issues addressed in many of the Wellesley panels were relevant. Yet the conference did not really succeed in achieving its objectives, though it helped to focus attention on how future conferences of this nature should be organized.

Its first basic weakness was the topic proposals. There were both a lack of historical perspective and insufficient appreciation of the historical experiences to which women in some of these societies, particularly the African ones, have been subjected. Although African societies have been responsive to many changes that have affected both men and women, one historical experience, namely, the colonial one, stands out as being of particular significance for any assessment of women's future role in development.

Questions at the Wellesley conference—for example, women's relationship to power, or male and female perceptions of women—would have been more meaningful in a historical perspective. Answers to such questions would both give an insight into the virtually total neglect of women's contributions by the powers that be during the colonial period and provide a useful framework for the examination of women in the transformation of former colonies into developed nations. Such a historical approach will also give leads into research needs and priorities.

Other elements in the Wellesley conference should engage our attention because of their implications for future international conferences and collaborative efforts among scholars from dissimilar backgrounds. Participation of Third World scholars at the three main levels of organizing, panel convening, and presenting papers was totally inadequate. The conference therefore became, in the main, one organized largely by women from the developed countries, especially from the United States, for Third World women. Input based on the experience of the developed world was minimal. Contributions from both white and black scholars from the United States, which might have provided useful comparative notes, were very few. Moreover, because of the inadequate representation of Third World scholars, expectations that such a well-supported international conference aroused were not realized. The small representation of panelists from the Third World also inevitably affected the quality of the papers. Many of the panelists who had only had some research experience of the areas they discussed showed inadequate knowledge of the problems they raised. This, of course, frustrated the collaborative efforts and the useful interaction which that type of gathering should engender.

Indeed, the experience at Wellesley provoked the fundamental question of who should do research in any country, developing or developed. While the observations of the foreign researcher can be useful, the time has now come when emphasis should be on indigenous scholars; by virtue of their permanent membership in their society they are likely to have a better insight into its problems and the areas that need closest attention. Because of the present position of women in developing countries, research on women must also be policy oriented, but initiated by local scholars who can best indicate priorities. Scholars from developing countries must set up their own area programs as well as regional centers for collecting data, outlining research priorities, getting research proposals, initiating projects, and generally "brainstorming" for government on matters that affect women. They must also be able to sponsor international conferences on relevant issues in their own countries.

Collaborative effort between local scholars and foreign ones remains important. On account of the poverty of many of the developing countries, cooperative work through funding agencies such as those of the United Nations and other international and national foundations is still a necessity. But there must be a new orientation in this joint exercise. Whatever the source of funding, foreign or indigenous, the local scholar must be fully acknowledged and designated, along with her foreign counterpart, as a principal investigator. Her role must not be reduced to that of an informant, and copies of whatever materials are collected must be left in the countries researched.

In spite of its shortcomings, the Wellesley conference laid the foundation for better scholarship on the study of women. It made it possible for scholars from the developing and developed countries to declare in categorical terms their stands and the basis for future collaborations. For the sake of true scholarship and the enrichment of our knowledge of women in development, this dialogue must continue.

Ministry of Education
Ibadan, Nigeria

Implications

Reflections on the Conference on Women and Development: II

Lourdes Casal

How should we evaluate a conference such as the one at Wellesley? The first obvious alternative—although clearly an insufficient one—would be to assess the extent to which the objectives of the conveners were fulfilled. The Wellesley conveners clearly attempted to bring together scholars devoted to women's studies from all over the world, with the goals of evaluating the "state of the art" in women-and-development studies and contributing to the growth of international scholarly networks in this field. As defined by its conveners, the conference was primarily an academic gathering, with certain expected results in terms of future research (i.e., fostering of exchanges and cooperation between United States–based scholars and researchers in various less developed regions, improved methodologies, etc.).

However, as this conference itself illustrated, "pure" academic gatherings are illusory. A meeting which dealt with the problems of development and the status of women was bound to become enmeshed in political controversies, because the definitions of development and even of the status of women *are* political. Furthermore, the Wellesley conference raised complex issues about the politics of research and particularly the politics of international research conferences. But the many controversies which erupted at Wellesley should not make us forget that the conference itself provided a setting in which such controversies could be aired.

As a first approximation to the evaluation question, the Wellesley conference must be considered a success. The conveners managed to raise funds; organize a very complex logistic operation involving five continents; tap existing scholarly networks to identify potential participants; establish linkages with scholarly associations devoted to area studies in North America; and develop a program which, although conceived along traditional academic-conference lines and within those limitations, was ambitious and comprehensive. However, the quality of presented papers was highly variable. Wellesley participants could hear some of the great original thinkers in women-and-development studies (such as Ester Boserup, Ulla Olin, and Heleieth Saffioti). But there was too much sophomoric (or, to be more precise, pompous graduate student) deadweight.

It also became obvious at Wellesley that networks between U.S. scholars and their Third World counterparts were at different levels of development in different areas. Latin American scholars and U.S. Latin Americanists, for example, have developed long-standing avenues of collaboration and communication. Similar channels in Middle Eastern studies of women and development await organization.

The traditional format of the Wellesley conference was seriously criticized by many participants, who desired more time for discussion of papers (as opposed to presentation) and a more flexible approach which would have allowed questioning of certain dominant orientations (emphasis on micro-level studies rather than macro-micro linkages, the rampant empiricism which permeates so many U.S. studies, fragmentation along traditional disciplinary lines and the further isolation of women's studies) and of the structures of domination themselves (including notions of expertise and unequal distribution of "scientific" resources).

The politics of international conferences also became a focus of debate. Planners of future conferences will have to deal with two basic issues raised at Wellesley. Can conferences on "development" properly be convened in "developed" countries? What is the proper input which participants from the less developed countries should have in decision making at the level of program planning, format selection, representation at the panel convener, panelist and discussant levels, etc.?

The underlying questions in the debate concern the purposes of research, its ideological functions, and the appropriate conceptual framework for women-and-development studies. The absence of scholars from the socialist world underlined the need to analyze the conception of development which seemed to prevail at the conference and, indeed, in the whole field of U.S. development studies.

From my perspective, the Wellesley conference underscored the need for a conceptual framework for women-and-development studies more adequate than the patchwork of unexamined "developmentalist" ideology which has prevailed so far. Even a cursory examination of Buvinic's bibliography suggests serious weaknesses in theoretical development, lack of conceptual clarity, and lack of consistent use of operational definitions of key concepts such as "women's status."[1] She stresses a handful of important issues (theoretical and operational definitions of status and role, the relationship of sexual inequality to socioeconomic inequality, the problem of unequal political participation, etc.) which also recurred in different forms in the papers and discussions at Wellesley.

However, looking back at Wellesley, I think the need for a more radical critique is obvious. We have to question the definition of development, emphasize the perils of simplistic indicators which fragment and distort complex historical processes, discuss the socialist alternative to capitalist underdevelopment, and analyze the relationship between science and ideology.

Department of Psychology
Rutgers University at Newark
Newark, New Jersey, U.S.A.

1. M. Buvinic, *Women and World Development: An Annotated Bibliography* (Washington, D.C.: Overseas Development Council, 1976).

IMPLICATIONS

Reflections on the Conference on Women and Development: III

Eleanor Leacock

Topics discussed at the Wellesley Conference on Women and Development ranged widely. Political questions concerned women's organizations and associations and women's relations to power, the law, and protest movements. Economic issues included women in the labor force, their relations to production and their significance as migrant workers. Other subjects dealt with were the structure of the family, past and present; decision making about family size; and religious sex-role definitions. From the papers and the discussion both about them and about the conference as a whole, it was evident that development per se was not seen as providing the means for women's release from oppressive social-economic and political institutions but, instead, as defining new conditions of constraint. To discuss the impact of development on women's status in society is to confront the fact that women's oppression is inextricably bound up in an exploitative world system of which development, as presently defined, is a part. Consequently, to analyze the status of women in order to change it is to analyze the possibility of fundamental social transformation.

Real development would mean ending the system whereby rich nations continue to "underdevelop" poor nations by consuming a huge proportion of the world's resources, while multinational corporations grossly underpay Third World workers. To talk of development also means facing the reality that "underdeveloped" national groups exist in the heart of the "developed" industrial world—black, Chicano, Hispanic, and native American minorities in the United States and immigrant workers from Third World nations in Europe. To talk of development means to talk about the desperate need for a peaceful and economically secure world in which people, not profits, are the central social value.

Although women bear the heaviest burden of oppression, they are often told that they should subvert their own cause at this time in the interest of the "larger" goals of national, racial, and class liberation from exploitation. One form of oppression should never be pitted against another in this way. The problem of ultimately transforming world capitalist society is so vast that one cannot begin to consider it without recognizing the need to combine the special drive for liberation of half of humanity, women *as women* with the drive of women and men as workers and as members of oppressed races and nations. Their oppression is so deeply embedded in the entire political, economic, and social structure of society that women, many of whom are workers and most of whom are members of oppressed races or nations, can help unify through their own fight for liberation diverse struggles for class, racial, and national liberation.

A major contribution of the Wellesley conference, in my view, was to make more concrete the vision of the enormous potential women can have when working together, across nations, classes, and races, to solve their problems. Along with conference papers and the richness of the data they offered on women's activities, extramural discussion and debate on problems of organizing, strategies for alliance, and the central role of Third World women workers gave evidence of the fact that, when women unite to move against their own oppression, they move against oppression generally. In contrast to the glimpse these discussions afforded of a fundamental historical process at work in the world, theories of female-male relations in biosocial terms of universal submissiveness and dominance seem pathetic and irrelevant. Unfortunately, however, they continue to be influential and cannot be ignored. Stereotypical views of female dependency as a universal norm pervade writings in the United States and in Third World countries. Assertions of women as the natural servitors of dominating men reinforce the notion that traditional family relationships in Third World countries were based on the same male dominance that characterized Europe, where the ideal wife in the Calvinist entrepreneurial family important to the rise of capitalism served dutifully and submissively as the "helpmeet" of her husband. The fact is glossed over that in much of the precolonial world women related to each other and to men in public and autonomous ways as they carried out their social and economic responsibilities. Female sodalities of various kinds figured importantly in many Third World social structures before principles of male dominance within individual families was taught by missionaries, defined by legal statutes, and institutionalized through the economic relations of colonialism.

As data accumulate about women around the world, passing statements about them as subordinate housewives and mothers, commonplace in anthropological writings, are being replaced by analyses of their decision-making roles in different types of society.[1] For example, ethnohistorical materials on native North American societies reveal the reciprocal roles women and men played in social, economic, and political decision making in early colonial days; indeed, a strong commitment to autonomy often still persists in American Indian communities.[2] Ethnohistorical and ethnographic data are also documenting the public functions of women's organizations and their lineage roles in Africa. Drawing on such work and on her own field research, a recent paper by Niara Sudarkasa makes a basic point. The distinction generally made between a male "public" sphere and a female "domestic" sphere distorts the very nature of the "preindustrial, precapitalist, and precolonial world," in which "power, authority, and influence within the 'domestic sphere' was *de facto* power, authority, and influence at certain levels within the 'public sphere.' "[3] In West African societies, the "public sphere" was not conceptualized as masculine.

Perhaps the most serious effect of constantly burgeoning arguments for male supremacy has been to deflect attention from women as decision makers and organizers. Certainly today we find ourselves spending too much time jousting with windmills and too little analyzing the present level of women's organizations and the future potentials, the bases—real and spurious—for schisms, and the foundations for alliance. The suggestion I brought away from the Wellesley Conference, in relation to directions for women's studies, is to emphasize women's organizations, broadly defined, of the past, present, and future.

Department of Anthropology
City College, City University of New York
New York, New York, U.S.A.

1. Rayna R. Reiter, ed., *Toward an Anthropology of Women* (New York: Monthly Review Press, 1975); and Alice Schlegel, ed., *Sexual Stratification: A Cross-cultural View* (New York: Columbia University Press, 1977).
2. Judith K. Brown, "Iroquois Women: An Ethnohistoric Note," in Reiter; and John Phillip Reid, *A Law of Blood: The Primitive Law of the Cherokee Nation* (New York: New York University Press, 1970).
3. Niara Sudarkasa, "Female Employment and Family Organization in West Africa," in *New Research on Women and Sex Roles,* ed. Dorothy McGuigan (Ann Arbor: University of Michigan Center for Continuing Education of Women, 1975).

Implications

Reflections on the Conference on Women and Development: IV

Vina Mazumdar

The basic problem of the Wellesley conference was the confusion in expectations. Was it to be an analytical exercise, an attempt to develop a methodological framework for research on women in developing countries? Or was it to be a shop window for display and exchange of academic knowledge of the position of women in Third World countries?

I think both these objectives were shared by the initial planners. But then the group should have been smaller, the themes less widespread, and the coverage more intensive. Above all, the papers and discussions should have included more people from the field of development and planning—the economists, geographers, and the new breed of academic experts who act as consultants and evaluators of development projects. The few who were there were apparently content with a listener's role—perhaps because they found themselves rather bewildered. One can guess that they had come looking for new insights and skills to help them in their tasks—to look at the impact of development on women or how development appeared from women's point of view. Many of them were disappointed because this aspect was missing during the greater part of the conference. It only emerged on the last day, primarily because of the determination of a few like Ester Boserup.

This account is based entirely on personal recollections, because to date I have not read the mass of papers; and beyond the panels that I attended the only memory of what went on in the other groups is filtered through reports presented on the last day—some vivid, some hazy, and some forgotten. It should therefore be taken as an impressionistic record of a personal experience, not a review.

For most of the academics who were looking for analytical tools, the conference must have been somewhat of a disappointment. Some significant theoretical issues did emerge in one or two panels, for example, in the Panel on the Informal Labor Market; but there was never sufficient time for interaction among the participants, the authors of the papers, and experts whose command of theoretical tools could have helped the conference to understand patterns of relationship among different social processes.

One of the best features of the event was the brave attempt to involve persons from different disciplines. One of the lessons that I learned was the remarkable role that anthropologists can play in explaining the hidden aspects of women's positions and roles in society. It is particularly important to expose economists and political scientists to the anatomical exercises undertaken by anthropologists. It is equally necessary for anthropologists to accept the politicoeconomic dimensions of the process of change that is disrupting the organization of traditional society. So many of the anthropological studies presented at the conference were like beautiful still photographs, taken through high-powered but narrow lenses.

One group of social scientists who were conspicuously absent were historians. Except for the Panel on Historical Development of the Family, the time dimension was very much absent. Development is an ongoing process, and it is difficult to achieve a proper perspective on its impact unless one can compare the present with the past. Nor were there attempts to compare the Third World experience with that of women in the developed world. I later discovered the enormous volume of research on women's history that is going on in the United States. The presence of some of these scholars at the conference and an opportunity for Third World women and women studying the Third World to observe the marked similarities in their current experience with that of American women in the eighteenth and the early nineteenth centuries would have been the best possible way to understand the patterns of relationship between economic development and changes in the roles and status of women.

The failure to project the American experience was one of the major reasons for the sense of disturbance among many of the Third World women. Had they been invited only to provide data for U.S. scholars doing research on the Third World? Was this yet another experiment in neocolonialism, using the potential sympathy of women for what appeared to be a venture in the women's cause—with a view toward undermining the increasing mobilization for the New International Economic Order? Why had not more Third World women been associated with conference planning, and why had so few of them been invited to present papers?

If the conference was planned to promote international cooperation in the women's movement, then the absence of the American experience was a serious omission. The feminist perspective was there among many of the academics, feminist passion and organizational experience less so. Some of the younger American women who came looking for sisterhood across the ocean were, I believe, equally disappointed. I have no doubt that many of them found Third World women lacking in feminist energy and too identified with their existing social establishments.

What is perhaps not really understood is that in the Third World feminist perspective or outlook is more likely to emerge among women who have their roots deep in their own cultures rather than among hybrid, half-alienated products of the modern sector of such societies. The highly educated professional women of the Third World are the beneficiaries of the development process. For most of them the time has not yet come to realize the darker side of this impact on the lives of other women in their own countries. For most of them the feminist revolt appears as a threat to well-earned and secure positions in their own societies.

The conference missed a great opportunity to correct the many distorted images of the feminist movement current in many Third World countries. The presence of some of the outstanding leaders of the movement could have helped not only to destroy these images but also to provide new insight and inspiration to many of the Third World women to look at their own society from different perspectives. This is of course a generalization. There were some who had already developed this insight. But they had little chance to contribute adequately during the conference. Some of them were of immense value in the Wingspread Workshop that came after the conference.

With all its limitations, it was a memorable experience. The speed with which one could make friends, the quick response to ideas coming from across the room, and a feeling of involvement in a massive effort—all this was in the atmosphere. So was an intense feeling of excitement—which left no room for the boredom that frequently characterizes large academic gatherings. With all its shortcomings, the Wellesley conference was definitely a "happening" in the feminist studies movement and should receive its due recognition.

Indian Council of Social Science Research
New Delhi, India

IMPLICATIONS

Reflections on the Conference on Women and Development: V

May Ahdab-Yehia

Most of the current literature on social and economic changes has neglected to give enough importance to the assessment of the nature and extent of women's participation in the process of development or to the impact of development itself on the status and roles of women in their own societies. Until recently, much of the literature on development has been stimulated, conducted, funded, evaluated, and disseminated by male researchers who have derived assumptions about the organization and operation of societies according to their own perspectives and middle-class limitations. While ongoing social changes have all too often negatively affected the productivity of women and deprived them of options and opportunities, the literature on development has generally categorized women as passive recipients of social and economic change. Their status as active participants in social life has been recognized only through implementation of their kinship roles, especially that of wives and mothers.

Nowhere is this assumption taken more uncritically for granted than in the literature dealing with the Arab world. Inherent in the analysis of these societies is the belief that women are segregated in a private world invariably described as domestic, narrow, and restricted. Women's power, role, and influence are thus limited to domestic affairs. On the other hand, men's worlds are described as public, political, broad, and general.[1] It is not surprising, then, that analysis of the role of Arab women in development has been considered unimportant com-

1. Cynthia Nelson, "Public and Private Politics: Women in the Middle Eastern World," *American Ethnologist* 1 (1974): 551–63.

pared with the assessment of the more evident participation of men in the public sphere and their active structuring of their environment.

In summary, research on development has singled out variables that are relevant for urban and middle-class Arab males. These biases have helped to underemphasize the economic and social contributions of the majority of women, especially those originating from lower-class, low-income families. Only when women become involved in the male model of economic roles does assessment of their contribution to the development of their countries begin.[2]

The research on the Arab world presented at the Conference on Women and Development showed an interesting combination of the biases inherent in all research about the Arab world and some refreshing perspectives that could outline a new theoretical orientation on the role of Arab women in development.

In the first group, some researchers, despite an awareness that women's roles and status vary greatly by class and productive unit (whether these are nomadic, village, or urban), have strongly emphasized stereotypic characteristics of Arab women. The harem; the veiling and seclusion of women; the role of Islam in fostering sexual asymmetry, polygamy, divorce, and inheritance laws favoring the male; and elaborate codes of honor and shame have all been presented without adequate documentation of individual, class, or group differences. Another problem has been the presentation of Arab female emancipation and women's rights primarily in terms of modern, middle-class ideas, borrowed from the now industrialized Western world. Evidence suggests that change in Arab women's roles and status is presently motivated by nationalistic rather than individualistic ideology. In this context, the ambivalence between the desire to develop and the wish to reaffirm certain traditional ways of life can be better explained. Most males, especially the educated ones, would like women to incorporate the new patterns of "modern" qualities, as these seem more compatible with ongoing structural changes, but only on condition that these new values are added to (not substituted for) the traditional qualities.[3] Arab women themselves are sensitive to these conflicts and react in an ambiguous way. Today they rather prefer to assert their right to change within the boundaries of a nationalistic ideology.

The most important subject brought to our attention was that of the ongoing contradictions between some of the cultural, traditional values and the economic realities facing rural, lower-class women.[4] Urbaniza-

2. Constantina Safilios-Rothschild, "The Current Status of Women Cross-culturally: Changes and Persisting Barriers," *Theological Studies* 36 (1975): 577–604.

3. Carmel Camirelli, "Modernity and the Family in Tunisia," *Journal of Marriage and the Family* 29 (1967): 590–95.

4. Amal Vinogradov, "Cultural Values, Economic Realities, and Rural Women in Morocco: Contradictions and Accommodations" (paper presented at the Conference on Women and Development, Wellesley College, June 2–6, 1976).

tion in the Arab countries has been described as occurring primarily through a population-redistribution process, characterized by large-scale rural-to-urban migration and concentration in only a few urban centers. In this situation, more lower-class women have been motivated to go to work, both because of financial necessity and because of an increasing demand for their labor in small, specialized industries (although wages for female workers are still very low compared with those of males in other industries). To understand better the contradictions women face when their families migrate to urban areas, the effects of technological improvements on lower-class women's economic activities, the competing influence and pressure of male-employment patterns, and changes in the women's own view of their familial and economic roles, careful study is required.

The analysis of the many different types of associations to which lower-class urban women belong has also made us aware of the opportunities such associations can offer for the integration of these women into particular development programs. Past discussions of social changes and clique formation associated with migration to urban settings have been studied only from male perspectives. Males have been presented as benefiting from the "modern" innovations which are perceived to flow from urbanization and broader contacts with diverse people, situations, and ideas. Analysis of the impact of recent mobility on rural women and the subsequent associations they form is much needed. Recently women migrants to cities have been presented as feeling isolated, excluded from any association with their "unfriendly" neighbors, and thus in turn forming temporary patterns of sociability with other newly migrant women.[5] A deeper analysis of women's participation in such groups may lead to a better understanding of social organization. For instance, do these temporary associations play the role of counterinstitutions to the more dominant institutions run by city-born women or by men in other social settings? Joseph, investigating some aspects of the problem, found that most women's networks tend rather to take on a village-like atmosphere. The women-based associations he studied were not counterinstitutions but were themselves manifestations of the traditional institutions employing the same cultural modes.[6] These different findings suggest that more research is needed on kinship and village norms and their influence on structuring women's roles and status in new situations.

These pioneering studies, along with Mernissi's paper,[7] make clear the need for more thorough analysis of the social mechanisms by which

5. Roxann Van Dusen, "Natives and Newcomers: Women in a Suburb of Beirut, Lebanon" (paper presented at the Conference on Women and Development).

6. Suad Joseph, "Counter-Institutions, Structural Constraints, and Potential of Women Networks in an Urban Lower Class Lebanese Neighborhood" (paper presented at the Conference on Women and Development); see the abstract in this volume.

7. Fatima Mernissi, "Women, Saints, and Sanctuaries," in this volume.

the majority of Arab women are confined to the traditional status-based mode of social relationships. Such an analysis can clarify the subsequent range of relationships women establish among themselves in order to achieve status in their respective communities.

* * *

Despite some progress in some areas, research on Arab women and development is only beginning. The status of the majority of women who live in the Arab world is still low, and ongoing social changes either do not affect women's primary roles or tend to deprive them even further of options and opportunities. The relationship between women's status and development is complex and must be understood in an interrelated historical, cultural, social, and economic environment. The interplay of such factors as the socioeconomic characteristics of a population, the nature and cause of attitudinal as well as behavioral changes toward women's roles, structural changes providing women with a wider range of opportunities and options, and structural barriers to social and economic change are all areas that should be further investigated. Much is still to be learned from studies of ongoing changes in the totality of the milieu in which women function.

Department of Sociology
Wayne State University
Detroit, Michigan, U.S.A.

Other Papers Presented at Conference on Women and Development, Wellesley College, June 2–6, 1976

Abadan-Unat, Nermin. Implications of Migration on Emancipation and Pseudoemancipation of Turkish Women." Kibris Sokak 6/12 Kavaklidere, Ankara, Turkey.

The paper deals with the impact of external migration on two distinct groups: (*a*) female migrant workers employed in industrial and tertiary sectors abroad, and (*b*) left-behind female members of the migrant's family in the home country. After discussing the nature of "intended versus unintended" migratory moves and its effect on consumption patterns, the entrance of Turkish women workers into new jobs and the indirect networks with the home country resulting from this exodus are evaluated in terms of emancipation and pseudoemancipation.

Aguiar, Neuma. "A Comparative Study of the Impact of Women's Work in the Plantations and Slums upon Family Dynamics." Rua Pinheiro Machado 25, Apt. 408, Laranjeiras, Rio de Janeiro G.B., Brazil.

Aklilu, Bisrat. "The Status of Female Migrants in Indonesia." Department of Economics, Boston University, Boston, Massachusetts 02215, U.S.A.

Awosika, Keziah. "Nigerian Women in Distributive Trade." Nigerian Institute of Social and Economic Research, University of Ibadan, Ibadan, Nigeria.

Beck, Lois. "Women and Islam: The Impact of Religious Ideology."

Department of Anthropology/Sociology, Amherst College, Amherst, Massachusetts 02181, U.S.A.

Berger, Iris, "Women, Religion, and Social Change: East and Central African Perspectives." Department of History, Wellesley College, Wellesley, Massachusetts 02181, U.S.A.

Material on selected rural areas of East and Central Africa suggests that, as women's socioeconomic status has declined in recent years, they have relied increasingly on religious activities to gain status and recognition, to express their attitudes toward change, and to maintain collective female control over fertility, childbirth, and family health.

Bledsoe, Caroline. "Kpelle Women's Status and Power." Department of Anthropology, University of New Mexico, Albuquerque, New Mexico 87131, U.S.A.

Kpelle men (Liberia) prefer marriage to control female production and reproduction, whereas women marry only for male labor or wealth. However, age rather than sex seems most important in individuals' strategies: both men and women try to get the young to support them and marry spouses who will support them.

Burkett, Elinor. "Race, Class, and Sex in Colonial Latin America." Department of History, Frostburg State College, Frostburg, Maryland 21532, U.S.A.

Cebotarev, E. A. "Rural Women in Nonfamilial Activities." Department of Sociology and Anthropology, University of Guelph, Guelph, Ontario, Canada.

Chaney, Elsa. "Women at the Marginal Pole of the Economy: The Case of Peru." Department of Political Science, Fordham University, Bronx, New York 10458, U.S.A.

Chaudhury, Rafiqul Huda. "Aspects of Social Self-Identity among Working Women in Bangladesh." Bangladesh Institute of Development Studies, Adamjee Court, Motijheel, Dacca 2, Bangladesh.

Dirasse, Laketch. "Setinya Adariwoch: Women and Informal Labor Market Organizations." Department of Anthropology, Boston University, Boston, Massachusetts 02215, U.S.A.

Ellickson, Jean. "Women of Rural Bangladesh: Variation in Problems of Self-Perception." Department of Anthropology, Western Illinois University, Macomb, Illinois 61455, U.S.A.

Elu de Leñero, Mariá del Carmen. "Education and Labor Force Participation of Women in Mexico: Some Significant Relationships." Instituto Mexicano de Estudios Sociales, Avenida Cuauhtemoc 1486, 5th Piso, Mexico, D.F.

Garrett, Patricia. "Some Structural Constraints on the Agricultural Activities of Women: The Chilean Hacienda." Department of Sociology, University of Wisconsin, Madison, Wisconsin 53706, U.S.A.

The paper analyzes the interaction between the Chilean land-tenure system and family organization to account for the disproportionate displacement of women from the agricultural labor force. The principal source of data is the agricultural censuses of Chile, supplemented by survey research referring to the 1970–71 agricultural year.

Gilfeather, Katherine. "Women—Changing Role Models and the Catholic Church in Chile." Centro Ballarmino—Cias, Almirante Barroso 24, Casilla 24, Santiago, Chile.

Women in Chile have taken great responsibility for the pastoral concerns of the Catholic Church. While in accepting pastoral responsibilities for the future of the Church these women are not intentionally out to change Church structures or invade clerical ranks, it is inevitable that the values and procedures of the ecclesiastical structure are being transformed and modified by their involvement.

Hahner, June E. "Changing Structure of Women's Employment in Urban Brazil, 1850–1920." Department of History, State University of New York at Albany, 1400 Washington Avenue, Albany, New York 12222, U.S.A.

The paper focuses on women working for pay or profit in Brazil's cities from 1850 to 1920, and explores the changing structure of employment as well as conditions under which women labored and their wages during a period of urban and industrial growth. An expanded version is published in Dauril Alden and Warren Dean, eds., *Essays Concerning the Socioeconomic History of Brazil and Portuguese India* (Gainesville: University of Florida Press, 1977).

Hamalian, Arpi. "Armenian Women in Urban Occupations: A Cross-cultural Analysis." Education Department, Concordia University, Montreal, Quebec H3G 1M8, Canada.

Hass, Paula Hollerbach. "Fertility Decision Making in the Latin American Context." Department of Sociology, Queen's College, Flushing, New York 11367, U.S.A.

The paper undertakes a review of Latin American survey research and field studies of rural and less-educated women, and notes that even when women have had all the children they desire there are rational reasons why they may decide not to use contraception/abortion. Some of these factors include: misperception of their susceptibility to conception; limited knowledge of sexual and reproductive functioning; limited knowledge and access to contraception; dissatisfaction with the family planning clinic; and dissatisfaction or fear of contraception/abortion, especially the actual and perceived side effects of various methods.

Infante, Isa Maria. "Women in Revolutionary Politics in the Dominican Republic." 4393 St. George Place, Riverside, California 92504, U.S.A.

Jahan, Rounaq. "Women in the Politics of Bangladesh." Ahmad Villa, 4 Elephant Road, Dharmandi, Dacca, Bangladesh.

Joseph, Suad. "Counterinstitutions or Institutions: Structural Constraints and Potential of Women's Networks in an Urban Lower-Class Lebanese Neighborhood." Department of Anthropology, University of California, Davis, California 95616, U.S.A.
Assessing whether the exclusion of women from dominant national institutions of society leads to their creation of counterinstitutions, the paper concludes that neighborhood social networks in Borj Hammoud are the local working out of institutionalized ways in which people secure their social needs in Lebanon.

Katzenstein, Mary F. "Women in India: Political Participation and Socioeconomic Equality." Department of Government, McGraw Hall, Cornell University, Ithaca, New York 14850, U.S.A.

Keddie, Nikki. "Methodological Problems in the Study of Middle Eastern Women." Department of History, University of California, Los Angeles, California 90024, U.S.A.

Kilson, Marion. "Women in African Traditional Religions." Radcliffe Institute, 3 James Street, Cambridge, Massachusetts 02138, U.S.A.
Following a preliminary discussion of methodological issues associated with studying women in African traditional religions, several ideological and structural aspects of the topic are explored, drawing upon information from thirteen African societies at various levels of social differentiation.

Leader, Shelah. "Development and Women: A Case Study." 3727 McKinley Street N.W., Washington, D.C. 20015, U.S.A.
Chinese women have benefited from the economic and cultural policies of Mao Tse-tung. Reliance on labor-intensive modes of production provides women with new job opportunities and a degree of economic in-

dependence. The party-controlled mass media present a new, heroic image of women. But, developmental strategies have not eliminated sexist attitudes or traditional marriage customs, nor has the burden of housework and child care been lightened for women. While the regime has eliminated the worst abuses of women, it has not created real equality between the sexes.

Leonard, Karen. "Indian Women in Family and Society: Caste, Class, and Regional Variations." Comparative Studies Program, University of California, Irvine, California 92664, U.S.A.

Nineteenth-century movements for girls' education and widows' marriages in two South Indian regions with relatively similar economic and social structures, Andhra and Madras, were contrasted. The widow-marriage campaign in Andhra, closely integrated with other social and political movements, was credited with increasing the participation of Telugu-speaking women in public life.

Lewis, Barbara C. "Female Strategies and Public Goods: Market Women in the Ivory Coast." Department of Political Science, Livingston College, Rutgers University, New Brunswick, New Jersey 08903, U.S.A.

While broadly defining "the political" to include domestic and local relations, we must ask also what impact women's political action has upon decision making in the emergent centralized states in Africa. This perspective is illustrated by a case study of market women in the Ivory Coast's capital.

Lobban, Carolyn Fleuhr. "Women in Radical Political Movements in the Sudan." Department of Anthropology and Geography, Rhode Island College, Providence, Rhode Island 02908, U.S.A.

Lomnitz, Larissa. "The Role of Women in an Informal Economy: Shanty-Town Networks in Mexico." Centro de Investigacion en Matematicas Aplicadas y en Sistemas, Apartado Postal 20-726, Mexico 20, D.F.

McHardy, Aba. "Cimarron Slave Communities: Women in Secret Societies." Goddard College, Plainfield, Vermont 05667, U.S.A.

Mann, Kristin. "The Changing Role of Women among the Modern Elite in Regional Variation." Department of History, Stanford University, Stanford, California 94305, U.S.A.

Mblinye, Marjorie. "Women's Education, Labor Force Participation, and Underdevelopment." Faculty of Education, University of Dar es Salaam, Tanzania.

Meesook, Oey Astra. "Working Women in Thailand." Faculty of Economics, Thammasat University, Bangkok 2, Thailand.
The exceptionally high female labor force participation rate in Thailand is explained by the absence of any religious or social barriers and the prevalence of family farms and enterprises. Household-related variables affect the female participation rate. Compared with men of similar characteristics, women are more likely to be unpaid family workers, and among paid workers women receive lower wages.

Merriam, Kathleen Howard. "The Impact of Educational Experiences upon the Professional Careers of Contemporary Egyptian Women." Political Science Department, Bowling Green State University, Bowling Green, Ohio 43403, U.S.A.
Expansion of education under the 1952 Revolutionary Regime in Egypt has opened up career opportunities for women and provided avenues for upward social mobility for hitherto less-privileged groups of society. Traditional wife-mother role expectations are challenged by the increased availability of state-run education at all levels and the economic requirements for women's employment, making desirable the acquisition of a modern secular education, the means to guaranteed government employment.

Nader, Claire. "Technology and the Legal Status of Women." Suite 1220, 1975 Connecticut Avenue N.W., Washington, D.C. 20009, U.S.A.

O'Barr, Jean. "Longitudinal Analysis of Political Efficacy and Support among Women and Men in Tunisia." Office of Career Development and Continuing Education, Duke University, Durham, North Carolina 27708, U.S.A.
The analysis focuses on three major issues: the relationship between sex and education-occupation indicators as predictors of political efficacy and support, the negative impact political modernization has on upper-class women's civic attitudes, and the differential influence unplanned aspects of social change have on women's orientations to politics. The data come from two surveys conducted in 1967 and 1973 in the urban area of Tunisia.

Ogundipe-Leslie, Omolara. "Women's Protest Movements in West Africa." Department of English, University of Ibadan, Ibadan, Nigeria.

Oppong, Christine. "Ghanaian Women Teachers and Their Families: Some Effects of Mobility on Family Dynamics." Institute of African Studies, University of Ghana, Legon, Ghana.

Palmer, Ingrid. "The 'Basic Needs' Approach to the Integration of Women in Development: Conditions for Success." Bureau International Du Travail, CH-1211, Geneve 22, Switzerland.

Pessar, Patricia. "Religious Models and Roles for Brazilian Women." Department of Anthropology, Duke University, Durham, North Carolina 27708, U.S.A.

Pharr, Susan. "Routes to Political Power for Japanese Women Elites." Department of Political Science, University of Wisconsin, Madison, Wisconsin 53706, U.S.A.

Pico, Isabel. "Political Participation of Women in Puerto Rico." Calle Sol No. 1, San Juan Puerto Rico 00901.

Rengert, Arlene C. "Female Out-Migration: A Focus on the Migration Process from Some Mexican Villages." Population Studies Center, University of Pennsylvania, 3718 Locust Walk, Philadelphia, Pennsylvania 19174, U.S.A.

Robertson, Claire. "Twentieth-Century Changes in the Organization of the Fish Trade In Accra." 1336 Linn Street, State College, Pennsylvania 16801, U.S.A.

Safa, Helen. "Changing Class Composition of the Female Labor Force in Latin America." Department of Anthropology, Livingston College, Rutgers University, New Brunswick, New Jersey 08903, U.S.A.

This paper deals with the changes occurring in the class composition of the female labor force in Latin America as women move out of family units of production in peasant agriculture into urban wage labor. It is suggested that middle-class women are entering the newer white-collar jobs and blocking the mobility of proletarian women who remain locked into menial jobs in the informal labor market.

Salaff, Janet. "Women's Work and Intended Family Size in Singapore." Department of Sociology, University of Toronto, Toronto, Ontario, Canada.

Sarkar, Lotika. "Social Legislation and the Status of Women." L-1/10 Hauz Khas, New Delhi 110016, India.

Seidman, Ann, and Pala, Achola. "A Model of the Status of Women in Africa." Center for Research on Women, Wellesley College, Wellesley, Massachusetts 02181, U.S.A.

Seidman, Robert. "Law and Women in Development: Search for a Paradigm." Boston University School of Law, Boston, Massachusetts 02108, U.S.A.

Sheik el Din, Dina. "How Sudanese Fare with Customary and State Law." Faculty of Law, University of Khartoum, Khartoum, Sudan.

Starr, June. "Western Law and the Position of Rural Turkish Women." Department of Anthropology, State University of New York at Stony Brook, Stony Brook, New York 11790, U.S.A.

Stichter, Sharon. "Women in the Urban Labor Force in Kenya: Problems and Prospects." Department of Sociology, University of Massachusetts, Boston, Massachusetts 02125, U.S.A.

Women's employment rates, incomes, and occupational levels have lagged behind those of men in Kenya, and since the 1950s women have been incorporated mainly into Western-defined "women's" jobs. In addition, dependent development has led to a widening gap between urban middle-class elite women and women of the working classes, urban poor, and peasantry.

Stiehm, Judith. "Measuring Women's Power." Department of Political Science, University of Southern California, Von Kleinsmid Center 327, University Park, Los Angeles, California 90007, U.S.A.

Strange, Heather. "Village Paths and City Routes: Rural Women's Perception of Urban Alternatives." Department of Sociology and Anthropology, University College, Rutgers University, New Brunswick, New Jersey 08903, U.S.A.

This paper explores rural Malay women's perceptions of urban life-style alternatives. The difficulty of establishing categories useful for comparing and contrasting village women's attitudes is discussed. Consideration is then given to interaction between young females and males, educational and employment opportunities, and other aspects of urban life as viewed by rural women.

Tadesse, Zenebework. "The Effect of Development Programs on Rural Women in Ethiopia." P.O. Box 3469, Addis Ababa, Ethiopia.

Van Allen, Judith. "Revolutionary Strategies for Change." 2620 College Avenue, Apt. 1, Berkeley, California 94704, U.S.A.

"Pragmatic" arguments for increasing women's access to education, employment, and politics ignore dependent capitalism's need for women's unpaid domestic and agricultural labor. Absence of autonomous women's organizations facilitates such exploitation. Revolutionary socialist societies (e.g., Guinea-Bissau, discussed here), committed ideologically and organizationally to women's equality and autonomy, offer significant possibilities for liberating women of all classes.

Van Dusen, Roxann. "Natives and Newcomers: Women in a Suburb of Beirut, Lebanon." Social Science Research Council, 1755 Massachusetts Avenue N.W., Washington, D.C. 20036, U.S.A.

Vinogradov, Amal. "Cultural Values, Eçonomic Realities, and Rural Women in Morocco: Contradictions and Accommodations." Queens College, Flushing, New York 11367, U.S.A.

Wasserspring, Lois. "Inequality and Development: Women in Latin America." 361 Harvard Avenue, Cambridge, Massachusetts 02138, U.S.A.

Wilson, Amy Auerbacher. "The Women's Federation of the People's Republic of China: An Analysis of Elite Transformation and Organizational Change in a Mass Organization." Department of Sociology, Douglass College, Rutgers University, New Brunswick, New Jersey 08540, U.S.A.

Zakaria, Mazida. "Life Cultures: Rural and Urban Malay Women." Department of Anthropology, University of Malaya, Kualalumpur, Malaysia."

Index